THE SOCIAL CONDITION AND EDUCATION OF THE PEOPLE

The Development of Industrial Society Series

Joseph Kay

THE SOCIAL CONDITION AND EDUCATION OF THE PEOPLE in England and Europe

Volume 2

IRISH UNIVERSITY PRESS
Shannon Ireland

First edition London 1850

This I U P reprint is a photolithographic facsimile of the first edition and is unabridged, retaining the original printer's imprint.

ISBN 0 7165 1565 2 Two volumes
ISBN 0 7165 1566 0 Volume 1
ISBN 0 7165 1567 9 Volume 2

T M MacGlinchey Publisher
Irish University Press Shannon Ireland

PRINTED IN THE REPUBLIC OF IRELAND BY
ROBERT HOGG PRINTER TO IRISH UNIVERSITY PRESS

THE SOCIAL CONDITION AND EDUCATION OF THE PEOPLE.

VOL. II.

LONDON:
SPOTTISWOODES and SHAW,
New-street-Square.

THE

SOCIAL CONDITION

AND

EDUCATION OF THE PEOPLE

IN

ENGLAND AND EUROPE;

SHEWING

THE RESULTS OF THE PRIMARY SCHOOLS,
AND OF THE DIVISION OF LANDED PROPERTY, IN
FOREIGN COUNTRIES.

BY

JOSEPH KAY, ESQ. M.A.

OF TRINITY COLLEGE, CAMBRIDGE;
BARRISTER-AT-LAW;
AND LATE TRAVELLING BACHELOR OF THE UNIVERSITY
OF CAMBRIDGE.

"The best way to help the Poor is to enable them to help themselves."
"The object of all Government should be the happiness of the *majority* of the people."

IN TWO VOLUMES.

VOL. II.

THE EDUCATION OF THE PEOPLE.

LONDON:
LONGMAN, BROWN, GREEN, AND LONGMANS,
PATERNOSTER-ROW.
1850.

CONTENTS

OF

THE SECOND VOLUME.

CHAP. VI.

CHAP. VII.

CHAP. VIII.

CHAP. IX.

CHAP. X.

CHAP. XIV.

CHAP. XV.

THE

SOCIAL CONDITION

AND

EDUCATION OF THE PEOPLE.

CHAPTER III.

THE GREAT DIFFUSION OF EDUCATION IN GERMANY. — SECTARIANISM HAS BEEN NO INSURMOUNTABLE OBSTACLE. — GENERAL VIEW OF THE PAROCHIAL AND LOCAL CHARACTER OF THE GERMAN EDUCATIONAL SYSTEMS.

I PURPOSE now to give a simple statement of the really wonderful efforts which Germany, Austria, Switzerland, France, Holland, Denmark, Norway, and Sweden are making to educate their people. Whether the methods, by which any of these different countries are carrying out their great design, are in any way applicable to this country or not, I shall not stop to consider, my desire being merely to show how different countries,— with different degrees of political freedom, with different political constitutions, whose people profess different religious tenets, where Protestants of different sects, Roman Catholics, and Jews are mingled up in every kind of proportion,— have all managed to overcome difficulties precisely similar to those, which stand in our way, and have all agreed to labour together to educate their poor. For it is a great fact, however much we may be inclined to doubt it, that throughout Prussia, Saxony, Bavaria, Bohemia, Wirtemburg, Baden, Hesse Darmstadt, Hesse Cassel, Gotha, Nassau, Hanover, Denmark, Switzerland, Norway, and the Austrian Empire, ALL the children are actually, at this present time, attending school, and are receiving a careful religious, moral, and intellectual education, from highly educated and efficient teachers. Over the vast tract of country, which I have mentioned, as well as in Holland and the greater part of France, *all* the children above six years of age are daily acquiring useful knowledge and good habits under the *influence* of moral, religious, and learned teachers. ALL the youth of the greater part of these countries, below the age of twenty-one years, can read, write and cipher, and know the Bible History, and the history of their own country. No children are left idle and dirty in the streets of the towns — there is no class of children to be compared, in any respect, to the children who frequent our "ragged schools" — all the children, even of the poorest parents, are, in a great part of these countries, in dress, appearance, cleanliness, and manners, as polished and civilised as the children of our middle classes — the children of the poor in Germany are so civilised that the rich often send their children to the schools intended for the poor; and, lastly, in a great part of Germany and Switzerland, the children of the poor are receiving a *better* education than that given in England to the children of the greater part of our middle classes! These facts deserve to be well considered.

And let it be remembered that these great results have been attained, notwithstanding obstacles *at least* as great, as those which make it so difficult for us to act. Are they religious differences which hinder us? Look at Austria, Bavaria, and the Prussian Rhine provinces, and the Swiss cantons of Lucerne and Soleure. Will any one say, that the religious difficulties in those countries are less than those, which exist in our own? Is Roman Catholicism in these countries free from that arrogance and haughtiness, which are, at the same time, the causes and effects of a vain belief in human infallibility, and which stimulate opposition, instead of conciliating opinion? Is the sectarianism of the Jesuits of Lucerne, or of the priests of Bavaria, of a more yielding character towards the Protestant "heretics," than that of one Protestant party in England towards another? And yet, in each of these countries, the difficulties arising from religious differences have been overcome, and *all* their children are brought under the influence of a *religious* education, without any religious party having been offended. But are they political causes, which prevent us proceeding in this great work, in which nearly all Europe has so long preceded us, notwithstanding that we need it more than all the European nations put together? Are they political causes, I ask? I answer by again referring my readers to the countries I have enumerated. Under the democratic governments of the Swiss cantons, where it is the people, who rule and legislate; under the constitutional governments of Saxony, Wirtemburg, and Baden, which were framed more or less upon the English model, and where the people have long had a direct influence upon the government; under the constitutional governments of France and Holland, and under all the different grades of absolute rule which existed, but a few months since, in Prussia, the German dukedoms and the Austrian states, the difficulties of the question have long been overcome, and with such entire satisfaction to all parties, that among the present representatives of the people, no member has ever been heard to express a desire for the change of the laws which relate to primary education.

But once again; perhaps there are some who say — but there is no country which is troubled, as we are, by the union of both religious and political difficulties. I again refer my readers to the cases of Holland and Switzerland. They will find in these countries the same strong love of independence of action, which we boast so proudly and so justly. They will find also, not only strong religious feuds existing among the Protestants themselves, and pushed to the most shameful extremities, as in the case of the canton of Vaud, from which one religious party has lately been driven as exiles, but they will find the still more formidable differences of the Protestants and Catholics arrayed against each other, and seemingly preventing all union on any subject whatsoever; and yet, in all these various countries, differing as they do in the state of their religious parties, and of their political regulations, in *all* of them, I say, have *all* parties consented to join on this one great and important question — THE EDUCATION OF THE PEOPLE.

The only reason, why we have not done as much is, that we have hitherto wanted the deep interest, which they have now taken, for so long a time, in the promotion of this question, as well as a due appreciation of the benefits to be derived from the undertaking. When peace was once again established in Europe in 1815, the governments I have enumerated, began to feel that the condition-of-the-people question was one of vital importance, and that there was no time to lose. Recognising this truth in all its magnitude, they all resolved to educate the children, knowing that this must be the *commencement* of their work, however much more they might find necessary to its perfection. It was this consciousness and this resolution, that carried them triumphantly through all difficulties to the attainment of their object. And did we only feel half the interest in this great subject, which we have shown in the improvement of our internal communication, or in the extension of our empire in foreign lands, we should long ere this have outstripped our neighbours. Once let Englishmen comprehend the importance and necessity of any undertaking, and nothing can hinder its accomplishment. In material creations we effect, in a single month, what would cost our neighbours years of efforts. But alas! the education of the people is not one of those labours, in which we can hope, as in material enterprises, to speedily correct, by our national activity, the sad effects of a long-deferred commencement. It is a labour of years, and its effects are future and not immediate. It is like sowing the acorns from which the oak forest is to grow. The planter must not hope to reap the benefits of his labour. That is reserved for his posterity or successors. A mere attendance at school is not sufficient for the creation of a useful citizen, when the scholar's home is an immoral one, and exerts an influence for evil, greater and more powerful, than the good influence of the teacher's precepts and example. The homes must be improved, before the schools will produce any very good results; and the reformation of the domestic life of a people is a work of years. Hence the still greater necessity of beginning our labours with as little delay as possible.

All this generation can hope to see from extended education and extended religious influences, is the slow and gradual improvement of the homes, and the *lessening* of the corrupting influences now at work upon the poor. But, if we could only remove the poor children of the towns from their present demoralising life in the streets, and from the daily spectacles of immorality there exposed continually to view—if we could only effect this, we should have made a great step towards reformation. I have always believed that the life of our town children was an explanation quite sufficient, independently of all others, to account for the length of our criminal records, and the character of the poorer classes in our towns. The difference between an English and a German town in this respect is most remarkable; no one can believe it till he has seen it for himself. In England, my readers know what spectacle presents itself: crowds of little children in a filthy state, free from superintendence, without occupation, often actually locked out of home, while the parents are absent, are left in all the dirt, subject to all the evil influences, and witnesses of all the demoralising scenes, which are too generally the necessary appurtenances of a town street. Let any one spend a day or two of observation in the back streets of London, or of any of our great towns, and he may perceive, that the life of crowds of poor children is passed altogether in the streets, entirely free from all surveillance. The companions they find in their earliest years are of the most degraded character; their pastimes, even from the age of seven, are, many of them, of the foulest and lewdest description; filthy and disgusting practices, and promiscuous intercourse, are common to nearly all of them: they are never accustomed to cleanliness, they are seldom washed; they are, from childhood, habituated to dirt, bestiality, and vice; and, with such a training as this, the young children in our towns grow up to manhood, with abominable habits, with no religious knowledge, with a long-engendered craving for the stimulants of vice, and with the coarseness of barbarians. This is the English picture: now look upon the German. All children are obliged to be in the school-room, or school-playground, in company with their teacher, during six hours of every week-day; they are obliged to present themselves in a perfectly clean state; this prevents them from indulging in the filthy and degrading amusements, which become the natural pastimes of a child, who is accustomed to a street life from its infancy; their parents are subject to punishment, if the children are not sent to the schools in a decent state; and, as some time is necessarily taken in eating their meals, and in preparing for the morning or afternoon classes, the consequence is, that no children are to be found playing in the streets, excepting in the evening hours, and are to be then found amusing themselves in a much more innocent, decent, and cleanly manner than in the back alleys of our own towns. This alone is sufficient to account for much of that difference, which exists between the moral and social states of the German and the English town labourers, and for the striking fact, that all the living criminals of Germany are at this moment lodged in prisons at home, and that the German governments are able to dispense altogether with the punishment of transportation. Where, I would ask, should we find room for all our transported convicts were we to bring them back from their distant lands of exile?

I can give a traveller, who is desirous of comprehending at one short view the workings of the German and Swiss systems of popular education, no better advice, than to direct him to notice the state of the streets in any German or Swiss town, which he happens to visit: no matter where it be, whether on the plains of Prussia or Bavaria, on the banks of the Rhine, in the small towns of the Black Forest, or in the mountainous cantons of Alpine Switzerland—no matter where—let him only walk through the streets of such a town in the morning or the afternoon, and count the number of children to be found there above the age of four or five—or let him stand in the same streets, when the children are going to or returning from the schools—and let him examine their cleanly appearance, the good quality, the excellent condition, and the cleanliness of their clothing, the condition of the lesson books they are carrying, the happiness and cheerfulness, and, at the same time, the politeness and ease of their manners; he will think he sees the children of the rich: but let him follow them home, and he will find that many of them are the offspring of the poorest artisans and labourers of the town. If that one spectacle does not convince him of the magnitude of the educational efforts of Germany, and of the happy results which they are producing—let him go no further, for nothing he can further see will teach him. Let him then come home, and rejoice in the condition of our poor; but, should he start at this extraordinary spectacle, as I have seen English travellers do, to whom I have pointed out this sign of advanced and advancing civilisation, let him reflect, that this has been effected, spite of all the obstacles which impede ourselves. Bigotry and ignorance have cried their loudest: Romanists have refused co-operation with Protestants, Protestants with Romanists, and yet they have co-operated. There has been the same strong jealousy of all government interference, the same undefined and ill-digested love of liberty, there has been the same selfish fear of retarding the developement of physical resources. In Bavaria, the war has been waged between Romanists and Protestants; in Argovie, opposition has been raised by the manufacturers; in Lucerne, by the religious parties, and by the political opponents of the government; and in Baden, the difficulties have been aggravated by the numbers of Jews, whom both Romanists and Protestants hated to receive into alliance, even more than they disliked to co-operate among themselves. But in all these countries the great principle has finally triumphed; and all parties have yielded some little of their claims, in the full conviction, that a day is dawning upon Europe, fraught with the most overwhelming evils for that country which has not prepared for its approach.

The man must be a wild enthusiast in the cause of education, who can imagine, that we have done all when we have built our schools and educated our teachers; but what must he be, who can hope that *until* this be done, we can effect any thing for the removal of those evils and dangers with which our social state is threatened? Between the years 1835 and 1846, the country expended 57,254,541*l.*, besides the immense outlay of private charity, in the temporary relief of pauperism, and we are now throwing into the same gradually widening lagune more than 5,000,000*l.* per annum, whilst we do not expend on the improvement of the notoriously deficient materials for the education of our poor more than 200,000*l.* per annum! In Prussia, the tables are strangely turned. She has within the last twenty-five years, spent many *millions* on the perfection of her schools, and of the materials necessary for the education of her people; while the funds necessary for the relief of pauperism have continued so small, as not to require any additional forced tax like our poor rates. What she requires for this purpose is obtained by parochial collections from those who are able to contribute. But here, in manufacturing England, 5,000,000*l.*

per annum, besides the immense contributions of private charity, for the relief of a steadily increasing pauperism, and 100,000*l.* per annum and private contributions amounting annually to not more than another 100,000*l.* for increasing the deficient materials necessary for the education of the people, is the epitome of the social question; while the accumulation of multitudes of poor is going on each year with increasing rapidity, and while even now greater masses of intelligent and uneducated operatives are crowded in our towns, than the world has ever before seen assembled together.

But there are some, who say, that if our means of direct education are worse, yet that our means of indirect education are better, than those of other countries, and that if our people have not schools and good teachers, they have long had a free press, the right of assembling together for political discussion, plenty of cheap and very liberal journals, good reports of all the debates of our Houses of Legislature, and a literature free in its spirit, suggestive in its writings, and anything but one-sided in its views of political and social questions, and that all this serves to stimulate the intellectual energies of the people. As far as regards the middle classes, this is all very true; but, as regards the poor, it is ridiculously false. Most of our poor are either wholly without education, or else possess so little as to be entirely out of the sphere of such influences, as those I have enumerated. What good can one of our boorish peasants gain from cheap literature, free parliamentary debates, free discussion, and liberal journals? What advantage is it to a starving man that there is bread in the baker's shop, if he has not wherewith to buy? What good is cheap literature and free discussion to a poor peasant who can neither read nor think? He starves in the midst of plenty, and starves too with a curse upon his lips.

It is utterly false to argue that the peasants would provide themselves with schools and education, if education would improve their condition in society. We can never hope to see the peasants supply themselves with schools. They never have done so in any country, they never will do so in our own. Such a step implies in them a great prior development of the intellectual and moral faculties; a development which can only be obtained by means of education. The peasants are neither wise enough, nor rich enough, to erect or support schools for themselves, and should government refuse either to do it for them, or to oblige all classes to assist the poor to accomplish this great work, we may rest assured that another century will see no further advances than we have made at present — our schools for the most part totally unfitted for their purpose, and our teachers the most ignorant, ill-paid, and least respected set of men in the community. Other countries have long since recognised these truths, and acted upon them.

Whilst in England we have been devoting most of our energies to the increase of our national wealth, the Germans and Swiss have been engaged in the noble undertaking of attempting to raise the character and social position of their poorer classes. To effect this, they have not vainly imagined that schools alone were sufficient, but to the accomplishment of this great end, every social institution and every social regulation has been rendered subservient. They began, it is true, by raising schools, and educating teachers; but they have continued this great work by reforming their prisons and criminal codes; by facilitating the transfer and division of their lands; by simplifying their legal processes; by reforming their ecclesiastical establishments; by entirely changing the mediæval and illiberal constitutions of their universities and public schools; by improving the facilities of internal communication; and, lastly, by opening the highest and most honourable offices of the state to all worthy aspirants, no matter of how low an origin.

Nor have their labours in the cause of social reform diminished, as there was seemingly less immediate need for them. On the contrary, to a traveller in these countries, who has not acquainted himself with all that has been going on there for the last thirty years, they would seem to be only now commencing, so vigorous and universal are the efforts which are *at this moment* being made.

Although I hope I shall not be understood to maintain that school instruction alone, and unaided by any other reforming principle, is able to raise our peasantry to that satisfactory condition, which it is confessed they occupy in Holland, Norway, and in many parts of Germany and Switzerland, yet sure I am, that without schools, teachers, and an early education, this never has, and never can be attained.

It is doubtless true, that the social polity of a country should be so ordered, that the whole life of any of its members should be a progressive and continued religious, moral, and intellectual education; but it is no less certain that this great work, if it is ever to have a commencement, must begin at home, and be continued, in the case of the peasant, in the village school, under the superintendence of the religious minister and village teacher, or it can never be accomplished at all. True it is, that at first the evil influence of the home will be stronger than the good one of the teacher and the school. But still, if he understand the conduct of his important work, he will know how to awaken those principles which, it may be, lie dormant, but which nevertheless exist in every child's mind, and which, if once aroused, would be certain in some degree to mitigate the evil influences of home. Thus might we hope, that the cottage firesides of the next generation, would prove less injurious than those of the present, to the children, who will cluster around them, and that the school would have an auxiliary, and not an antagonist, in the powerful, though now, alas! too often misdirected influences of home. It is only, when we have attained this happy result, that we can hope to realise the full benefits, which education is capable of conferring, and which, in other lands, it is at this day conferring upon the people.

So long as the early *domestic* training is in direct opposition to the education of the schools, so long must the improvement in education be very slow; but, however slow, it is the only sure means we have of counteracting the effects of a vicious domestic training, and of cleansing the very fount of immorality. The labourer is occupied from twilight on to twilight, and the religious ministers have but few opportunities of bringing higher influences to bear upon him. Those, too, who most need improvement, are generally the most unwilling to receive it; and those whose homes act most injuriously on the younger inmates, are precisely those, who oppose most strenuously the entry of the religious minister, and who are most rarely brought under any ennobling influence whatever. Thus it often happens, that the only way, by which we can introduce reform into a home, is through the children; for, most happily, there is among the poor such a great idea of the benefits to be derived from education, that it very rarely happens, that the parent cannot be persuaded to send his child to school, *when he is enabled to do so.*

But there are some who maintain, that eight hours' association with the good and enlightened teacher on the Sunday, and in the Sunday school, are quite sufficient to counteract the bad influences of the immoral home to which the child has, perhaps, been exposed through the whole week!—that *eight* hours of religious exercises on Sunday can obviate the effects of the *one hundred hours* of immoral association of the past six days! This ignorance is even more fatal, than it is ridiculous; how little would those who profess such opinions like to submit their own children to such an ordeal. How contrary is their practice to their profession! Who would expect to save his child from vice, if he turned him out into the streets during weekdays, and only gave him instruction and religious education on the Sunday? and yet this pittance of education is thought more than enough for the poor. If we would raise the character of our labourers, we must reverse this order of things.

It is delightful to see how thoroughly this truth has been recognised in Western Europe. From the shores of the Baltic and the North Sea to the foot of the great Alpine range, and from the Rhine to the Danube, *all* the children of both rich and poor are receiving *daily* instruction, under the surveillance of their religious ministers, from long and most carefully educated teachers. Throughout the plains of Prussia, Bohemia, and Bavaria, among the hills and woods of Saxony and central Germany, in the forests and rich undulating lands of Wirtemburg and Baden, in the deep and secluded Alpine valleys of Switzerland and the Tyrol, in most of the provinces of the Austrian empire, throughout Holland, Denmark, and almost the whole of France, and even in the plains of Italian Lombardy, there is scarcely a single parish, which does not possess its school-house and its one or two teachers. The school-buildings are often built in really an extravagant manner; and in Switzerland and South Germany, the village school is generally the finest erection of the neighbourhood. In the towns the expenditure on these monuments of a nation's progress is still more remarkable. Here the municipal authorities generally prefer to unite several schools for the sake of forming one complete one. This is generally erected on the following plan:—A large house is built of three or four stories in height, with commodious play-yards behind. The one or two upper stories are used as apartments for the teachers; the lower rooms are set apart for the different classes. A town school has generally from *eight* to *ten*, and sometimes twelve or fourteen, of these class-rooms, each of which is capable of containing from 80 to 100 children. An educated teacher is appointed to manage each class, so that there is generally a staff of at least *eight* teachers connected with each town school of Germany, and I have seen schools with as many as twelve and fourteen teachers. The rooms are filled with desks, maps, and all the apparatus which the teachers can require for the purposes of instruction. I generally noticed, on entering a small German or Swiss town, that next to the church, the finest building was the one set apart for the education of the children.

It is impossible to estimate the enormous outlay, which Germany has devoted to the erection and improvement of school-houses alone, during the last fifteen years. In the towns, hardly any of the old and inefficient buildings now remain, except where they have been improved and enlarged. In Munich, I directed my conductor to lead me to the worst school buildings in the city, and I found all the class-rooms measuring fourteen feet high by about twenty-five square, and ten of such class-rooms in each schoolhouse, each of which rooms was under the constant direction of an educated teacher. In whatever town I happened to be staying, I always sought out the worst, in preference to the best schools. In Berlin the worst I could find contained four class-rooms, each eight feet in height, and about fifteen feet square; and in the Grand Duchy of Baden I found that the Chambers had passed a law prohibiting any school-house being built, the rooms of which were not fourteen feet high.

Throughout Germany no expense seems to have been spared to improve the materials of popular instruction.

This could never have been effected had not the expenses of such an immense undertaking been equally distributed over all the parishes of the different states. The burden being thus divided amongst all, is not felt by any; but had the government started in the vain hope of being able to bear even a third of the expense, popular education would have been no further advanced in Germany than in England. But wiser, or more interested in the real success of the undertaking than ourselves, the governments of the different states have obliged each province to provide for the expenses necessary for its own primary education.

It is very strange, however, to hear the unfounded and untrue aspersions, which are cast upon all these noble efforts. When one speaks in England of German education, one is sure to be assailed by cries of "Centralisation," "Irreligion," "No local liberty of action," "No union between the schools and the churches," "All done by the state," and so forth. Now I assure my readers that all these are only so many untruths, or most unwarrantable exaggerations.

Of all these errors, the greatest perhaps is, the belief that every thing connected with the education of the people in Germany is done by the state, and that the parochial affairs are managed by an exterior and distant authority. Nothing can be a more utterly unfounded supposition. It has not been so either in Prussia or in any other German state, no matter how absolute the government. The systems, so far from having been systems of excessive centralisation, leaving no freedom of action to the parishes, have been always and still are *essentially* parochial systems, merely under the surveillance, and subject to the check of the central authority. It is the parishes and towns, which tax themselves for educational purposes; it is the parishioners and citizens, who elect their own teachers; it is the parishioners and citizens, who pay their own teachers, and provide all the materials for the education of their own poor; it is the parishioners and citizens, who determine whether they will have separate schools for their different religious sects, or common schools for them all; it is the parishioners and citizens, who choose the sites of their school-houses, and the outlay they will make on their erection; and although they have not the power of dismissing a teacher after they have once elected him, without first showing to government a sufficient ground for such a step, yet they are afforded every facility of forwarding any complaints they may have to make of any teacher they have elected, to the educational authorities appointed to judge such matters, and to protect the teachers from the effects of mere personal animosities or ignorance.

I have sometimes been almost inclined to doubt the possibility of conveying any just idea of the present state of education in Germany on account of the extraordinary prejudices which exist in this country against the very name of a German school. One hears people talking about it, as if it were the prison of the village, where the poor children are immured for six hours *per diem* against their parents' inclinations, and where mere instruction, entirely divested of all religion, is forced into the scholars in true military fashion. It is said too, that the inhabitants of the village have no control over the school, and that the teacher is a man imposed upon them by an arbitrary king. The school-house too, according to these writers, is built by an architect sent down from the metropolis, and after plans drawn out by the minister's own hand, and is looked upon by the people as a gaol, where their children are drilled as soldiers. Even Mr. Laing, liberal-minded and philosophical as he is, comes home, after inquiries made in Berlin, tainted with these prejudices, and utters all the common platitudes against this monstrosity of centralisation. Now let me ask, what does this centralisation mean? Let us look this terrible enigma in the face. If my readers can once be taught, that it is in this case a mere delusion of their own fancy's creating, perhaps I shall not labour against such disheartening odds, in my efforts to give them an account of what German education really is.

I ask them, then, to accompany me to a Prussian village. It shall be one of those solitary collections of hamlets found scattered at long intervals over the great central plains of Prussia, and unconnected with any other village or town, except by miles of long and sandy roads.

Imagine a plain stretching in every direction as far

as the eye can reach, as level as the sea in a calm, without a solitary tree or hedge to break the disheartening distances — a vast prairie of the flattest and most unbroken corn land, with four roads crossing it in different directions. Such is a true picture of a great part of the country on the line of railroad leading from Magdeburg to Berlin.

In the middle of this plain is our village, surrounded by a few trees, and by the kitchen gardens of the villagers. The houses are built of wood, and of a sort of composition, which is whitewashed continually, for stone or brick cannot sometimes be obtained in these great sandy prairies. We enter into a long straight street of houses nearly all built as I have described, and whitewashed over. It is worth our while to look through the windows and see the beautiful cleanliness of the interiors. Every room looks as if it had been whitewashed only yesterday; and the substantial appearance of the furniture, and, above all, the intelligent and good-natured faces of its inmates, offer us the best possible proof of the happy, intelligent, and thriving condition of the Prussian peasantry.

But if we are still disposed to doubt, let us, before going further, just take one turn into the village gardens. Remember, these, as well as all the fields and lands around, in most cases belong to the peasant inmates of the villages, round which the plain lies spread out like a cultivated prairie. The tenants of the Prussian cottages are generally their owners also. Look how beautifully these gardens and the fields around are cultivated. There are no weeds. There is no rubbish. Every particle of soil is used. The clods are finely broken, and the prairie seems to have been all turned up and loosened by the spade. These small allotments and the fields around them are the garden, the kitchen garden of the village. If we visit these allotments in the evening, when the peasants have left their own corn fields, we shall find the men and women all out, assisted by the children, and engaged in watering and tending their little kitchen gardens, with all the interest, with which our landed gentleman watches the labours of his gardener. This fact of peasant proprietors is the true secret of peasant nobility, and also of peasant conservatism. The German peasants, who are also the German landowners, have had until lately much less political liberty than the English peasant, but they have had property and intelligence, and have been consequently much better satisfied with their condition in life, and consequently truly conservative in their principles. Look at the reverse of this in Ireland.

But to return to the village,—we find in one part the Protestant church; in another, it may be a chapel of the Romanist, and here the village school. Now we are far enough from Berlin, and from that centre so odious to Englishmen; but are we free from its tyranny? This is the question, and this I shall now attempt to answer.

First then, I own there is a representative of this odious centre in this quiet village. One of the more intelligent villagers has been chosen by the magistrates of the bezirke or county, in which the village is situated, to direct its civil affairs. He has been appointed by these county magistrates to superintend the repair of the roads, the collection of the taxes, and the direction of the police, and he is empowered to interfere to a certain extent in the educational affairs of the district. We shall see presently how far. Suppose, that, at the period of our visit to this oasis of the Prussian plains, for some reason or other no school had been established, and that the government inspector had just paid them a visit in order to notify to them, that the laws require, that parish, as every other, to provide itself with sufficient school-room for its children.

The inspector makes this notification to the village magistrate of whom I have just spoken; this officer immediately informs the villagers of the message he has received, and requests the householders to elect three or four from among themselves to attend a meeting or committee, in which the best course to be taken in respect to these educational matters will be considered. This is accordingly done, and on the appointed day these delegates, the religious ministers of the village, and the village magistrate assemble together. As the law *obliges* them to build school-rooms for their children, they have only to consider how this is to be effected. According to our English notions, it would be utterly impossible for them ever to come to a decision, as the inhabitants of our village consist, as I have said, of Romanists and Protestants. But although the churches of each sect are regularly filled with the poor, and although there is every symptom, which would lead a traveller to say, that the religion of the Prussian peasantry exercised a powerful influence upon them, yet the different religious parties in Prussia do find it possible to co-operate in their efforts to improve the condition of their poor. The first point then, which the village committee have to decide, is, whether they shall have *one* school for both religious parties, or a *separate* school for each. Perfect liberty of choice on this subject is secured by law to each different religious sect. All that the government says, is, "*You (the different parishes)* MUST *provide sufficient school-room for your children, but we leave it entirely to your own choice how you will do this.*" It is true that the government encourages the erection of separate schools, whenever this is possible, but it never attempts to interfere, when any religious party of a parish wishes to have a separate school, if it can only find sufficient funds for the purpose. And if any one religious sect should not happen to be represented in the committee, still this party has the right of dissenting from the resolutions of the committee, should they be in favour of a mixed school, and should the unrepresented sect be willing to bear the expense of a separate school for themselves alone. It is important to bear this fact in mind, viz., that the question of mixed or separate schools is, in Western Europe, left *entirely* to the decision of the parishioners, and local religious ministers, and that it consequently occasions no difficulty whatsoever. The governments do not attempt to fetter the people's right to decide this point, and *therefore* no one is jealous of the result of the parochial deliberations, as every religious party has the power of acting as it may desire.

When this point is decided, the village committee chooses a site for a school, and decides on the amount of the outlay, and on the plan of the school buildings. The several determinations are then sent up to the county magistrates for approval, which is given as a matter of course, unless an unhealthy site or a positively defective plan has been adopted, in which case, the resolutions are sent down to be reconsidered, with recommendations from the magistrates on the subject.

When these several matters have been arranged, the village committee elects its own teachers, subject, however, to this limitation, — that no person can engage in any branch of instruction, until he has obtained from learned examiners, appointed by Government, a diploma certifying, that his religious, moral, and intellectual qualifications are such, as to render him worthy to be entrusted with the exercise of a teacher's duties.

Of the school and teacher, when thus constituted, the parochial religious ministers of the different sects educated in the school are *ex officio* inspectors. They are required to send periodical reports of the state and progress of the parochial education to the superior county authorities. The schools are also inspected two or three times a year by several government inspectors, who are sent round on periodical visitations, to see that all is conducted in an efficient and proper manner.

The village committee continues to meet at regular intervals; and its members make periodical visits of inspection to the school, and report to the county magistrates. It is also the business of the committee to provide the necessary school apparatus, and the funds required for the necessary repairs ; and it is its especial duty to protect and encourage the teacher. In this manner are the villagers and village ministers immediately connected with, and interested in, the progress of the education of their own little neighbourhood.

Now, I would ask every candid man, supposing that I have given you a true idea of the way in which German parochial education is managed, can you see any thing so very horrible in it? Is there really in all this any great excess of contralisation? Is it true, that the people have nothing to do with the management of their own education? Is it not rather the people themselves who manage the schools?

And yet, this is the system pursued, not only over the Prussian plains, but in the forest villages of Central Germany, Wirtemburg, and Baden, in the lovely valleys of the Tyrol and Switzerland, in the Rhine Provinces, among the hills of Saxony, and in the plains of Bavaria.

It is this simple, religious, and parochial system which has been abused and vilified in this country in every possible manner. It has been called tyrannical, illiberal, irreligious, and has been stigmatised by every opprobrious epithet that ignorance and bigotry could invent. But truth in the end will conquer, and Germany will one day be lauded by all Europe, as the inventor of a system securing, in the best possible manner, guidance by the greatest intelligence of the country, the cheapest manner of working, the fostering of local activity and of local sympathies, and the cordial assistance of the religious ministers.

Disputes about separate or mixed schools are unheard of in Prussia, because every parish is left to please itself which kind it will adopt. One of the leading Roman Catholic Counsellors of the Educational Bureau in Berlin assured me, that they never experienced any difficulty on this point. "We always," he said, "encourage separate schools when possible, as we think religious instruction can be promoted better in separate than in mixed schools; but, of course, we all think it better to have mixed schools, than to have no schools at all; and when we cannot have separate schools we are rejoiced to see the religious sects uniting in the support of a mixed one. When mixed schools are decided on by the parochial committees, the teacher is elected by the most numerous of the two sects; or, if two teachers are required, one is elected by one sect, and the other by the other; and in this case each conducts the religious education of the children of his own sect. But when only one teacher is elected, the children of those parents, who differ from him in religious belief, are permitted to be taken from the school during the religious lessons, on condition that their parents make arrangements for their religious instruction by their own ministers."

I went to Prussia with the firm expectation, that I should hear nothing but complaints from the peasants, and that I should find the school nothing but a worthy offshoot of an absolute government. To test whether this really was the case or not, as well as to see something of the actual working of the system in the country districts, I travelled alone through different parts of the Rhine Provinces for four weeks before proceeding to the capital. During the whole of my solitary rambles,

I put myself as much as possible into communication with the peasants and with the teachers, for the purpose of testing the actual state of feeling on this question. Judge, then, of my surprise, when I assure my readers that, although I conversed with many of the very poorest of the people, and with both Romanists and Protestants, and although I always *endeavoured* to elicit expressions of discontent, I never once heard, in any part of Prussia, one word spoken by any of the peasants against the educational regulations. But on the contrary, I every where received daily and hourly proofs, of the most unequivocal character, of the satisfaction and real pride with which a Prussian, however poor he may be, looks upon the schools of his locality.*

Often and often have I been answered by the poor labourers, when asking them whether they did not dislike being *obliged* to educate their children, — "Why should I? The schools are excellent; the teachers are very learned and good men; and then think how much good our children are gaining: they behave better at

* A remarkable proof of the truth of these remarks is, that since the commencement of the German revolutions of 1848, the only change in the educational regulations, which has been demanded by the people, is, that they should be allowed to send their children to the parochial schools free of all expense, and that the present small weekly pence required from the parents for the education of each child should be paid out of the regular parochial school-rates. This has been conceded, and the peasants themselves will now as rigorously enforce the compulsory educational regulations, as the Swiss peasants enforce laws *at least* as stringent. In France, the republican party in the first assembly laid before the assembly, immediately after the Revolution, the scheme of a law to oblige every parent to send his children to school. The republicans of France desire such a law.

home, they make our families all the happier, and they are much better able in after life to earn their own livelihood. No, no; we do not dislike the schools. We know too well how much good our children are gaining from them." And one very poor man at Cologne added, "you see, if we are not rich enough to pay the school fees, or to give our children clothes decent enough for the school-room, the town does this for us; so really we have not the least reason to complain." I have heard this said over and over again in different parts of Prussia, Saxony, Bavaria, Wirtemburg, and Baden; and, indeed, I may add, that throughout Germany, I never heard one single word of discontent uttered against these truly liberal and Christian establishments.

Every one of the richer classes, with whom I conversed, corroborated the truth of all that the peasants had told me. I particularly remember a very intelligent teacher at Elberfeld saying to me, "I am quite convinced that, if we had a political revolution to-morrow, none of the peasants would think of wishing to have any great alteration made in the laws which relate to the schools." Recent facts have proved the truth of the assertion.

The laws now in force in Switzerland and America show, that the freer the people are, the more stringent will be the regulations affecting the education of their children.

Several travellers have fallen into the strangest errors in their investigations on this subject, from having confined their attention to the schools of the capitals, or of one or two other large towns. Very few have seen the working of the system in the villages and remote provinces. But it is there only that a fair idea can be formed of the effects it is producing, and of the manner in which it is regarded by the people themselves.

CHAP. IV.

PRUSSIAN EDUCATION. — THE POLITICAL DIVISION OF THE COUNTRY. — THE LOCAL MAGISTRATES. — THEIR DUTIES WITH REGARD TO THE SCHOOLS AND TEACHERS.

It is now many years since the first regulations relating to the education of the people were issued by the Prussian government. The earliest extant dates from 1770; but a long period elapsed ere these decrees of the central power were productive of any great results. Before the beginning of the present century, but little was attempted, and, during the wars of Napoleon, all the energies and all the resources of the nation were devoted to a fierce struggle for existence, and to those patriotic and really gigantic efforts, which were finally crowned by his overthrow. It was only after the settlement of Europe, in 1815, that any great progress *began* to be made, towards the actual realisation of that end, which they have now attained. It must not be thought, however, that the following year saw the country supplied with schools and educated teachers. Such a result required, and will here in England require, many years of labour.

Thousands of schools for the children, and many great colleges for the education of teachers, had to be erected. Teachers had to be trained; the whole system had to be set in motion; so that a long time elapsed, ere it could be said, as at present, "*all* the young children in Prussia, between the ages of six and fourteen, are actually attending daily schools; *all* the schools are supplied with highly educated teachers, and with a sufficiency of books and apparatus; *every* parish has its school; *all* the Prussian people below thirty years of age are taught the great truths and doctrines of their religion; *all* of them can read, write, and sing; *all* of them understand arithmetic; and *most* of them know the history of their own country, and the geography of the world."

In order to understand the working of this system, it is necessary to understand the political division of the country. To enable my readers to do this, I shall give to the German divisions the names of such English territorial divisions, as most nearly correspond to them, so that it may be easier, hereafter, to recollect this somewhat complicated subject.

Prussia, then, is divided into eight provinces, viz., Prussia, Posen, Pomerania, Brandenburg, Silesia, Saxony, Westphalia, and Lower Rhine.

Each of these provinces is again subdivided into two or three Regierungsbezirke or counties.

Each of these counties is again subdivided into Kreis, or Unions of several parishes, and each of these Unions (as I shall term them) into Gemeinde, or parishes.

In each of the towns, all the parishes are united together under a Burgomaster or Mayor, who is elected for six years by the citizens, and who is assisted by a council of persons, elected also by the different parishes in the town. The number of the persons, composing these councils, depends on the population of the towns over which they preside. Of these municipal corporations I shall have to speak more at large hereafter; for the present it is only necessary to bear in mind, that, while in the country it often happens, that each parish has a separate and distinct civil organisation, this is not the case in all the Prussian towns, for in most of these, all the parishes are united together under one municipal corporation elected by the citizens.

Each parish is presided over by a magistrate (Schulze), who is elected from among the inhabitants of the parish, and appointed by the county council, of which I shall speak hereafter. I shall designate this parochial officer the *village magistrate*. His duties are to superintend all the civil concerns of his locality. He is the head of the parochial police, takes care of the public roads, and collects the taxes in his little department.

Each union (Kreis) or collection of parishes has also its civil officer or union overseer (Landrath), who is in reality the civil inspector of the county government. He takes care that the subordinate officers perform their civil functions, and conveys to them all the orders of the county council.

This county council it is very important that my readers should clearly understand, as it is through it that the government acts upon the parochial and municipal schools.

In each county, then, there is a council of magistrates, appointed by the central government, and selected invariably, I believe, from among the ablest men of the county. They are salaried by the state, and form the real *local* government. It is particularly necessary to take notice, that these representatives of the central power are chosen from among the inhabitants of their respective localities, so that they may be able to understand the actual wants and sympathise with all the different prejudices of their respective districts.

This county council (or Regierung, as it is termed) is composed of four sections, one of which presides over the police, another over the collection of the taxes, another over the administration of justice, and another over the *primary schools*. The council itself is under the superintendence of one magistrate, who presides over the four sections; and, in conjunction with these, over all the municipal corporations and parochial authorities in the county.

The section, whose duty it is to superintend the county schools, is composed of a president, who is termed Schulrath, and who is always selected from among the members of that religious party, which includes the majority of the inhabitants of the county; of two inferior counsellors, one acting as representative of the Roman Catholic, and the other as representative of the Protestant schools; of the president of the committee for the administration of justice, and of the president of the committee for the collection of taxes, both of which committees form, as I have before mentioned, part of the Regierung or county court.

Now, it is by means of this educational committee, thus composed, that the state directs the parochial and municipal *primary* schools of the county.

This committee, formed of men who thoroughly understand the peculiar wants of their district, and who are chosen from those inhabitants of the county who have shown themselves most interested in the education of the people, and by their intelligence most worthy of being entrusted with such an office, are instructed to assist the parochial committees with advice, to act for them, if they refuse to act for themselves, and to check their operations, when these operations are manifestly tending to unsatisfactory results.

Some such sort of intelligent surveillance and direction is always necessary, in order to secure the actual realisation of parochial education.

There are always some districts in every country, which are too ignorant of the importance of education, or too careless, or too selfish, to put themselves to the trouble and expense of supporting a sufficient number of schools and teachers if they are not compelled to do so; or which are too ignorant or prejudiced to act rightly, without the aid and advice of some enlightened, disinterested, and impartial advisers. It is to remedy these necessary and inherent evils of totally unrestrained liberty of action, that the county councils are appointed. It is their business to see, that every parish is supplied with able teachers and good schools. The parish can act for itself if it will; but if it will not, the county council is there to take care that the general interests of the country do not suffer from parochial negligence.

Besides, even when a parish has provided itself with schools and teachers, it is always necessary to have some kind of constant intelligent surveillance; or else, owing to the neglect of the parishioners, who are obliged to devote most of their time and attention to their own daily concerns, and who have consequently little time, even when they have sufficient intelligence, to attend to the school concerns,—the teacher, if he be not a very conscientious man, would often become dispirited by neglect, or careless from want of being inspected, or would be thwarted in his labours by the ignorance or unreasonable prejudice of the parishioners who live around him. Now, the educational section is intended to remedy both these evils. It watches over the parochial schools by means of its inspectors, and it mediates between the parishioners and teachers, when any dispute arises between them. Of both these functions I shall have to speak more hereafter, when I enter upon the subject of the inspectors and the teachers. Suffice it then, for the present, to repeat, that while the school affairs are committed to the immediate management of the parishioners, the government interferes with the parochial action, through these educational committees, to advise, to negative injudicious plans of proceeding, and to supply the defects of local efforts. It takes care, that schools are established, that they are established in an efficient manner, and in healthy sites, and that their efficiency is not afterwards allowed to lessen, but that it shall be continually increased. In fine, the Prussian government is the *guardian,* but not the sole director, of the primary schools. The educational section of the county council, as I have said, has the surveillance of the *primary* schools of the county, but not of the *higher* schools, normal colleges, or gymnasia; for these are placed under the surveillance of the *provincial* authorities.

The Schulrath, or president of the educational section in each county, corresponds directly with the Minister of Instruction in Berlin, and with all the county inspectors of schools, who are all chosen from among the clergy. He himself, also, makes his yearly tour of inspection in his county, enters the schools without giving previous notice of his visit, assists at the teacher's lessons, and makes his own separate report to the Minister of Public Instruction. He is the representative of this latter high functionary in the county, and by his immediate supervision, and by his direct connection with the central government, stimulates, in an extraordinary degree, the efforts of all the different localities and teachers of his county.

Above all the county courts in each province, is the *provincial* president and *provincial* consistorium. The president is for the province, what the landrath is for the union. He is the chief officer of government in the province, and conveys to the different county courts the orders and regulations issued by the government in Berlin. He receives all the reports of the county courts, and communicates them to the Minister of the Interior, and he presides over the provincial government or consistorium. This consists of three parts. The first, or Consistorium, properly so called, has the direction of ecclesiastical affairs. The second, or Schulcollegium, has the direction of the superior colleges and of the Normal colleges. It is also before a committee of this body, that the teachers are examined for diplomas; it is from this committee that they receive their diplomas or certificates of capability, without which they are not allowed to teach in the schools; and it is the schulcollegium also which must give its sanction ere any book can be employed in the primary schools. The members of this body are all laymen, chosen from among the most learned men of the province by the Minister of Education. It will be seen hereafter, that the concurrence of the bishops is necessary to render several of their acts valid, and especially the one relating to the certificates of the teachers. All the directions relating to the interior management of the schools and of the lesson plans, showing between what subjects and in what manner all the hours of the week devoted to education are to be set apart, are also issued by this schulcollegium.

The third section of the provincial consistorum, of which I have not yet spoken, is the medicinal college, and has the direction of all matters relating to the public health.

The Minister of Education at Berlin, aided by a council, superintends all these various local administrations, and watches over the general working of all parts of this great and admirably organised system of national education.

It must, however, be most carefully borne in mind, that the actual administration is *parochial* and *municipal*. The superior authorities only act as a check on, and as guides to, this parochial action. It is not the minister or the county councils, who actually manage the parochial affairs. They only assist the parishes with their advice, and check them, when about to take any injudicious step.

The three great results, which the Prussian government has laboured to ensure by this system of education are —

1. To interest the different parishes and towns in the progress of the education of the people, by committing the management of the parochial schools to them, under certain very simple restrictions;

2. To assist the parochial school-committees in each county with the advice of the most able inhabitants of the county; and, —

3. To gain the cordial cooperation of the ministers of religion.

These results the government has gained, to the entire and perfect satisfaction of all parties. The provincial and county councils act as advisers of the parochial committees. These latter are the actual directors of parochial education; and the clergy not only occupy places in these parochial committees, but are also the *ex officio* inspectors of all the schools.

The system is liberally devised; and I am persuaded that it is solely owing to its impartial, popular, and religious character, that it has enlisted so strongly on its side the feelings of the Prussian people.

I know there are many in our land who say, " But why have any system at all? Is it not better to leave the education of the people to the exertions of public charity and private benevolence?" Let the contrast between the state of the education and social condition of the poor in England and Germany be the answer. In England it is well known *that not one half of the country is properly supplied with good schools, and that many of those, which do exist, are under the direction of very inefficient and sometimes of actually immoral teachers.* In Germany and Switzerland, *every* parish is supplied with its school buildings, and *each* school is directed by a teacher of high principles, and superior education and intelligence. Such a splendid social institution has not existed without effecting magnificent results, and the Germans and Swiss may now proudly point to the character and condition of their peasantry.

So great have been the results of this system, that it is now a well known fact, that, except in cases of sickness, every child between the ages of six and ten in the whole of Prussia, is receiving instruction from highly educated teachers, under the surveillance of the parochial ministers. And, if I except the manufacturing districts, I may go still farther, and say, that every child in Prussia, between the ages of six and fourteen, is receiving daily instruction in its parochial school. But even this assertion does not give any adequate idea of the vastness of the educational machinery, which is at work; for the Prussian government is encouraging all the towns throughout the country to establish infant schools for the children of parents who are forced, from the peculiar nature of their labour, to absent themselves from home during the greater part of the day, and who would be otherwise obliged to leave their infants without proper superintendence; and, as all the children in the manufacturing districts, who are engaged in the weaving-rooms, are also obliged to attend evening classes to the age of fourteen years, I may say, with great truth, that *nearly all the Prussian children between the ages of four and fourteen are under the influence of a religious education.* And let it not be supposed that an arbitrary government has forced this result from an unwilling people. On the contrary, as I have said before, the peasants themselves have always been at least as anxious to obtain this education for their children, as the government has been desirous of granting it.

A proof of the satisfaction, with which the Prussian people regard the educational regulations, is the undeniable fact, that all the materials and machinery for instruction are being so constantly and so rapidly improved over the whole country, and by the people themselves. Wherever I travelled, I was astonished to see the great improvement in all these several matters that was going on. Every where I found new and handsome school-houses springing up, old ones being repaired, a most liberal supply of teachers and of apparatus for the schools provided by the municipal authorities, the greatest cleanliness, lofty and spacious school-rooms, and excellent houses for the teachers; all showing, that the importance of the work is fully appreciated *by the people,* and that there is every desire on their part to aid the government in carrying out this vast undertaking.

CHAP. V.

PRUSSIAN EDUCATION. — THE LAWS OBLIGING EACH PARENT TO EDUCATE HIS CHILDREN. — THE LAWS OBLIGING THE VILLAGE TO PROVIDE SUFFICIENT SCHOOL ROOM, ETC., FOR THEIR CHILDREN. — THE LAWS RELATING TO THE EDUCATION, ETC., OF CHILDREN EMPLOYED IN THE FACTORIES. — THE LAWS OBLIGING THE TOWNS TO PROVIDE SUFFICIENT SCHOOLS, ETC., FOR THEIR CHILDREN. — THE LAWS OBLIGING GREAT LANDED PROPRIETORS TO EDUCATE ALL THE CHILDREN ON THEIR ESTATES.

THROUGHOUT all Germany and Switzerland, every parent, no matter what his station in life, whether nobleman or pauper, is obliged, by law, to provide for the education of his children, either by educating them at home, in an efficient manner, or by sending them to some school which is open to the government inspectors. He may consult his own taste, whether he will send them to a private tutor, private school, or public school. In making this choice, he has entire and uncontrolled liberty; but educated they must be. No German or Swiss government will suffer a child to grow up to manhood, without having passed through a most careful religious, moral, and intellectual training.

Germany has long perceived this truth, that the morality and social order of an uneducated people will always be immeasurably below that of one, which has been enlightened and civilised by a sound religious and intellectual training. Hence the same laws on this point have been for many years in force throughout Germany, Switzerland, and the Austrian Empire. The people themselves so perfectly well understand the necessity of enforcing this duty, that they would as soon think of dispensing with all laws whatsoever, as of being freed from these reasonable and moral regulations. "Schulpflichtigkeit," as they call this legal obligation of educating the children, has, in truth, become an integral part of their national moral codes; and it is very curious to observe, that the freer the people have been, the more strenuously do they put in force this law. In Austria it has, until lately, been observed less than in any other German country; in Prussia, where the enforcing of it has been entrusted, as I shall presently show, in great measure to the people, it has been much more rigorously observed; in the states of Wirtemburg and Baden, which have long enjoyed political liberty, still more so; whilst in the democratic states of Switzerland and North America, a very much stricter observance of these laws has been required than in any other part of the world.

It is very important to clearly understand the meaning of this "Schulpflichtigkeit," as some very strange prejudices have arisen from its being misapprehended. Many persons imagine, that the German governments oblige each parent to send his children to school; that they define to *what* school they must be sent; and that they themselves organise the school, and regulate the tone and spirit of the instruction given in it. Now these three suppositions are and have been entirely unfounded. It is not the government, but the particular locality, whether it be town or village, which organises the school and chooses the teacher; and when it is so organised, and the teacher so selected, the law does not say to the parent, you must send your child there. Far otherwise. The German and Swiss governments have always left to the parent the greatest possible liberty of choice, as to the manner in which he will educate his children; they have only said, "the happiness and social prosperity of every country require, that all its members should be, capable of thinking, intelligent, and, above all, religious; he who does not educate his children is an offender against his country, inasmuch as he lessens the probability of its future prosperity and happiness; therefore, such a person must be punished, that other careless citizens may be deterred from following his example." Induced by such a train of simple reasoning as this, the Prussian government, as well as all the governments of Germany, Denmark, Switzerland, Sweden, and America, obliges every parent to educate his children. He may send them to any school he pleases, in any part of the country; he may have a private tutor at home if he pleases; he may educate them himself; or the mother may perform the office of the teacher. In all this the government will not interfere. All that is demanded is, that as the country is immediately and essentially interested in the right development of the mind of each one of its citizens, the country should have satisfactory proof, that the children of every parent are being properly educated in one way or another. Surely there is nothing so very unreasonable in all this. We interfere with the parent's right, so far as to say, he shall not teach his children to steal, or to trespass on the property of others, or to blaspheme. Why, then, should it be so much worse to require, that he shall not allow them to grow up in idleness, filth, and immorality, contemners of the laws both of God and man, and curses to themselves and to all their neighbours?

But we have an idea, that if a government does this, it necessarily follows, that it must interfere with the religious education of the children, and that it must define what religious education is to signify. But is this so? Look at the governments of Germany, Switzerland, Denmark, Sweden, and America. The Protestants, Romanists, and Jews, in these countries, are each of them satisfied with the guarantees, that the several governments have given them, that they will not interfere with their religious education, and that they will leave the surveillance of this, the most important part of education, to the clergy of the different religious parties.

All this shows, that it is not *impossible* for religious parties to work together on this great question, when there is only an honest desire to advance the real interests of the poor. If these three sects of Romanists, Protestants, and Jews can really work together in Germany, Bohemia, Austria, Switzerland, Holland, Denmark, and France; is it not disgraceful that we Protestants, differing from one another as we do merely on points of so much less significance, than those which separate Romanists, Protestants, and Jews from one another, — is it not disgraceful, I repeat, that we should find it impossible to unite upon this important question, when, by our disunion, we are ruining the best interests of our poor fellow citizens? Are we not forced to the conclusion, that we are much less deeply interested in the welfare and advancement of the poor, than the countries I have named?

M. Cousin has quoted a great deal from a law on Schulpflichtigkeit, which was only projected, and which never received the royal sanction. Indeed, the greater part of his excellent report is a translation of the same *proposed* ordinance; and though this law was not much more, than a projected codification of the different scattered regulations then and now in force, yet it did contain some rather important alterations, which were never carried out, but which are erroneously represented by M. Cousin as in force.

The laws, which are in force on this subject, are as follows: —

"Every parent may educate his children at home.

"Those parents, however, who undertake the education of their own children, must satisfy the proper authorities, that they are capable of undertaking this duty.

"All parents or guardians, *who cannot give proof that they provide for the education of their children at home,* shall be obliged, by compulsion or punishment, to send each of their children to school, as soon as it has completed its fifth year.

"But if a village or hamlet is separated from the school-house by more than a quarter of an hour's walk, the child must commence its attendance after it has completed its sixth year.

"Regular attendance at school must be continued, until the child, in the opinion of its religious minister, has obtained all the knowledge necessary for an intelligent person in its station of life.

"Admission into the public schools shall be denied to no child on account of difference of religious belief.

"Those children, who are brought up in a religious belief different to that taught in the public school, shall not be obliged to remain in school whilst the religious education is being given."

The children generally remain in school, until the completion of their fourteenth year; and a law has been issued, for one or two of the provinces, appointing this as the time, after which the parents may remove their children. But if the parents are very poor, and their children have learnt the doctrines of their religion, as well as to read, write, and cipher, their religious minister can, in conjunction with the teacher, permit them to discontinue their attendance at the completion of their twelfth year.

"No child, without the permission both of the civil magistrate of the town or village of which its parents are inhabitants, and also of their religious minister, can be kept from school beyond the completion of its fifth year, or afterwards discontinue its attendance on the school classes for any length of time."

If a parent neither provides at home for the education of his children, nor sends them to the school, the teacher is bound to inform the religious minister of the parent; the minister then remonstrates with him; and if he still neglects to send his children, the minister is bound by law to report him to the village committee, which has power to punish him by a fine, of from one halfpenny to sixpence a day, for neglecting the first and greatest duty of every parent. If the village committee cannot induce him to educate his children, he is reported to the union magistrates, who are empowered to punish him with imprisonment. But it is hardly ever necessary to resort to such harsh measures, for the parents are even more anxious to send their children to these admirably conducted schools, than the civil magistrate to obtain their attendance. In order, however, to ensure such a regular attendance, and as an assistance to the parents themselves, each teacher is furnished by the local magistrate, every year, with a list of all the children of his district, who have attained the age, at which they ought to attend his classes. This list is called over every morning and every afternoon, and all absentees are marked down, so that the school committees, magistrates, and inspectors may instantly discover if the attendance of any child has been irregular. If a child requires leave of absence for more than a week, the parent must apply to the civil magistrate for it; but the clergyman can grant it, if it be only for six or seven days, and the teacher alone can allow it, if for only one or two days.

At the German revolutions of 1848, one of the great popular cries was for *gratuitous* education. The governments of Germany were obliged to yield to this cry, and to make it the law of nearly the whole of Germany, that all parents should be able to get their children educated at the primary schools without having to pay anything for this education.

There are now, therefore, no school fees in the greatest part of Germany. Education is perfectly gratuitous. The poorest man can send his child free of all expense to the best of the public schools of his district. And, besides this, the authorities of the parish or town, in which a parent lives, who is too poor to clothe his children decently enough for school attendance, are obliged to clothe them for him, and to provide them with books, pencils, pens, and every thing necessary for school attendance, so that a poor man, instead of being obliged to pay something out of his small earnings for the education of his children, is, on the contrary, actually paid for sending them to school. This latter is an old regulation, and is one which has aided very greatly to make the educational regulations very popular among the poor of Germany.

I made very careful inquiries about the education of children in the principal manufacturing district of Prussia. I remained several days in Elberfeld, their largest manufacturing town, on purpose to visit the factory schools. I put myself there, as elsewhere, in direct communication with the teachers, from whom I obtained a great deal of information; and I also had several interviews on the subject with the educational councillors at Berlin, who put into my hand the latest regulations on this subject issued by the government.

The laws relating to the factory children date only from 1839, so that no notice of them whatever will be found in M. Cousin's report. They are as follows:—

"No child may be employed in any manufactory, or in any mining or building operations, before it has attained the age of *nine* years.

"No child, which has not received three years' regular

instruction in a school, and has not obtained the certificate of a school-committee, that it can read its mother tongue fluently, and also write it tolerably well, may be employed in any of the above-mentioned ways, before it has completed its sixteenth year.

"An exception to this latter rule is only allowed in those cases, where the manufacturers provide for the education of the factory children, by erecting and maintaining factory schools."

If a manufacturer will establish a school in connection with his manufactory, and engage a properly educated teacher, he is then allowed to employ any children of nine years of age, whether they have obtained a certificate or not, on condition, however, that these children attend the school four evenings in every week, as well as two hours every Sunday morning, until they have obtained a certificate of proficiency in their studies.

The "schulrath," or educational minister in the county court, decides whether the factory school is so satisfactorily managed, as to entitle the manufacturer to this privilege. This minister also regulates the hours which must be devoted weekly to the instruction of the factory children.

"Young people, under sixteen years of age, may not be employed in manufacturing establishments more than ten hours a day."

The civil magistrates are, however, empowered, in some cases, to allow young people to work eleven hours a day, when an accident has happened, which obliges the manufacturer to make up for lost time, in order to accomplish a certain quantity of work before a given day. But these licenses cannot be granted for more, at the most, than four weeks at a time.

After the hours of labour have been regulated by the "schulrath" and the manufacturer, the latter is obliged by law to take care that the factory children have, both in the mornings and in the afternoons, a quarter of an hour's exercise in the open air, and that at noon, they always have a good hour's relaxation from labour.

"*No young person, under sixteen years of age, may, in any case, or in any emergency, work more than eleven hours a day.*" The children of Christian parents, who have not been confirmed, may not work in the mills during the hours set apart by the religious minister, for the religious instruction, which he wishes to give them preparatory to their confirmation.

The manufacturers, who employ children in the mills, are obliged to lay before the magistrate a list, containing the names of all the children they employ, their respective ages, their places of abode, and the names of their parents. If any inspector or teacher reports to the civil magistrate, that any child under the legal age is being employed in the mills instead of being sent to school, or if the police report the infringement of any other of the above-mentioned regulations, the magistrate is empowered and obliged to punish the manufacturer by fines, which are increased in amount on every repetition of the offence.

I examined the actual state of things in Elberfeld, one of the most important of the manufacturing districts of Prussia, and I found these regulations most satisfactorily put in force. No children were allowed to work in the mills, before they had attained the age of nine years, and after this time, they were required to attend classes four evenings every week, conducted by the teachers of the day-schools; or, if their work was of such a nature as to prevent such attendance, then they were obliged to attend classes every Sunday morning for two hours; and this attendance was required to be continued, until the children could obtain a certificate from their teacher and religious minister, that they could read and write well, that they were well versed in Scripture history, and that they knew arithmetic sufficiently well to perform all the ordinary calculations, which would be required of them. As a check upon the parents and manufacturers, no child was allowed to labour in the mills, without having obtained a certificate, signed by its religious minister and its teacher, that it was attending one of these classes regularly. If the attendance was irregular, this certificate was immediately withdrawn, and the child was no longer allowed to continue working in the mills. But, from all I saw of these schools, and from what the teachers told me, I should say, they had no difficulty in enforcing attendance; and, so far from it being evident, that the parents were anxious to send their children into the mills, as soon as possible, I was astonished to find even the *daily* schools filled to overflowing, and that with children, many of whom were thirteen, fourteen, and fifteen years of age.

It is very easy for the traveller, who is merely passing through the *manufacturing* towns of the Rhine Provinces, to prove to himself, how anxious both the people and the government are to carry all these regulations into effect. Let him only take the trouble of wandering into the streets of such a town, at a quarter to eight in the morning, or at a quarter to one in the afternoon, and he will find them alive with children of remarkably courteous and gentle appearance, all *very* neatly and cleanly dressed, each carrying a little bag containing a slate and school books, and all hurrying along to school. Let him visit the same streets at any time during the school hours, and he will find an absence of young children, which, accustomed as he is to the alleys of our own towns, swarming with poor little creatures growing up in filth, and coarseness, and immorality, will be even more astonishing and delightful.

Before Prussia began in good earnest to promote the education of the people, it was thought there, as it is in England at the present day, that private charity and voluntary exertions would suffice, to supply the country with all the materials of education. In the early part of the eighteenth century the government enunciated, in formal edicts, that it was the first duty of a parish to educate its young. For nearly one hundred years, it trusted to the voluntary principle, and left the work in the hands of generous individuals; the result was what might have been expected, and what may be observed in England: the supply of the materials of education did not keep pace with the growth of the population. Prussia was little or no better provided with schools in 1815, than it had been in 1715; as to the teachers, they were poor, neglected, ignorant persons. Educated persons would not become teachers of the poor; and the poor were neither able nor willing to pay for the education of teachers for their children. A sufficient number of benevolent individuals could not be found to bear the whole expense of educating the nation; and even in those parishes, in which the benevolent part of the richer classes had managed to collect funds, sufficient for carrying on such a work for a year or two, it was found, that they were unable or unwilling, for any length of time, to bear alone such a great and ever-increasing burden.

After a long trial of this unfair voluntary system, which taxed charitable individuals in order to make up for the default of the selfish or careless, it was found, in 1815, as in England at the present day, that great numbers of parishes had no schools at all; that of the schools which were built, scarcely any were properly supplied with the necessary books and apparatus; that there were no good teachers in the country, and no means of educating any; and that the science of pedagogy had been totally neglected, and was universally misunderstood.

If, then, the people were to be educated,—and the French Revolution of 1789 had taught the Prussian government the necessity, of enlightening the poor and of improving their social condition,—it became but too evident, that the government must act as well as preach. In a word, the experience of one hundred years taught the Prussians, that it was necessary to *compel* the ignorant, slothful, and selfish members of the political body to assist the benevolent and patriotic, or that sufficient funds would never be found for educating the whole of the labouring classes. The following regulations, therefore, were put into and are still in force throughout Prussia.

The inhabitants of each parish are obliged, either alone, or in company with one or more neighbouring parishes, to provide sufficient school room, a sufficient number of teachers, and all the necessary school apparatus for the instruction of all their children, who are between the ages of six and fourteen. I shall show by what parochial organisation this is effected.

I. *Where all the inhabitants of a village are members of the same religious denomination.*

In these cases, whenever more school room, or a greater number of teachers, or more apparatus, or any repairs of the existing school-buildings is required, the village magistrate, having been informed of these deficiencies by the district school-inspector, immediately summons a committee of the villagers, called the "Schulvorstand."

This Schulvorstand consists:—

1. Of the religious minister of the parish. He is the president of the committee or Schulvorstand. In some parts of Prussia, however, there are still some few remnants of the old aristocracy, who possess great estates; and where the village is situated on one of these estates, there the landlord is the president of the school-committee. This, however, is so rare an exception, that it is not necessary further to notice it.

2. Of the village magistrate, who is selected by the

county magistrates, from the most intelligent men in the parish.

3. Of from two to four of the heads of families in the parish. These members of the committee are elected by the parishioners, and their election is confirmed or annulled by the union magistrates. If the union magistrate annuls the election, because of the unfitness of the persons chosen, the parish can proceed to a second election; but, if they again select men, who are not fit to be entrusted with the duties of the school-committee, the election is again annulled, and the union magistrate himself selects two or four of the parishioners, to act as members of the committee. When the village is situate on the estate of a great landed proprietor, he also can annul the choice of the parishioners; but these cases, as I have before said, are very rare, and are confined almost entirely to the eastern provinces of Prussia, where the Polish nobles still retain some of their former possessions; for in the other provinces of Prussia, the land is now almost as much subdivided as in France, and is generally the property of the peasants.

The members of these committees are chosen for six years, at the end of which time a new election takes place.

If several parishes join in supporting *one* school, each of them must be represented in the school-committee, by at least one head of a family. The county court, however, has the power of preventing this union of parishes for the support of one joint school,—

1. When the number of children is so great, as to make it difficult to instruct them all in two classes;

2. When the parishes are separated too far apart, or when the roads between them are bad, dangerous, or at times impassable.

In such cases, there must be separate schools; or else the great law of the land, that "*all the children must be educated*," would often be infringed.

II. *Where the inhabitants of a village are members of different religious denominations.*

Sometimes it happens, that a parish contains persons of different religious opinions; and then arises the question, which has been a stumbling-block to the progress of primary education in England, "how shall the rival claims of these parties be satisfied, so that the great law of Germany, that '*all the children must be educated*,' may be carried into effect?"

In these cases, the governments of Germany leave the parishes at perfect liberty to select their own course of proceeding, and to establish separate or mixed schools, according as they judge best for themselves. The only thing the government requires is, that schools of one kind or another shall be established.

If the inhabitants of such a parish in Prussia determine on having separate schools, then separate school-committees are elected by the different sects. The committee of each sect consists of, the village magistrate, the minister, and two or three heads of families, of the religious party for which the committee is constituted.

If the inhabitants, however, decide on having one mixed school for all the religious parties, the committee consists of, the village magistrate, the religious ministers of the different parties, and several of the parishioners, elected from among the members of the different sects, for which the school is intended.

In these cases, the teacher is chosen from the most numerous religious party; or, if the school is large enough to require two teachers, the head one is elected from the members of the most numerous party, and the second from those of the next largest party. If there is only one teacher, children of those parents, who do not belong to the same religious sect as the teacher, are always allowed to absent themselves during the hour, in which the teacher gives the religious lessons, on condition, that the children receive religious instruction from their own religious ministers.

One of the educational councillors at Berlin informed me, that the government did not *encourage* the establishment of mixed schools, as they think, that, in such cases, the religious education of both parties, or at least of one of them, often suffers; but, he continued, "of course we think a mixed school infinitely better than none at all; and, when a district is too poor to support separate schools, we gladly see mixed ones established." The gentleman who said this was a Roman Catholic. In the towns, there are not often mixed schools containing Romanists and Protestants, as there generally are sufficient numbers of each of these sects in every town, to enable the citizens to establish separate schools. The children of Jews, however, are often to be found, even in the towns, in the schools of the other sects; but, owing to the entire and uncontrolled liberty of decision that the people themselves possess on this point, there seems to be little difficulty in arranging matters, and no jealousy whatever exists between the different parties. If a mixed school is established in any parish, and the teacher is chosen from the most numerous sect, and if the minor party becomes discontented or suspicious of the education given in the school, it is always at liberty to establish another school for itself; and it is this liberty of action, which preserves the parishes, where the mixed schools exist, from all intestine troubles and religious quarrels, which are ever the most ungodly of disputes. In leaving the settlement of this matter to the parishes, the government appears to have acted most wisely; for, in these religious questions, any interference from without is sure to create alarm, suspicion, and jealousy, and cause the different parties to fly asunder, instead of coalescing. All that the government does, is to say, "You must provide sufficient school room, and a sufficient number of good teachers, but decide yourselves how you will do this." The consequence is, that the people say, "We can try a mixed school first; and, if we see reason to fear its effects, we will then amicably decide on erecting another separate one." So that the great difficulty arising from religious differences has been easily overcome.

The duties of the school-committees, when once formed, are:—

1st. To take care that the parish is supplied with sufficient school room for all the children, who are between the ages of five and fourteen.

2nd. To supply the school-rooms with all the books,

writing materials, slates, black-boards, maps, and apparatus necessary for instruction.

3rd. To provide the teachers with comfortable houses for themselves and families.

4th. To keep all the school-buildings, and the houses of the teachers, in good repair, often whitewashed, and well warmed.

5th. To take care that the salary of the teachers is paid to them regularly.

6th. To assist those parents, who are too poor to provide their children with clothes sufficiently decent for their school attendance.

7th. To assist, protect, and encourage the teachers.

8th. To be present at all the public examinations of the school; at the induction of the teachers, which is a public ceremony performed in church before all the parishioners; and at all the school fête days.

If the school is not endowed, the committee is empowered to impose a tax on the householders for its support, and for the payment of the schoolmaster; and it is held responsible by the higher authorities for his regular payment, according to the agreement, which was made with him on his introduction. The school-committee, however, cannot discharge the teacher, it can only report him to the higher authorities; for in Prussia none of the *local* authorities, who are in *immediate* contact with the teacher, and who might, consequently, imbibe personal prejudices against him, are allowed to exercise the power of dismissing him. This is reserved for those, who are never brought into personal connection with him, and who are not, therefore, so likely to imbibe such prejudices. Neither can the committee interfere with the interior discipline of the school; it can only inspect the condition of the school, and report to the county authorities. When the committee has once elected the teacher, he is entirely free to follow his own plans of instruction, unfettered by the interference of local authorities, as he is presumed to understand his own business, better than any of those about him. If the school-committee neglects its duties, or refuses to furnish the teacher with the necessary apparatus, or to keep the school-house in proper repair, or to pay the teacher regularly, he has always the power of appealing to the inspectors, or to the county courts, who instantly compel the local authorities to perform their appointed duties.

When a new school is required, the school-committee selects the site and plan of the buildings, and sends them for confirmation to the county magistrate. If this magistrate sees any objection to the plans, he returns them to the committee, with his suggestions; the plans are then reconsidered by the committee, and returned with the necessary emendations to the magistrate, who then gives his sanction to them. Before this sanction has been obtained, the plans cannot be finally adopted by the committee.

It is already very evident, by what I have said, how very much liberty of action is left to the people themselves. True it is, that in the election of members of the committees, as well as in the choice of plans and sites for school-houses, and in the determination of the amount of the school-rate, the county magistrates have a negative; but this is only a necessary precaution against the possibility of a really vicious selection of members, or of unhealthy or otherwise unsuitable sites for the school-houses, or of a niggardly and insufficient provision for the support of the school. Such a limited interference is always necessary, where the interests of the acting parties might otherwise tempt them to disregard the spirit of the law, and to sacrifice some great public good to the selfishness or ignorance of private individuals.

Every landed proprietor is obliged by law, to provide for the education of the children of all labourers living on his estates, who are too poor themselves to do so. Every such proprietor is also obliged by law, to keep the schools situated upon his estates in perfect repair, and in a perfect state of cleanliness; to conform to all the regulations, of which I shall speak hereafter, and which relate to the election and support of the teachers; and to furnish all the wood necessary for the repairs and warming of the school-buildings, and all the apparatus, books, &c., necessary for instruction.

This is what ought to be done in England. If it is right, that the law should grant to the proprietors such full powers over their property even after death, and should enable them to tie up their land in their own family for so long a time, and thus prevent the land dividing and getting into the hands of the poor, as it does abroad, it is but just, that the landlords should be compelled by law to do, at least, as much for their tenants in this country, as they are compelled to do in countries, where the poor are much more favoured than they are here, and where the interests of landlords are much less protected by law, than they are with us.

It sometimes happens, that a parish is so poor, as not to be able to build the new school-house, of which it stands in need. In these cases, in order that the great law of the land "*that every child must be educated*" should be carried into execution, it is necessary, that the poor parish should receive assistance from without. This is provided for by a law, which requires that each county court shall assist, within its district, every parish, which is not able to provide alone for the expenses of the education of its children. If a county court should, from the number of calls upon its treasury, find itself unable to supply enough to assist all the parishes of the county which need assistance, the government at Berlin grants assistance to the county court; for, whatever else is neglected for want of funds, great care is taken, that all necessary means for the education of the people shall be every where provided.

The school organisation of the Prussian towns differs somewhat from that of the Prussian villages. I have already mentioned, that the superior *village* magistrates are appointed by the state, and that in each village there is one of these civil magistrates, who is a member of the village school-committee, and is held responsible, if sufficient means are not provided for the education of the people of his district. But, in the towns, the magistrates are elected by the citizens; and, strange as it may seem, the municipal corporations have long been, on the whole, liberally constituted. The privilege of citizenship in any town is acquired, by good character and honest repute. The magistrates, who have been themselves elected by the citizens, can admit such inhabitants of the town, as they think worthy of the position, to the rank of citizens. But all citizens, who possess any ground of the value, in small towns, of 50*l*., or in large towns, of about 250*l*. in Prussian money, and all citizens who, without possessing any ground, have incomes of at least 35*l*. per annum, in Prussian money, are by law entitled to a vote in the election of the town magistrates. The citizens, who are entitled to a vote, elect, every three years, a number of representatives, or, as they are called, town councillors. No person can be elected to the office of town councillor, unless he possess land of the value, in small towns, of at least 150*l*., and in large towns of at least 200*l*., or whose income does not amount to at least 35*l*. per annum. The number of these councillors depends on the size of the towns; no town can elect fewer than nine, or more than sixty. The manner, in which they are elected, differs in different towns, but I believe the ordinary custom is, for each division of a town to elect one or more to represent it in the general council. These councillors, when elected, proceed to the election of a certain number of magistrates, whose offices last from six to twelve years, and these magistrates appoint from among themselves a mayor, who is chosen also for twelve years. The county court, under which the town finds itself ranged, has the power of annulling the election of the mayor, and of any of the magistrates, whom it may judge unfit for their office; and, in such a case, the magistrates or the town councillors, as the case may be, are obliged to proceed to another election. Such is a bare outline of the Prussian municipal system. With the various civic and political duties of the different authorities, I have no concern here, further than they relate to the education of the people.

In each town a committee is chosen, which is called the "*schuldeputation*," or, as I shall translate it, the school-committee. It consists of from one to three, but of never more than three, of the town magistrates, of an equal number of deputies from the town councillors, an equal number of citizens, having the reputation of being interested and skilled in school matters, (these are commonly selected from among the religious ministers), and also of the several representatives of those privately endowed schools in the town, which are not supported by the town, but yet fall under the surveillance and direction of its municipal authorities. The number of these representatives varies, according to the size of the town. With the exception of the representatives of the *private* schools, the members of this committee are chosen by the magistrates, who are themselves, as I have before said, elected by the citizens; but the representatives of the private schools, which are not supported by the town funds, are nominated by the county courts. To these members, thus elected, is joined one member from each of the committees, which are elected from the magistrates and town councillors for the different municipal affairs, if the former election should not have admitted any such members into the school-committee. The first ecclesiastical authority of the town is also *ex officio* a member of the committee; and if the town contains both Romanists and Protestants, the committee must be composed of equal proportions of members of the different parties. The county courts have the power of annulling the election of any member, if they see reason to deem him unfit for the exercise of the duties of his office, and in such a case, the town authorities are obliged to proceed to make a new election.

The duties of the town school-committees are to provide sufficient school room for all the children in the town; to elect a sufficient number of teachers; to pay them their salaries regularly; to provide all needful apparatus for the schools; to keep the class-rooms and the teachers' houses in good repair, well whitewashed, and well warmed; to take care that all the children of the town attend school regularly; to inspect the schools at stated intervals; *to provide each school with a play-ground;* and to take care that the teachers exercise the children there every morning and afternoon. The funds, required for the maintenance of the town schools, are provided from the treasury of the corporation.

The town councillors are responsible to the county magistrate and to the central government for the due performance of these several duties. If they neglect any of them, the teachers and inspectors complain to the higher authorities, who oblige them to conform immediately to the general law of the land.

Besides these municipal authorities, for the superintendence of the education of the whole town, it often happens, that each school in the town has its peculiar schulvorstand, corresponding to the village committees, which I have already described. These committees, where they do exist in the towns, elect their own teachers, and collect, in their several districts, the necessary school funds from the heads of families dwelling there; but if any one of the district school-committees is not able to provide for the expenditure, required to supply the wants of its district, the town school-committee is obliged to come forward and assist it, from the general town funds. The latter committee is the general superintendent and assistant, but the former little district societies, where they exist, are the actual labourers. Difference of religion creates no greater difficulty in the towns than in the country parishes, since the Romanists, Protestants, and Jews can, if they prefer, manage their own schools separately, by means of the little school societies, and are never forced into any sort of connection, unless, where it is agreeable to themselves.

The Prussian government seems to have considered the education of the children of the towns, of even higher importance, than that of the children of the villages; and to have required the formation of these superior committees in the towns, as a sort of additional security, that all the districts of a town should be amply provided with every thing necessary for the careful education of their children.

These committees assemble every fortnight, and oftener when necessary, at the town halls; they have the power of inviting any number of the clergy and teachers of the towns to assist at their conferences, and to aid them with their experience and counsels.

In many parts of Prussia these central town committees are superseding the smaller district school societies, so that the funds of all the town schools, and the choice and induction of all the teachers, rest entirely with the one central town school-committee; and in the case of towns containing different religious sects, as far as I could gather from what I heard in Berlin — for on this point I could find no express regulation,—the Protestant members of the town committee appoint the teachers of the Protestant schools, and the Romanist members the teachers of the Romanist schools.

But in every town every religious party is at liberty, if it pleases, to separate itself from the central town committee, and to form its own separate school-committee, for the management of its own educational affairs. And wherever the union of the different religious parties occasions any strife or disputes, the small district committees are sure to be formed. Where these smaller committees do exist, they elect the teachers for the schools under their management.

Great advantages are, however, insured, when the management of all the schools in any town can be put under the direction of ONE committee, instead of each being placed under the direction of its separate committee; or when all the Romanist schools can be put under the direction of one committee, and all the Protestant schools under the direction of another. For in these cases, instead of creating a great number of *small* schools in different parts of the town, each containing only one or two classes, in which children of very different ages and very different degrees of proficiency must be necessarily mingled and taught together, to the manifest retarding of the progress of the more forward as well as of the more backward, several schools are generally combined, so as to form one large one, containing five boys' classes and five girls' classes. In these classes, the teachers are able to classify the children in such a manner, that one teacher may take the youngest and most deficient, another the more advanced, and so on. In this manner, as each teacher has a class of children, who have made about the same progress in their studies, he is enabled to concentrate his whole energies upon the instruction and education of *all* his scholars at the same time, and for the whole time they are in school, instead of being obliged to neglect one part of his class whilst he attends to another, which is necessarily the case, where children of different degrees of proficiency are assembled in one class-room, and which is always necessarily the cause of considerable noise and confusion, tending to distract the attention of both teachers and children.

But, besides the good classification, a further advantage, which results from this combination of schools, is the greater economy of the plan. When each school contains only two class-rooms, four times as many schools are required, as when each school contains eight rooms. And it is by no means true, that a school-building containing eight class-rooms costs as much as four school-buildings, each of which contains two class-rooms. Not only is a great expenditure saved, in the mere erection of the exterior walls and roofs of the buildings themselves, but a still greater saving is effected, in the purchase of land, as, instead of increasing the area on which the school is erected, it is always possible to increase its height.

Nothing can be more liberal, than the manner in which the Prussian towns have provided for their educational wants. The buildings are excellent, and are kept in most admirable order.

The town authorities are held responsible for all this; and, wherever I went, I found large, commodious, and beautifully clean school-rooms, furnished with all that the teachers could possibly require. Along the length of the rooms, parallel desks are ranged, facing the teacher's desk, which is raised on a small platform, so that he may see all his scholars. On either side of him are large black boards, on which he illustrates the subjects of his lessons. On his right hand, there is generally a cabinet, for the reception of all the books and objects of instruction which belong to the school; and all around, on the walls of the room, hang maps of different countries, and, generally, several of Germany, delineating, in a strong and clear manner, all the physical features of the different provinces and kingdoms which compose the "Fatherland."

The school-rooms are continually whitewashed; and should there be any neglect on the part of the town or village authorities to keep the school-buildings in proper order, or to provide all the necessary apparatus, the teachers have always the power of complaining to the inspectors, or to the county magistrates, who immediately compel the authorities to attend to these important duties.

Besides the schools, which are managed by school-committees in the villages and towns, and which might be denominated public schools, there is another class, which would fall more properly under the designation of private schools.

If a private individual is desirous of establishing a school, as a means of earning his livelihood, or from a desire to offer to the poor of his neighbourhood a better education, than they could obtain in the public schools, he is at liberty to do so, on the following conditions: —

1st, That the school be opened to public inspection, on the ground, that, as the nation is directly interested in the moral education of its citizens, so it ought to be assured, that none of the children are subjected to immoral and corrupting influences, during the time when their minds are most susceptible of impressions of any kind and most tenacious of them when received:

2ndly, That no person be employed as teacher in such school, who has not obtained a teacher's diploma, certifying his character and attainments to be such, as to fit him for the office of teacher.

3rdly, That the school be supplied with a playground, and that the children be allowed to take exercise there in the middle of the morning and afternoon school hours:

4thly, That at least a certain fixed amount of instruction in reading, writing, arithmetic, geography, history, singing, and science be given in the school:

5thly, That a sufficient number of teachers be provided for the children: and,

6thly, That the rooms are kept clean, well warmed, lighted, and ventilated.

The profuse expenditure on all the materials of education in the Prussian towns astonished me greatly, accustomed as I had been to the dame schools of England, and to the empty and repulsive interiors of many of our national school rooms, with their bare floors and uncovered walls.

I took the greatest pains not to be deceived on this point; and hearing that, owing to some municipal disputes, education had made less progress in Berlin than elsewhere, I requested Professor Hintze of Berlin to direct me to the worst school in the city, and, having visited several of the more perfect ones, I started one morning to see what was considered a poor school in Prussia.

It was managed by a teacher, who had established a school for the poor at his own expense, as a private speculation, and unconnected with the town committees.

I found a good house containing *four* class-rooms, each of which was fitted up with parallel desks, and was under the direction of a teacher, who had been carefully educated, and had obtained his diploma.

I found a good, dry, and roomy playground attached to the school, a very agreeable and seemingly intelligent head master, who was owner of the school and manager of one of the classes; and the only causes of complaint, I could discover, were, that the rooms were lower than the generality of school-rooms in Prussia, not measuring more than nine feet in height; that there was a paucity of maps, black boards, &c.; that the desks were placed too closely together; and that the walls were not so white and clean as in the town schools. But I could not help thinking, while walking through the rooms of this building, if these people could only see some of our dame, and some of our dirty and unfurnished national schools, what a palace would they not consider this to be!

The regulations which I have been describing, by means of which the enormous expenses of such a vast educational scheme are divided between all the different districts of the kingdom, and by means of which each parish is held responsible for the education of its children, have been followed by this splendid result — that, notwithstanding that most of their town schools contain five or six times as many class-rooms as those of our country, the Prussian people have established 23,646 schools, which in 1844 were attended daily by 2,328,146 children, and were directed by 29,639 highly educated teachers, of whom nearly 28,000 were young professors, who had obtained diplomas and certificates of character at the normal colleges! Now, could this magnificent result have been attained if the people, the clergy, and the government had not been at unity on this great question? Could it have been attained, if there had been no organisation of the parishes and towns, by which the duties of the different educational authorities were clearly and distinctly defined? Could the government alone have borne the enormous expenses of establishing such a system? Could the government have even afforded to carry it on? And, above all, could private charity alone have effected so vast and splendid a result? These are questions for my readers to answer for themselves.

The central committees of each town are required by law to establish, in addition to the primary institutions, which I have described, one or more *superior primary* schools, the number of which varies according to the population of the town. The education given in them is superior to that given in the primary schools themselves, but is inferior to that given in the *gymnasia*. It is of a more practical character than the latter, and is quite as good as the education of the children of our middle classes. These *superior primary* institutions are intended for all those children, who have passed through the primary schools, and whose parents wish them to receive a better education than that given in the latter establishments, without their having to go through the classical course of the gymnasia.

The education given in these superior schools, as in all the public schools of Prussia, is gratuitous, and open to all classes of society. All the children of the small shopkeepers and artizans, many of the boys, who afterwards enter the teachers' colleges, as well as many others, whose parents are to be found in the very humblest walks of life, and even children of the nobles and of the richest classes of society, are to be found pursuing their studies there together, in the same class-rooms and on the same benches. I have myself seen sons of counts, physicians, clergymen, merchants, shopkeepers, and poor labourers working together in one of these classes in Berlin.

Above these *superior* schools are the *real* schools and *gymnasia,* or colleges, where a *classical* and *very superior* course of education is pursued, and where the children of the more wealthy classes are instructed. They are under an entirely different direction; and all I have to do with them here, is to mention, that even these institutions are open gratuitously to all, who wish to avail themselves of the education which they offer. Even in these *classical* colleges children of poor labourers are sometimes to be found studying on the same benches on which sit the sons of the rich. It is very instructive to observe, that in Prussia, where one would imagine, according to the doctrines preached in England, that the government should, until the late revolution, have feared to advance the intelligence of the people, no one has seemed to have an idea, that too much instruction could be imparted to the children of the poor. On the contrary, every one has acted, as if the public order and public morality depended entirely upon the people being able to think. A theoretically arbitrary government has been doing everything in its power to stimulate and enable the people to educate their children as highly as possible, and has been for years telling them, that the prosperity and happiness of the country depend greatly on the training of the children; while here, in our free country, we still find people speaking and acting, as if they feared, that education was the inevitable harbinger of immorality and disaffection.

There are also in Prussia a great number of *endowed* schools, which derive their incomes from the rents of lands, or from the interest of money bequeathed to them by charitable individuals, or which have been founded and endowed at different times by the government. For each of these cases, there is an exception made in the operation of the municipal regulations, which I have described;—neither of these classes of schools are directed by Schulvorstände, or by the town committees. The teachers for the *former* class are chosen by the trustees, appointed by the will of the devisor; the county courts being enabled to annul the elections, if a bad selection is made. The trustees, however, are unable to appoint any person, as teacher, who has not obtained a diploma * of competency from the provincial committee, appointed to examine all candidates for the teachers' profession. In fact, no person can officiate as teacher, in *any* Prussian school, unless he has obtained such a diploma. This is the parents' guarantee, that he is a person, to whom they may safely entrust their children. The teachers of the class of schools, which have been founded and endowed by government, are appointed by the county courts. The town-committees have, however, the surveillance and inspection of all these schools, and are obliged by law to assist them from the town funds, if their own do not suffice for their efficient maintenance. The municipal authorities are

* See next chapter for an account of the diplomas.

also obliged to assist all the parents, who are too poor to do it themselves, to purchase the books, slates, pencils, &c. required for the class instruction; and they are also obliged to provide decent clothing for such children, as are too poor, to obtain a dress sufficiently respectable for school attendance. And here, I cannot help remarking, on the general appearance of the children throughout the provinces of Prussia, which I have visited. They were generally very clean, well dressed, polite, and easy in their manners, and very healthy and active in their appearance. In whatever town of Prussia the traveller finds himself, he may always satisfy himself on this point, if he will take the trouble to walk out into the streets, between twelve and two o'clock in the morning, *i. e.*, between the hours of the morning and afternoon classes. In some towns, a stranger would imagine, either that the *poor* had no children, or that they never let them go out of doors. All the children he would see in the streets would appear to him to be those of respectable shopkeepers. This is a very satisfactory proof of the good effects of the school system, as cleanliness and neatness among the poor are invariable symptoms of a satisfactory moral and physical condition.

Among the defects of the Prussian system, especially as regards its working in the towns, is the want of infant-schools. It is impossible to exaggerate the importance of these institutions in towns. The earliest impressions are always the strongest, whether for bad or good. It is necessarily a rare case, when either of the poor parents is able to stay at home and watch over the house and the children. During their absence, the child, who is too young to go to school, is left, as in England, to play in the streets with any companions he can find; and though there is *none* of the loathsome juvenile degradation to be seen in the back streets of the Prussian towns, which is to be found, openly displaying its disgusting character, in so many forms, in the back streets of our own crowded cities, yet it is quite impossible for a child to be left days together to itself, exposed, necessarily, to many injurious influences, without gaining considerable harm. This the Prussian government has felt; and though it has made no positive regulation on this subject, it has directed the county courts to encourage the erection of as many infant-schools as possible; and I am happy to say, they are now beginning to spring up over the face of the whole country.

The law requires that every school, both in town and country, shall have an open space of ground adjacent to it, where the children may take a little exercise in the mornings and afternoons. This is a very important regulation, and is well worthy our imitation. The children, in Germany, are never detained more than an hour and a half in the school-room at one time, except when the weather is too bad, to allow of their taking exercise in the open air. Every hour and a half, throughout the day, they are taken into the playground for ten minutes' exercise by one of the teachers; the air of the school-room is then changed, and the children return refreshed to their work. In the towns this regulation ensures other and greater advantages, as it keeps the children out of the filth and immorality of the streets. In most cases, our town-schools have no yard attached to them, so that, if the children do change the bad and noxious air of the school-room, it is only for the dirt and depravity of the streets, where they are brought under evil influences, much more powerful for injury, than those of the schools are for good.

In some provinces of Prussia, there are still some few of the old class of great landowners, between whom, in former days, the whole of Prussia was divided, until Stein and Hardenburg put the laws in force, which destroyed the old feudal system, and gave the peasants an interest in the soil. It is, therefore, an interesting question to examine, what the law requires these landlords to do for the education of the people on their estates. I have already mentioned, that the selection of the teacher is left to them, but that the government reserves the right of a veto upon their choice, in all cases where an injudicious election is made. The landlords are required to keep in good repair the schools upon their estates, and to pay the school-fees for the children of all the poor labourers living upon them, and not able to pay it themselves. They are also obliged to furnish the materials, required for the erection or repair of all necessary school-buildings; the fuel required for the school-rooms and teachers' houses through the winter; and, where the school is not endowed, the sum which is necessary for the teachers' salaries. The children of the landed proprietors themselves, often attend the village schools, and work at the same desks, with the sons and daughters of the poorest peasants,—a proof of the excellent character of the education given in the primary schools, and of the high estimation, in which the teachers are generally held by all classes of society.

CHAP. VI.

PRUSSIAN EDUCATION. — THE PRUSSIAN TEACHERS. — THEIR SOCIAL POSITION. — THEIR EDUCATION BEFORE ENTERING INTO THE NORMAL COLLEGES. — THE COLLEGE ENTRANCE EXAMINATIONS. — THE EDUCATION OF THE TEACHERS IN THE COLLEGES. — THE EXAMINATION OF THE TEACHERS FOR DIPLOMAS. — THEIR ELECTION TO SCHOOLS. — THEIR INDEPENDENCE OF LOCAL INTERFERENCE WHEN ELECTED. — THEIR RELATION TO THE INSPECTORS. — THE SALARIES OF THE TEACHERS. — THEIR AMOUNT. — HOW AND BY WHOM PROVIDED. — THE TEACHERS' CONFERENCES. — PROVISION FOR SUPERANNUATED TEACHERS, AND FOR THE WIDOWS AND ORPHANS OF DECEASED TEACHERS. — THE TEACHERS' JOURNALS AND READING SOCIETIES.

THE PRUSSIAN TEACHERS.

DURING my travels in different provinces of Prussia, I was in daily communication with the teachers. I had every opportunity of observing the spirit, which animated the whole body, and of hearing the opinions of the poor respecting them. I found a great body of educated, courteous, refined, moral, and learned professors, labouring with real enthusiasm among the poorest classes of their countrymen. I found them wholly devoted to their duties, proud of their profession, united together by a strong feeling of brotherhood, and holding continual conferences together, for the purposes of debating all kinds of questions, relating to the management of their schools. But what gave me greater pleasure than all else was, to observe in what esteem and respect they were held by the peasants. If you tempt a Prussian peasant to find fault with the schools, he will tell you, in answer, how good the school is, and how learned the teachers are. I often heard the warmest panegyrics bestowed upon them by the peasants, showing in the clearest manner how well their merits and their labours were appreciated.*

I could not but feel, how grand an institution this great body of more than 28,000 teachers was, and how much it was capable of effecting; and, when I regarded the happy condition of the Prussian peasantry, I could not but believe, I saw some of the fruits of the daily labours of this enlightened, respected, and united brotherhood.

Upon the parochial ministers and parochial teachers depend, far more than we are willing to allow, the intelligence, the morality, and the religion of the people. The cordial co-operation of these two important and honourable professions is necessary to the moral progress of a nation. The religious minister acts upon the adults, the teacher on the young. The co-operation of the religious ministers is necessary to secure the success of the teachers' efforts; and, on the other hand, without the earnest aid of the teacher, the fairest hopes of the religious minister are often blighted in the bud.

* Since these remarks were written, the course of public events in Prussia has given a very remarkable proof of their correctness. To the National Assembly, which met in Berlin in May 1848, the people of the provinces elected no fewer than eight teachers as representatives; giving this striking proof of the people's respect for the ability and high character of the profession.

We must educate the child, if we would reform the man. But, alas! this education is a labour, requiring a long, persevering, careful, intelligent, and most tender handling. It were much better left alone, than to be attempted, so as to create disgust, or to embitter early associations, or to render virtuous and ennobling pursuits disgusting throughout after life. On the teacher depends the training of the poor man's child, for poor parents have, unhappily, too little spare time to allow them to perform the greatest duty of a parent. And thus, as the character of every nation mainly depends upon the training of the children, we may safely affirm, that, such as our teachers are, such also will be our peasantry.

How essential is it, then, to the moral welfare, and therefore to the political greatness of a nation, that the profession of the teachers should be one, ensuring the perfect satisfaction of its members, and commanding the respect of the country!

The teacher's station in society ought to be an honourable and a comfortable one, or few learned and able men will be found willing to remain long in the profession, even if any such men can be induced to enter it; and it is much better to be without teachers altogether, than to leave the training of our children to men of narrow minds, unrestrained passions, or meagre intelligence. The Prussian government has fully recognised these truths, and has therefore done all within its power, to raise the character and social position of the teachers as much as possible. As these efforts have been heartily seconded by the provincial governments and the people, the result has been most remarkable and satisfactory.

The first exertions of the government were wholly devoted to the improvement of the intellectual and moral character of the profession, and to the increase of its numbers. They determined to make the name of "teacher" an honour, and in itself a guarantee to every parent of the character and attainments of the man who bore it. To attain this end, they denied all access to the ranks of the profession to any but those who proved themselves worthy of admittance. No person can be a teacher in Prussia, or in any part of Germany, France, Austria, Switzerland, or Holland, until he has passed a very severe and searching examination, and until he has produced testimonials, from those well acquainted with him, of the irreproachable nature of his moral life and character. This examination, which includes both intellectual and moral qualifications, is conducted by able and impartial men, among whom are to be found the candidate's religious minister, the professors of the normal college at which he was brought up, and at least one of the educational magistrates of the county of which he is a native. He who passes the ordeal is allowed to be a teacher, whether he was educated at a normal college or not. The ranks of the profession are open to all educated and moral men, wherever or however they were educated; but educated and moral they must prove themselves. It is not, then, to be wondered at, that the men, who are known to have satisfactorily passed this scrutiny, are regarded by all their fellow-countrymen with respect and consideration, and as men of great learning and of high character.

This once attained, the next great efforts of the

government were directed to the improvement of the social position of the teachers. The government placed them under the immediate protection of the county courts. They also made a law that no teacher, who had been once elected, whether by a parochial committee, or by trustees, or by private patrons, should be dismissed, except by permission of the county magistrates. This protected the teachers from the effects of the mere personal prejudices of those in immediate connection with them. They then defined the *minimum* of the teachers' salaries, and this *minimum* they have ever since been steadily increasing.

It is absolutely necessary, that my readers should not connect their preconceived ideas of an English village schoolmaster with the learned and refined teacher of Prussia. They might just as well think of comparing the position and attainments of the vast majority of our teachers with those of the scholars of our universities, as of comparing those of our schoolmasters with those of the Prussian teachers. I felt, whenever I was in the company of a Prussian teacher, that I was with a gentleman, whose courteous bearing and intelligent manner of speaking must exert a most beneficial influence upon the peasantry, among whom he lived. It was, as if I saw one of the best of our English curates performing the duties of a schoolmaster. I never saw any vulgarity or coarseness, and still less any stupidity or incapacity for their duties, displayed by any of them.

The Protestant teachers of Germany occupy situations of importance in connection with the religious ministers and religious congregations. They fulfil several of the duties of our curates, clerks, and organists. In both Romanist and Protestant congregations, they lead the choir and play the organ. They act, too, as clerk; and when a Protestant minister is indisposed, and unable to conduct public worship, the parochial teacher officiates in his stead, reads the church service, and sometimes also preaches. The musical part of public worship, in both Romanist and Protestant churches and chapels, is always directed by the parochial teacher. The small salary, which they receive for the performance of these duties, serves to increase their incomes; but what is of much more importance is, that this connection of the teachers with the religious congregations and ministers serves to bind the religious ministers and teachers together, to lessen the labours of each by mutual assistance, and, above all, to raise the teacher in the estimation of the poor, by whom he is surrounded, and thereby materially to increase the effect of his advice and instructions.

It was very curious, and pleasing, to observe the effects of the intercourse of this enlightened and excellent body of men with the peasantry during the last twenty years. I do not hesitate to say, that, at the period of my visit to Prussia, I had never before seen so polite and civilised, and so seemingly intelligent, a peasantry as that of Prussia. Were a stranger introduced into some of the lowest schools, I am quite convinced he would not believe he saw peasants' children before him. They were generally so clean and neatly dressed, and their manners were always so good, that I was several times obliged to ask the teachers, if I really saw the children of the poor before me. The appearance of the girls was particularly gratifying; their dress was so respectable, their manners were so good, their way of dressing their hair showed so much taste, and their cleanliness was so great, that no one, who had not been informed before-hand to what class they belonged, would have believed them to be the children of the poorest of the people. The lowest orders of Germany are so much more refined than our poor, that the children of the rich very often attend the primary schools, while the children of the tradespeople and middle classes almost invariably do so. The richer parents know that their children will not come into contact with any coarseness, and that the teacher is certain to be an educated and refined gentleman. This mingling of the children of the higher and lower orders tends to civilise the peasantry still more, and to produce a kindly feeling between the different ranks of society. But the primary cause of the great and ever-increasing civilisation of the Prussian peasantry is, undeniably, their contact with their refined and intelligent teachers. For, whilst the clergy are labouring among the adults, the teachers are daily bringing under the influences of their own high characters and intelligence ALL the younger portions of the community.

The social position of the teachers in Prussia and in England are so TOTALLY different, that those who do not divest themselves of their acquired notions of an English village schoolmaster, will not be able to understand the true position or character of a Prussian teacher. Of course I do not mean here to speak of the *character* of some of the educated men who have left the normal colleges of Battersea and Stanley Grove; but it is well known what a mournful exception these are to the general class of village teachers in England. And even these men have to struggle against all the obloquy which years of neglect have heaped upon their profession. No better summary of their position in England can be given than the words which I once heard Mr. Coleridge, the excellent principal of Stanley Grove, use, when speaking of the extreme difficulty he experienced in instilling into patrons of schools the necessity of paying ordinary respect to teachers. He said — "*I have been obliged several times to make an express stipulation with the patron, that the teacher, when in his house, shall not be sent to eat with the menial servants in the kitchen.*" It is, indeed, a very common thing to see a well educated young teacher, who only requires a better social position to enable him to exercise the most important moral influence over the poor in his neighbourhood, treated by his patrons with less respect and consideration than the house servants! The following is only a solitary instance of the position and character of a great number of the English schoolmasters. It occurred in 1846, in one of the southern counties of England, and shows, at least, what is *possible* in England.* In a certain parish in this county, which it is not necessary to name here, there is a village school endowed with 20*l.* a year. There is no teacher's house, no garden for him, and no perquisites of any kind. The donor, no doubt, expected

* The reports of the Welsh commissioners and of the inspectors, show that such cases are very numerous.

that the parish would generously make the situation worth a good teacher's acceptance. The parish had not, however, such an appreciation of the value of education, and thought it did enough, in appointing a recipient of the donor's bounty, no matter how unworthy he might be. They, however, could not but feel that 20*l.* a year would hardly enable the poor man to keep body and soul together, without some additions from other sources; so they put an advertisement into the local paper, stating, that this excellent situation was open to competition, that a candidate, who had practised some trade or calling, would be preferred for the place, and that they were inclined to favour applications from young tailors! The teacher, to gain his livelihood, must mend clothes in the school-room! I might fill my pages with such instances; but I shall content myself with saying, that it is *utterly impossible* for such a public insult to the teacher's calling to occur in Prussia. So totally different is the state of things there, that when I told the story in society in Berlin, or to the Prussian teachers, it always excited shouts of laughter, and more than once, I had auditors, who utterly disbelieved its truth.

The teachers in Prussia are men respected by the whole community, men to whom all classes owe the first rudiments of their education, and men in whose welfare, good character, and high respectability both the government and the people feel themselves deeply interested. In birth, early recollections, and associations, they are often peasants; but in education and position they are *gentlemen* in every sense of that term, and acknowledged officers of the county governments. There are more than 28,000 such teachers in Prussia. This great profession offers, as I shall presently show, a means, by which an intelligent peasant may hope to raise himself into the higher ranks of society, as the expenses of preparing for admission into the profession are borne by government. But, as the number of candidates for admission is consequently always large, the government takes every possible precaution, that only such shall be chosen, as are in every respect qualified to reflect honour upon the profession, and carry out its objects in the most effective manner. And so well satisfied are the teachers with their position, that, although their pay is often but poor, yet it rarely happens that any one quits his profession to seek another situation. They are contented with their profession, even when it affords only a bare living, as it always confers a station of respectability and honour, in direct communication with the provincial governments. I made the most careful inquiries upon this subject, and can speak with great confidence upon it. I was in daily communication with the teachers from the day I entered Prussia, and I tested the truth of what they told me, not only by comparing their statements together, but also by many inquiries, which I made of the educational counsellors and government officers in Berlin. Next to Dr. Bruggeman, one of the head counsellors of the Minister of Education, the gentlemen to whom I am most indebted for information on this subject are Counsellor Stiehl, the Chief Inspector of

Prussia, who is employed by the Minister on particular missions of inspection in all the provinces of Prussia; Professor Hintz, one of the young professors in Dr. Diesterweg's normal college; Dr. Hennicke, the director of the normal college at Weissenfels; Herr Peters, a teacher at Bonn; one of the teachers at Cologne; several of the teachers at Berlin; and several of the teachers at Elberfeld. From these gentlemen, and many others, I gathered the following information: — When a boy is intended for the teachers' profession, he remains in the primary school, until he has completed the whole course of primary instruction, *i. e.* until he has learned to write and read well, and until he knows the principal rules of arithmetic, the outlines of the geography and history of his native country, a little natural history, and the Scripture history. This knowledge he does not generally acquire before he is fifteen years of age. From the age of fifteen to the age of eighteen, before which latter age a young man cannot be admitted into any normal college, the education of young candidates, who are the sons of townspeople, is different to the education of those, who are the sons of country people.

The young candidates for admission into the teachers' profession, who are the sons of townspeople, enter at fifteen into the classes of the *superior public schools* of the town, in which schools a number of endowed places are always reserved for poor boys, who have distinguished themselves in the primary schools. The education given in these schools is of a higher character, than that given in the *primary* schools. It comprehends mathematics, and the rudiments at least of the classics, besides lectures in history, physical geography, and drawing. They remain in these *superior public schools* until their eighteenth year, when they can seek admission into a normal college. The young candidates for admission into the teachers' profession, who are the sons of poor country people, do not enjoy all the advantages which the children of townspeople possess, as there is seldom a superior primary school in their neighbourhood, in which they can continue their studies, after leaving the primary school. If the son of a peasant aspires to enter the teachers' profession; after leaving the primary school, he engages the parochial teacher to give him instruction in the evenings, attends the teacher's classes in the mornings and afternoons, and assists him in the management of the younger children. He continues to improve himself in this manner, until he has attained the age, at which he can apply for admission into a normal college.

There are, however, a great many schools in Prussia, established for the purpose of preparing the sons of the peasants for admission into the normal colleges. These preparatory schools generally belong to private persons. Every young person admitted into them is obliged to pay a small fee for his education there. This fee is generally very trifling, but is still sufficient to prevent the sons of the poorest peasants entering them; and, consequently, these latter, if they live in a country village, are obliged to content themselves with the evening lessons given by the village teacher, and with the practical knowledge gained by attending his classes in the mornings and afternoons. But it is always possible for the peasants' children, with industry, to prepare themselves, by the aid of the village teacher, for admission into a normal college. Of these latter admirable institutions for the education of teachers I shall hereafter speak at length; suffice it here to say, that there are between forty and fifty of them in Prussia, supported entirely by the state, and under the direction and surveillance of the provincial committees called Schulcollegium. There are five or six normal colleges in each province, some of which are set apart for the education of the Romanist, and the others for that of the Protestant teachers. Each of them is generally put under the direction of a priest or of a Protestant minister, according as it is intended for the education of Romanist or Protestant teachers, and is provided in the most liberal manner, with every thing necessary for the education of the young students. The education given in them is nearly gratuitous; no young man being called upon to pay for any thing, but his clothes and his breakfast, whilst, in many cases, even this trifling charge is paid for the poor student out of the college funds.

All young men who aspire to the office of teacher in Prussia, and who aspire to enter a normal college, when the yearly vacancies take place, are obliged to submit to an examination, conducted by the professors of these colleges, in presence of the educational counsellor from the county court. No young man can enter the examination lists, who has not produced certificates of health, and freedom from all chronic complaints, or who has a weak voice or *any* physical defect or infirmity.

None but picked men are selected as teachers in Prussia. The examination is very severe and searching. For, as there are always a great number of candidates for admission into each college, and as the favoured candidates are only chosen, on account of their superior abilities, the competition at the entrance examinations is very great.

The subjects of this examination are, Reading, Writing, Arithmetic, Geography, History, Singing, Chanting, and the Scripture History.

The young man, who has just obtained admission into a normal college in Prussia, and whose education as a teacher has only just begun, is much better educated, *even at the commencement* of his three years' education in the college, than almost any of our teachers are, when they enter upon the performance of their duties in the schools, and when their education is considered to be completed! How much superior, therefore, in intellectual acquirements, the Prussian teacher is, when he has completed his collegiate course, I need not observe. When the examination is concluded, as many of the most promising of the candidates are selected as there are vacancies in the college; and, after a strict examination has been made into their characters and previous life, each successful candidate is required to sign an agreement, promising to officiate as a teacher, after leaving the college, for a number of years, equal to those during which the government educates him gratuitously in the college. They are then admitted, and are only required to provide themselves with clothes, and to pay about 3*l.* per annum. All the other expenses of their education, maintenance, &c. are, as I have said before, borne by the state. They remain in these colleges two or three years — never less than two, or more than three. Here they continue the studies which they had previously followed in the primary and superior schools. They perfect themselves in writing, arithmetic, history, geography, and Scripture history, and receive a careful education in the physical sciences, and particularly in mathematics and botany. In some of the normal colleges, the young men also study Latin and the modern languages. Besides this, they *all* learn the violin, the organ, and pianoforte. I have seen as many as a hundred violins, three organs, and three pianofortes in one normal college. They also continue the practice of chanting and singing, which they had commenced in the village schools; and when the college is situated in the country, and intended for village teachers, the students learn gardening and agriculture. I became acquainted in Bonn with the teacher of the *poorest* school in the town. He could speak French very tolerably, as well as a little English; he was acquainted with many of our first writers, and knew the rudiments of the Latin language, in addition to the necessary attainments of a teacher.

But the government and the people are not satisfied that, because a teacher has passed through one of these training establishments, he is therefore fit to undertake the management of a village school. Far from it. When the normal college course is finished, the young aspirants are obliged to submit to another examination, which is conducted by the professors of the college in the presence of a counsellor from the provincial schulcollegium, the educational counsellor of the county court, and a delegate from the Roman Catholic bishop, or Protestant superintendent of the county, according as the school is for Romanist or for Protestant students. These different personages *ought* to be present, but I was assured that, in general, only the educational counsellor of the county court assisted at the examination. At its conclusion, if the directors and professors have been satisfied with the conduct of the young men, during their residence in the college, and have no reason to doubt the excellence of their moral character, and the orthodoxy of their religious belief, the young candidates receive diplomas marked according to the manner in which they acquitted themselves in the examination, "1," "2," or "3," and signed by the director and professors, and by the members of the provincial schulcollegium.

Those who obtain the diplomas marked "1," are legally authorised to officiate as teachers, without further scrutiny, but those who only obtain those marked "2" or "3," are only appointed to schools for two or three years on trial, and, at the end of that time, are obliged to return to the normal college and undergo another examination.

It is not, however, *necessary* that a young man should pass through a normal college, in order to obtain a diploma enabling him to officiate as teacher. Any person, who has received so good an education as to enable him to pass the examination at a normal college, can obtain one, if his character is unimpeachable.

By far the greatest proportion, however, of the teachers of Prussia are educated in the normal colleges. When they have obtained these diplomas, the county courts present them to such school-committees as require teachers; and if these parochial committees are satisfied with them, they are elected. In such a numerous body as that of the Prussian teachers, there are always numerous vacancies. The number of colleges and students are so arranged, as to regularly supply that, which is found to be the average number of yearly vacancies.

The candidates who have only obtained the diplomas marked "2" or "3" hold their offices, as I have said, only provisionally; and, in order to be definitely appointed, are obliged, at the termination of their specified period of trial, either to obtain the approval of the local inspector, or to undergo another examination; and I was assured, that they are sometimes obliged to return three or four times to be examined, ere they can obtain a definite appointment — such care does the country take, that none but fit persons shall occupy this responsible position. When he is once appointed, however, the teacher is thenceforward a county and not a parochial officer. No person or set of persons in *immediate* connection with him can turn him out of his situation, without having first obtained the sanction of the county magistrates. After the parochial ministers and householders have once elected him, they have no power to deprive him of his salary or his situation. No one but the county magistrates or the union inspector, who, by living at a distance, are not likely to be affected by personal prejudices or parochial disputes, can interfere directly with the teacher, and should the latter deem the interference of even the inspector uncalled for, he can always appeal to the superior authorities, or even to the Minister of Education himself. The parochial committees have, however, the power of complaining of the teacher to the county magistrates, if they think he is acting unwisely or immorally; and such complaints always receive immediate and special attention. When any such complaints are made, the county court despatches an inspector to examine into the matter, and empowers him, if he thinks the teacher worthy of censure, fine, or expulsion, to act accordingly. If, however, the teacher is not blameable, the inspector explains the matter to the parochial authorities, and effects a reconciliation between the parties. If the inspector should deem the teacher worthy of punishment, and this latter should be dissatisfied with the sentence, he can carry the matter before a justice of the peace; and if he is not satisfied with his decision, he can appeal to the provincial schulcollegium, thence to the Minister of Instruction, and thence, if he desires, to the King himself — of so much importance does the Prussian government deem it, to protect the teachers, and to raise their office in public opinion. I have mentioned that a Prussian teacher seldom leaves his profession; but that many change their positions. When a good and well paid situation falls vacant in any parish, an experienced teacher, who already occupies some worse paid situation in another parish, and who has obtained credit for his excellent school-management, is preferred by the school-committee to the young adepts fresh from the normal colleges. On this account, the young men generally commence with an inferior position, and earn better ones, according as they manage the first they entered. It is evident, how important a regulation this is, as the teachers of the poorest schools are saved from becoming listless and dispirited, and are rendered earnest and industrious, in the hopes of bettering their situation. The country is, however, gradually improving the salaries of all the teachers. No village or town is ever allowed to *lessen* the amount it has once given to a teacher. What it has once given, it is obliged to continue to give in future. It may increase it as much as it likes, and the county courts have the power of interfering, and saying, "You have hitherto paid your teachers too little; you must augment the teacher's salary." This is only done, however, when it is known, that the parish or town is capable of increasing the school salaries and is unwilling to do so.

The importance of enabling the teachers to command the respect of the people, of rendering them independent of those in immediate connection with them, and of protecting them from ignorant interference and mere personal animosity, is so fully recognised in Prussia, that even when the school is endowed, and managed by trustees, these trustees, after having once elected a teacher, are not permitted to dismiss him, unless they can prove to the county court that they have sufficient cause for complaint. The teacher, elected by trustees, has the privilege of appealing to the Minister of Education in Berlin, against the act of the trustees and county magistrates, just as well as all the other teachers of Prussia.

The reasons, which have induced the Prussian government to render the teachers, after their election, so independent of those in immediate connection with them, appear to have been:—

1st. Because the teachers of Prussia are a very learned body, and, from their long study of pedagogy, have acquired greater ability than any other persons in the art of teaching. They are, therefore, better qualified than any other persons to conduct the instruction of their children; but, if those persons who have never studied pedagogy could interfere with them, and say, "You shall teach it in this way or in that, or else leave the parish," the teachers would often be obliged to pursue some ridiculous, inefficient method, merely to please the whims of persons not experienced in school management, and the enlightenment of the people would thus be often considerably retarded.

2nd. Because, if the parishioners or the parochial ministers had a right to turn away a teacher, whenever he chanced to displease them, the teachers would always be liable to, and would often suffer from, foolish personal dislikes, founded on no good ground. They would thus lose their independence of character, by being forced to suit their conduct to the whims of those around them, instead of being able to act faithfully and conscientiously to all; or by being exposed to the insults or impertinence of ignorant persons, who did not understand and appreciate the value and importance of their labours; or by being prevented from acting faithfully towards the children, from fear of offending the parents; or by being forced to cringe to and flatter the ignorance, and even the vices, of those around them, instead of being able to combat them; and they would thus generally, by one or other of these ways, forfeit at least some part of the respect of the parents of their children, and would, consequently, find their lessons and advice robbed of one half their weight, and their labours of a great part of their efficiency.

For these reasons, the Prussian government endeavours to give as much liberty as possible to the teachers, and to fetter their hands as little as possible. In the normal colleges they receive instruction in the different methods of teaching; and, out of these, each teacher is at liberty to follow whichever seems to him the best calculated to promote the growth of the intelligence of his scholars. It is felt, that without this liberty, a teacher would often work unwillingly, and that a discontented or unwilling teacher is worse than none at all. In the choice of their books and apparatus, the teachers are allowed an almost equal freedom. If a teacher finds a book, which he thinks better calculated for instruction, than the one he has been in the habit of using, he sends it through the inspector to the educational counsellor of the county court, who forwards it to the schulcollegium for approval; and, as soon as this is obtained, the teacher can introduce it into his school. There are, already, a great many books in each province, which have been thus sanctioned; and, out of these, every teacher in the province can choose whichever pleases him most. These school-books are, generally, written by teachers; and, from what I saw of them, they seemed to evince a profound knowledge of the science of pedagogy. Until a book has been thus sanctioned by the schulcollegium, which has the management of the normal colleges and gymnasia of its province, it cannot be introduced into a parochial school.

The teachers are not assisted by monitors in Germany, as in Switzerland, France, and England; and this I think a very great error. I have often been in schools in Prussia, where the teacher had about one hundred children of different degrees of proficiency to instruct in the same class-room, without any assistance whatever; the consequence was, that while he was teaching one class, the others were in disorder, and making noise enough to distract the attention of the children, who were receiving instruction, as well as that of the teacher, who was giving it; while the teacher, instead of being able to devote his time to the higher branches of instruction, and to the children, who more particularly needed his care, was obliged to divide it among all, and to superintend himself the very lowest branches of instruction; and this, too, at the sacrifice of the order and quiet of his school. When I represented this to the teachers, I was always answered, "Yes, that is true; but then we think, that a young monitor is unable to educate the minds of the children under his care, and is, consequently, likely to do them much injury." This is, no doubt, the result, if the teachers leave the education of any of his children *entirely* to monitors; but he has no need to do this: he ought to employ his monitors merely in superintending the more mechanical parts of instruction, such as writing, and learning the alphabet, and also in preserving order; he might then himself conduct the *mental* education of all the children. But this they will not do in Prussia; they are so afraid of injuring the mental culture of the children, that they positively throw away a very important means for the attainment of this end. In Switzerland a very different course is pursued; the teachers are assisted in keeping order, and in teaching the more mechanical parts of instruction, by monitors, chosen from among their most advanced pupils. These monitors remain with the teacher, until they are of sufficient age to go to a normal college; they are paid, I believe, by the parishes, and are instructed by the teachers in the evenings. From among them, the young candidates for the vacant places in the normal colleges are chosen; so that the Swiss teachers have often been engaged in schools, and in school management, from their earliest years. Besides this advantage, the country is spared a great expense; for in Prussia, where they have no monitors, they are obliged to augment the number of their teachers very considerably; and I have found in a small school, which could have been very easily managed by one teacher and some well-trained monitors, as many as three teachers, for each of whom good salaries had to be provided, as well as houses and gardens. Doubtless, it is much better to have experienced teachers, than young monitors; and hence it is that the town schools in Prussia are very much better than those of other countries, as the town committees can afford to engage a sufficient number of teachers; but in the poor country parishes this is not the case, and there it is, where the want of monitors is most severely felt, as a large school is often left entirely to the unaided care of a single teacher. But this very defect in the Prussian system arises from the great anxiety of the educational authorities, that the religious and moral education of the young should not suffer. Still I think it is a very great mistake; and I am sure that many schools I saw in Prussia suffer grievously from this regulation.

But it will be asked, how are the salaries of the teachers provided, and what is their amount? The regulations on this subject are particularly deserving of attention. The Prussian government clearly saw, that nothing could tend more strongly to nullify their efforts to raise the teachers' profession in the eyes of the people, than to leave the salaries of the teachers dependent, either on uncertain payments, or on private benevolence. To have done so would have been to destroy the independence of the profession.

The Prussian government, therefore, decreed that, however small and from whatever source the teacher's salary should be derived, its *amount* should always be *fixed* before his appointment, and that the payment should be *certain* and *regular*.

As I mentioned before, each succeeding teacher must be paid, *at least*, as much as his predecessor received. The county magistrates have the power of obliging each town or parish to increase the amount of the salaries of their teachers, whenever they think the town or parish is paying too little, and can afford to pay more. These salaries are now wholly paid by the school or town committees, from the funds raised by local taxation. Before the late law, which made education gratuitous, they were derived, in part, from the school fees. But the amount of the salary did not, in any case, depend on that of the fees, nor was the teacher ever placed in the invidious position of being obliged himself to collect these monthly payments. They were always collected by a tax-gatherer, appointed by the village or town magistrate; and when they did not amount to the fixed salary, which the school-committee had agreed to pay to the teacher, they were increased by a parochial rate, levied on the householders. In many cases, however, the schools are endowed, and for admission into these, no school fees were ever required. But where fees were required, and where a parent was too poor to pay them, the parochial or town authorities were always obliged, by law, to pay them for him. The following are the regulations, which define the *minimum* of the salaries of the Prussians.

Some of the country schools have each as many as three teachers; but the number of teachers in a country school in Prussia does not, generally, exceed *two;* and, in many of these schools, there is only one teacher. Where there are several, one is the head master, and the others are his assistants. The laws relating to their payment are as follow: —

"The first teacher in a country school, or, if there be only one, then the single teacher shall receive, as his yearly salary and the perquisites of his office, at least,—

"1st. Free lodging.

"2nd. The necessary fuel for the warming of the

school-room, and of his own dwelling-house, and for his household economy.

"3rd. A piece of land, as near as possible to the school, of from one to three Prussian acres large; the tillage and manuring of which are to be done at the expence of the parish.

"4th. A kitchen-garden behind his house, of not less than half a Prussian acre.

"5th. The necessary building for his little farming operations.

"6th. Free summer pasture for at least two cows.

"7th. Twelve bushels of rye meal, two cart-loads of hay, and two cart-loads of straw.

"8th. 7*l.* 10*s.* in money." [It must be remembered that 7*l.* 10*s.* in Prussia, is worth about as much as 12*l.* in England, and that this is only the sum which has been fixed by law as the *legal minimum*, and by no means gives an idea of the amount of salaries paid to the Prussian teachers.]

"If the field, garden, or summer pasture for his cows cannot be provided by the parish, the county court must determine what equivalent in money must be given him.

"The second, third, &c., teacher in a country school must receive —

"1st. Free lodging.

"2nd. The fuel necessary for warming his house.

"3rd. 9*l.* in money (or about 15*l.* in English value).

"The teachers of the towns must receive —

"1st. Free lodging and fuel.

"2nd. The first teacher should receive at least 40*l.*

per annum, and the other teachers at least 30*l.* per annum," in English values.

I found these regulations among some educational laws issued by the government in 1845 for one of the provinces; but Dr. Bruggeman assured me, that similar laws were in operation for the whole of Prussia. The above emoluments are the lowest the teachers can receive according to law. The government is about to raise this *minimum* considerably, and to increase the salaries throughout Prussia. Hitherto many have been paid but poorly; very few, however, have deserted their profession, or engaged in other occupations, as they are generally proud of their position, and satisfied with it.

Herr Peters, a teacher of a primary school in Bonn, with whom I spent some time, said to me, one day, "The Prussian teachers do not receive high salaries; but," he added, with emphasis, "however little the salary of a teacher may be above the legal minimum, it is certain, and collected for him by the parochial authorities, without his having to trouble himself about it." The law, as I have mentioned, is very strict in requiring the payments of the salaries to be made with the utmost regularity.

It is easy to see how invaluable, for any country, a great privileged class, like that of the Prussian teachers, must be, especially when many of its members are, as in Prussia, chosen by the state from amongst the most highly gifted of the peasant class, and educated at the expense of the country. It is, in fact, for modern Prussia, just what the Roman Catholic Church was, for Europe in the Middle Ages — it is a ladder, by which all the genius of the lowest orders may ascend into a suitable field of action. A young peasant boy of promising abilities, pushed on by the restless spirit, which so often characterises youth of real genius, and anxious to better his position in the world, or to gain some sphere of action more congenial to his taste, than the farm-yard or the workshop, finds, in Prussia, the teacher's career open to him. If he can only distinguish himself in his village school, and pass the entrance examination of a normal college, he gains a high education at no expense, and is then sure (if he conducts himself well, and distinguishes himself in the normal college) to obtain a teacher's place, to put himself in immediate connection with the government, and to gain a very honourable situation, affording him the amplest field for the development and exercise of his talents. A clever peasant in Prussia, instead of becoming a Chartist, enters a normal college, and becomes a teacher. There is no need for a young peasant to despond in Prussia, and say, "Here I am, endowed with talents fitting me for another sphere, but shut out by doors, which can only be opened with a golden key." Far otherwise. Free places are retained in the gymnasia for poor boys, who wish to continue their studies; and from these colleges they can enter either into the ranks of the Protestant or Romanist clergy, or into those of the teachers; and, in the last case, without having any thing to pay for their education. It is easy to comprehend, how this tends to allay political strife and discontent. In our country, this is often occasioned, or, at least, increased, by some one or two clever individuals, who find themselves confined within a sphere, too narrow for their talents and energies, and who, by their own restless murmurs, arouse the dormant passions of their neighbours. The German governments have been wiser in their day than our freer countries. They have separated the fiery spirits from the easily excited masses, and converted them into earnest, active, and indefatigable fosterers of the public morality, and into guardians of the common weal.

In considering the salaries and privileges of the teachers, it must also be borne in mind, that they are exempt from taxation, and that they are free from all obligation to serve in the army, and to attend the yearly military exercises.

On the installation of a new teacher, the parochial or school authorities are obliged, either to send conveyances for the transport of his family and goods, or to pay the expenses of such transport, for any distance less than fifty English miles. But, if the teacher leaves his situation before the expiration of five years, he is obliged to repay to the local authorities the expenses of this conveyance.

Whenever a new teacher is introduced into a parochial school, his installation is a public ceremony, at which all the parochial authorities assist, in order to impress the people with a sense of the importance of his office and his duties, and to encourage among them a respect for him, without which his hopes of success in his labours must be necessarily very small.

The ceremony of installation generally takes place in the parochial church, where the new teacher is presented, by the religious minister, to the civil authorities, and to the inhabitants of the parish. The children, whose education he has to conduct, are always present at the ceremony.

The Prussian government feels that, unless it can render the profession honourable and worthy of men of high characters and attainments, all its attempts to raise the religious and moral tone of the education of the people will be ever unavailing.

I have not hitherto mentioned Prussian schoolmistresses, because there are but few; and because the regulations, with respect to their education, examination, and appointment, are precisely similar to those relating to schoolmasters. Among the Protestants of Prussia there are scarcely any schoolmistresses; the greatest part of the Prussian female teachers are Romanists, and for their education there are several normal colleges established in the Romanist provinces of Prussia. I inquired of the Romanist counsellor, in the Bureau of Public Instruction in Berlin, whether it was not found difficult to retain the female teachers long at their posts, on account of their making such eligible wives, even for the farmers. But he assured me, that this was not the case, as far as their female teachers were concerned, as they form among themselves a body like the order of the Sisters of Charity, with this distinction, that, instead of actually taking a solemn public vow of celibacy, it is generally understood among them, that they shall not marry, but shall devote themselves, during the remainder of their lives, to the duties of school management and instruction. In this respect the Romanists have a great advantage over the Protestants; for I found, in the Protestant cantons of Switzerland, just the same objection to the employment of female teachers, as that which is experienced among the Protestants of Prussia and of England, viz., that a young woman, who has been carefully trained in a good normal college, until she is twenty years of age, makes so good a wife for men, even in the middle classes of society, that she always marries, soon after leaving the college; and, consequently, that a much greater supply of students and colleges are required, in order to supply the constant vacancies, which occur in the ranks, and that the expences of educating a sufficient number of female teachers are therefore too great in general to be supported, unless the students pay for their own education, which very few of the young women, who are desirous of being teachers, are able to do.

In the Romanist cantons of Switzerland, the Sisters of Charity conduct the education of the girls; and their schools are the best and most pleasing female schools I have ever seen. Herr Stiehl, one of the Protestant educational counsellors and chief inspector of Prussia, confirmed all that the Catholic minister had told me, and stated that, for the reasons above mentioned, the Prussian Protestants found it impossible to keep the female teachers long in their situations; and that the expence of constantly educating fresh female teachers, to supply the places of those who married, was too great to be borne. The Prussians, however, in general, prefer male teachers for the girls, *even where they can obtain female*; so that in nearly all the schools I visited, I found schoolmasters, and not schoolmistresses, instructing the girls' classes.

The Prussians would ridicule the idea of confiding the education of the girls to uneducated mistresses, such as those in our dame, and in most of our female schools. They cannot conceive the case of a parent, who would be willing to commit his child to the care of a person, who had not been educated, most carefully and religiously, in that most difficult of all arts, the art of teaching. They think, that a teacher *must* either improve and elevate the minds of his children, or else injure and debase them. They believe, that there is no such thing as being able to come into daily contact with a child, without doing him either good or harm. The Prussians know, that the minds of the young are never stationary, but always in progress; and that this progress is always either a moral or an immoral one, either forward or backward; and hence the *extraordinary* expenditure the country is bearing, and the *extraordinary* pains it is taking, to support and improve its training establishments for teachers.

There are at present in Prussia forty-two normal colleges for the education of the teachers of the people! These great, admirable, and well-endowed institutions are supported by the central government. All the German states, as well as Denmark, Holland, Switzerland, France, and Austria, have recognised the absolute necessity of supporting these teachers' training establishments. Holland has two very large ones, Baden two, Wirtemberg two, Saxony eight, Hanover five, Bavaria eight, Switzerland thirteen, Austria fourteen,

France ninety-six; and each of the smaller German States several. But in England we care so little about the profession of the teacher, that we have not more than twelve worth mentioning. I shall show hereafter the character of the admirable normal colleges of Prussia.

In order to increase the feeling of union and brotherhood, which already exists in a high degree among the Prussian teachers, and in order to encourage them to renewed exertions, and to diminish, as much as possible, the feeling of isolation which must always exist, in some degree, where an educated man finds himself placed in a solitary country parish, surrounded by peasatry less cultivated than himself, and cut off from the literary society, to which he had been accustomed at the normal college, the government promotes the frequent holding of teachers' conferences, for the purpose of mutual improvement and encouragement. These conferences are held very often, over the whole of Germany, Switzerland, France, and Holland, and the benefits resulting from them are very great indeed. In Prussia, there are three kinds of such conferences, of which I shall now give a short account. The first is that of the province. In several of the provinces of Prussia, all the teachers, both Catholic and Protestant, assemble once a year, in some town, which has been agreed upon at their last meeting, and on a predetermined day. The duration of the meeting is different in different parts; sometimes only for one and sometimes for several days. Their objects, too, are different. Sometimes it is for mutual instruction, whilst at others it is for pleasure. But, whatever be the *nominal* purpose of their assembling, the real end of it is, to produce the feeling of association and brotherhood, which is one of the strongest encouragements to isolated and single efforts.

Besides these yearly provincial assemblies, there is also another meeting of teachers held monthly in every kreis or union. The principal ecclesiastical authority or school-inspector of the union summons and presides over it. This meeting is more especially intended for the purposes of instruction, than that of the province. It lasts only one day; the teachers meet early in the morning, and disperse again in the evening. They dine together at noon, and spend the morning and afternoon in conference and mutual improvement. They assemble at some town or village in the union on an appointed day, of which the union inspector gives them each notice some weeks beforehand. In the morning, they all meet in one of the schools, or in some great room of the town. A class of children, taken from one of the schools of the town, is assembled there. One of the teachers, generally one of the younger ones, is chosen by his companions to give these children a lesson, on some subject of instruction in the primary schools. The teacher, who is selected, gives the lesson before all the others assembled at the conference. When the lesson is ended, the children are dismissed, and the remaining teachers then begin to criticise the manner, in which the instruction was given, and each shows, how he thinks it might have been improved; and then a debate ensues on the merits of different methods of teaching and of different plans of school management.

This plan of debating at the conferences, on methods of instruction, makes the teachers think, and stimulates them to inquire, how they can impart instruction in the most efficient manner. It makes them also eager to improve their manner of teaching, as each one fears to exhibit any ignorance of his profession, or any unskilfulness before his professional brethren, and desires to win their applause by his ability; and, it makes them properly attentive to all the minutiæ of their profession, as well as to the more interesting studies connected with it.

I was present at one of these teachers' conferences. It was attended not only by the teachers from the primary schools, but also by professors from the superior schools and colleges, and was presided over by the director of a normal college. I do not think the importance of these meetings can be exaggerated. They are not only, as I have before said, a great encouragement to the isolated teachers; but they are a continual source of instruction and improvement to all in their most important duties. The teachers continue at these meetings the instruction they commenced at the normal colleges; they discuss all the new school-books that have appeared, all the new regulations that have been issued, all the new plans that have been tried; and they inform one another of the progress of their different districts. In France and South Germany, they have so strongly felt the importance of these meetings, that the expenses of the teachers in travelling to them are borne by the government; and in Holland and the Duchy of Baden, the government inspectors assist at them, and join in the debates. In some parts of Switzerland, also, they are very well organised; and in the canton of Neufchâtel, I remember to have read a number of a very interesting periodical, which was published after each conference, and which contained several most instructive and very able papers, which had been read at the previous meeting of the village school professors. One cannot help regretting, that here in England, with our rapid means of transit, something of the sort is not done in each county. I believe the government would find it a very easy matter, to prevail upon the different railway committees to allow each teacher four journeys a year, so as to enable all the teachers of a county to assemble in their own county, free of expense, at least four times a year.

Besides those conferences, which I have already mentioned, there is still another kind, which is held in Prussia. This is when a parish is very large, and contains several schools and many teachers. In such cases, the chief ecclesiastical authority summons a meeting of all the parochial teachers once a month, for purposes of mutual instruction, similar to the meetings in the unions. Sometimes the clergyman himself gives them a lecture on religious instruction, and, at other times, they debate among themselves on questions of pedagogy, or criticise one another's methods of teaching; but in all cases the object of the meetings is the same, viz., mutual encouragement and improvement. As the religious ministers preside at these parochial and union conferences, they have an opportunity of addressing the teachers on their religious duties, and of giving them advice and instruction respecting the true end they ought to keep in view in their school lessons, and on the care they ought to take to keep this end constantly in sight. The ministers also give the teachers advice and counsel respecting the manner, in which their religious lessons ought to be given, in order the more strongly to impress the minds of their scholars with the serious import of the truths of the Scriptures; and they have the opportunity of reminding the younger teachers of the particular parts of the Scripture, which they ought more particularly to lay before the different classes of their children, and of the method of religious instruction which they ought to pursue. But it is impossible to detail all the great and obvious advantages, which result from these meetings of the clergy and the school professors, or to enumerate the different subjects of reflection, debate, and conversation, which are started and discussed at them. They are the supplements, so to speak, of the normal colleges, and serve, in an admirable manner, to carry forward the education, which the young aspirants to the teachers' profession commenced at these institutions, and to continually revive through after life the knowledge imparted in them.

I have now shown how the government provides for the education, appointment, payment, protection, encouragement, and continual improvement of the teachers.

It remains for me to show, how the Prussian government secures the teacher from all fear of being disabled, by sickness or old age, from pursuing his labours or providing for his family. It would be a great disgrace for a profession, such as that of the Prussian teachers, were the fate of a superannuated teacher to be the same as in our country; where there is in general no other refuge for such a person, than the workhouse or the hospital. Doubtless, if Prussia did not feel more interested, than we do, in the protection of this most important class of public servants, it would not care what became of them, when they were too old or too weak to attend the schools. But Prussia fully appreciates the value of the labours of her teachers, and has a sincere respect for them, and a lively concern in their welfare. The government has felt, that to cast off and forsake all the old and faithful teachers, when they could work no longer, would be to disgust the whole body, to break off the sympathies, which unite them to their profession, and to shut out of it many noble spirits. It has, therefore, most carefully guarded against these results, by the regulations, which I shall now proceed to describe.

If a teacher, who has been definitely appointed, becomes unable to fulfil the duties of his station, either through the utter breaking up of his health, or by old age, the authorities who appointed him, whether they were the county court, the town school commission, or the parochial school-committee, are obliged to pension him for the remainder of his life.

This pension must, according to law, amount to at least one third of his former income. Whether the committee settles more than this upon a teacher or not, depends upon the manner in which he has laboured, whilst he was yet able to do so, and upon the resources which the committee finds at its disposal. When, however, the teacher is not so far incapacitated for exertion as to be unable to do any thing, but only so far as to require assistance, the local committee or county court is not *allowed* to dismiss him on a pension, but is required to provide him an assistant, who must be chosen from among the young men, who have been educated in the normal colleges, and who have obtained certificates of qualification for their duties.

If the school, to which a teacher has been appointed, is supported by or belongs to a landed proprietor, this latter is obliged to pension the teacher, when incapacitated for his duties by illness or old age; and if the school is one of royal foundation, the court of the county, in which it is situated, must pension him. The Prussian government, although professedly a military state, has shown itself *at least as deeply* interested in the welfare of its teachers, as in that of its soldiers, whilst we, who disown the appellation of a military people, take greater care of our soldiers than of our teachers.

Besides the provisions for the pensioning of the superannuated teachers, there is another law in force in Prussia, which relates to the future provision of the widows and orphans of deceased schoolmasters, and which is deserving of equal praise.

In each union a society is formed, of which the principal ecclesiastical authority in the union is the president, the object of which is to provide for the support of the widows and orphans of deceased teachers. The regulations of these societies differ a little, I believe, in the different provinces; but it will not be necessary here to examine them so minutely, as to show what is peculiar to each. I shall only attempt to give a brief sketch of them, as I have collected it from the laws, which have been framed for some of the eastern counties of Prussia, and which I have now before me.

Every definitely appointed teacher, whether in town or country, must become a member of the society established in his union, for the assistance of the widows and orphans of deceased teachers.

Every teacher must pay a small entrance-fee on his becoming a member, and afterwards a small yearly sum. The amounts of these sums are in all cases confined within certain limits, and can neither fall below nor rise above them. On the amount of the yearly subscription paid by the teacher depends the value of the pension, which his widow or children will be entitled to receive, after his death, from the director of the union society. There are generally three different pensions, varying in value, for either of which the teacher may subscribe at his own discretion, but for one of which he must pay his annual subscription. If he pay to the first and best, his widow or children will receive the greatest pension given by the society, and this is always very much more than the interest of his money, calculated on life averages, would have entitled him to receive, as the societies are not commercial enterprises, but charitable institutions. To enable the societies, therefore, to meet the calls upon their treasuries, it is often necessary, that they should be assisted in some extraordinary manner, and this is done by collections made in the union churches by the ecclesiastical superintendent, and by

CHAP. VII.

PRUSSIAN EDUCATION.—THE TEACHERS' COLLEGES.—THE WEISSENFELS NORMAL COLLEGE.

A FEW years ago, any one used to be thought clever enough to be a teacher. Even now, in many parts of our country, any poor fellow who can read and write decently, is thought fit to teach in a village school, so low is the idea of many of the education which should be given to the children of the poor, and of the character of the men who ought to train our citizens!

Forty years ago there were not twenty colleges for the education of teachers in the whole of Europe; now there are several hundreds of such institutions! Within the last forty years, Holland has established *two* great normal colleges, expressly intended for the scientific education of the teachers of the poor; Baden, two; Wirtemberg, two; Saxony, eight; Hanover, five; Denmark, five; Bavaria, eight; Switzerland, thirteen; the Austrian Empire, fourteen; Prussia, forty-three; and France, ninety-six. Besides these, many others have, I believe, been established in the smaller German States, as well as in Norway and Sweden. And what is now the consequence? At this moment, in almost every village of France, Germany, Austria, Denmark, Holland, Switzerland, Norway, and Sweden, a learned and good man, who has been highly educated at some one or other of these great and well endowed colleges, and whose character has received the approbation of the religious minister of the village, in which he grew up to manhood, is now teaching and associating with the poor. Is it possible that such a moral influence could exist without result? No; each year has witnessed, and is still witnessing, a visible and steady improvement in the character and social habits of the poor of these countries. There can be no possible doubt to an unprejudiced traveller, that the physical and moral condition of the German and French peasants has within the last twenty years greatly improved. Every one bears witness to this fact. The villages themselves tell the same tale.

In proportion, as the tastes of the peasants of these countries have been raised, so have their providence, their morality, and their prosperity been increased. They eat better food, they wear better garments, they inhabit better houses, than they used to do only twenty years ago. Squalid pauperism is rapidly disappearing; comfort, contentment, and industry are taking its place. It is impossible to shut one's eyes to these facts. Whatever be the cause, most certain it is, that the German peasant is a happier man than the English farm labourer. His cottage is cleaner, more roomy, and more comfortable; his children look like the children of the gentry—clean, well-mannered, and intelligent; his wife is comfortably clothed; his food is good, and he has plenty of it; his amusements are healthy, and he has time for their enjoyment; and his own countenance is happy and intelligent, and bespeaks contentment. I was constantly told, as I wandered among the people "You cannot conceive what a change for the better has taken place within the last thirty years, and that change is still going on." I did not need this testimony. I saw enough on every side to convince me of the happy effects arising from the combined influence of *peasant proprietorship and education.* I only wish that every Englishman was able to travel in these countries, to learn what has been done for the people, and what it is possible to do.

In each of the different provinces of Prussia the government has established five or six great colleges, intended expressly for the education of the teachers. There are now forty-three of these magnificent foundations scattered throughout the kingdom. Each county possesses at least one, nearly all have two of them. They are all endowed, partly by the state and partly by private benefactors. The education given in them is perfectly gratuitous; *at least* one-half of the cost of boarding each student is borne by the state, or defrayed out of the funds of the college, on the most liberal scale; and every thing is provided, which can possibly contribute to the perfection of the training and education of the students.

No attempt has been made to give the education of the teachers any political bias. The normal colleges are widely dispersed throughout the country. They are situated close to the homes of the students, and at great distances from the centre of government; so that the patriotic sentiments naturally resulting from the humble origin of the young teachers are not weakened;

nor are their local sympathies ever interrupted by the young men being removed, during the period of their education, into a distant and uncongenial political atmosphere. Neither does the government undertake the actual direction of these great and important establishments. Each of them, with only two or three exceptions, is put under the care of a religious minister of the sect, for the education of whose teachers it is destined.

In each province, there are, as I have before stated, five or six of these institutions. In each county, there are generally two. If the inhabitants of a county are composed of Romanists and Protestants in pretty equal proportions, one of these colleges is devoted to the education of the Romanist teachers, the other to that of the Protestant. If nearly all the inhabitants of a county are of one faith, both of the normal colleges are devoted to the education of the teachers of this faith; and the teachers of the minority are educated in one of the colleges of a neighbouring county. There are only two normal colleges in Prussia, where Romanist and Protestant teachers are professedly educated together. The directors of these great institutions are chosen from among the clergy. The director of a Romanist college is chosen by the Romanist bishop of the province, in which the college is situated; and the director of a Protestant college is chosen by the ecclesiastical authorities of the province, in which the college is situated; subject, however, in both cases, to the approbation of the Minister of Education in Berlin, who has the power of objecting, if an unsuitable or injudicious choice is made.

The normal colleges are thus put under the supervision of the religious bodies. The government itself directs their management. It recognises the importance of these colleges having a decidedly religious character; and, at the same time, of the education given in them being of the most liberal kind. On the one hand, therefore, it entrusts the direction of them to the clergy; and, on the other hand, it reserves the right of examining them, so as to have the power of interfering, in case the *secular* education of the students should be injudiciously curtailed. The director of each college appoints all the professors and teachers. The religious ministers have, therefore, a considerable share of the direction of these institutions. Their character is decidedly religious, and a union between the clergy and the teachers is effected, which is productive of the best possible results.

The students remain in these colleges about three years. They live in the institution. Almost the whole of the expenses of their education, and of their board, are paid out of the funds of the college.

If a young man wishes to enter into one of these normal colleges, he need not travel far from home. Within a day's journey of his own village, is to be found one of the normal colleges of his country. If he is able to pass the preparatory examination, and to procure carefully attested certificates of character, he is received as an inmate of the college on a vacancy occurring. During the time of his sojourn there, and during the continuance of his arduous studies, he is in constant communication with all his old associates and friends, and constantly revisits the scenes of his boyhood. His sympathies with his people are thus preserved intact. None of his old connections with his village are broken; he remains the son, the brother, and the companion of the peasants. His life in the normal college is very simple and laborious; the change from its arduous discipline and duties, to those of a village teacher, is a change for the better. The teacher is not rendered discontented with his simple village life, by being pampered in the college; the laborious and self-denying discipline of the college teaches him, how to combine the simplicity of the peasant, with the learning of the scholar. It is the design of these Prussian colleges to send forth simple-minded, industrious, religious, and highly educated peasant teachers; and not affected pedagogues, or mere conceited and discontented gentlemen. Nobly, most nobly, have they fulfilled their mission! Prussia may well be proud of her 30,000 teachers.

Each one in his village, and in his district, is labouring among the poor, not so much to teach them their A, B, C, and mere school-room learning, as to enable them to think; to show them the present, as well as the future advantages of manly virtue, and to explain to them, how much their own prosperity in life depends upon their own exertions. This is education.

Oh! if we could once be taught to recognise the vast benefits, which education *must* confer upon the people—if we could once be taught to understand, the meaning of the term, and the nature of the undertaking—it would not be long, ere each one of our counties would possess its two normal colleges, and each one of our villages its educated teachers and its school. We have the power, but not the will. We do not understand the vast importance of education to the people.

It has been said, by persons desirous of screening our own shameful neglect of the people's education, by the abuse of the great efforts of our neighbours, that the teachers of Prussia have been, in reality, nothing more than the paid servants of an absolute power, intended to prepare the minds of the people to passive submission to a despotic government. Nothing can be more shamefully and ignorantly false than this assertion.

I have a right to speak on this subject, as I have seen more, perhaps, of the Prussian teachers, than any of my countrymen; and of this I am certain, that the sympathies of the Prussian teachers have always been notoriously with the people, and not with the government. The Prussian government has always, in fact, bitterly complained of the too liberal spirit which actuates the teacher's profession, but without effect; the body is popular in its origin, its position, its education, and its sympathies. Many of the warmest friends of constitutional progress in Prussia have always been found among the teachers; and, it is a fact, well worthy of consideration, that liberal and constitutional ideas never made so rapid a progress in Prussia, at any period of its history, as they have done since the establishment of the present system of education. I believe, that the teachers and the schools of Prussia have been the means of awakening in that country that spirit of inquiry and that love of freedom, which forced the government to grant a *bonâ fide* constitution to the country.

An evidence of the free spirit, which has pervaded the Prussian teachers, may be derived from the fact, that the Prussian government found itself compelled, in 1831, to address a circular order to the teachers, in which, after reciting that the government had been informed, that some of the teachers had converted their class-rooms into political lecture rooms, and had selected the political topics of the day as the subject of remark, if not of instruction,—it prohibited such subjects being introduced into the lessons by the teachers, and ordered the inspectors to prevent the teachers perverting their schools to such objects as these.

The very fact, that such a prohibition was found necessary, proves that my own observations were correct. If further proof were needed, it might be told, that the people have elected many teachers as their representatives in the different Diets; thus proving their esteem and respect for the able instructors of their children.

As nearly all the expenses of the young teacher's education in the normal colleges, are borne by the country at large, and not by himself, it has been thought advisable to require some kind of guarantee, that those, who are educated in the colleges, will really, when their education is completed, labour as teachers in the village schools, and not merely use their college education as a preparation for other more lucrative situations.

In order, therefore, to secure an adequate return for

the expenditure of the country, it has been decreed by the government: —

"1st. That every young man, who is received into a normal college, shall bind himself, by an agreement, to remain, for three years, after leaving the college, at the disposition of the government; and during such three years, to take any situation, which the authorities of the district, in which the normal college is situated, should offer him, or to which they should wish to translate him.

"2nd. That if he does not comply with this condition as soon as required to do so, he shall repay to the normal college the cost of the education and maintenance, which had been gratuitously given to him."

Every year, at a fixed period, of which public notice has been previously given in the local papers, the directors and professors of each of the normal colleges hold a public meeting, at which the magistrates of the county and the religious ministers are present, for the purpose of examining all young men, who are desirous of obtaining admission into the normal college for the purpose of being educated as teachers.

These examinations are open to all young men, even of the poorest classes, many of whom enter the lists, as almost all the expenses of the collegiate course are, as I have said, borne by the state, or defrayed out of the funds of the college.

Every competitor at one of these examinations must forward to the director of the college, a fortnight before the examination takes place, —

1. A certificate signed by his religious minister, and

certifying that his character and past life have been moral and blameless;

2. A certificate from a physician, certifying his freedom from chronic complaints, and the soundness of his constitution and health;

3. A certificate of his having been vaccinated within the last two years;

4. A certificate of his baptism (if a Christian);

5. A certificate, signed by two or more teachers, of his previous industrious and moral habits, and sufficient abilities for the teachers' profession.

On the day appointed, all the young candidates, who have complied with the preceding regulations, and who have attained the age of seventeen, are examined at the college, in the presence of the county magistrates, and of the religious ministers, by the directors and professors of the college, in all the subjects of instruction given in the highest classes of the primary schools; *i. e.*,

Biblical History,
The History of Christianity,
Luther's Catechism,
Writing,
Reading,
Arithmetic (Mental and Common),
Grammar,
Geography,
German History,
Natural History,
The first principles of the Physical Sciences,
Singing,
The Violin.

When the examination is concluded, a list is made out, in which the names of the young men are inscribed in order, according to the proficiency and ability they have displayed in their examination. As many of the highest in the list are then elected, as students of the college, as there are vacancies that year, occasioned by the departure of those who have left the college to take the charge of village schools.

Those who are elected, as well as their parents or guardians, are then required to subscribe the agreements I have before mentioned; and the successful candidates are then admitted as residents of the college for two or three years, according to the length of residence required by the rules of the college.

The time of residence in Prussia is generally three, and never less than two years. The time of residence in the normal colleges in the neighbouring kingdom of Saxony is always FOUR years. When the young men have been once admitted into the normal college, their education as teachers commences. It must, however, be borne in mind, that the Prussian teacher, when he first enters a normal college, has generally before that period enjoyed a much better education, and knows much more then, than an English teacher does when he undertakes the management of a school. Unless he did, he would not be able to obtain admission into a normal college. When he leaves the normal college, he has had a better general education, than nine out of every ten men who leave our Universities.

The education of a good teacher is a very difficult matter, and, principally, for this reason:—Nothing, but a very high education, can fit an individual for the proper performance of that most delicate, difficult, and important duty, the education of a child. Great learning, even when accompanied with good principles, is often apt to *unfit* its possessor for the humble duties of a teacher's life — the mingling, living, and conversing with, and the advising the peasants; the laborious and often unnoticed and unrequited labours of the schoolroom; the constant and wearying struggle with sloth, ignorance, filth, bad habits, and immorality; with the opposition of the prejudiced, and the ignorance of the uneducated parents; with the misrepresentations of his scholars; and with the neglect of the community. The learned teacher has all this, and more than this, to contend with. He finds himself in such a situation, having received an education fitting him for a very different sphere of action, deserving much higher emolument, and inclining him to seek a very different kind of employment. Such a man, if he has received *only* an intellectual training, is sure, sooner or later, to fly from his profession, and seek out an employment more congenial to his newly-acquired tastes, or, if he remains at his post, he remains discontented, and, by discontent, totally unfitted to perform his duties aright.

Now the Prussian and the German normal colleges have avoided this difficulty in the following manner: — They give the teachers a very high intellectual education, but they give them something more: they educate *their habits* also; they accustom the young men, whilst they are in the colleges, to the most laborious and most menial duties; to combine high intellectual endowments with the performance of the humblest duties of a peasant's life; and to acquire high literary attainments whilst living on a peasant's diet, wearing a peasant's dress, and labouring harder than any peasant is ever called upon to do. When, therefore, the students leave the colleges, they find their positions, as village teachers, situations of less labour, of less real drudgery, and of more comfort, than those, which they formerly occupied in the colleges. By these means, their sympathies for the labours and simplicity of the class, from which they sprung are cherished, whilst the labours of the class-room are rendered light and easy by comparison with the labours and daily duties of the normal college. Thus, the college does not engender discontent, but braces the young teacher to his work, and prepares him to encounter it with pleasure.

The education given in the normal colleges of Germany and Switzerland may then be said to consist of two distinct parts:

1st. The intellectual training.
2nd. The industrial training.

1st. THE INTELLECTUAL TRAINING.—This, I have before said, is of a very high character. I have shown what knowledge a young man must have acquired, before he can gain admittance into a normal college. This is only the *groundwork* of his education in the college. During his three years' residence he continues his studies in—

Biblical History,
The History of Christianity,
Luther's Catechism,

Reading, Writing, and Arithmetic, — and
Grammar.

He further enters upon a new and regular course of study in —

Geography,
History,
Natural History,
Botany,
The Physical Sciences,
Pedagogy,
Singing and Chanting,
Drawing,
The Violin, Pianoforte, and Organ.

Besides these subjects of study, the young men generally learn the Latin and French languages, and very often the English also. I met several teachers who knew all three. These latter acquirements are not, however, required; but without the former, a young man could not obtain a teacher's diploma, or officiate in any school as a teacher, nor would he be accepted by the inhabitants of a parish.

The first two years of a teacher's residence in the normal college are devoted almost exclusively to these studies; the third year is divided between them and the daily practice of teaching in the model schools, connected with the college. Here they first practise as teachers, under the eye and direction of an experienced professor, who is able to show them how to impart knowledge in the best manner, and how to manage and direct all the minutiæ of school discipline. Those who imagine, that any one is fit for the performance of these duties without any preparation, show themselves as ignorant of the duties of a teacher, as they are careless about the improvement and happiness of the people.

Besides the subjects of instruction I have noticed, the law requires, that each student shall be taught how to distinguish poisonous herbs; what are, and how to use, the antidotes of different poisons; how to treat the more common accidents, which labourers are liable to meet with; and what remedies and treatment to make use of in cases of scalds, burns, and bites of mad dogs. The teachers are required to impart this instruction to the scholars of the primary schools, so that every person may be capable of acting for himself and without delay, in cases of such daily occurrence, and where a short delay in administering a simple and necessary remedy often proves fatal.

The teacher is thus qualified in simple cases to act as the village doctor; and in country villages, where no surgeon or medical adviser lives within many miles, the teacher's medical knowledge proves invaluable, both to himself and to the people, among whom he dwells. As the uneducated always esteem a man much more if he exhibits a knowledge of the practical arts and appliances of life, the benefit and use of which they can understand, than for any reputation he may have of learning, of the use of which they have generally but a vague idea; so this practical knowlege of the teachers tends greatly to raise them in the estimation and respect of their poorer neighbours, and by this means to give greater influence and effect to their advice and teachings.

2nd. THE INDUSTRIAL TRAINING.—This consists, generally, of the performance of all the ordinary household work, preparing the meals, taking care of the sleeping apartments, pruning the fruit-trees, and cultivating, in the lands always attached to the colleges, the vegetables necessary for the use of the household.

The students are required to rise at five o'clock, and to retire to rest by ten at the latest; and in turn to wait upon the professors and on one another; to ring the bell for classes, &c.; to pump the water required for the daily use of the establishment; to go to the post-office for letters; and to teach in the class-rooms of the village school attached to the college.

The whole of every day is occupied by the regular routine of these duties, and by attendance at the lectures of the principal and the professors. There is no unoccupied time, and, therefore, no time for the formation of idle or immoral habits. The college course is a laborious, severe, but healthy course of life; bracing up the mind, the body, and the habits, to the exertions of the future career.

It is a more than Spartan discipline.

Every year, during its continuance, the young men are rigorously examined, to see whether they are making such progress in their studies, as to afford satisfactory reason for hoping that, at the end of their course of study, they will be able to succeed in gaining a diploma or certificate of competence. When it is found that a young man is incapable, or idle, and that his progress is not such, as to ensure his probable success in the final examination for diplomas, he is removed from the college, to make room for some more worthy recipient of the national bounty, and of some more worthy candidate for the teachers' profession.

This training continues, as I have said before, for *three* years in most of the Prussian colleges. During the whole of this time the young men are urged and stimulated to the greatest exertion, by the knowledge that, at the end of it, they will have to submit to a severe and searching public examination, conducted in the presence of the educational magistrates of the county, of the religious ministers, and of the professors of the college; and that on the results of that examination, and on the manner in which they succeed in it, their admission into the teachers' profession, and their future course of life, entirely depend.

Unless they can pass this final examination creditably, they cannot become teachers; and, even if they do pass it, the value of the situation, to which they may be afterwards appointed, depends entirely on the degree of efficiency and diligence which they display at the examination.

Every year at a certain period, fixed and publicly announced beforehand, a meeting is held in each normal college, by the director and professors of the college, and by the religious ministers and the educational magistrates of the county, at which all the young men, who have been three years in the college, are summoned to attend, for the purpose of being examined in all the subjects, in which they have received instruction, during their residence in the college. This examination generally lasts two days.

The young men who have completed their third year's residence in the college are then examined in, —

1. Biblical History;
2. The History of Christianity;
3. Luther's Catechism;
4. Reading, Writing, and Arithmetic;
5. Grammar;
6. Geography, Local and Physical;
7. History;
8. Natural History;
9. Botany;
10. The Physical Sciences;
11. Pedagogy, and Class Management;
12. Singing and Chanting;
13. Drawing;
14. The Organ, the Pianoforte, and the Violin.

According to the manner, in which each student acquits himself in this examination, he receives, as I have before shown, a diploma marked "1," "2," or "3," or else is rejected, *i. e.* refused admittance into the teachers' profession on the ground of incompetency.

If a student has succeeded so well in his examination, as to gain a diploma marked "1," he is qualified to take a situation in any school as principal teacher, and to enter at once into the highest and most lucrative situations in the country. This diploma is a guarantee to all to whom he shows it, that he is a young man of good ability, high character, and great attainments, and fit to be entrusted with the education of any children of any class in the community.

If a student obtains a diploma marked "2," or "3,"

he cannot, as I have before shown, for the first two or three years, take any situation as principal teacher in a school, but can only officiate as assistant teacher until, by further study and diligent application, he has qualified himself to attend another of the general annual examinations, and has there succeeded in obtaining one of the first diplomas. Those students who obtain the diplomas marked "3," are obliged to return, *the following year*, to the college examination; and, if they do not give proofs of having improved themselves, in the interim, in the branches of education in which they were deficient, they are, generally, deprived of their diplomas altogether.

Any person, whether he has been educated at a normal college or not, may present himself at one of them, at the time when the great annual examination is held, and may demand to be examined for a diploma. If he shows a requisite amount of knowledge, and can produce all the certificates of character, health, &c., which are required of the other students at their entrance into the normal college, he may, equally with the rest, obtain his diploma, and afterwards officiate as a teacher.

But no person without a diploma, *i. e.*, without having given to the country undeniable proofs of high character, well regulated temper, high attainments, and a thorough knowledge of the science of pedagogy, is permitted to officiate as teacher in Prussia.

The connection of a German teacher with the normal college does not, however, close when he has obtained a diploma marked "1", and when he has entered upon his duties as parochial teacher.

The principal of the normal college is commanded by the laws, to pay at least one yearly visit of inspection to each of the teachers, who have been educated in his college. The expense of these journeys of inspection, advice, and encouragement is borne by the state, or rather, as indeed a great part of the expenses of the normal college itself, by the provincial magistrates.

If on these tours of inspection, he perceives that any one or more of the teachers requires some further instruction or practice in any department of school instruction — if he perceives, that a teacher has allowed his knowledge of any branch of instruction to lag behind the progress of the science of pedagogy, or to grow dull from want of exercise — or if the teacher should himself require it, — the principal is empowered to remove the teacher for a few months to the normal college, and during the interim, to fill up his place with a young student, or with some young teacher, who has not yet obtained a situation. All the extra expenses, attendant upon this removal, as, for instance, the payment of the young substitute, as well as the keep of the teacher himself during his renewed sojourn in the college, are defrayed by the provincial government. The teacher's salary continues to be paid by the school-committee, and serves to support his family during his absence.

I need not here remark upon the great munificence of these arrangements, and upon the sad and disgraceful contrast which our own efforts make when compared to them.

The normal college in Prussia is, so to speak, the

home of all the teachers of the district, in which it is situated. They know they can always apply there for advice; that they will always find friends there, ready to sympathise with them and to render them assistance; and that the director and professors understand all their difficulties, and are always able and willing to aid them in obtaining a remedy from the superior authorities. The college is thus the protector and the adviser of the teachers; it is their refuge in all troubles; it is the central point for their meetings and reunions; and it is the place, from which they can, at all times, gain every kind of necessary information, respecting the various objects connected with their profession. They can see there all the best and newest works on the different branches of pedagogy; all the lately improved apparatus and materials for school instruction; and all the more recently adopted methods of teaching. They can obtain information there about the general progress of education in general, and of the different arts and sciences in particular; about their old friends and associates; and about the character and efficiency of particular books, schools, and methods of instruction.

I cannot speak too highly of these great and liberal institutions. The spirit in which they have been conceived, is so liberal; the way in which they have been endowed is so munificent; their tone and teaching are so truly healthy and patriotic; they are so free from the ignorant cant of dogmatism and from the narrow-minded feeling of pedantry; their discipline is so severely moral and so invigorating; their domestic life is so simple, laborious, and happy in its arrangements;

and they are so entirely in unison with the religious institutions of the country, that no one can visit them without profound satisfaction. It is in these great institutions that all the guides and teachers of the youth and children of Prussia are educated for their noble but most arduous profession. No wonder then, that the children of the poor of Prussia, who are ALL brought up from their earliest years, by men educated as these Prussian teachers are, should be so much in advance of the children of our poor, in the scale of civilisation.

In order to give a clearer idea of the real character of the great normal colleges of Prussia, I shall describe one of those, which I inspected in 1846, viz., the normal college of Weissenfels in Prussian Saxony. After having visited the celebrated normal college, then conducted by Dr. Diesterweg at Berlin, which has acquired a European reputation, and after having been conducted over the more extensive institutions at Bruhl, in the Rhine Province, and at Potsdam, I determined to proceed to Weissenfels, in Prussian Saxony, as I had heard from several high authorities, that the Weissenfels training establishment for Protestant teachers, was considered one of the most complete and satisfactory in Prussia, although not so large as some of the others.

The Minister of Education at Berlin gave directions, that I should be furnished with letters of introduction to the director of this institution, as well as to those of any others I might desire to visit. I reached Weissenfels in the latter end of September, 1846, and was received there, as well as everywhere else throughout Prussia, with the greatest politeness. The director, Dr. Hennicke, put into my hands the fullest accounts of all the plans he pursued, and enabled me to verify these statements by personal inspection and examination. The institution is a very interesting one, and so much exceeded my expectations, that, even at the risk of some repetition, I shall venture to describe it here.

The buildings, devoted by the provincial government of Prussian Saxony to the Weissenfels normal college, formed at one time a large monastery. They are situated in a garden of about four or five English acres in extent, near the small town of Weissenfels, in the south of the Prussian province of Saxony. One building is used as the residence of the director and his family and of the students, who are sixty in number; the other contains the apartments of the professors, the chapel, the class-rooms for the students, and the class-rooms for the model school, which is attended by about 300 children from the town.

This model school was divided into five classes, each containing from fifty to eighty children. Each of these classes occupied a separate class-room, and was instructed by an able and experienced teacher, who had obtained his diploma.

The rooms of this school were lofty, and excellently proportioned. They were beautifully clean, very well ventilated, and all furnished with rows of parallel desks, with large and excellent maps, large engravings for the lectures on botany and natural history, black boards, slates, and every thing which could assist the professors and teachers.

In the college itself, there were five distinct lecture-rooms for the use of the students of the institution; five large class-rooms for the model or practising school, which I have just mentioned; a noble music and general lecture hall, containing an excellent organ; a library for the use of the students; a second music-room, with another organ; three smaller rooms for the practice of instrumental music, each containing a piano-forte; a large dining-room, containing two pianofortes; a washing-room; a bath-room; an infirmary; large and well-ventilated dormitories; and excellent kitchens, larders, and offices for the management of the domestic economy of the household. There were also three or four other rooms used as a school for deaf and dumb children; and a third building, outside the garden, used as another model school. In this and the above-mentioned model school, as I shall hereafter show, the students first commence to practise teaching under the *surveillance* of the director and professors. There were also two large exercise-grounds fitted up with gymnasiums, where the students and the children from the model schools practised, daily, all kinds of bodily exercises. No expense seemed to have been spared in making all the arrangements as perfect as possible, and in keeping the whole premises in a state of the most excellent order, preservation, and cleanliness. The gardens were well stocked with trees, and nearly all the vegetables used by the household, were cultivated in them by the students themselves, under the superintendence of a scientific gardener.

The province of Prussian Saxony contained, in 1840, a population of 1,637,221 inhabitants. It is divided into three counties or regierungsbezirke. *Each one* of these counties has THREE teachers' training colleges. The province, therefore, possesses NINE normal colleges, which, in the year 1843, contained 238 young students preparing to enter the ranks of the teachers; while Lancashire and Cheshire, with about twice as many inhabitants, have only *one* training establishment for the whole of that populous district.

The Weissenfels institution is under the direction and *surveillance* of the provincial school college in Magdebourg, the members of which, as I have before said, are immediately appointed by the government.

The number of the students in the Weissenfels normal college generally amounts to sixty. They remain THREE years in the institution, before they are examined for diplomas; the first two of these years being devoted to study, and the latter more particularly to the practice of teaching. At the time of my visit the students paid nothing for their lodgings or dinners; but they provided their own bread and milk for breakfasts and suppers, and for dinner, if they wished to eat bread with their meat. I inquired, if they could have what they liked for breakfasts and suppers, but the answer was — "No; we only allow milk and bread, as we wish to accustom them to the plainest fare, that they may never find the change from the normal college to the village school a change for the worse; but always one for the better." The young men furnished themselves with all the necessary class-books; but their instruction was entirely gratuitous; and, I believe, that the sum total, which a young student had to pay annually, exclusive of the cost of bread and milk for breakfasts and suppers, and of his clothes, did not exceed three pounds, so that there was nothing to hinder young men, of the humblest ranks of society, entering the college, and being educated there for the teachers' profession. On the contrary, the government, as my readers will perceive, offered every inducement and assistance to such candidates.

All candidates for admission present themselves at the institution, at the annual candidates' examinations, which are conducted by the director and professors, in the presence of the educational magistrate for the county. The most able and forward of the candidates are then, after a careful examination, elected and admitted. There are generally, in each of the Prussian provinces, some special regulations, limiting this choice of students for the normal colleges. Thus, the regulations of the province, in which the normal college of Weissenfels is situated, prescribe, that "no short-sighted, deaf, or feeble candidates shall be admitted." The same regulations also direct the examiners to give a preference to those candidates, who have a broad chest and a good voice. They also forbid any young man being admitted, before he has completed his seventeenth year, or, "unless he is a young man of a good character, moral habits, and unimpeachable conduct."

All candidates for admittance are required to give

satisfactory proof, that they know the Biblical history, and the outlines of the history of religion; that they are able to repeat Luther's catechism, the maxims of Scripture, and the more beautiful of the Psalms; that they can write clearly, pronounce their words distinctly, and read well; that they are conversant with the principal rules of the German grammar; that they understand the doctrine of proportions and fractions; that they can sing simple pieces of music at sight, and play the violin; and that they have made such a progress in geography, history, natural history, and physics, as may be expected from young men, who have completed their education in a higher municipal school. I have translated literally, that part of the Weissenfels' college prospectus, which mentions, what the provincial committee of Prussian Saxony has ordered the examiners of candidates to require, from every applicant for admission to one of the normal colleges of that province, before their education as teachers is even commenced. I believe that there are not 500 village teachers in the whole of England and Wales, who know so much as the candidates for admission into the Prussian normal colleges are by these laws required to know, before they can even begin their course of study in these great institutions.

I have already mentioned, that the young men are prepared in various manners for admission into the normal colleges. Many of the young men at Weissenfels, at the time of my visit, were teachers' sons, whom their fathers had educated. Others were the sons of peasants or small shopkeepers, and had been either educated in the evenings by the village teachers, or had attended one of the preparatory normal schools, where they had had to pay something for their board and instruction. I was informed that these schools were not generally very good. They are often the enterprizes of private individuals, who cannot afford to expend the funds requisite to complete the internal arrangements in a proper manner. I have already shown that it would be much better to close these schools, and to allow each teacher to have at least one monitor, whom he might train, and employ in assisting to teach the more mechanical parts of education. From these trained monitors might be chosen, with great advantage to the general education, the candidates for the normal colleges. France is pursuing this system, and, I believe, with great advantage, as the country obtains much better candidates for admittance into the normal colleges, and at a much smaller expenditure, whilst the teachers, by being freed from the more mechanical part of school teaching, such as writing and the rudiments of reading, are enabled to devote more of their time, attention, and energies to the more intellectual parts of instruction.

A part of the young students educated in the Weissenfels institution are prepared for admission in a preparatory normal college, situated not far from the principal establishment. This preparatory institution contains about sixty boys, most of whom are destined for reception into the principal college. Some of them, however, make such satisfactory progress in their studies during their residence in the preparatory institution, as to be able to present themselves at the annual examination for diplomas, without going through the normal college at all. The course of study at this preparatory school is of two years' duration. The boys, who are destined to be teachers, and whose parents can afford to pay for their education, enter it about the end of their fifteenth year, after leaving the primary parochial schools. There are two classes in this school. The first class is intended for the boys during their first year's residence in the establishment, the second contains all those who have spent more than one year in the establishment.

The subjects of instruction in the first class of this preparatory school are ; religious instruction, Scripture history ; composition ; a clear pronunciation in reading and speaking ; arithmetic, writing, the German language ; agriculture and farming ; drawing ; singing, the violin, and pianoforte.

The subjects of instruction in the second class are; religious instruction, Scripture history, Scriptural interpretation ; the German language ; writing, arithmetic, geometry, natural philosophy, geography, history, drawing ; choral singing, the violin, the pianoforte ; and exercises in teaching.

This institution is, as I have said, close to the normal college, from whence two of those students who have spent two years in the college, are sent every day to conduct the instruction of the youths. Each boy in the preparatory school pays for his board and education a sum, which is equal to about 10*l.* or 12*l.* per annum, if the relative value of money in Weissenfels and in England is considered.

The normal college in Weissenfels has a public examination every year at Easter, at which the educational counsellor of the county court assists, when all candidates for admission are examined, in order that those, who are the best qualified, may be selected to fill up the year's vacancies. A public notice of the day, on which this examination will take place, is given in the principal provincial newspaper; and each young man, who wishes to offer himself as a candidate for admission, is obliged to send the director notice of his intention to be present, at least a fortnight before the examination takes place, and to forward to him a certificate of his baptism; the certificate of a physician of his freedom from chronic complaints, and from every weakness and physical imperfection, which would prove an obstacle to his performance of all the necessary duties of a teacher; a certificate of his having been vaccinated within the last two years; a certificate signed by two or more teachers of his possessing industrious and moral habits and sufficient ability for the profession he has chosen.

Such is the care, which is taken to prevent any unfit person being received into the college and trained for the important profession of a teacher. It has often happened, that many young men who had presented themselves at these entrance examinations have been rejected, as not having made sufficient progress in their studies, even when there still remained several unoccupied vacancies in the establishment, which the director was desirous of filling up. But the maxim in Prussia is, that it is better to have no teacher, than to have an incapable or an immoral one.

As soon as a candidate has been admitted into the Weissenfels College, he is required, with the approbation of his parent, or guardian, to bind himself by writing: —

1st. During the first three years after leaving the normal college, to accept any situation in the county in which the college is situated, to which he should be presented by the county magistrates; and during these three years, to avoid all engagements which would prevent him fulfilling this condition.

2nd. If he should not, during the first three years, accept any situation, which the county magistrates offer him as soon as it is offered, to repay to the college all the outlay, which was made by the institution while he remained there, upon his maintenance and education.

The Prussian government has, however, enacted, that as long as any candidate, who has been educated at one of the normal colleges of a county, is unprovided with a situation, neither the county magistrates nor any parochial committee, nor any patron of a private school, shall elect any other person as a teacher, even although such person shall have obtained a diploma certifying his fitness to be a teacher.

The above-mentioned regulations are intended to prevent unprincipled men making use of the gratuitous education of the college, merely for their own advancement in life, without any intention of ever acting as teachers in the parochial schools of the county; to prevent the young men commencing to teach, before they have satisfied the magistrates of their fitness and capability; and to oblige the young and unpractised teachers to begin their labours, in the worse-paid and poorer situations, from which they are afterwards advanced to the more important and lucrative posts, if they prove themselves deserving of such advancement. Were it not for the former of these two regulations, the poorer situations would never be filled, while the worse-paid teachers would seldom have any hopes of any advancement; and were it not for the latter, unprincipled men would be able to avail themselves of the gratuitous education of the college in order to prepare for more lucrative situations than those, which the teachers generally occupy during the first three years after obtaining their diplomas.

Desertions from the teachers' profession are very rare in Prussia and Saxony. This, as I have said before, proves how well contented the teachers are with their position. But what shows this still more clearly is, that a great proportion of the young students, who are generally to be found in the normal colleges preparing for entrance into the teachers' profession, are the sons of the parochial teachers, who have educated and partly trained them in their own schools. This is the case, not only in Prussia, but in the neighbouring kingdom of Saxony also, where the teachers have hitherto been scarcely so well paid as in Prussia.

When the successful candidates have been admitted into the Weissenfels normal college, the director presents them to the professors and teachers, and then addresses them, in the presence of all the members of the institution, on the duties they will be expected to perform during their three years' residence. He enters minutely into an enumeration of these duties, and what is thus intended more especially for the instruction of those who have just entered, serves also to call to the remembrance of all the others, the great end of their studies and labours, and the importance of religion, morality, order, and industry to enable them to attain their object.

The staff of professors in the Weissenfels training college consisted, at the time of my visit, of:—

1st. The director, Dr. Hennicke, who had been educated as a Lutheran clergyman, although I believe he had not actually entered into holy orders. He was the first professor, and conducted the religious instruction and the lectures on pedagogy, and he superintended the whole institution. He had the appointment of all the professors and teachers of the establishment.

2nd. The *second* professor, who conducted the musical instruction of the students, and superintended the lecture-rooms of the normal college.

3rd. The *third* professor, who gave instruction in the German language and in the history of Christianity, and superintended the school life of the students.

4th. The *fourth* professor, who gave instruction in geometry and arithmetic, in physical geography and natural history, in writing and drawing, and who superintended the domestic life of the students.

5th. The teacher of the deaf school, in which there were between twenty and thirty children. The young men in the normal college studied under him how to conduct this particular kind of instruction.

6th. SEVEN assistant teachers, five of whom directed the classes in the model school, whilst the other two assisted the teacher of the deaf school. All these teachers assisted also in the superintendence of the students in the normal college. One of them acted as the assistant of the second professor, in superintending the lecture-rooms; and a third, as the assistant of the fourth professor, in superintending the domestic life of the young men.

7th. A gardener, who superintended the out-door labours of the students.

There were also, in addition to this large staff of professors and teachers, a housekeeper and a female servant, who prepared the meals, made the fires, and cleaned the house. All the other household duties were performed in turn by the young students themselves. Each young man had his appointed days, when he was expected to ring the bell for the different lectures and meals, to bring the letters from the post, to attend the sick, to carry the director's dinner to his room, to light the lamps, &c., &c. By the performance of these humble duties, and by their labour in the gardens, where they cultivate the vegetables for the use of the household, they learn to combine simplicity and humility with high mental attainments; and are taught to sympathise with the peasant class, with whom they are afterwards called upon to mingle, and to whom, it is the principal duty of their lives, to render themselves good counsellors, instructors, and friends.

At the commencement of each year, a table is drawn out, showing the arrangement of the hours of study in the lecture-rooms, and of those of labour in the open air. This table is hung up in different parts of the establishment, so that all may know in the morning, to what duties each hour of the day is devoted, in order that all loss of time and all confusion may be avoided. The director put into my hands the time-division plan for 1846; and I shall now proceed to show from it, the ordinary arrangement of the hours of study in the Weissenfels institution.

The young student who is on duty for the week, rings the bell at five o'clock in the morning to rouse the household to its day's labours. All then rise, wash, and assemble in their different class-rooms at half-past five o'clock. Each class sings a hymn, the teacher reads a prayer, and they then commence work.

At seven o'clock breakfast is served, at eight o'clock the young men return again to the lecture-rooms, where they remain until twelve o'clock. At twelve o'clock dinner is served. At one o'clock they return again to their classes, where they remain until four. From four o'clock until half-past six, the young men are allowed to employ themselves as they please, save that a certain number must work one hour every evening in the garden. This is performed in rotation, so that every young man should labour a certain time *every week*, in cultivating the vegetables for the use of the household. At half past six, they take their simple supper, and then resume their studies for about an hour; and at a quarter past nine in summer, and at a quarter to nine in winter, they all assemble together for prayers, and afterwards, retire to rest. In summer, the first and second classes of the students, attended each by a professor, make long walks into the country to botanise, for botany is studied carefully by all the teachers in Prussia, as they are required to teach at least the elements of this science to the children in the country parishes, in order to give them a greater interest in the cultivation of plants, and to open their eyes to some of those wonders of creation, by which they are more immediately surrounded. In winter also, long walks and excursions in the country are made by all the students, whenever the director thinks, that their health requires such exercise.

On Sundays, the day is commenced by all the students being assembled together for prayer, reading the Scriptures, and singing. At half-past twelve, one half of the young men go to church, whilst the others remain at home for religious instruction. In the afternoon, those who remained at home in the morning go to church, whilst the others receive religious instruction in the college.

The education given in this normal college consists of: —

I. Religious intruction, including lectures on the Scriptures, Luther's catechism, and the history of Christianity.

II. The German language, including exercises in composition, writing, grammar, and reading.

III. Mathematics, history, physical geography, botany, natural history, and gardening.

IV. Drawing, including geometrical and perspective drawing.

V. Music, including lectures on the theory and practice of music, and constant practice in chanting and singing, and in playing the organ, pianoforte, and violin. Every schoolmaster in Germany is required, as I have said before, to be able to play these instruments.

VI. Pedagogy, or the art of teaching. The young men are taught the art of teaching in the classes of the model school, by the teachers who superintend these classes. They afterwards practise it alone, or are only subject to occasional inspection, in the classes of the smaller model school attached to the college, but standing outside the college grounds. I was present at a very interesting lesson in pedagogy, conducted by one of the superior professors. About fifteen or twenty of the students were assembled in one of the lecture-rooms, where a small class of from six to ten children were brought from the model school. One of the young men was then desired, to give them a lesson in etymology, in the presence of all his companions, and under the criticism of the professor. Whenever he was guilty of any bad mannerism, of any involved or verbose explanation, or of any neglect of discipline, the professor called upon the class of students to correct him. Those of the students, who imagined they detected an error in any of these respects, then held up their hands; and out of those who did so, the professor chose one to explain the fault, of which the student, who was teaching, had been guilty.

VII. Arithmetic, including mental arithmetic, ciphering, and mensuration.

VIII. Medicine. — The law, as I have already remarked, requires that every student in a Prussian college should be taught, how to treat cases of suspended animation, and wounds occasioned by bites of mad dogs, or by fire, &c., how to distinguish poisonous plants, and how to employ some of the more ordinarily used antidotes for poisons. These subjects the young men are required to teach in their schools afterwards, so as to enable the people to act for themselves in accidents, &c. of common occurrence.

A great deal of time is devoted to the musical part of the education of Prussian teachers, and the proficiency attained is perfectly astonishing. I was present at an exercise in musical composition in the Weissenfels College. It was the second class that was examined, so that I did not see what the most proficient students were capable of performing. The musical professor wrote upon a black board a couplet from an old German song, which he requested the students to set to music. In ten minutes this was done, and though every composition was not equally good, yet, out of a class of twenty, I have six different pieces of music, the compositions of six of the students, which deserve no little praise for their harmony and beauty. The director afterwards assembled all the professors and students of the college, in the hall, that I might hear them sing some of their national songs together. The performance was most admirable; the expression, time, and precision, with which they managed the great body of sound, which they created, was quite wonderful. My readers must remember, that every German child commences to learn singing, as soon as it enters a school, or, in other words, when it is five or six years of age; that the young students continue the practice of singing and chanting from six years of age, until the time when they enter the normal colleges; and that during their residence there they daily practise the most difficult musical exercises, besides learning three musical instruments. It is not, therefore, surprising that they attain very remarkable proficiency. I have mentioned several times that every teacher in the normal colleges in Prussia (and the same is the case throughout Germany) is obliged to learn the violin and the organ. They are required to know how to play the violin, in order with it to lead the singing of the children in the parochial schools, as the Germans think, the children cannot be taught properly how to modulate their voices, without the aid of a musical instrument. They are required to learn the organ for a reason which I will now explain.

The German teachers, as I have before shown, have almost always some duties to perform, in connection with their respective places of religious worship. If the teacher is a Romanist, he is expected to attend upon the priests, to play the organ, and to lead the chanting and singing. If he is a Protestant, he has to give out the hymns, to play the organ, to lead the chanting and singing, and if the clergyman should be prevented officiating by illness, or any other cause, the teacher is expected to read the prayers, and in some cases also to read a sermon. This connection of the teachers and of the religious ministers is very important, as it raises the teachers' profession in the eyes of the poor, and creates a union and a sympathy between the clergy and the schoolmasters.

In order, therefore, to fit the teachers for these parochial duties, it becomes necessary for them to pay a double attention to their musical education, and particularly to render themselves proficient upon the organ.

Hence a traveller will find, in each of the German teachers' colleges, two or three organs, and three, four, and sometimes six pianofortes, for they commence with practising on this latter instrument, and afterwards proceed to practise on the organ.

They had two organs in the Weissenfels institution; one in the great lecture-hall, and another in one of the largest of their lecture-rooms.

As I have already mentioned, time-tables were hung up in different parts of the establishment, showing how the different hours of the day are to be employed. Before visiting any of the classes, the director took me to one of these tables, and said, "You will see from that table, how all the classes are employed at the present moment, so you can choose which you will visit." In this manner, I chose several classes one after the other, by referring to the table; and I invariably found them pursuing their allotted work with diligence, order, and quiet.

The education of the young students, during their three years' residence in the training college, is, as I have said, gratuitous. The young men are only required to pay part of the expenses of the board. Even this small expenditure is, in many cases, defrayed for them, so as to enable the poorest young men to enter the teachers' profession; for the Prussians think, that a teacher of the poor ought to be a man, who can thoroughly sympathise with the peasants, and who can associate with them as a friend and a brother; and that no one is so well able to do so as he, who has known what it is to be a peasant, and who has personally experienced all the wants, troubles, and difficulties, as well as all the simple pleasures of a peasant's life. For these reasons, they have endeavoured in many ways, to facilitate the admission of peasants into the teachers' profession. They have founded, in the *superior schools*, a great number of free places, which are reserved expressly for boys of the poorest classes, who are unable to pay any thing for continuing their education, beyond the course of the primary schools. These places are generally awarded to the most advanced of the poorer scholars, who have creditably passed through all the classes of a primary school, and who are desirous of pursuing their education still further. This liberal and excellent plan enables a young man, however poor, to prepare himself for the admission examinations of the normal colleges.

But even if a young peasant is enabled to enter a normal college, there is still the expense of maintaining himself there; and this, unless provided for, would, in the case of most peasants, be an effectual bar to his entering the teachers' profession. To obviate this difficulty, the Prussians have founded, in each of their forty-two normal colleges, a certain number of what are called *stipendia*. These stipendia correspond with the foundations at our public schools. They are endowed places, intended for poor and deserving young men, who would not, without them, be able to bear the small expenses of residence in these institutions. These foundations or endowments are created, sometimes by charitable individuals, sometimes by municipal corporations, and sometimes by the government, but the object of them is always the same; viz., the assistance of very poor young men of promising abilities, who are desirous of entering the teachers' profession, but who would not be able to aspire to it without such assistance. There are ten of these foundations in the Weissenfels institution, varying in amount, and created, some by the municipal authorities of Weissenfels and other towns in the province, and others by private individuals.

There are no Romanist students in this institution; all the young men are Protestants. There are only two colleges in Prussia where Romanists and Protestants are educated together. As each county has two, and sometimes three, training establishments, it is always easy to arrange that one or two of them shall be devoted to the instruction of Romanist teachers, and the others to the instruction of Protestant teachers, according to the relative proportions of the two religious bodies in the county. The Prussian government never encourages simultaneous or mixed teachers' colleges or parochial schools, when separate colleges or separate schools can be provided. With respect to the parochial schools, government never interferes directly, except advice is requested; and the parochial committees are left at perfect liberty to please themselves.

The normal colleges, however, are under the direction

of the Minister of Public Instruction; and the government is therefore enabled to carry out the plan, which it deems to be the best calculated to insure the perfection of these institutions. When, however, I say that they are under the direction of the Minister, I do not mean that they are so immediately, but only through the medium of the provincial school-committees, which, as I have before said, consist of the chief president of the province, and of several other learned men, inhabitants of the province, and elected by the Minister, as being qualified to direct the superior educational establishments of their native province; for all the higher schools, such as the schools for the richer classes, the gymnasia, and the normal colleges, are directed by these provincial school-committees, and not by the parishes.

The young students, during the first two years of their residence in the Weissenfels normal college, devote nearly the whole of their time to the advancement of their education in Biblical knowledge, history, geography, mathematics, natural philosophy, arithmetic, music, &c.; and do not receive much instruction in the science of pedagogy. The principal part of their instruction in pedagogy is reserved for their third year's residence in the normal college. They then begin to practise teaching at regular hours. One or two of the students, who have passed two years in the establishment, are sent daily into each of the five classes of the model school, each of which classes has a separate class-room assigned to it, where one of the five trained teachers of the model school is always engaged in instruction. Under the superintendance, and subject to the criticism and advice of these able teachers, the young students make their first attempts in class-teaching. After they have attended these classes for some months and have gained a certain proficiency in class management and direction, they are allowed by turns to take the direction of the classes of the other school for children, which is attached to the institution. Here they are left more at liberty, and are subjected to no other *surveillance* than that of the casual visits of the director, or of one of the superior professors, who pay occasional visits to the school, to see how the students manage their classes, and what progress they make in the art of teaching. They also attend, during their third year's residence, regular lectures given by the director on pedagogy; indeed, their principal employment during their last year's residence in the college is to gain an intimate acquaintance with both the theory and practice of this difficult art. With what success these labours are attended, all will bear witness who have had the pleasure of hearing the intelligent and simple manner, in which the Prussian teachers convey instruction to the children in the parochial schools. There are none of the loud, and illogical discourses, or of the unconnected and meaningless questions, which may be heard in many of our schools; but the teacher's quiet and pleasant manner, the logical sequency of his questions, the clearness and simplicity with which he expounds difficulties, the quickness of his eye in detecting a pupil who does not understand him, or who is inattentive, and the obedience of the children, never accompanied with any symptom of fear, show at once, that the Prussian teacher is a man thoroughly acquainted with his profession, and who knows how to instruct without creating disgust, and how to command respect without exciting fear.

There are three vacations every year in the Weissenfels College: one in August of three weeks, one at Christmas of two weeks, and one at Easter of three days' duration. Previous to each vacation, the young men are called together, when the director reads aloud a paper, containing the opinions of himself and the professors of the abilities, industry, and character of each student. Each young man is then required to write out the judgment, which has been passed upon himself. These copies are signed by the director, and are carried home by the young men to be shown to their relatives. The students are required to present these copies to their religious ministers and to their parents, and to obtain their signatures, as a proof that they have seen them. They are then brought back, at the end of the vacation, to the normal college, and are delivered up to the director, that he may be satisfied, by the signatures, that their friends and religious minister have seen and examined them. It is not necessary to show how great a stimulus to exertion these written characters afford.

The following regulations are a literal translation of some, which are contained in a published description of the Weissenfels Institution, which was put into my hands by the director.

"Since the state considers the education of good teachers a matter of such great importance, it requires that all young students shall be removed from the establishment, concerning whom there is reason to fear that they will not become efficient schoolmasters. The following regulations are therefore made on this point: —

"If at the close of the first year's course of study, it is the opinion of *all* the professors of the normal college, that any one of the students does not possess sufficient ability, or a proper disposition, for the profession of a teacher, he must be dismissed from the establishment. But if only *three* of the professors are of this opinion, and the fourth differs from them, they must inform the provisional authorities of their disagreement, and these higher authorities must decide. Should the unfitness of any student for the profession of a teacher be evident, before the end of his first year's residence in the normal college, the director must inform the young man's friends of this fact, in order that they may be enabled to remove him at once.

"If any student leaves the institution without permission before the end of his three years' course of study, and yet desires to become a teacher, he cannot be admitted to the examination for diplomas sooner than the young men who entered the normal college when he did.

"In cases of theft, open opposition to the rules and regulations of the establishment, and, in general, in all cases of offences which merit expulsion from the college, the superior authorities, or provincial committee, must carry such expulsion into execution."

When the young men have completed their three years' course of study in the Weissenfels College, they can present themselves for examination for a diploma. Until a student has gained a diploma, he cannot instruct in *any* school, or in *any* private family. The knowledge that he has procured one, serves to assure every one that he is fitted for the right performance of his duties. If he can show this certificate, granted by impartial and learned men, after rigid inquiry into the merits of the claimant, every one feels that he is a man to be trusted and to be honoured. It assures them that he entered the Weissenfels College with a high character, that he maintained it while there, and that he has attained that amount of knowledge which is required of all elementary school teachers. These examinations for certificates are common to Holland, France, Prussia, Saxony, Nassau, Hesse Darmstadt, Cassel, Bavaria, Baden, Wirtemberg, and Austria. In none of these countries, I believe, is a young man allowed to officiate as teacher, until he has proved his capability for such an employment to a committee of examiners, chosen by the central power on account of their learning and of their knowledge of what a teacher ought himself to be acquainted with in order to be able to instruct, and until he has obtained from this committee a diploma stating his capability.

A young man who has not been educated in the Weissenfels College may obtain a diploma if he can pass the examination, and can furnish the county magistrates with the following certificates: —

1st. A certificate of a physician that he is in perfect health, and has a sound constitution.

2nd. An account of his past life composed by himself.

3rd. Certificates from the civil magistrate of his

native town or village, and from the religious minister under whose care he has grown up, of the blameless character of his past life, and of his fitness, in a moral and religious point of view, to take a teacher's situation.

The committee of examiners at the Weissenfels Institution consists of Dr. Zerrener, the educational councillor (schulrath) of the provincial school-committee under which the normal college is ranged; of Dr. Weiss, the educational councillor (schulrath) of the court of the county in which Weissenfels is situated; and of the director and professors of the normal college.

The examination is conducted by the professors in the presence of these two educational councillors; and when it is over, the young men receive their diplomas, marked "1," "2," or "3," according to their merits. Only those who obtain the first kind, or those marked "1," are capable of being definitely appointed to a school; those who obtain either of the other kind of diplomas, can only take a situation on trial for one or two years; at the end of which time they are obliged to return again to the normal college, and to be re-examined, when they again receive diplomas, marked according to their merits, as before. Until a young man has obtained a diploma "1," he cannot obtain an independent situation, and it sometimes happens that a young man returns three or four times to the normal college ere he can obtain a permanent appointment as a teacher.

The examinations at the Weissenfels College are very strict, and last for two days. The young men are examined both *vivâ voce* and also by writing in all the subjects of instruction in the college and the examinations are rendered all the more imposing by the presence of the two representatives of the Minister of Public Instruction. Religious instruction, history (both sacred and profane), music (both theoretical and practical), geography (both topographical and physical), grammar, arithmetic, mental calculation, mathematics, botany, natural history, and particularly pedagogy, are the subjects of this searching investigation. If the young candidate passes it creditably, his diploma is signed by the two representatives of the Minister, and by the professors of the establishment; and from that time forward he is a member of the profession of teachers. His long course of study is then at an end; the continual examinations to which he had been previously subjected are passed. He is, from that moment, the recognised servant of his country, which protects him and encourages his efforts.

But even after a teacher has obtained his diploma marked "1," and after he has been appointed to a permanent situation, the directors and professors of the college do not lose sight of him.

If they, or the inspectors of the county court, perceive that a teacher, after leaving the college, neglects to continue his education, or that he has forgotten any of the knowledge or skill he had acquired when there, they require him to return to the college for a few months or weeks, where he is made to attend the lectures and to submit to the discipline intended for the regular students. The county magistrates are empowered to provide for the support of his family, and for the management of his schools, during the time of his residence in the college.

The director of the college is directed to make at least one tour of inspection every year through the whole of the district, for which his normal college educates teachers, at the expense of the county magistrates, for the purpose of inspecting the progress and attainments, and of making inquiries about the character of the teachers, who have been educated in his college.

It is not necessary for me to point out how these different regulations tend to raise the character of the teachers' profession in Prussia, and to gain for them the estimation and respect of society. As it is laid down in one of the circular rescripts of the Prussian government, " the chief end of calling the teachers back to the normal colleges at intervals, is to increase the earnestness, zeal, and enthusiasm of the teachers in their duties; to regulate and perfect the character of the teaching in the village schools; to produce more and more conformity and agreement in the methods of instruction used in the schools; to make the teachers look upon the normal college as their common home, and the place to which they may all apply for advice, assistance, and encouragement; to make the professors of the college better acquainted with those parts of the education of teachers which particularly require their attention, and which are necessary to form efficient village school teachers; to inspire the professors of the normal college with a constant zeal in the improvement of the district in which their college is situated; and to impress upon the young students of the normal college, from their first entrance into it, a full sense of the importance of the work in which they are about to engage." Every one knows that any person, who is officiating as teacher, must necessarily be a learned and moral man. Every one knows that he has passed through a long course of education in religious and secular instruction, continuing from his sixth to his twentieth year; that he has passed two or three different severe examinations with honour; that he is well versed in Scripture history, in the leading doctrines of his religion, in the history of Germany, in the outlines of universal history, in geography, and in arithmetic; that he is a good singer and chanter; that he can play the organ, pianoforte, and violin; that he is acquainted with the elements of the physical sciences, with natural history, and botany; and that he is profoundly versed in the science which is more peculiarly his own, viz., that of pedagogy. I have already said, that it is no uncommon thing for a Prussian teacher to be acquainted with the Latin language, that very many speak and read French fluently, and that not a few can also, at least, read English. Now, I do not ask whether we have a class of *village* teachers who can be compared to these men, for it would be ridiculous to put such a question; but, I ask, have we *any* set of teachers in the country who, in *general* attainments, can bear comparison with them? Very few of the masters of our private schools are gentlemen who have been educated at our universities; but of even those who have been brought up at our great seats of learning, I would ask any university man, whether one man in ten receives any thing like so general an education as the Prussian schoolmasters must have obtained, in order to enable them to pass the examination for diplomas? Do the students at our universities generally learn anything of church history, of music, or of physical geography? Do they learn even the outlines of universal history? Are they acquainted with botany or natural history? Do many study carefully the history of their own country or its geography? Do any of them know any thing of pedagogy? If not, where shall we find a class of teachers of even the children of our gentry nearly so highly educated as the Prussian parochial schoolmasters?

Still I am delighted to say, that we have two teachers' colleges, that may well challenge comparison with any of the forty-two great Prussian institutions which I have been describing. The two I refer to are the training colleges at Battersea and Stanley Grove. From what I have now seen of the most celebrated of the training colleges in France, Germany, and Switzerland, I believe Mr. Coleridge's Teachers' College, at Stanley Grove, to be one of the best in Europe. I believe that the richer classes of England will soon so fully appreciate Mr. Coleridge's labours, that they will beset him with petitions to allow them to take his students into their families as tutors of their children. He is giving England the most satisfactory proofs of the necessity and importance of a special and peculiar education for those who are destined to teach others. No one can visit either this admirable institution, or the one at

Battersea, without feeling how fatally blind we have hitherto been to all that relates to the education necessary to make a good teacher. The earnest and unostentatious manner in which Mr. Coleridge is pursuing his great work, is as instructive as it is delightful. He is evidently impressed with the full consciousness of how much remains to be effected, ere the people of this country will properly appreciate or understand the importance of the calling and profession of the teachers.

The college at Battersea, would at least equal that at Stanley Grove, could the section of the National Society of which it is the college be only taught the importance of complying with the wishes of the principal to lengthen the time of the students' residence. At present, students do not remain in this college more than fifteen or eighteen months; whereas, the experience of all the European countries, and our own common sense, ought to teach us, that a young man cannot acquire in so short a period, either the habits or the knowledge necessary to qualify him to become a teacher of the young. The practical character of the Battersea College which was impressed upon it, by its founders, Sir James P. Kay Shuttleworth, and Mr. Tufnell, is, however, deserving of the highest commendation. Its principal, the Rev. Thomas Jackson, is fully alive to the importance of developing the peasant, and not of turning out the gentleman. He labours to inculcate in the students' minds sympathy with the peasants, by accustoming the young men to humble manual toil. He, himself, associates with his students in their labours, as well as in their studies. He seeks to send forth, among the peasants, highly educated peasants, — men who, notwithstanding their education, will be peasants still — and not mere learned gentlemen. He labours to form teachers, endued with the spirit of the early apostles, not too proud to labour with their hands in the humblest manner, or to associate with the humblest of our citizens, but learned enough to teach the nation. Simple diet, hard labour, early hours, and the religious influences of a religious home, characterise the students' life at Battersea. If the time of residence were but prolonged, this college, which was the first institution deserving the name of a teachers' college ever established in England, would realise the views of its founders, as it did when under their management, and would send forth religiously educated men to mingle with our labourers, who would combine high mental acquirements and ability, with the simplicity and humility of those with whom they were called upon to associate.

All persons in Prussia seem to be entirely agreed, that the shortest period during which a student ought to remain in a normal college is three years, and this, be it remembered, after a previous education from his sixth to his seventeenth year. In the neighbouring kingdom of Saxony, the students remain four years in the normal colleges, after a similar previous training, and cannot then be definitely admitted into the teachers' profession, until after two years' practice as assistants under other teachers in parochial schools; and until they have creditably passed through four different examinations, conducted by three different examining bodies, two of which examinations last two days each, from seven in the morning until eight in the evening. It does seem very grievous then, when we have so lamentably small a number of these colleges, that we should injure the efficiency of several of those we do possess, by limiting the term of residence to the ridiculously short space of one year. Even our shoemakers receive a longer training. There are two schools in England which profess to prepare teachers in six months; but I pass them over in silence, merely remarking how sad a sign it is of our ignorance of the meaning of education, that such caricatures of teachers' colleges should be suffered to exist.

CHAP. VIII.

PRUSSIAN EDUCATION.—THE SYSTEM OF PUBLIC INSPECTION OF THE SCHOOLS.

HITHERTO I have only had to speak of the efforts, which the parishes are making to promote the education of the Prussian people. I have had hardly any occasion as yet to mention the part, which the Prussian government takes in this great work. Indeed, as I have often assured my readers, the interference of the state in this national undertaking is so indirect and so limited in its operations, as to occupy a very subordinate place, in any consideration of this truly popular system of a people's education.

It is impossible to conceive a more liberal scheme than the one adopted in Prussia, and throughout Germany.

It is the people who select and appoint their own teachers; it is the people who pay, support, and superintend them; it is the people who choose the sites and plans of their school-buildings, and who determine the numbers of teachers to be employed, and, the amount of the stipends to be given them; and, lastly, it is the people who decide, whether they will have separate schools for the separate sects, or common schools for several of them.

I had the pleasure of being in company with a celebrated German professor, whose name is very well known to most of my readers, and will be remembered by all, when I mention Frederic von Raumer. He has travelled both in England and America, and understands our prejudices almost as well as he recognises our merits. The conversation turned to the subject of primary education, when he said, addressing me, "Your countrymen have some strange ideas about our educational regulations. They imagine that the government in Berlin directs all the parochial schools throughout Prussia, and that it drives the children to school by means of the police. If they would only believe it, they might be told that it is the people of the parishes who manage their own educational affairs, and that there is no need of the police to send the children to school; for the parent who could be capable of keeping them at home would be deemed nothing better than a fool." This is literally the case; for the parents so fully appreciate the great importance of education, that they cannot comprehend a complaint being made against the educational regulations.

But if the parishes and teachers were left *entirely* to themselves, without *any central* and public supervision, what would be the result? Here and there a schoolmaster, who had entered the profession merely for the sake of its emoluments and privileges, but without any real interest in his duties, would become careless, idle, and sometimes immoral.

The careless and idle man, being free from scrutiny, would neglect his duties, or would perform them inefficiently, or would become irritable, and find a vent for his unreasonable sensitiveness on the children themselves; so that, in many cases, the careless as well as the immoral teacher, so far from educating his children in morality, would only injure and demoralise them. But, say some, this would always be prevented by the parents themselves. They would be sure to hear of the unfitness of such a teacher, and would remove their children to some other school. Let us suppose, however, as is constantly the case, that there is no other school within five or six miles, what are the parents to do in such a case, *even supposing* them to hear of the unfitness of the teacher? Should they remove their children? How would they then be able to educate them?—how would they be able to comply with the law which obliges them to provide for their childrens' instruction? Should they petition for the teacher's removal? But whom?—the central government? How could it pay any attention to the murmers of one or two individuals, if not supported by the evidence of some one qualified to form a sound opinion? Why, every parent would have some complaint to find with the best teacher. Were the government to listen to these murmers, they would render the efficient teachers discontented, and would waste their own time in examining into innumerable idle tales. Thus the complaints, even when well founded, would often pass unnoticed, or be outweighed by the teacher's assertions, and really vicious schoolmasters would often be continued at their posts. But I doubt whether the parents would, in the majority of cases, ever hear what kind of man the teacher was, or how he taught. How should they?

They have no time to go in and attend the school-classes, or, if they had, they are not capable of being judges of the teacher's management of his classes; nor could they put any confidence in the tales of their children, as to what was going on in school, even if such tales ought to be encouraged. Nor would the matter be any better, if the school were under trustees, or a private patron. I have heard of several instances of such schools in England, never having been visited by any person, clergyman, trustee, or any one else, for months and years together. And this is quite natural. The trustees are generally small farmers or shopkeepers, and have so much to do to provide for their families' maintenance in the world, as not willingly to undertake other duties, except when absolutely necessary. They either never go into the school, or, if they do, the day is arranged between themselves and the teacher, everything is prepared for their reception, the scholars are clean, the lesson has been got up beforehand, and they go away perfectly satisfied, saying, "What a fine fellow our teacher is!" when, if they could have broken through the crust, and looked beneath — if they could have put unexpected questions to the children — they would have found them destitute of the veriest sham of knowledge; and if they could have made an unexpected visit to the school, they would most probably have found it in disorder and confusion, whilst the schoolmaster was attending to his own concerns; or else they would have discovered, in maltreated children, the sad evidence of his ungoverned temper and of the progressive demoralisation of his school. These were some of the causes, which rendered it necessary to establish a system of public inspection, by means of which the schools and teachers should be continually examined, and by means of which the government and the country should be always immediately informed, when a teacher deserved either dismission or promotion.

But there is another great evil which arises from a want of a well organised system of inspection. This is the feeling of discouragement, which a teacher is sure to experience, if not supported by the consciousness, that the public is interested in his success and watches his progress. A learned man who, from his previous education, has imbibed literary tastes, and has experienced the pleasure and the benefit of literary society, cannot but feel at times a certain degree of disgust and despondency, when sent out into a distant country parish to labour among poor and illiterate persons, without any educated friends, and often without any one companion with whom he can exchange ideas, or in whose sympathy he can seek for solace or encouragement. The evils of such a situation are tenfold increased, when the teacher feels that none of his exertions will be known or appreciated by his countrymen, and when he is unable to encourage himself by information of the progress of other members of his profession in other districts. To cut off a teacher from society, from the world, and from his own profession, in this manner, soon induces disgust or despondency, and either lessens his efforts and his efficiency, or drives him out of his profession into a sphere better suited to his tastes and to his intellects. These reasons, among others, have induced all the European states to pay the greatest attention to the formation of a good working system of *public inspection*, and to the maintenance of a sufficient number of good and able inspectors. These public officers may be found travelling from school to school throughout the whole of Germany, Switzerland, France, and Holland. In each canton of Switzerland there is a board of public inspectors, who divide between them the labours of visiting and examining the progress of all the central schools. In France, in the year 1843, 201 of these officers had been appointed by government in the different departments, and in that year these gentlemen had visited and examined 50,996 schools, all their travelling expenses having been defrayed by the state in addition to their salaries. In Holland there are 70 such officers, and not only is the number greater in that country, in proportion to the population, than elsewhere, but the whole system is perhaps better organised. And even the little kingdom of Bavaria has more than 200 of these important public servants. But it is with Prussia that I am here more particularly concerned; and to its system of inspection I beg to call the attention of my readers, as in this part of the Prussian system they will perceive the influence which government and the religious ministers of all the different sects exercise over the schools of the parishes.

First, then, in every parish the religious ministers are *ex officio* inspectors of the schools of their respective religious sects, as well as presidents of the managing committees of their respective schools. These committees have the surveillance of the schools, are always present at the examinations of the children, and can visit the schools when they like. Of course it is not often that they do this, as their time is fully occupied with other avocations, such as the care of their farms and shops. But with the religious ministers it is otherwise. They not only have the right to visit the schools, but they are obliged by law to do so several times in the year, and to forward a report of their progress to the union inspector, of whom I shall presently speak. If they think the teacher is unfit for his situation, or if they think that he is pursuing faulty methods of instruction or correction, they can remonstrate with him; and if he does not follow their advice, they can report him to the superior authorities. The principal duty, however, of the parochial ministers of the different religious sects is, to watch over the *religious* instruction given by the teachers, and to show them how they may improve it, when they consider it imperfectly or injudiciously imparted. In this way all the schools of the country are put under the surveillance and protection of the religious ministers, so that no irreligious or immoral teacher can long remain undetected; for the school is, so to speak, an open house, and is sure to be inspected each year by several officers, and that at times which the teachers cannot ascertain beforehand; so that if a careless or immoral man has managed to creep into the profession, under a false disguise, he is under restraint at all hours, and is sure in the end to be detected. I have laid great stress on the clergy being *obliged* to visit the schools, as they are but men, and among them would be found many who would not be inclined to give themselves much unnecessary trouble, were it not a matter of legal obligation.

The next superior inspector is the one I have had occasion to mention several times already, viz., the Kreisshul inspector, or union inspector. The unions almost always contain schools both for Romanists and for Protestants. In such union there are two union inspectors. The one for the Protestant schools is the ecclesiastical superintendent of the union; the one for the Romanist schools is the dean. So that the second grade of inspectors is also ecclesiastical equally with the first. Great care is taken, in the appointment of the superintendents and deans, to select men, who understand the details of school management, and who have paid considerable attention to the subject of elementary instruction. These inspectors are in direct communication with the county courts, and with the synods and bishops, so that they can furnish every required information, both to the ecclesiastical authorities and to the government.

They are required to visit all the schools of their respective districts at least once a year; and when there are two inspectors of different religions in one union, each must confine his visits to the schools of his own sect. They also receive regular periodical reports of the state of the schools from the school-committees and from the parochial clergy, and are obliged themselves each year to prepare a report on the state of education in their respective unions, and to forward the same, when completed to the county court. All the expenses they incur in making the necessary journeys are defrayed by the county courts; but no especial salary is allowed them for their labours as inspectors. These duties form part of those appertaining to their office as superintendents or deans; and the salary they receive for the performance of them is included in the emoluments of their office.

The Protestant superintendent is appointed by the Minister of Public Instruction, on the nomination of the provincial consistory. The Romanist dean is nominated by his bishop, and appointed by the Minister of Public Instruction, who, in Prussia, is also the Minister or head director of the religious churches of the country. If the Minister does not approve of the selection that has been made, he has the power of withholding his confirmation, and in such cases a new nomination must be made.

Every school in the union, whether it be public or private, whether it be endowed or the property of the schoolmaster himself, or whether it be supported by some rich landed gentleman — every school, I say, is open to the visit of the union inspector. It is through him that all new laws and regulations are conveyed to the parochial authorities; and it is through him that the schoolmasters are brought into immediate connection with the government. It is the duty of these inspectors to encourage the teachers, to support and advance the deserving, to admonish the careless, and, if their admonition is not attended to, to report them to the higher authorities. It is through the inspectors that the teachers correspond with the county courts, when they wish to obtain permission to introduce into their schools, and to use in their classes, any book which had not previously received the licence of the provincial authorities; and to them the teachers always apply, if the parochial committees do not provide them with all necessary apparatus, or do not keep their school-buildings in proper repair, or, in fine, if they have any reason to complain of the negligence or misconduct of the proper authorities.

Is is from the yearly reports of these inspectors that the higher ecclesiastical authorities receive information of the state of religious education, and of the moral and religious condition of the schools; and it is from them, too, that the government obtains all its reports of the actual state of education, of the number of children attending school, of the conduct of the teachers, and of the state of the school-buildings; so that, when necessary, it may interfere by means of its regular organs, the county courts.

It is these officers, also, who take the first steps towards the formation of new school-committees, when any new schools are required; and, in fine, it is these officers, who are at the head of the union education, and are answerable for its progress.

Thus far, then, by means of this system of inspection, is the *moral* and *religious* education of the children put under the surveillance of the religious ministers of the different sects to which their parents belong. The clergy superintend the schoolmasters; and, although they cannot interfere to alter the prescribed school rontine or to diminish the required amount of secular instruction, yet, by appeals to the county courts, they can prevent the schoolmasters diminishing the amount of religious instruction which ought to be given, and can bring upon them the censure of the higher authorities, if the religious instruction is imparted in a careless or irreverential manner, or if the moral discipline of the school is imperfectly maintained.

The Prussian teachers are very anxious that the kreis or union inspectors should be chosen out of the ranks of the teachers. They say, with great truth, that it is ridiculous, that teachers, who have been trained for many years in the science of pedagogy, and in the many delicate and difficult duties of a teacher, should be subject to the criticism and examination of men, who have never studied pedagogy at all, and who have had no experience in school management. Many, too, of the ablest men of Prussia think, that the inspectorships ought to be given solely to teachers, in order to encourage the whole profession to zealous emulation of one another's exertion, by holding out to them all, the prospect of gaining the honourable and more lucrative position of an inspector.

I entirely concur in these views. I know, as a fact, that both in Prussia and in England, many of the more learned teachers are greatly disheartened in their labours, by being subjected to the inspection of a gentleman of great talents, it may be, but who knows nothing whatever of the difficulties, with which the teacher has to strive, and who is, often, totally unfitted to form any rational opinion of the merits of the teacher's management and exertions. Several of the ablest teachers in different parts of England and Germany have expressed themselves at different times to me, in the following manner: —

"We earnestly wish, sir, that the government would consent to select its inspectors from men who have actually *practised* teaching; as it is, many of the inspectors are quite ignorant of all the details of school-management. They come into our schools with the crudest and most ill-digested ideas; each has some pet plan of his own; many of these plans have never been tested by their authors; many of them are quite incapable of application. But, however that may be, the inspector judges us and our efforts by comparing them with his own preconceived and often really irrational ideas. It very often happens that teachers of the greatest ability, and of the highest merits, but not carrying out the fanciful or impossible plans or methods of the unpractical and inexperienced inspector, are set down as ignorant or unskilful men. Imagine, sir, what our feelings must be, when, after having gained our diplomas at the college—after having earned the praise of our professors—after having earnestly carried out for years methods, of the excellence of which there can be no doubt to any one, who has given any attention to pedagogy—and after having been encouraged in our efforts by the directors and professors of the normal college—imagine, sir, what our feelings must be when an inspector, who knows nothing about pedagogy, and who has all sorts of fancies of his own, quite at variance with the views of all pedagogists, comes down to our school, and, instead of praising our efforts and congratulating us on our success in carrying out the methods taught us at the normal college, finds fault with us, because we do not carry out his own fanciful and ill-digested views, and reports us unfavourably to the government, when all those who are qualified to judge, commend us for what we have done. You cannot imagine, sir, what a feeling of despair this situation engenders; and yet this is what constantly happens, and what must constantly happen, until the inspectors are selected *solely* from among men skilled in pedagogy."

But there is another very strong reason why the inspectors should be chosen from among the teachers.

We all know that, in any profession, a small chance of winning a high station reconciles many men to work for many years in an inferior and badly paid one. Thus in the church, and at the bar, the chance of winning one of the great prizes, however small the chance may be, encourages many men to long years of self-denial and hard labour in the inferior and ill-requited ranks. So in the profession of the teachers, we could not adopt a better expedient for stimulating the labours and exertions of the primary teachers, and of the professors of the normal colleges, than by filling the ranks of the inspectors with the most learned and efficient of the primary school teachers. By adopting this plan, we should raise the character of the whole profession; we should stimulate their industry, and we should encourage their efforts more than by any other plan we could adopt.

The Prussian government has, within the last two years, made a law that every young student for holy orders shall in future produce, at his examination for, and before his admission into holy orders, a certificate of his having attended a normal college for six weeks, and of his having passed an examination in pedagogy, conducted by the principal of the college and his professors. This is clearly a great step in the right direction; and it has, I believe, given general satisfaction to the teachers. But they are not yet contented; for they say, and with great reason, "We spent many years of severe study in acquiring a knowledge of the science of pedagogy; and yet we are examined, criticised, and reported upon by men who have only studied the science for six weeks! Is it likely that such men should be able to instruct us how to manage our classes?" This is doubtless true; and it does seem desirable, for the reasons that I have mentioned above, that the government should choose the inspectors from the teachers' ranks.

Above the two grades of inspectors of which I have already spoken, and which, it will be seen, are composed of the clergy, there are yet two others, of which I shall now proceed to speak. The first of these are the county inspectors: I have had occasion often to speak of the Schulrath, or the member of the county court, who has the *surveillance* of all educational affairs in the county. This magistrate is appointed by the Minister of Public Instruction at Berlin, and is usually chosen from among the most learned and able men of his county; he is assisted generally by two inferior counsellors, one of whom represents the Romanist and the other the Protestant schools. He is the representative of the government in his county. All the reports of the different union- or kreis-inspectors are forwarded to him; he arranges them, and communicates them to the Minister at Berlin: he has a negative upon the appointment of members of the school committee; and can oblige the parishes to proceed to a new election if he thinks the man whom they first elected, is unfitted for his duties.

He has also a negative upon the proposed acts of the parishes, *i. e.* upon their choice of sites, plans of school-buildings, augmentation of the school-funds, payments of teachers, &c.; as he is required to take care that no unwise and really prejudical steps are taken by the inferior authorities. He has power also to dismiss or reprimand a schoolmaster, if any one has deserved such punishment, though the teacher can always appeal from his decisions to the Minister at Berlin. But one of his most important duties, and that with which we are here more particularly concerned, is that of school inspection. Not only is he required to be present at the examination of young men, who desire to enter the normal colleges, and also at the still severer examinations of those who, having remained two or three years in such an establishment, are desirous of obtaining diplomas, and not only is his concurrence necessary in granting these diplomas, but he is also obliged to visit the elementary schools themselves, and to personally inspect the progress of education in his county. He is not required to go through every elementary school in his county every year, (for such a labour his duties as director of the education of his county does not leave him sufficient time,) but he is required to visit a part of these schools every year; and as his visits are, I believe, undetermined beforehand, so each parish of the county is uncertain when it may expect this high functionary, and is consequently always on the alert, that he may not find the schools in a neglected condition. In some counties the Schulrath, or the county educational magistrate, is also the director of one of the normal colleges; and in all cases he is selected as a learned and able man, who thoroughly understands the affairs over which he is called upon to preside. There are twenty-five counties in Prussia, and in each a county a Schulrath; so that, besides all the parochial and union inspectors, there are twenty-five superior inspectors and directors of the education of the people.

These county inspectors are laymen. The superior ecclesiastical authorities of the Romanist and Protestant churches take a part in the educational affairs by means of the union inspectors and the parochial clergy, but over the superior educational officers they have no control.

The religious ministers in Prussia are presidents of the school committees; they are inspectors of the parochial schools; they have a vote in the election of the teachers; and they have the power of reporting them to the superior authorities, when dissatisfied with their conduct. It is from the clergy that the union inspectors are chosen, and it is the higher ecclesiastical authorities who have the nomination of these influential officers. No attempt is made in Prussia to sever the education of the people from the Churches. The great ends which the government has attempted to attain are —first, to foster the morality and religion of the people; and, secondly, to increase their intelligence, and by means of their intelligence, their prudence, foresight, and happiness, by sound, liberal, and effective instruction in all useful knowledge. It has effected these objects by making the religious ministers the inspectors of the *religious* education of the people, by reserving to itself the inspection of the *secular* education of the people, and by making the people themselves the fosterers and guardians of their own instruction in both religion and knowledge.

Last of all in the scale of inspection comes that of the central government at Berlin. The Minister of Public Instruction is assisted by a number of councillors, to whom various duties are assigned in the *bureau* of educational affairs, and of these councillors there are three, who are sent every year from Berlin by the Minister, on special missions of inspection into the different counties, in order to investigate the condition of the schools in particular districts, where the Minister has reason to fear that the education of the people is not making a sufficiently rapid progress, and in order to obtain information respecting the state of different parts of the country, where particular circumstances may require some modifications in existing regulations.

Such is the great system of school inspection in

Prussia, by which the government, the churches, and the people insure the strictest observance of the educational regulations; the religious, moral, and intellectual character of the teachers; and the continued development of the intelligence of the people. If my readers will compare these really gigantic efforts, made by a government, whose whole annual revenue does not amount to 10,000,000*l.*, and for a population of 16,000,000 souls; with those which our rich country has been making for a population equal in amount, but amongst whom so much pauperism exists as to require aid from the nation to the amount of 7,000,000*l.* per annum, I think they will be struck by the startling contrast.

CHAP. IX.

PRUSSIAN EDUCATION. — THE PAROCHIAL SCHOOLS — THEIR INTERNAL MANAGEMENT. — THE SYSTEMS OF INSTRUCTION PURSUED IN THEM. — THE SUBJECTS OF INSTRUCTION. — THE STATISTICS OF PRUSSIAN EDUCATION. — COMPARISON OF THESE STATISTICS WITH THOSE OF OTHER COUNTRIES. — DEDUCTION FROM THEM WITH RESPECT TO ENGLAND.

It is generally admitted thoughout Germany, Holland, and France, that no one unaided teacher can direct the instruction of more than sixty children, in one school-room, without serious injury to the individual education of each scholar. Where one hundred are assembled in one room under one teacher, it will almost always be found, that the whole class makes very unsatisfactory progress, and that the children who are the least studious and clever, and who consequently more particularly require the teacher's attention, are almost wholly neglected. Moreover, where great numbers are left to the unaided efforts of one man, it is always found that order cannot be properly maintained; and, therefore, that the advancement of the whole class is retarded. These evils are tenfold increased when the whole of the children do not form one but several classes, and when the teacher's eye must be removed from one part of the scholars, whilst he is instructing the others; and even where they do form but one class, a careful observer may always discover that the education of at least one half of the children is almost entirely neglected.

I have often been present, both in England and in different parts of Germany and Switzerland, at lessons given to large classes by teachers noted for their power of managing a great number; and I have always observed that in the back rows there were a great number of children, who never answered a single question, who sat listless and inattentive, or who distracted the attention of all the others by their disorderly conduct. In Saxony, where the greatest pains are taken to perfect the village schools, a law has been passed by the Chambers, which forbids any teacher assembling more than *sixty* children in the same class; and so much importance is attached to this regulation, that if a parish cannot afford to support one teacher for every sixty children, the Chambers have decreed, that the children must be divided into two classes, one half of which is required to attend the morning, and the other the evening school; it being esteemed much better that each child should have only three or four hours of careful instruction per day, than that one half should be neglected, in order that the other half should receive the whole of the teacher's attention.

About eight or ten years since all the German schools were conducted on the Bell and Lancasterian methods, the children being left almost entirely in the hands of young and half-educated monitors, as in our own parochial schools at the present day. The results of this system were so unsatisfactory that they soon occasioned a powerful re-action in the contrary direction.

The German governments, perceiving how grievously the mental education and mental development of the children were retarded by subjecting them to the imperfect care of half-educated monitors, prohibited all employment of monitors in the parochial schools. Hence it became necessary to considerably increase the staff of teachers, as well as the expenditure required for their support. In the towns this has been productive of beneficial results, as the towns can always raise sufficient funds for the support of a sufficient number of teachers. I generally found that each of these schools throughout Germany had a staff of from six to twelve teachers attached to it, each of whom had attained the age of twenty years, had been specially educated in the classes of the primary, secondary, and normal schools, from his sixth to his twentieth year, and had obtained a diploma certifying his fitness for the profession to which he had devoted himself.

But in the village schools the results of this rejection of all monitorial assistance has been less satisfactory. The villages are not generally rich enough to support more than two teachers, and often not more than one, and this, too, in many cases, where there are 150 children who attend the school. In these cases, therefore, monitors are greatly needed to assist in maintaining order among one part of the children, while the teacher is instructing another part, and to relieve the teacher from the more mechanical part of class instruction, so that he may apply his undivided attention to those branches of instruction, in which his superior skill, knowledge, and experience are most needed.

But the prejudices which the Germans have imbibed against the monitorial system, are, as yet, too strong to allow them to perceive the necessity of employing monitors in the village schools. Whenever I addressed a German teacher on this subject, he immediately answered, "Oh! we have had enough of your Lancasterian methods; depend upon it, we shall never try them again." It was very surprising to me to see, how universal and how strong this antipathy to monitors was throughout Germany; but it served to show me, how deep an interest all classes took in the prosperity of the schools, as it was evident that they only rejected this means of lessening the parochial outlay in the support of teachers, because they believed it to be essentially injurious to the sound mental progress of the children.

No doubt that the old monitorial system was deserving of all their maledictions; but it would well become the Prussian educational authorities to consider, whether the mean between the old system and the present, such, viz., as the monitorial system pursued in Holland and France, is not the true state of things to which they ought to aspire. In these countries, the teachers train the most promising of their oldest and most advanced scholars as monitors. They give them instruction in the evenings when the day's work in the schoolroom is over. These monitors are paid by the parochial authorities just enough, to make it worth their while to remain at their posts as assistants to the schoolmasters until about seventeen years of age, after which time they are removed to the normal colleges to be trained as teachers, whilst other children take their places in the village schools. To these trained and paid monitors nothing is intrusted, but the mere mechanical parts of school teaching, *such as the elements of reading, writing, and arithmetic.* All the higher and more intellectual parts of school education, such as religious instruction, history, geography, and mental arithmetic, are conducted by the schoolmaster himself. But the principal service which the monitors render to the teachers is, in preserving order and silence in the school, and in watching over those classes, which are not for the time being receiving instruction from the schoolmaster. By this means, one able master, with the aid of two intelligent monitors, may conduct a school of 100 children; whenever the number however exceeds 100, there should in all cases be, at the least, two superior teachers.

But in Prussia this rule is not observed. They have resolved, as I have already mentioned, to employ no monitors in the schools; and as they are conscious, that without them they require a much greater number of teachers, they have directed the inspectors to inform the county magistrates when two or more teachers are required by a parish, and the magistrates are, in these cases, authorised to oblige the parochial authorities to elect and support as many additional teachers as are necessary. It often happens, however, that a parish, although very populous, is very poor and unable to do more than support one teacher, even when the number of its children of an age to attend school, is 120 or 130. In these cases, all the children of different ages and different degrees of proficiency are assembled in one schoolroom, under the care of only one teacher. Now it is evident, that no matter how clever such a teacher may be, it is utterly impossible for him to conduct such a school properly. Even if the children were all of the same degree of proficiency, it would be impossible for one man to promote the individual development and education of so many scholars; how much more so, when they are of different ages and of different degrees of proficiency? This is the great fault of the Prussian village schools. They are, at present, actually retarding the progress of their own education by their too blind fear of doing so. They fear the evil effects of our old, absurd monitorial systems so much as to refuse to reason calmly on the subject of monitorial assistance. But the evil will soon bring its own cure. They find that many parishes with more than 100 children cannot afford to support more than one teacher; they clearly see that one is not enough for so many; and that owing to this paucity of masters, the education of the less intelligent children is neglected. They are really anxious to perfect their schools; and where there is such a will, and such an experience as is possessed by the educational authorities in Prussia, or, in other words, by the Prussian people themselves, there the remedy will soon be applied. They are already, in some few quarters, beginning to see their error, and not many years will pass ere a change will be introduced.

As I have already said, the want of monitors is felt most in the village schools; for the town schools are conducted in a totally different manner. In a town a greater number of children are found assembled together, and greater funds are always found at the disposal of the school authorities, who, it will be remembered, are elected by the people. In each of the Prussian towns, several great school-houses are generally built, each containing from four to sixteen class-rooms. The number does not, I believe, generally exceed eight in one school-house, and some have not more, but hardly any fewer than four. In Germany, except in the poorest villages, different classes are never instructed in the same room. Even in the villages, there are generally two or three class-rooms in the village school-house, for each of which a separate teacher is maintained. This plan of teaching the different classes in different rooms, adds incalculably to the efficiency of the education given. In each room, only one voice is heard at a time — the voice of the teacher or of one of the children. The attention of the children is not disturbed or diverted from the teacher by what is going on in another class. Each room is perfectly quiet. The teacher can be heard distinctly, and can hear every noise in his class. Besides all this, for equal numbers of children four or five times as many teachers are employed in Germany as in England. Each child receives, therefore, four or five times as much assistance and attention from a learned man as a child does in England. The individual progress, therefore, of the children in the German schools (and the same may be said of the Swiss schools), is very much greater than that of the English children. Over each school-house one head teacher is appointed, who is an elderly and experienced man, and who himself takes the management of the highest class. Under him are appointed a number of younger teachers, corresponding to the number of class-rooms in the school-house. These younger masters board with the head teacher in his house, which is generally constructed large enough to afford lodgings for the staff of masters required for all the classes. If the class-rooms do not exceed four, the boys and girls are mixed together in the different rooms, and are divided into four classes, according to their proficiency. If, however, the school contains more than four class-rooms, then the girls and boys are separated into two distinct divisions, each of which is divided into three or four classes according to the proficiency of the children. In the town schools, therefore, it is much easier to dispense with monitors, as no teacher is perplexed with having to direct different classes in the same room. Each teacher has only to instruct a small number of children of about the same proficiency in the same subject, at one time and in a separate room. He can, therefore, at all moments engage all his children in the same occupations, keep them all under his constant inspection, and direct their operations much better than where these operations themselves are necessarily of three or four different kinds at the same time. But even in such case, the teachers require the assistance of monitors, in the writing, drawing, and ciphering exercises; or else, as I have often observed, when the teacher's attention is withdrawn from the class, or when he is attending to some individual pupil in one part of the school, the juvenile spirit is sure to begin to effervesce in another, and to produce noise, disorder, and interruption. This want of assistance for the principal teachers was almost the only fault I could find with the Prussian schools.

The school-buildings were generally excellent, and often handsome; the class-rooms numerous, lofty, capacious, and *always* clean; for the inspectors take great care that the parochial authorities do not neglect the whitewashing and repairs. The scholars themselves were always exquisitely clean. The rooms were constantly whitewashed and scoured. The law obliges the school-committees to do this. If any neglect in these particulars is evident, the inspectors and county magistrates are empowered and required to act for the parochial committee, and to raise the funds necessary for the purpose by a parochial rate levied upon the householders. But from the beautiful neatness and cleanliness and from the excellent repair of the school-rooms which I saw in different provinces of Prussia and Germany, it appeared to me, that the people fully understood and appreciated the importance and utility of these regulations.

The class-rooms were always well fitted up with parallel desks and forms, and almost always with excellent maps of Germany, on which all the leading physical characteristics of the country were delineated in a strong and forcible manner, and on a large scale; and also with smaller but excellent maps of other parts of the world.

At one end of each class-room is the teacher's desk, raised a little above the others. Behind and on each side of him hang great black boards, fastened to the wall by moveable hinges. On these he writes copies of the writing exercises, and draws all his figures, &c. for the illustration of his lessons: and on these also each child is called upon in turn to explain arithmetical operations, or to fill up or draw the outlines of a map of some part of Europe, or of one of the principal countries of the world. The space between the teacher's desk and the other end of the room is filled with parallel rows of desks and forms, at which the children work; for the Prussians are too anxious to make the children interested in their school duties, to think of making education more disagreeable to them than it necessarily is, by forcing them to stand through nearly the whole of their lessons, as they do in many of our National Schools to this day. Each school has also a yard, where the children take exercise in the middle of the morning and afternoon school hours, to refresh themselves, and to awaken their faculties, while the windows of the class-rooms are thrown open, and the air of the rooms is thoroughly purified.

Our town schools are often without any yard, so that the children are either kept for three or four hours at a time in the close air of the school-room, or are turned loose into a dirty back street, to mix with all the frequenters of such a locality, no matter who they may be.

Some persons seem to imagine that, if a school-room is built and children attend it, the results must needs be good; but it behoves them to examine whether they have left any influence at work upon the children's minds, stronger than the influence for good which the school affords. If it is so, it seems a little sanguine, to say the least of it, to hope for happy results. The whole system of things in Germany is so entirely different to that in England, that any one who attempts to describe it to Englishmen must necessarily appear to exaggerate. I can only say, let doubters go and inspect for themselves, and I am convinced they will own, that I have not said nearly so much as I might have done, in favour of the wonderful efforts the people and the governments are making to advance the great cause of popular instruction.

Each child buys its own books and slate. Those children, however, who are too poor to pay the small school-fees, and who are consequently sent to school at the expense of the town or parish in which they dwell, are provided with books, &c. by the town or parochial authorities. The children generally carry their books home with them; and every morning at a quarter to eight o'clock, a traveller may see the streets of a German town or village filled with boys and girls, neatly dressed and very clean, hurrying to school; each of the boys carrying his school-books in a small goat-skin knapsack on his back, and each of the girls carrying hers in a small bag, which she holds in her hand. The cleanliness and neatness of dress which I generally observed among the children very much surprised me, and always served to convince me how the educational regulations were tending to civilise and elevate the tastes of the lower classes throughout Germany. At first I was often disposed to doubt the veracity of my companions, when they assured me that the children I saw were the sons and daughters of poor labourers.

The very way in which children of different ranks of society are to be found mingled in the same school, serves to show how superior the civilisation of the lower orders in Germany is to that of the English peasants. With us it would be impossible to associate, in the same school, the children of peasants with those of even the lowest of our middle classes. But in Germany I *constantly* found the children of the highest and of the lowest ranks sitting at the same desk, and in almost every school I saw the children of the lowest and of the middle classes mingled together.

In Berlin, one of the teachers, on my asking him whose sons the boys at one of his forms were, requested them to tell me in what occupations their fathers were engaged. From these boys I learned, that one was the son of a clergyman, another of a physician; that others were the sons of small shopkeepers, and others the sons of errand men and porters. Now, were not the children of the errand men and porters very much more civilised, polished, and, if I may use that much abused word, more *gentlemanly* than the same class of children in England, such an association would be totally impossible. And yet this to us incredible state of things, exists with infinitely less discontentment and social disturbance than we find among our labouring classes in England.

But it must not be imagined that the educational system is in a stationary state, that the people and the government are resting upon their oars, or that they now think that they have done enough, and that they can let the stream bear them on without further exertion. Far, far otherwise: on every hand extensive improvements are going on, as if they had only commenced last year, to take any interest in the question, and as if they were only now beginning the work, like fresh labourers. Here I found a new and handsome school-house just finished; there, another one in building; and here, again, old houses being altered and enlarged. In one town I found them preparing a great building for a normal college; in another, I found them preparing to remove one of these noble institutions to a more commodious and larger set of buildings; and wherever I travelled, I found the authorities labouring to establish infant schools, as well as to perfect the educational institutions of their several localities. It sometimes appeared to me as if all the resources of the government must be devoted to this object; whereas my readers must recollect that, except in the cases of the normal colleges, this great work is effected by the people themselves; and that the enormous expenditure, by being divided between all the different towns and parishes in the kingdom, is scarcely felt. Since 1816, every year has witnessed a further progress: old schools have been pulled down, new ones have been erected; the old and less efficient teachers have gradually died off, and their places have been supplied by excellently trained masters who now direct the schools; the young men who are about to enter holy orders have been obliged to study pedagogy, in order to fit themselves to be inspectors; the regulations respecting the factory children, which I have given in an earlier part of this work, have been put in force; the *minimum* of the teachers' salaries has been considerably raised, and the system of teachers' conferences has been perfected, and put into operation. What the full fruits of all this will be, cannot yet be foretold, as the system has scarcely been long enough in operation; but the most casual observer may already discern the generally prosperous and happy condition of the lower orders of the people.

I have already cursorily mentioned the regulations respecting the books used in the village schools; but I reserved all particulars on this head, until I came to speak of the interior of the schools themselves. I shall now show what restrictions exist on the free choice of books by the teachers. The Prussian government has here had two evils to guard against: one of these was the retarding of the gradual reform of school books, which reform will always take place, when the teachers themselves are learned men, when they thoroughly understand the theory and practice of pedagogy, and when they are not fettered by unwise restrictions; and the other was, the admission into the practical schools, of books of an irreligious or immoral tendency. These two evils are guarded against in the following manner: —

No book can be used in any school in any of the provinces, until the authorities composing the provincial Schulcollegium, which has the direction of the higher schools and gymnasia, as well as of the normal colleges of the province, have licensed it, or sanctioned its admission. Any book which has been so sanctioned, can be employed by any schoolmaster of the province in which it was licensed. There are, in every province, a great number of works on religion, history, science, &c., which have been thus licensed, and from which the teachers are at liberty to choose. But, if a schoolmaster writes a book, which he deems better qualified for school use than those already published, or if he desires to employ a work written by some one else and which is not licensed, he forwards a copy of it, through the inspector, to the provincial authorities, in order to obtain their consent, which is only refused, where the book is positively imperfect or unfit for the young. In the schools, which I personally inspected, I generally found the school-books very excellent, and written either by teachers, or by some person engaged in the educational profession. Coming as they do from men of very long experience in the practice of pedagogy, they are generally well adapted to answer the wants, which the writers themselves have experienced, in the exercise of their professional duties. With the above restrictions, the choice of books is left entirely to the schoolmasters.

The character of the instruction given in all the German schools is suggestive; the teachers labour to teach the children to educate themselves. There is little or no "cram" about it, if I may use an old university phrase. In most of the best primary schools of England, the teacher still contents himself with the old cramming system; that is, he tries to crowd the memories of his scholars with facts, and continually exercises their memories, without ever attempting to develope and strengthen any of their other intellectual faculties. Now, we know but too well, that a man may have the most retentive memory, and the best-stored mind, and yet remain as incapable of reasoning, as improvident, and as irrational as ever. He may be full of facts; but may be as unable to make any use of them, or to turn them to any good account, as one bereft of the faculties of speech, sight, and hearing. If a man cannot use his reasoning powers, he is much better without knowledge; to impart facts to a fool, is like entrusting fire to a madman. The great *desideratum* for the poor, as well as for every one else in this world, is a capability of using the reasoning faculties; not that this will always save a man from false ideas and from irrational conduct, but that a man who possesses it will be *more likely* than any other, to take a right view of his position in life, his duties, and his advantages, and will be more likely to understand the best means of improving them.

Next, then, to implanting good principles in the child, the first object of every system of instruction should be, to teach it how to use the high and important faculties, which Providence has given it, as the means by which to insure its temporal happiness and continued self-improvement. Facts are necessary, but facts alone are not enough: to cram a child's mind with facts, without constantly exercising its reflection and its reason, is like feeding it with quantities of rich viands, and denying it all bodily exercise.

The German teachers are, therefore, taught that their duty is to awaken the intelligence of their children, far more than to fill their heads with facts, which they would not know how to use, unless their reasoning powers had been first cultivated. The schoolmasters do not therefore hurry over many facts in one lesson; but endeavour to make them think and reason about the subject of instruction.

The method of instruction is left to the unfettered choice of the teachers, so that it is impossible to speak with certainty of the methods pursued in the majority of the schools; but in all that I visited, I invariably found the simultaneous method pursued. By this the scholars are divided into different classes, and each class is instructed separately. This is not done on the old shouting plan, where one or two clever boys give the answer, and all the others follow in the same breath, and often without having known what the question was. Not so: the class under instruction first reads a section or chapter from the school-book, relating to the subject of instruction; the teacher then endeavours to illustrate what the children have been reading, to make them clearly understand it, to assure himself that they do *understand* it, and to impress it more clearly and firmly upon their memories. All this he does by suggestive questions, which he himself does not answer, until he has first tried, whether any of the children can answer them for themselves. When a question is put, all the children, who are prepared to answer it, are told to hold up their hands, and the teacher then selects one child, who stands up and gives what he conceives to be the answer; if he is wrong, another is selected to correct him, and so on in like manner; but until the teacher has called upon some one to answer, not a single word is allowed to be spoken by any member of the class. If no one can answer the question, the teacher, before answering it for the children, excites their curiosity about it by questions and hints, and stories illustrating or partially explaining the subject under discussion; and when he has succeeded in interesting the whole class in the answer, he then gives it, but not before. By these means, the reflective powers of the children are exercised and trained—they are taught to think, to inquire and to reason, and their minds acquire strength and activity. During every lesson the teacher stands, and the children sit before him at their desks. The most perfect silence is observed, except when broken by the answer of the scholar fixed on to reply, or by a question made by a scholar seeking explanation, or by a laugh at some amusing story or joke of the teacher. No lesson is continued long. The subjects of instructions are changed about three times in every two hours; and, at the end of every two hours, the children of all the different classes meet in the playground, under the charge of one of the teachers, to get some fresh air and a little exercise.

The great object of all this is to make the lessons as interesting and attractive as possible to the children, to keep up their attention, and to gradually develope all the powers of their minds.

This system enables the German teachers to watch and tend the progress of each individual child. No child can screen idleness or ignorance behind the general shout of the class. The teacher sees instantly, if a scholar fails often to hold up his hand; and as he questions those, who do hold up their hands, by turns, he soon finds out if a child is really attending or not.

One thing which greatly surprised me in all the German and Dutch schools was, the great interest the children evidently took in the subjects of instruction. This is to be explained entirely by the manner, in which they are treated and instructed by the teachers. The teachers address them as intelligent, rational beings, and in a conversational manner, as if they expected them to listen and to understand.

The teachers further excite their interest by showing them, in all their lessons, the practical use of the knowledge they are acquiring. Constant references are made to the different pursuits, in which the children will be engaged after leaving school; to the commerce of the country, and the way in which it is supplied with the various articles of foreign produce which it requires; to the duties of citizens; to the history of the country; to its produce, its physical characteristics, and its political relations; to farming, in its various branches; to the great inventions and vast undertakings of the day; to the wonders of foreign countries; and, in fact, to all the newspaper topics of the day.

I have myself been obliged to answer questions in the German and Dutch schools about the navy of England, the wealth of England, our metropolis, our colonies, and the miseries of Ireland.

Instruction, or amusement which will excite the scholars to seek instruction, is sought from all the subjects and allusions started by the lesson. The children are made to see the end of instruction and the object of schools in every lesson which is given them. The teachers encourage them by words and looks of approval. A few words, such as "that's right, Charles," "that's a very good answer," "you have explained it very well," "well done indeed," and such like explanations, stimulate the children as if they were at a game. Added to this, that the teachers are so admirably drilled in the art of teaching, that they perfectly understand how to make every thing clear and comprehensible to the least intelligent scholar of the class, while they are so well educated, that they are able to illustrate each lesson by a hundred interesting stories or descriptions.

It is quite beside the purpose of this work to enter into any long examination of the methods of teaching pursued abroad in the different subjects of instruction. I hope I may be able, some future day, to offer some few remarks upon this subject; but I cannot deny myself the pleasure of calling attention to the admirable account of the manner of teaching in the Prussian schools as given by Mr. Mann, in his Educational Tour; one quotation from which work I shall here subjoin, to show how geography is taught in the schools throughout Germany.

Mr. Mann says*: —

"In describing the manner in which geography was taught, I must use discrimination; for in some respects it was taught imperfectly, in others pre-eminently well.

"The practice seemed to be uniform, however, of beginning with objects perfectly familiar to the child — the school-house with the grounds around it, the house with its yards or gardens, and the street leading from the one to the other. First of all, the children

* Educational Tour, p. 134.

were initiated into the ideas of space, without which we can know no more of geography than we can of history without ideas of times. Mr. Carl Ritter of Berlin—probably the greatest geographer now living—expressed a decided opinion to me that this was the true mode of beginning.

"Children, too, commence this study very early—soon after entering school; but no notions are given them which they are not perfectly able to comprehend, reproduce, and express.

"I found geography taught almost wholly from large maps suspended against the walls, and by delineations on the black board. And here the skill of teachers and pupils in drawing did admirable service. The teacher traced the outlines of a country on the suspended map, or drew one upon the black board, accompanying the exhibition by an oral lecture; and at the next recitation, the pupils were expected to repeat what they had seen and heard. And in regard to the natural divisions of the earth, or the political boundaries of countries, a pupil was not considered as having given any proof that he had a correct image in his mind, until he could go to the black board and reproduce it from the ends of his fingers. I witnessed no lesson unaccompanied by these tests.

"I will describe, as exactly as I am able, a lesson, which I heard given to a class a little advanced beyond the elements—remarking that, though I heard many lessons given on the same plan, none of them were signalised by the rapidity and effect of the one I am about to describe.

"The teacher stood by the black board, with the chalk in his hand. After casting his eye over the class to see that all were ready, he struck at the middle of the board. With a rapidity of hand which my eye could hardly follow, he made a series of those short diverging lines, or shadings, employed by map engravers to represent a chain of mountains. He had scarcely turned an angle or shot off a spur, when the scholars began to cry out—'Carpathian Mountains, Hungary;' 'Black Forest Mountains, Wirtemburg;' 'Giants' Mountains (Riesen Gebirge), Silesia;' 'Metallic Mountains' (Erz Gebirge), 'Pine Mountains' (Fichtel Gebirge), 'Central Mountains (Mittel Gebirge), Bohemia,' &c. &c.

"In less than half a minute, the ridge of that grand central elevation which separates the waters, that flow north west into the German Ocean, from those that flow north into the Baltic, and south east into the Black Sea, was presented to view — executed almost as beautifully as an engraving. A dozen crinkling strokes, made in the twinkling of an eye, represented the head-waters of the great rivers, which flow in different directions from that mountainous range; while the children, almost as eager and excited, as though they had actually seen the torrents dashing down the mountain sides, cried out 'Danube,' 'Elbe,' 'Vistula,' 'Oder,' &c. The next moment I heard a succession of small strokes or taps, so rapid as to be almost indistinguishable, and hardly had my eye time to discern a large number of dots made along the margins of the rivers, when the shouts of 'Lintz,' 'Vienna,' 'Prague,' 'Dresden,' 'Berlin,' &c. struck my ear. At this point in the exercise, the spot which had been occupied on the black board was nearly a circle, of which the starting-point, or place where the teacher first began, was the centre; but now a few additional strokes round the circumference of the incipient continent, extended the mountain ranges outward towards the plains — the children calling out the names of the countries in which they respectively lay. With a few more flourishes, the rivers flowed onwards towards their several terminations; and by another succession of dots, new cities sprang up along their banks. By this time the children had become as much excited, as though they had been present at a world making: they rose in their seats, they flung out both hands, their eyes kindled, and their voices became almost vociferous, as they cried out the names of the different places, which, under the magic of the teacher's crayon, rose into view. Within ten minutes from the commencement of the lesson, there stood upon the black board a beautiful map of Germany with its mountains, principal rivers and cities, the coast of the German Ocean, of the Baltic and the Black Seas, and all so accurately proportioned, that I think only slight errors would have been found, had it been subjected to the test of a scale of miles. A part of the teacher's time was taken up in correcting a few mistakes of the pupils; for his mind seemed to be in his ear as well as in his hand; and notwithstanding the astonishing celerity of his movements, he detected erroneous answers, and turned round to correct them. The rest of the recitation consisted in questions and answers respecting productions, climate, soil, animals, &c. &c. . . . . . .

"Compare the effect of such a lesson as this, both as to the amount of the knowledge communicated and the vividness, and of course the permanence, of the ideas obtained, with a lesson, where the scholars look out a few names of places on a lifeless atlas, but never had their imaginations abroad over the earth; and where the teacher sits listlessly down before them, to interrogate them from a book, in which all the questions are printed at full length, to supersede on his part all necessity of knowledge."

In the study plans of most of the schools and teachers'-colleges of North Germany, the following subjects of lessons are entered: — "exercises in thinking;" "knowledge of nature;" "knowledge of the world;" "knowledge of society." Speaking of these lessons Mr. Mann says: —

"These lessons consisted of familiar conversations between teacher and pupils, on subjects adapted to the age, capacities, and proficiency of the latter: with the youngest classes, on things immediately around them — the school-room and the materials of which it had been built; its different parts, as foundation, floor, walls, ceiling, roof, windows, doors, fireplace; its furniture and apparatus; its books, slates, paper; the clothes of the pupils, and the materials from which they were made; their food and playthings; the duties of children to animals, to each other, to their parents, to their neighbours, to the old, to their Maker — these are specimens of a vast variety of subjects embraced under one or another of the above heads. As the children advanced in age and attainments, and acquired full and definite notions of the visible and tangible existences around them, and also of time and space, so that they could understand descriptions of the unseen and remote, the scope of these lessons was enlarged so as to take in the different kingdoms of nature, the arts, trades, and occupations of men, and the more complicated affairs of society.

"When visiting the schools in Leipsic, I remarked to the superintendent, that most distinguished educationist, Dr. Vogel, that I did not see on the 'Study Plan' of his schools, the title, 'exercises in thinking.' His reply was 'No: for I consider it is a sin in any teacher, not to lead his pupils to think, in regard to all the subjects he teaches.' He did not call it an omission, or even a disqualification, in a teacher, if he did not awaken thought in the minds of his pupils; but he peremptorily denounced it as a 'sin.' Alas! thought I, what expiation will be sufficient for many of us who have had charge of the young?

"It is obvious, from the account I have given of these primary lessons, that that there is no restriction as to the choice of subjects, and no limits to the extent of information that may be engrafted upon them. What more natural, than that a kind teacher should attempt to gain the attention and win the goodwill of a brisk eager-minded boy just entering his school, by speaking to him about the domestic animals which he plays with or tends at home — the dog, the cat, the sheep, the horse, the cow? Yet, without any interruption or overleaping of natural boundaries, this simple lesson may be expanded into a knowledge of all quadrupeds, their characteristics and habits of life, the uses of their flesh, skins, fur, bones, horns, or ivory, the parts of the world where they live, &c. So, if a teacher begins to converse with a boy about domestic fowls, there is no limit, save in his own knowledge, until he has exhausted the whole subject of ornithology—the varieties of birds, their plumage, their uses, their migratory habits, &c. &c. What more natural, than that a benevolent teacher should ask a blushing little girl about the flowers in her vases or garden at home? And yet this having been done, the door is opened that leads to all botanical knowledge — to the flowers of all the seasons and all the zones, to the trees cultivated by the hand of man, or the primeval forests that darken the face of continents. Few children go to school who have not seen a fish — at least a minnow in a stream. Begin with this, and nature opposes no barrier until the wonders of the deep are exhausted. Let the school-house, as I said, be the first lesson; and to a mind replenished with knowledge, not only all the different kinds of edifices — the dwelling-house, the church, the court-house, the palace, the temple — are at once associated; but all the different kinds of architecture — Corinthian, Ionic, Doric, Egyptian, Gothic, &c., rise to the view. How many different materials have been brought together for the construction of the school-house — stone, wood, nails, glass, bricks, iron bars, paints, materials used in glazing, &c. &c; each one of these belongs to a different department of nature; and when an accomplished teacher has once set foot in any one of these provinces, he sees a thousand interesting objects around him, as it were soliciting his attention: then each one of these materials has its artificer; and thus all the mechanical trades may be brought under consideration — the house-builder's, the mason's, the plumber's, the glazier's, the locksmith's, &c. A single article may be viewed under different aspects — as, in speaking of a lock, one may consider the nature and properties of iron — its cohesiveness, malleability, &c. — its utility, or the variety of utensils into which it may be wrought: or the conversation may be turned to the particular object and uses of the lock; and upon these a lesson on the rights of property, the duty of honesty, the guilt of theft and robbery, &c., be engrafted. So, in speaking of the beauties and riches and wonders of nature — of the revolution of the seasons, the glory of spring, the exuberance of autumn, the grandeur of the mountain, the magnificence of the firmament — the child's mind may be turned to the contemplation of the power and goodness of God. *I found that these religious aspects of nature were very frequently adverted to, and I was daily delighted with the reverent and loving manner in which the name of the Deity was always spoken:* — 'Der liebe Gott,' the *dear* God, was the universal form of expression; and the name of the Creator of heaven and earth was hardly ever spoken without this epithet of endearment.

"It is easy also to see that a description of the grounds about the school-house or the paternal mansion, and of the road leading from one of these places to the other, is the true starting-point of all geographical knowledge; and this once begun, there is no terminus until all modern and ancient geography and all travels and explorations by sea and land, are exhausted. So the boy's nest of marbles may be the nucleus of all mineralogy; his top, his kite, his little wind-wheel or water-wheel, the salient points of all mechanics and technology; and the stories he has heard of the last king or the present king, the first chapter in universal history. . . . . .

"The Prussian teacher has no book. He needs none. He teaches from a full mind. He does not cumber or darken the subject with any technical phraseology. He observes what proficiency the child has made, and then adapts his instructions both in quality and amount to the necessity of the case. He answers all questions. He solves all doubts. It is one of his objects, at every recitation, so to present ideas that they shall start doubts and provoke questions. He connects each lesson with all kindred and collateral ones; and shows its relation to the every-day duties and business of life; and should the most ignorant man, or the most destitute vagrant in society, ask him 'of what use can such knowledge be?' he will prove to him in a word, that some of his own pleasures or means of subsistence are dependent upon it, or have been created or improved by it."

By these means the children are amused and interested in their studies. They go to their school with the same pleasure as a child to its nurse when expecting to hear a story told. Throughout their after life the school-days are a happy recollection; and all that was learned there, is cherished and loved; because it awakens agreeable, happy, and virtuous associations.

The perceptive powers of the children are exercised and strengthened. They are taught to think and inquire about all they see around them in life. Their reflecting and inventive faculties are thus developed, while their moral sentiments are cultivated. "Instead," as Mr. Mann says, "of any longer regarding the earth as a huge mass of dead matter, without variety and without life; its beautiful and boundless diversities of substance, and its latent vitality and energies gradually dawn forth, until at length they illuminate the whole soul, challenging its admiration for their utility, and its homage for the bounty of their Creator."

The subjects of instruction in the primary schools vary in the different classes. In those for the younger children, who have only just entered the school, they are confined to Scripture history, reading, writing, arithmetic, and singing; but, in the classes for the elder children, not only are higher and more advanced exercises in the above subjects given, but the scholars learn also German history, geography, drawing, and mental calculation. In this last subject of instruction, I sometimes found astonishing progress made. Besides the above lessons which the school-masters are obliged by law to teach in all schools, the children learn to recite the most beautiful of the Psalms and the finest passages of Scripture, as well as the most celebrated national melodies. In the higher elementary schools, or, as they are called, the higher burgher schools, which are open to all children who like to enter them after leaving the elementary schools, and which are attended by the sons of small shopkeepers and of labourers also, the course of education is much higher, embracing not only a continued exercise in the different subjects of instruction which I have enumerated, but in addition to these, geometry, universal history, and the French language. No child is *obliged* to attend these schools; but all are admitted, who wish to continue their education there after leaving the primary schools. These schools are, as I have before said, only to be found in towns; but each town is *obliged* by law to support *at least* one of them. They are generally, I believe, very well attended by the children of small shopkeepers, and contain also many children from the poorest ranks of society.

The great intelligence that pervades all ranks of the people, may be seen from the number and character of the country newspapers. Every small town which possesses a press, sends out at least one newspaper, and generally several. These journals appear sometimes every day, and sometimes only two or three times a week. To give an idea how cheap some of them are, I may mention, that I found one lying on the table of a little village inn in the kingdom of Saxony, which was of quarto size, contained eight pages of information, and appeared twice a week. In English value this paper cost about six shillings per annum. It was printed at the little town of Pirna, and contained all the latest news from England, France, Spain, Italy, and the different German countries. There was an account of the actual state of the negotiations then pending on the Spanish marriage question, of the progress of good government at Rome, and of the procession of Mr. Wyatt's great horse through the streets of London.

There was little or no original writing on political questions affecting Germany; but all the latest news of Germany, and of all other European countries, were given in it. This used to be the general character of German newspapers. Now, however, the press is free, and these papers contain original articles like our own. The greater the size of the town where they are published, the larger is the size of the journal, the more circumstantial the information given in it, and the more frequent the appearance of the paper. They are all remarkably cheap, the *daily* papers published at Dresden costing not more in English value than 26*s.* per annum. Now, not only do several of these papers lie on the table of the smallest village inn, for the peasants to read; but the labourers themselves and the poorest work-people in the towns take them in. Several families club together and take in a paper among them, which is passed from hand to hand. If my readers will consider the character of these journals giving, as they all do, original articles on literature and politics, and epitomes of the news of all foreign countries and of Germany, they will comprehend what different ideas a German and an English peasant have of what is going on in the world, and of political events in general.

I shall now proceed to give the statistics of Prussian education, as they were published in 1845. The Reports, from which these statistics were extracted, are forwarded to the government from all the counties every year, and are published in a collected form once every three years by the Director of the Statistical *Bureau* in Berlin.

In the end of the year 1843, the population of Prussia amounted to 15,471,765. For this population 23,646 elementary schools had been established. This is a great number; but it will appear all the more extraordinary, if we remember the size of the town-schools, which seldom contain less than *four* and *often* as many as TEN class-rooms and teachers. For the direction of the instruction given in these schools, the following number of teachers had been appointed, and was paid and supported by the different parishes and towns: —

Definitely appointed head teachers - - -	25,150
Assistant teachers - - - - -	2,680
Schoolmistresses - - - - -	1,801
Total number of teachers in Prussia, at the end of 1843	29,631

We shall still more fully comprehend the real worth and meaning of these statistics, if we bear in mind what the education of these 29,631 home missionaries has been; how they are protected and encouraged by the state, and how they are watched over, checked, and counselled by the inspectors. Could we find 2000 such teachers as these, in the *whole* of England and Wales? Each of these 29,631 has received a most careful preparatory training of FOURTEEN years' duration; each of them has been examined by committees of public examiners appointed by the state; each of them is well acquainted with the theory and practice of pedagogy, with the best methods of teaching reading, writing, and arithmetic; with Scripture and profane history, geography, drawing, and singing; each of them can play on the violin, the organ, and pianoforte; while nearly all of them have studied the elements of physics, botany, and natural history. Where can we find such a class of teachers in England?

The number of children who were receiving instruction in the 23,646 *day*-schools of Prussia, in the year 1843, were —

Boys - - - - - -	1,184,864
Girls - - - - - -	1,143,282
Total number of children attending the elementary *day*-schools of Prussia, in 1843 -	2,328,146

If to these be added 14,795 children, who were attending the higher class of elementary schools, which exist in the Prussian towns, and of which there are 100 in the kingdom, we shall arrive at the highly satisfactory result, that 1 child in every 6·5 of the population was attending a primary school, in 1843.

For the education of the great army of 29,631 teachers, the Prussian government has founded 43 seminaries or normal colleges, which contained, in 1843, 2546 young persons preparing to enter the teacher's profession, and to fill up the place of the superannuated, and of those who annually die at their posts or leave the profession.

A comparison of the statistics of Prussian education with the latest statistics of French and Swiss primary schools, will furnish us with some very useful and important conclusions. From the statistics of Prussian education we find that, in 1843, there was, notwithstanding the great size of the town-schools —

1 primary school in Prussia for every	653	inhabitants.
1 teacher for every	662	"
1 normal college for every	377,300	"

In *France*, the number of primary schools, in 1843, was 59,383, the number of normal colleges for the instruction of teachers was 96, and the number of teachers actually engaged in instruction 75,535; and as the population of France, in 1843, amounted to 34,230,178, it follows, that there was in that year —

1 primary school in France for every	558	inhabitants.
1 teacher for every	446	"
1 normal college for every	356,564	"

In *Switzerland*, there were, in 1843, 13 normal colleges, and the population was 2,300,000; so that there was, in that country —

1 normal college for every 176,923 inhabitants;

and in the canton of Bern, and also, I believe, in Lausanne, Zurick, Argovie, and Thurgovie, there was —

1 teacher for every 480 inhabitants.

In the kingdom of *Saxony*, there was, in the year 1843,

1 primary school for every	900	inhabitants.
1 teacher for every	588	"
1 normal college for every	214,975	"

In the duchy of *Baden*, in the year 1841, there was—

1 primary school for about every	700	inhabitants.
1 normal college for about every	500,000	"

In the kingdom of *Bavaria*, in the year 1846, there was—

1 teacher for every	508	inhabitants.
1 primary school for	603	"
1 normal college for every	550,000	"

Now, let me suppose that we are a moral people; that we require *fewer* schools, *fewer* teachers, and *fewer* normal colleges, in proportion to our population, than either France, Prussia, Switzerland, or Bavaria; and let me suppose that it would suffice to have—

1 primary school for every	700	inhabitants.
1 teacher for every	600	„
1 normal college for every	400,000	„

The proportions in all Germany, in Holland, and in Denmark, correspond very nearly with those of France and Prussia, so that when I adopt this low estimate for England, I am adopting one lower than the proportions existing in the greater part of Europe. But taking this estimate, which is the lowest we can *possibly* imagine, if we would supply all the people with the means of education, what result do we arrive at? WHY, THAT WE REQUIRE FOR ENGLAND AND WALES, AT LEAST—

23,531 SCHOOLS,
26,500 TEACHERS, AND
41 NORMAL COLLEGES.

If we had all these, we should not even then be nearly so well provided with the materials of education as Prussia, France, Switzerland, or Bavaria.

The whole number of children in Prussia, in the year 1843, between the ages of six and fourteen (between which ages all children are obliged to attend school), was 2,992,124; it follows, therefore, from the statement above given of the number of Prussian children attending school in 1843, that there were in that year 663,978 children, who had not attained the age of fourteen years, and who were not attending school. Many children, however, between the ages of six and fourteen were attending the classes of the higher schools and gymnasia, during the same year. The number of these was not exactly known, but it was supposed to be about 93,276; so that according to this calculation, there remained 570,702 children between the ages of six and fourteen, who were not attending the elementary schools, in 1843. But the Director of the Statistical *Bureau*, by whom these statistics are collected and published, goes on in his report to observe—"That it would be utterly false to suppose, that there were 570,702 children in Prussia, in 1843, between the age of six and fourteen, who received no instruction whatever." According to him, a great number of girls receive private instruction, and are not reckoned in the numbers of children attending school, while a still greater number of very poor children leave school at the end of their twelfth or thirteenth year, after having obtained the necessary certificate of being able to read, write, cipher, and of having acquired a knowledge of the outlines of Scripture history. There are, besides, always a number of children in every part of the country who are kept at home by sickness, and others, who are too delicate to begin school attendance with their sixth year. If these several circumstances be taken into account, it will be easily seen that the 570,702 children between the ages of six and fourteen, who were not attending the primary schools in 1843, are by no means children who have not received, or will not in future receive, any education; but that this apparent defalcation from school attendance arises from the number of girls who are receiving private instruction; from the number of poor children who leave a little earlier than the others, and who have gained a knowledge of reading, writing, arithmetic, and Scripture history (for, before they have gained this knowledge they are never permitted to leave school); and also from the number of those, who are absentees from ill-health or weakness of constitution. Hence it may with perfect truth be said, that, in 1843, with the exception of those children, who were suffering from bad health, nearly every child in Prussia between the ages of six and fourteen was, either actually receiving instruction in the parochial schools, or had already learned reading, writing, arithmetic, and the outlines of Scripture history. This is a very great result, and the Prussians may with reason boast, that, in a few years, when the oldest generation has passed from the stage, and has gone to rest with its fathers, there will not be one man in the whole kingdom, who will not be able to read and think. Already this consummation has been nearly attained; for, according to an investigation, which the government ordered to be made in 1845, it appeared, that, of the young men who were between the ages of twenty and twenty-two years, there were, in the whole of Prussia, only TWO IN EVERY HUNDRED WHO COULD NOT READ, WRITE, AND CIPHER! The appearance of the peasants themselves, is sufficient to satisfy any unprejudiced observer of the widely diffused and great intelligence of the people.

The difference, too, in the appearance of the children

of the poor in this country, and in those of Great Britain and Ireland, is quite extraordinary. Always clean, and generally very neat and tidily dressed, they have such intelligent countenances, and from their constant association with the children of the middle classes, and their having educated and civilised parents at home to correct them, they have such excellent manners, and are so free from vulgarity and coarseness, that I was often wholly unable to make out, whether those I saw were the children of peasants or of tradespeople; nor did I ever feel certain, unless when with the teachers, whom I almost invariably questioned, concerning the relative occupations and stations of the children's parents. The interiors of the cottages of the poor are very clean and comfortable; their little plots of land, which are their own property, are beautifully cultivated; the villages are very neat and orderly; the exteriors of the houses constantly whitewashed; and the whole appearance of the people in those provinces where the land is divided, is that of a contented and intelligent, and thriving peasantry. All this must needs seem great exaggeration, and I was oftentimes tempted to doubt the evidence of my own senses. It is true also, that I did not see the poorest part of the country, viz. the province of Posen; but, on the other hand, I did not visit the most prosperous and best-educated province, viz. that of Silesia. I have, however, no fear of bearing public testimony to the truth of all I have said as regards the provinces of Westphalia, the Rhine, Saxony, and Brandenburg; and, as I have already said, it is well known that the state of the great province of Silesia is still more satisfactory than that of those I have mentioned. The very fact of the children of such different classes of society being mingled together in the same schools, will serve to prove to any unprejudiced mind the excellence of the schools themselves, as well as the civilisation of the poorer classes; for if the schools were not good enough for the children of the rich and noble, or if the poor children were as rude and unrefined, as the children who frequent our ragged schools in England, we may rest assured, that the richer parents would not allow their children to attend the same classes with them. The same association of children of different ranks of society takes place, to even a greater degree, in Switzerland and South Germany than in Prussia.

I could mention a lady, who moves in the first circles of London society, and who is rich enough and sufficiently interested in the improvement of her young relations to engage private tutors for them, if it were necessary, whose young grandchildren I found attending a village school for peasants, situated near the Lake of Geneva, where her son, who was till lately a member of the government of the canton, resided. To prove to me, that it was not carelessness about the children, that had led the parents to remain satisfied with the education given in the village school, she gave me an introduction to the teacher, and begged me to visit his classes. I accordingly went, and found there, what you may find in nearly every village in Germany and Switzerland, an educated and gentlemanly man, who appeared qualified to act as private tutor in any gentleman's family. In Bavaria I found the same proofs of the excellence of the primary schools. I remember particularly a visit paid to one school in Munich, which may be fairly taken as an example of all; for all the schools in that city are remarkably good. When I entered, I did not know any thing about the children, or to what ranks of society they belonged. The appearance of all was so clean, respectable, and orderly, that I imagined they were all the children of tradespeople. I therefore asked the teacher to tell me what their parents were. He answered: — "The two boys you see here are the sons of counts; yonder is the child of a tradesman; there is the son of a physician; there, a son of one of the court servants;" and so he continued to point out others, who were the children of professional men, shoemakers, tailors, &c. I then said — "Have you any here, whose parents are so poor, as not to be able to pay any thing for their education, and who are consequently dependent on the town charity for their instruction?" "Oh! yes," he immediately answered; "the one you see yonder (pointing to a very clean and respectable-looking child) is one, and there is another;" and so he continued to single out several others, who were paid for, and clothed, at the expense of the city. Now, I am not arguing that this mixture of children of different classes in society is desirable, though it doubtless tends to render the intercourse of all classes in Germany more easy, and to lessen the jealousy with which one class of society generally regards another, which keeps proudly aloof from it; all that I wish to infer from it is, that the primary schools in Germany must be very excellent, that the instruction given in them must be of a very high order, and also that the lower orders of people must be far advanced in civilisation, or that such an association between the children of the different classes of society in Germany and of Switzerland would be no more possible than it is at present between those of England or of Ireland. These are facts well worthy of deep consideration.

I have said that the number of primary schools in the Prussian provinces, in 1843, was 23,646; and that 2,328,146 children were attending them. It follows, therefore, that the average number of children in each school was 99. But, as I have shown, the town-schools, and also many of the country-schools, are divided into many separate class-rooms, each of which is presided over by a trained teacher; and, as the number of these teachers was, in 1843, 29,631, it follows, that the average number of children under one teacher was only 73. In the towns the average number is less, and in the country greater. If the Prussian government would consent to the training and employment of paid monitors, it would be very easy to reduce the average number of children under one teacher from 73 down to 40; and I do not doubt that many years will not elapse before this will be effected. In the northern part of Prussian Poland the average number of children to one teacher is only 61; in the northern part of the province of Pomerania it is only 48; in another county of the province of Pomerania it is only 51; and in Berlin only 41. The highest average is in the southern and mountainous district of the province of Silesia, where it is 116.

One strong symptom of the deep interest which the Germans are taking at present in the question of the people's education, is the fact of the astonishing number of works on pedagogy which are constantly appearing. The press is literally teeming with such publications. They treat the subject of pedagogy as a science, while every question relating to it is debated in these works with the greatest minuteness and enthusiasm. But besides these books and pamphlets, which are daily appearing on the subject of the people's schools, there are several periodicals published, which are very widely disseminated among all engaged in education, and which are devoted exclusively to this subject. These periodicals contain original articles on different questions relating to pedagogy; biographies of celebrated teachers; descriptions of particular schools, which are noted for any particular excellencies; and all the news of education, not of Germany only, but of all Europe, and, indeed, of all the world. I have seen articles in them on the progress of the people's education, in all the European countries, including even Russia and Turkey, in America, and even in China. All the educational statistics of every European country are given, and all the recent regulations issued by any particular government, whether the French, the English, or a German government, are criticised in the most unsparing manner. The principal part of the news, however, relates of course to Germany. The most minute and circumstantial accounts are given from time to time of particular institutions in the different states. All the new works, too, upon the subject of education are carefully reviewed in these periodicals; all the new methods introduced into any particular school are discussed; and, in this manner, the teachers throughout Germany are, as it were, bound together; and the efforts of each one are stimulated, by teaching him to consider himself a member of a great and widely spread association, labouring together for the improvement of mankind.

It is very interesting to see, how steadily and rapidly the means for the instruction of the people in Prussia have been improving, since 1819. The following statistics show only a part of the progress, which has been made, as a vast number of old schools have been pulled down and rebuilt, and a still greater number thoroughly remodelled and repaired, neither of which facts is exhibited by them. It appears, then, that —

1. In 1819, the number of schools in Prussia was -	20,085
In 1825, " " -	21,625
In 1831, " " -	22,612
In 1843, " " -	23,646
2. In 1819, the number of teachers in Prussia was -	21,895
In 1825, " " -	22,965
In 1831, " " -	27,749
In 1843 " " -	29,631
3. In 1825, the number of children between seven and fourteen years of age, was - - -	1,923,200
And the number of these who were attending the schools was - - - -	1,664,218
In 1831, the number of children between seven and fourteen years of age, was - - -	2,043,030
And the number of these who were attending the schools was - - - -	2,021,421
In 1843, the number of children between seven and fourteen years of age, was - - -	2,992,124
And the number of these who were attending the schools was - - - -	2,328,146

These statistics will prove better than any thing I can say, how steadily the primary education of the people is advancing, and how much the country is doing to raise the character and condition of the poor. And it is not only in Prussia, that these extraordinary results have been attained, by the united efforts of both the people and the government; but the same is the case all over Germany, France, Switzerland, and Holland. Every German state has been doing, in comparison to its means, as much as Prussia. It is impossible to estimate the enormous sums, which have been expended by the German states, within the last ten years, on the erection of new buildings alone. In France, the expenditure of the central government, between 1833 and 1843, on school-houses alone, amounted to more than 50,000,000 francs.

Surely these facts ought to stimulate us to some degree of energy in this great cause of the people's improvement. Difference of religion opposes no obstacle in Germany, for every one is persuaded that the work must be done; and where there is a will, a way is always to be found. Thus Bavaria, with a population three-fourths of which are Romanists, and the remainder Protestants; Wirtemburg, with a population two-thirds of which are Protestants and one-third Romanists; and Baden, with a population two-thirds of which are Romanists and one-third Protestants; are all as far advanced in the enlightenment of their people as Prussia: and Baden, it is said, has even outstripped her in the wide dissemination, and in the high character of the intelligence of her people. And let it be remembered, the peasants are more contented, more orderly, and more peaceful in their habits, more moral, and, in a word, more civilised, than those of any country in the world. If Englishmen would only candidly consider these things, we should soon find out a way, in which we could all consent to labour together for the improvement of our poorer countrymen. And if we only once commence this great work, we shall soon cover our land with noble schools conducted by good teachers; for what, as a nation, we take in hand, we love to do liberally, rapidly, and well: but, alas! we always hesitate to begin, and, in this case, hesitation is likely to prove fatal to our country.

CHAP. X.

THE EDUCATION OF THE POOR IN SAXONY.—THE LAWS OBLIGING THE PARENTS TO EDUCATE THEIR CHILDREN.—THE WAY BY WHICH ALL THE PARISHES ARE SUPPLIED WITH SCHOOLS, TEACHERS, AND APPARATUS.—THE CHARACTER OF THE SCHOOL BUILDINGS.—THE SUNDAY SCHOOLS. —THE TRAINING AND EDUCATION OF THE TEACHERS.—THE SOCIAL SITUATION OF THE TEACHERS.—THE EXCELLENT SYSTEM OF CLASSIFICATION IN THE TOWN-SCHOOLS. —THE METHOD AND SUBJECTS OF INSTRUCTION IN THE SAXON SCHOOLS.—THE TEACHERS' COLLEGE AT DRESDEN. —THE STATISTICS OF EDUCATION IN SAXONY.

BEFORE 1820, the education of the people had not made any very remarkable progress in Saxony. Several teachers' colleges had certainly been instituted, and good schools had been opened in all the towns. But the means of education were by no means perfect in the villages. Many parishes were totally unprovided for. Some had not sufficient school room, some had no efficient teachers, whilst others were badly supplied with school apparatus, books, &c., or had not provided any adequate and respectable maintenance for the teachers. After the people had won for themselves a share in the government, and had forced their former rulers to consent to a constitution, and to a regular periodical assembly of the representatives of the nation, the great subject of the people's education was immediately taken into consideration, and the admirable system which I am about to describe, was adopted by the Saxon Chambers and immediately put into force. It is then to be borne in mind, that the educational laws of Saxony have originated from the Saxon people, and that the laws requiring the parents to educate their children have been actually put into force by the people themselves.

For very much of the following account of the Saxon educational system, I am indebted to the great kindness of the Minister of the Interior for Saxony, and of Professor Dr. Otto *, director of the celebrated normal college at Dresden, and president of the examinations of candidates for admission to the teacher's profession, in the kingdom of Saxony.

The educational system of Saxony resembles those of Prussia and the rest of Germany in its leading principles. The people act, whilst the government inspects and advises. The state is not allowed to interfere any further than is absolutely necessary to insure the education of the people.

The Chambers have decreed, that every child MUST be educated, in order that the state may be able to carry out the great end of its own existence, viz. the promotion of the virtue and happiness of the people.

The law requires that every child shall receive, for eight years, an uninterrupted and efficient education.

Each parent is obliged to begin to educate his children at home or to send them to some school at

* Dr. Otto most kindly spent every evening with me for several weeks, in order to explain to me all that they were doing in Saxony.

the commencement of their sixth year, unless the child is sickly and unfit to bear any mental exertion. After a child has once commenced attending a school, it must continue such attendance regularly, summer and winter, for eight years; and even on the attainment of its fourteenth year, it may not discontinue such attendance, unless it has obtained a certificate, stating that it can read, write, and cipher, and that it is well acquainted with the doctrines of its religion and with the truths of the Scripture history. The examinations for these certificates are conducted by the religious ministers, in conjunction with the teachers. In some few cases, however, where the parents are very poor, the school-committees are empowered to permit the parents to remove their children from school at the end of their tenth year, if they can read, write, and cipher, and know the leading facts and doctrines of the Scriptures. But before they have attained this age, they cannot be taken from school, except when they are too sickly or too weak to attend the classes.

No child may be employed in any manufactory, or in any manual labour, before it has attained the age of TEN years.

The Saxons consider the education of young children as a matter of primary importance, to which all else must be made to give way. The morality and the liberty, as well as the social and physical condition, of the people are all considered to be dependent on the early and full development of their moral and intellectual faculties. To the attainment of this end, therefore, every other consideration is made to yield. The Saxons are, as is well known, a commercial people. But still commercial requirements have not outweighed moral considerations. From the age of six to the age of fourteen, every child must receive a sound, efficient, and religious education. Those children, however, who are wanted to work in the manufactories, and who have attained a tolerable proficiency in Scripture history, reading, writing, and arithmetic, are permitted to discontinue their attendance on the *daily* classes, at the age of ten; but are required to attend afternoon classes, two or three times a week, during the next four years. Thus, even the factory children receive regular periodical instruction from highly educated teachers, until they attain the age of fourteen.

As nearly all the children are obliged to attend some school, it became necessary to provide a sufficient number of schools and teachers. I proceed to show how this was effected.

The kingdom of Saxony is divided into Regierungsbezirke, or counties, and each of these counties into school-divisions, which correspond generally with the parishes. Where, however, a parish is very large or populous, it is generally divided into two or three school-divisions.

In each of these school-divisions, all the inhabitants whose income exceeds a certain fixed sum, have a vote in the election of a committee for the management of the school. This committee is composed of at least three lay-members, and of one of the Protestant clergy of the parish. Its duties are to provide for the erection, support, and effective maintenance of the necessary school-building; for the supply of all the necessary school-books and apparatus; and for the support, protection, and encouragement of the teachers.

Difficulties arising from religious differences, do not operate in Saxony, to any great degree. There are not more than 30,000 Roman Catholics in the kingdom; and as these are dispersed, it does not often happen, that sufficient numbers are to be found in any one locality, to enable them to support a separate school for themselves. The law allows them to do this however, whenever they are desirous to do so; and in such a case, they elect their own separate school-committee. But when they are not able to provide a separate school for themselves, they are obliged to send their children to the Protestant school to learn reading, writing, spelling, history, and geography; and are allowed to remove them from the school, whilst the religious instruction is being given; on condition, however, that they furnish the inspector with satisfactory proofs, that they are providing elsewhere for the instruction of their children, in their own religious doctrines.

In the towns, each religious party elects one committee for the management of all its schools, instead of electing a separate committee for each separate school.

When these committees have been elected, they are obliged to furnish sufficient school room for all the children of their respective districts; good and suitable houses for the teachers; all the necessary books and apparatus for the schools; and prizes and premiums for the most industrious and clever of the children. They are also required to keep the schools constantly whitewashed and in good repair; to provide the stipends of the teachers regularly, and to take care, that the school buildings are kept well warmed during the winter months. The funds for these several purposes are obtained in different ways. Where the school has been endowed, the annual revenue derived from the endowment sometimes suffices; but where it does not, and also where the school is not endowed, the necessary funds are collected by means of collections in the churches, by the fines imposed upon offenders against the laws, and by means of a tax upon the householders who have a vote in the election of members of the school-committee.

If the parochial committees refuse to collect these funds, the county magistrates are empowered to act for them, and to collect them by means of one of their own officers. By these regulations, the country has provided against the possibility of any parish or village in the kingdom, remaining unprovided with as many schools and as many teachers as it requires for the instruction of its children.

It will be observed that, although in some cases, part of the school expenditure is defrayed by the charitable collections in the churches, yet it is never left wholly dependent upon the amount of such uncertain and precarious supplies.

The amount of the teacher's stipend can never be reduced, in any case, below a certain *minimum* fixed by the Saxon Chambers, and is always settled at the time of his entering upon his situation; and this, as well as all the other expenses of the school and school-buildings, must be provided by the school-committee by means of a school-rate, when the funds obtained from other sources fall short of the necessary amount.

The school-rate is generally a property-tax. Each householder is obliged to contribute in proportion to the value of his property. If the village is situated upon the estate of a rich landlord, he is obliged to provide *all* the required funds; and if the land *around* the village belongs to him, he is required to pay a *third* of the required annual amount. Throughout the whole of Germany, the great proprietors are always *obliged* by law to support sufficient schools and teachers for all the children of all the labourers resident upon their estates. The German governments never leave the education of the children upon the great estates dependent upon the chance benevolence of the rich.

If the parochial committee or the great landlord neglects to provide the necessary funds for the payment of the teachers or for the purchase of apparatus, &c., at the regular fixed periods, or to keep the school-buildings well whitewashed, well warmed, and in good repair; the teacher can appeal to the county magistrates, who *are bound* immediately to attend to his request, and are empowered to enforce the punctual performance of the neglected duties.

The most minute and particular regulations are in force in Saxony respecting the school-buildings. The law prescribes that they shall be situated as nearly as possible in the centre of the parish, and that a quiet and perfectly healthy site shall be selected. To use the words of one of the regulations of the Saxon Chambers on this subject—"If there is any building which deserves the careful consideration of the architect, it is that, which is intended for the village school." The government has prepared several plans, with specifications of the cost, &c., for the guidance of the county authorities and village committees.

To follow the words of the regulations themselves,—

"Every school-room must be

"Sufficiently roomy,

"Lofty,

"Well lighted,

"Perfectly dry and free from damp,

"Of a convenient and suitable form for the management of the school-classes, and

"In a healthy, open, and quiet situation."

On each of these several heads, a great number of minute and most carefully digested regulations have been made, for the purpose of insuring the attainment of these ends. The *minimum* of the size and of the height of the school-room has been laid down, and very particular regulations have been made relative to the warming, cleansing, and ventilating of the school-rooms; to the proper draining of the land, upon which the school is to be built and upon which the play-grounds are to be laid out; to the lighting of the class-rooms; to the disposition of the desks; and even to the position and construction of the doors. Nothing which regards the school-rooms or school apparatus has been deemed too unimportant, to deserve the most careful consideration, or too insignificant, to require the most minute and scientific regulations. The school-rooms in Saxony, as indeed throughout Germany, are well supplied with parallel desks, forms, maps, illustration boards, and all the apparatus necessary to enable the teacher to instruct his children in an effective manner. In the towns the schools generally contain eight or nine classes. A separate room is provided for each class. A learned teacher, who has received *fourteen* years' preparatory education, presides over each separate class. One of these teachers is the general director and superintendent of the whole school.

Each of the class-rooms contains about sixty children. The law forbids any teacher to allow more than sixty to be instructed in the same class-room. Each of these rooms is fitted up along its length with parallel desks and forms, facing the teacher's desk, which is raised on a platform about a foot high at one end of the room. They are continually whitewashed and scoured, and are well ventilated. They are lofty, and always well lighted. The children are never kept in the rooms more than about two hours at one time. They are all taken down into the play-grounds at the end of every hour and a half, for ten minutes' exercise, and during this time, the windows of the class-rooms are all opened and the air purified.

The law requires every school-committee in Saxony to furnish their school-rooms with at least the following apparatus: —

1. A supply of school-books, slates, slate-pencils, lead-pencils, pens, paper, &c. for the use of those

scholars, whose parents are too poor to buy these things for their children.

2. Some black-painted,, smooth, wooden boards on which the teacher may assist his class-lessons by delineations or writing.

3. A moveable easel on which to raise the black boards.

4. Some maps, and among these one of the Holy Land; also some large copies for drawing and writing.

5. A reading-machine, like those now used in some of the best of our infant schools:—and

6. The school-committees are advised to furnish, whenever they can afford to do so, a collection of objects for the illustration of the lessons in natural history and physical geography.

Besides this apparatus, many village schools are supplied with a library of reading books, from which any villager can take books home, on payment of about a halfpenny a week. This is very liberal, when it is remembered that books are more expensive in Germany than in England.

Of the education given in the Saxon primary schools, I shall have to say more hereafter; but to give a general idea of the subjects of instruction in the schools, where the children of the people are brought up, I subjoin a table, which will show what is taught in the primary schools of the city of Dresden, and how the hours of the day are apportioned to the various subjects of instruction. I beg my readers to compare it with what they have each seen of the generality of English schools.

TIME TABLE in the DRESDEN PRIMARY SCHOOLS, showing the Number of Hours devoted each Week to the different Branches of Instruction.

Class I.		Class II.		Class III.		Class IV.		Subjects of Instruction.
Boys.	Girls.	Boys.	Girls.	Boys.	Girls.	Boys.	Girls.	
6	6	6	6	6	6	5	5	Religious instruction.
1	1	1	1	1	1	1	1	Recitation.
3	3	4	4	6	6	8	8	Reading.
3	3	4	4	3	3	3	3	Writing.
3	3	3	3	3	3	2	2	German language. IV. Mental and *vivâ voce* exercises.
4	4	4	4	4	4	3	3	Arithmetic.
3	3	3	3	2	2	0	0	Geography, History, and Natural History.
2	1	2	0	0	0	0	0	Drawing.
1	1	1	1	0	0	0	0	Singing.
0	10	0	6	0	4	0	0	Instruction in feminine duties — such as sewing, knitting, &c.
2	2	1	1	0	0	0	0	Preparation for the classes under the superintendence of one of the teachers.
28	37	29	33	25	29	22	22	Total Number of Hours in each Week devoted to Instruction.

To explain this table it is necessary to remark, that in the town schools, there are generally eight classes instructed in eight separate class-rooms, four for boys and four for girls; that the fourth class contains the least and the first class the most advanced of the children; that each class is under the charge of a separate teacher; and that the girls generally remain in the afternoons for an hour and a half after the boys have left, in order to be instructed in sewing, knitting, &c., by a woman who is paid to conduct this necessary branch of feminine instruction.

In the towns, there used to be two descriptions of elementary schools. Those for children, whose parents could afford to pay a small weekly fee for their children, and those for the poor children, or, in other words, for the children of parents who could not afford to pay any thing. There was also in every town an officer, whose duty it was to examine into all applications for admission into the poor schools, and to decide, whether the parents were really too poor, or not, to pay any thing for the instruction of their children. In the villages, however, where there were not enough poor children to require a separate school; the really poor parents were allowed by the village committees to send their children into the regular village schools free of all expense.

Since the Revolution of 1848, however, the education in all the primary schools has been made perfectly gratuitous, so that *every* parent can send his children to any school free of all expense; except that, which is incurred by providing them with respectable clothing.

Besides the day-schools, of which I have been speaking, and in which the Saxon people first learn to think, and from which they first derive their ideas of God, of liberty, and of national and social virtues, and their love of honest and industrious independence; there is still another class of schools, which merits our attention. These are the Saxon Sunday schools. They are to be found in all the towns, in the great parishes, and in the manufacturing districts. They are opened on the Sunday mornings or Sunday evenings, and are intended for the instruction of all persons of whatever age they may be, who desire to continue their education, and who are prevented, by their week-day duties, from attending any of the primary or superior schools. They are frequented principally by adults, or by young people above the age of fifteen, who have left the primary schools. These classes are opened every Sunday for about three or four hours, and are conducted by some of the district teachers, who are paid for this extra labour by the county authorities. The education given in them is not confined to religious teaching. It comprehends besides this, instruction in reading, writing, arithmetic, history, geography, the physical sciences, drawing, and the new inventions of the age. These classes generally assemble on the Sunday evenings, in one of the day-schools of the town or district. The incidental expenses necessary for warming and lighting the room, and for the purchase of the necessary books &c., are generally defrayed by the voluntary contributions of the students, who attend the classes, and by the benevolence of rich people, who are interested in promoting these useful institutions. When the funds derived from these sources do not suffice, the Minister of Public Instruction is empowered to assist the town or other locality, in perfecting and supporting these schools. In many towns and parishes, however, they are entirely maintained by public subscriptions, and in these cases the students do not pay any thing for their education.

So eager are the Saxon people to gain knowledge, and so well do they understand its value, that wherever any of these schools are opened on the

Sundays or other holidays, they are, as in France, immediately filled to overflowing, with people of all ages from eighteen up to fifty, who are desirous of increasing their stock of information, and of unfolding the powers of their minds. The importance of these institutions cannot be over estimated. By their means, the people of Saxony are always learning, that they have more to learn, and are always renewing the instruction given in the primary schools. The lessons of the primary schools are here continually enforced; morality and prudence are inculcated; the union between the teachers and the people is continually strengthened; the value of education and intelligence is each week shown in a still clearer light; the people are continually brought into a closer connection with persons of a much higher order of intelligence; the tastes and habits of the people are raised; and by these means, their independence of character, their prudence, their energies, and all their political as well as social virtues, are progressively developed.

These schools must not be confounded with our Sunday schools. The subjects of instruction are more varied, the character of the instruction is much higher, and the whole system of teaching in them is much more scientific, than in the Sunday schools of England. And then it must also be remembered, that the Saxon Sunday schools are *only* supplements of excellent day-schools. They do not pretend to supply the place of day-schools. They contain scholars of all ages, young and old, and their teachers are persons, who have studied pedagogy as a science, and who are, in every sense of the word, qualified to teach. The Germans smile at the idea of a Sunday school, even of such a one as those of Saxony, *sufficing* for the purpose of educating a child. They understand the meaning of education too well to think, that one day of education is sufficient to counterbalance six days of neglect and idleness.

But inefficient as the Sunday school is, when employed as the *sole* place of instruction, it is nevertheless a most important engine of moral civilisation, when employed as the assistant of the day-school. In England, it is the means of bringing the middle and the lower classes together, in the most beneficial manner. It is an education for both. It makes them better acquainted with one another, more interested in one another, and more friendly towards one another. It does all this, and much more than this; but still, when considered as the *only* means of educating the poor, as is the case in very many parts of England, it is miserably and ridiculously inefficient. What would our middle classes think, of a school for their children, where the teacher professed to instruct the boys on the Sunday, and to give them holidays on all the week days? And yet such is the Sunday school, when unassisted by a good day-school. But to all this we close our eyes in England; because we do not yet understand, either the real necessity of educating our poor, or what education really means.

I am far from wishing to speak slightingly of our English Sunday schools. It is to be hoped, that the time will come, when there will be a *really efficient* one, connected with every place of worship in our country; whether that place of worship belong to the Church of

England, or to the Dissenters. There never can be too many labourers in the great work of the people's enlightenment. But it is also to be hoped that the Sunday schools will be formed on a more liberal basis than at present among us; and that, in conjunction with Bible teaching and religious instruction, we shall introduce some instruction in the history of the Scripture times, in the manners and customs of the Jews, and in the history of Christianity; and, above all, it is to be hoped, that these schools will be SUPERINTENDED by learned teachers worthy of being compared with those of Germany, Switzerland, France, and Holland, and capable of directing the efforts of all the benevolent persons, who attend these schools, in order to take a share in the instruction of the children, but who have never themselves studied the science of pedagogy. When we once begin to comprehend what the education of the people really means, all this will soon follow.

As an example of what a Sunday school is in Saxony, I may mention one of those instituted at Dresden for adults. It is supported partly by charitable subscription and partly by the municipal authorities of Dresden. Five paid teachers conduct the instruction given in it. It is open every Sunday morning from 8 o'clock until 12, during which time the teachers attend and instruct the different classes. The instruction is perfectly gratuitous, and a great part of the necessary materials, such as paper, pens, ink, and drawing materials, are provided for the scholars free of expense. The object of the institution is to awaken the religious feelings of the scholars; to strengthen their moral principles; and instruct them in reading, writing, the German language, geography, history, arithmetic, and drawing. The way in which the four hours of study are divided between these different studies, may be seen from the following table: —

Lesson Plan of a Sunday School at Dresden.

Morning.	1st Class.	2nd Class.	3rd Class.	4th Class.
From 8 to 8½.	Prayers and Religious Instruction.			
From 8½ to 10 o'clock.	Arithmetic and Elementary Geometry; Extraction of Square Root and the Rules of Proportion, and their application to mechanics.	Mental and Slate Arithmetic; Fractions, both common and decimal.	Geography and History of Germany; Use of the Globes and Physical Geography, especially as regards Germany and Saxony.	
From 10 to 11 o'clock.	Drawing joined with constructive Geometry and Architectural Drawing.	Drawing; Light and Shadow Exercises in Lead, Chalk, Pen and Ink, and Colors.	German Language; Orthography, Etymology, and Dictation Exercises.	Arithmetic, both Mental and Slate Exercises.
From 11 to 12 o'clock.	German Language; various Exercises in Composition.	German Language; various Exercises in Composition.	Drawing principally from Models.	Writing and Elocution.

But it matters not how many schools a nation has, nor how richly it has endowed them, if it has not good and efficient teachers, to whom to confide their management. All depends upon the teacher. Good schools and good books are all so much sunk capital, if the teacher is wanting; and if the teacher is what he ought to be, it matters comparatively little what the schools and books are. The character of the poor, the morality of the poor, the religion of the poor, the prosperity of the poor—how often does all this depend, in a great measure, upon the influence of the teacher on the child. There is not any more important public servant in a state than the primary school teacher. In England, there is no public servant who meets with so little encouragement, protection, or reward. A policeman, in England, is a gentleman compared to many a village teacher. Who ever heard of a gentleman asking a teacher to dine with him? how often has not every one heard of a teacher dining among the servants of his patron in the servants' hall? Who ever considered a teacher to be a gentleman, or his profession to be as respectable as that of the Bar, or of the medical faculty? The answer we must nearly all of us give to these questions, explains an Englishman's appreciation of a teacher's duties, of a teacher's qualifications, and of a teacher's profession. But not so in Saxony. There the greatest pains have been taken to raise the character and position of the teachers' profession, and to secure for the teachers the respect of the peasants. The people of Saxony feel that the character of the future citizens of their country depends mainly on the character and reputation of the village teachers. The greatest pains have, therefore, been taken to perfect this important national profession. Indeed, in no country is so much being done for the education of the people's teachers as in Saxony.

No person may officiate as teacher in any school in Saxony, until he has obtained from a committee of learned professors, expressly appointed for the purpose of examining candidates, a diploma certifying in precise and definite terms his fitness for admission into the profession. And, even when a candidate has passed this examination, he cannot be appointed head teacher of any school, until he has been tried, for two years, as assistant teacher in some elementary school, and until he has after this passed another severe examination.* The preparation for these examinations continues for many years. It begins at the elementary schools. If a boy wishes to enter the teacher's profession, he must gain a testimonial from his teacher, stating his diligence and his success in his studies. After leaving the village school, he still continues his studies, either in one of the higher burgher schools, or in one of the real schools or gymnasia, until he attains the age of fifteen. When he has attained this age, he lays testimonials of his character and his acquirements, signed by his teacher and his religious minister, before the magistrates of his county. He is then examined before these magistrates, together with all the other candidates, at the yearly entrance examinations of the normal colleges of his

* In the literal words of the law—

"No one can be appointed teacher,

"1st. Who has not satisfied the examiners appointed by the Minister of Education, of his fitness to be admitted into the teachers' profession, by passing an examination conducted by them.

"2dly. Who has not, after the above-mentioned examination, *practised for two years as assistant teacher*, or, at least, as private tutor, under the direction, if possible, of an able teacher; and who has not, during this time continued his education, and obtained the entire approbation of his superior teacher.

"3dly. Who has not, after these two years, satisfactorily passed a *second* examination conducted by the above-mentioned body of examiners.

"4thly. Who has not attained his twenty-first year."

Das Elementar-Volkshulgesetz
für die Sachsischen Lande
von Dr. Schultze.

county, in all the subjects of instruction in the elementary schools. The most promising are then chosen out, and are sent by the magistrates to fill up the vacancies in the normal colleges, of which there are always one or two in each county.

There are NINE of these colleges in Saxony, *i. e.* in a country containing a population less than that of London, there are nearly as many teachers' colleges as in all England and Wales!

These colleges are supported by the government; and have, in one or two instances, been richly endowed by private individuals. All the teachers' colleges in Saxony are Protestant; but the Romanist teachers are educated in them, being permitted to absent themselves during the time of the religious lessons.

The young students remain FOUR years in these colleges, continually engaged in preparing for their entrance into the teachers' profession. The education given in these colleges is, however, perfectly gratuitous, or it is manifest no poor young men would be able to bear the expenses of such a training. At the end of this long and careful preparation, they are called before the board of examiners. If the young man is a Protestant, his religious examination is conducted by the board of examiners themselves; but if he is a Romanist, a priest is joined to the board, and conducts the religious part of the examination.

The examination lasts *three* days.

On the first day the subjects are —

From 1 to 10 o'clock,	A. M.	Scripture history.
10 to 12	,,	,,	Pedagogy.
2 to 4	,,	P. M.	Mathematics and the theory of music.

The answers to the questions of the first day's examination are given in writing.

On the second day the subjects are —

From 7 to 11 o'clock, A. M.	Catechising a class of village school children on some subject of elementary instruction.
11 to 12 „ „	Reading; Arithmetic; and An object lesson given to school children.
1 to 2 „ P. M.	A *vivâ voce* examination — In religion; The Scriptures; Luther's catechism; and Pedagogy.
4 to 5 „ „	German language; Logic; and Psychology.
5 to 6 „ „	History; Geography; Natural philosophy; and Natural history.

On the third day the subjects of examination are —

Organ playing;
Singing;
Pianoforte; and
Violin.

If the young candidate, who has been educated for FOUR years in a teachers' college, cannot pass this examination so as to satisfy the examiners, he is obliged to continue his studies until he can do so. But if he passes the examination in a satisfactory manner, the examiners grant him a diploma, which is marked "excellent," "good," or "passable," according to the manner in which he acquitted himself in his examination.

If the young candidate does not obtain a certificate marked "excellent," but only one marked "good" or "passable," he cannot officiate as teacher, until he has spent two years in some school as assistant to an experienced teacher.

At the end of this time, he is obliged again to present himself to the board of examiners, who examine him again in the most careful and searching manner. If he passes this examination, he receives another diploma marked "excellent," "good," or "passable," ac-according to his merit, and if he obtains a diploma marked "excellent" he is enrolled among the members of the teachers' profession, and is allowed to officiate either as a private tutor or as a village teacher. But if he cannot obtain this diploma, he is obliged to continue to act as an assistant teacher until he can do so. Seminar Director Dr. Otto, the principal of the first normal college in Saxony, and a member of the board of examiners, assured me, that it was a common thing for candidates to be examined four or five times, before they succeeded in obtaining a teacher's diploma. When they have at last succeeded, they, as well as those, who obtained the diploma marked "excellent" in the first examination, are eligible as teachers.

The school-committee of the different parishes elect their own teachers. The only condition, to which this right is subjected, is, that they may not elect any person, who has not obtained a diploma of competence from the board of examiners.

When a teacher dies or vacates his situation, the school-committee is required by law to elect another within two months to fill his place. All candidates for the vacant office are examined in the presence of the school-committee and of those inhabitants of the parish or town who desire to be present; and after the examination, the school-committee proceeds to elect the candidate whom they consider the best qualified to fill the vacant situation. But even after this examination before the parochial or municipal school authorities, the successful candidate is generally obliged to present himself to another committee in Dresden, called the Landconsistorium, for examination, before he can finally be inducted into his hard-won office. Such is the great, the seemingly exaggerated precautions, which are taken by the Saxon people to secure good and efficient teachers for the schools. If, at any of these different examinations, anything is discovered against the moral or religious character of the candidate, he is immediately rejected. His moral as well as his religious character is carefully scrutinised before his reception into the Training College, and by each of the different bodies of examiners, before whom he is obliged afterwards to appear. If his previous life cannot bear this scrutiny, or if the principal or professors of his college cannot bear testimony to his morality and to his religious demeanour during his residence, he is rejected, and is not permitted to enter the profession.

It is easy to perceive how high a teacher, who has passed all these examinations and scrutinies, must stand in the estimation of his country and of those who sur-round him more immediately. As Seminar Director Dr. Otto said to me, "The great number of examinations, that a young man must pass through, before he can become a teacher, is important, not only in preventing any unworthy person ever being admitted into the teacher's profession, but also, and more especially, in raising the profession in the estimation of the public. The people have a great respect for men, who have, as they know, passed so many and such severe examinations. They attend with more attention and respect to their counsels and instruction." And certes, until the teacher is respected by the people, his teaching will be productive of but little profit. To be a teacher in Germany is necessarily to be a man of learning and probity. None but such a person can be a teacher. Can we say the same in England? How many of our teachers are only uninstructed women, or poor uneducated artizans; or rude and unlettered pedagogues; or even immoral and low-minded men? How many have never been educated in anything more than reading, writing, and a little ciphering? How many have never been into a teacher's college? How many have only been instructed in such a college for the ridiculously short period of six months? How many have never been educated at all? And yet over Germany, Austria, Switzerland, Denmark, Holland, and France, every teacher has been carefully trained for some twelve or fourteen years, in preparation for his duties; has passed at least two, generally three, and often four years, in a teachers' college, under the instruction of learned and high-minded men, conscious of the importance of their work; has passed with credit several severe examinations, and has only finally been received into the teachers' profession, after a most careful scrutiny into his character and accomplishments has given an assurance to his country of his fitness for the important duties of his profession.

But strange and humiliating as is the contrast between the care, that is taken in Saxony and in England to prepare and elect efficient teachers for the village schools, the contrast between the situations of the teachers in the two countries, after election, is no less sad. In Saxony, as indeed throughout Germany, Switzerland, Holland, Denmark, and France, great pains are taken to make the teacher's rank in society, and his situation, worthy the acceptance of an educated man. The teacher is never left dependent upon uncertain charity. If his salary is sometimes small, it is at least fixed and certain. The minimum is fixed by government, and no parish or town-committee may offer less than this salary to its teacher. Moreover, the teacher is never degraded into being his own tax-gatherer. The parish or town is obliged to arrange with the teacher, before his appointment, how much he shall receive, when he shall receive it, and how he shall receive it. The committee is obliged to collect the funds necessary for cleansing, warming, repairing, and furnishing the school-buildings, *and for paying the teachers*. If they neglect to pay the teacher regularly, he can always appeal to the county magistrates, who oblige the parochial or town-committee to perform its duty.

When a teacher has become too old, or too weak to perform all his accustomed duties in the school-room, the inspector of the district decides, whether he shall be dismissed with a pension; or, whether the committee shall engage an assistant teacher, to aid him in the school-room. The widows and children of deceased teachers are pensioned off in Saxony, in the same manner as in Prussia, and the funds for this purpose are raised by the same means.

Another most important regulation is, that no person or persons in immediate personal connection with a teacher, shall have the power of dismissing him, after he is once elected. It must be evident to all, how much this is tending to lower the independence and respectability of the teachers of England. A private patron, a clergyman, or a committee of parishioners has the power in almost every case, in our country, of dismissing a teacher. How often this has been done merely on account of some personal pique, or because the teacher would not submit to their crude notions of how a school ought to be managed; or from misrepresentation; or from mere village squabbles, I have no need to remind any of my readers. That such a dismissal is possible, every one will admit. How such a possibility must often damp a good and earnest teacher's energy, or undermine his honesty and destroy his usefulness, or at least lower his profession in the eyes of the people around him, is but too evident. But in Germany, no person in immediate connection with the teacher can dismiss him on any pretext whatsoever. His judges are distant, unprejudiced, and impartial persons. In Saxony, after the parish has elected its teacher, it loses all direct power over him. The parochial minister or committee can inspect the school, when he or they please. Indeed, it is their duty to do so at stated times. They can advise the teacher and counsel him, but they cannot directly interfere with him. He is supposed to understand, how to manage his school, better than any other person in his parish. If he did not, his long preparatory training would have been of little avail.

If the clergyman, or any of the parishioners, have any cause of complaint to find with the teacher, and desire to have him either dismissed or reprimanded, and obliged to change his plans of proceeding, a complaint must be made to the county educational magistrate, and by him, to the minister of education in Dresden, who, in Saxony, is the only person, who can dismiss a teacher. The county magistrate, on receiving the complaint, immediately sends an inspector to the spot, to inquire into the ground of complaint or dispute; and after having received his report, the complaint of the parish, and the defence of the teacher, sends them to the minister of education in Dresden. It remains with the minister alone to pronounce the final judgment. This impartial mode of proceeding tends to raise the teachers' profession in the eyes of the people. They see that the teachers are men, who are considered worthy of the protection and support of the government. But above all, it enables the teachers to act honestly and fearlessly, to follow out the plans they know to be the best, and to devote their whole energies and minds to their duties, without any embarrassing fears of offending employers or patrons, or of endangering their continuance in office.

There are 2925 teachers in Saxony, or one teacher to every 588 inhabitants. For a poor country like Saxony, this is a very large body of teachers to educate and support. But still it is not large enough for the wants of the country. In Saxony, as throughout Germany, they will not make any use of monitors. At present Germany is suffering a strong reaction of feeling against the old monitorial systems. In Saxony the want of monitors, is making itself felt much more than in other parts of Germany. The Saxons have discovered, that one teacher cannot undertake the management of more than fifty children at one time, so as to promote with any great success their individual development, and at the same time, they cannot afford to support a greater staff of teachers. As they will not avail themselves of the assistance of educated monitors in the more mechanical parts of school teaching, they have therefore been obliged to adopt the following expedient. The law ordains, that when there are more than sixty children in any parochial school, and the parish cannot afford to support more than one teacher, the children shall be divided into two classes, when there are not more than 100, and into three classes, when not more than 150 in number; that when there are two classes, the teacher shall instruct one in the morning, and the other in the afternoon; that when there are three classes, he shall instruct each class for three hours daily at separate times; and that all the children not under instruction shall not attend the school, while either of the other classes is there.

This is doubtless better, than to assemble all the children at the same time in school; as in such a case, those who were not under the care of the teacher, would only interrupt the labours of the others, and the attention of the teacher to them, without gaining any good themselves. But if the Saxons were only to make use of educated monitors, all the children might, in every case, receive their six or eight hours' daily instruction, and that without hindering one another, or dividing the attention of the teacher; as the monitors might direct the more mechanical parts of the instruction, such as the writing and reading, and might assist in preserving order and silence in the school-room. But the Saxons think that, because a monitor cannot educate the mind of a child, and cannot awaken either its dormant principles or its dormant powers, that therefore it can do nothing. Here, however, they are clearly wrong, as a monitor may be of the greatest use, in preserving order, and in teaching writing, reading, spelling, drawing, and mere local geography. He may thus spare the teacher a great deal of mere drudgery; and for these minor branches of instruction, he is even better fitted than the teacher himself; as the latter is not always able to repress his impatience, in being forced to spend his time in such mere drudgery, or to apply himself to it, so patiently as the younger monitor, who still remembers his own difficulty in acquiring this elementary knowledge, and in what that difficulty consisted; whose education has not yet given him a distaste for such simple duties, and who is encouraged by a feeling of satisfaction at their being entrusted to him.

It is only in the poorer village schools, however, that the need of monitors is felt, as the town school-committees can generally raise sufficient funds to support several teachers. Each town has generally one central school-committee, elected, as I have before said, by the citizens. These committees generally form one or two large schools for the whole town, each containing eight or ten class-rooms, instead of building a greater number of smaller schools. This arrangement, as I have already shown, offers great advantages, as it enables them to classify the children much better, than where the school-house only contains two or three school-rooms. All the children are divided according to their acquirements, into as many classes as the school contains rooms; one educated teacher is placed over each class, and by having only children of the same degree of knowledge under his care, he is able to give his class-lessons to all his children at one time, without being obliged to divide them, and his thoughts and attention also. It was very delightful to enter into one of these well classified German schools, accustomed, as every one is in England, to the wretched disorder of many of the schools of our National School Society, and to the jaded and fatigued looks of the poor little scholars who are forced to stand and shout in them for so many hours every day. I remember taking an English clergyman over the noble school in Leipsic, which contains, I think, fourteen class-rooms. Each room is about fourteen feet high, twenty-five feet long, and fifteen broad, and was fitted up with rows of parallel desks and forms, at which the children work. In front of them stood a teacher's desk, raised on a slightly elevated platform, so as to enable him to see all his scholars. Behind it, and on either side, hung swinging black boards, on which he might illustrate his lessons; and round each room, hung maps of Germany, and of the different quarters of the world; those of Germany delineating, in a strong and forcible manner, all the physical characteristics of the fatherland. There was about the whole an air of science, which was irresistibly pleasing. Every thing showed us, that all the details of instruction had been thoroughly and carefully considered. The size, careful ventilation, and cleanliness of the rooms; their arrangement and furniture, and the character of the apparatus, with which they were filled, all told us, that the Saxon people and the Saxon government understood the importance of the great work of the people's education, and knew that its perfection depended, on a scientific regulation of all the details of school management. I could not help turning to the English clergyman and asking, "Where will you find such schools in England?" I visited, also, several of the primary schools in Dresden, in company with one of the students of Dr. Otto's normal college, and found them equally admirable for their classification, for the number, size, cleanliness, ventilation, and good arrangement of their class-rooms; for the character and numbers of the teachers connected with them; for the scientific character of the instruction given in them; for the order, quiet, and excellent discipline of the class-rooms; for the suggestive and awakening nature of the methods of instruction pursued in the classes; for the gentlemanly and intelligent bearing of the teachers; for the cleanly, healthy, and comfortable appearance of the children, and for the friendly relations of scholars and teachers.

In a Saxon class-room one finds a learned professor, who has been educated for many years in preparation for his duties, standing before his class lecturing his children, as if they and he were rational beings. The aim of a German teacher is to awaken the minds of his scholars; to enable them to think, and to teach them to instruct themselves. He never tries to cram. The method which is pursued is the suggestive one. The teacher selects the subject of the lesson, whether it be on history, natural history, geography, arithmetic, or grammar; and after the class has read some few pages together, the teacher commences his lesson by questions. When a question has been put by him to the class, all those children, who think they can answer, hold up their hands; the teacher calls upon them by turns to answer his questions, or to correct the answers of their companions. If the lesson is in history or geography, the teacher increases the interest of the children by anecdotes or descriptions, and enlists their sympathies on the side of virtue, heroism, and patriotism, by pointing out for notice the brilliant deeds of their country's heroes, and the exploits of their ancestors in resisting the foreign invader, or in conquering the national foes. The teacher addresses his children as thinking beings; as those, who will one day be men, and who will one day themselves influence the destinies of their nation. *The scholar will one day become a citizen;* that is the truth engraven on the German teachers' minds: their duty and their aim is to awaken and to nurse into maturity the virtues of the people.

How different is the state of things in England! A short time ago I visited two large schools, situated in a great and populous parish in the south of England: one belonging to the National Society, and the other to the British and Foreign School Society. They had both been built within the last few years: the one belonging to the British and Foreign School Society was only just finished. The teachers were men, who deserved no better description, than that of half-educated peasants: one had enjoyed the advantage of *six* months' instruction in the schools at Westminster; the other *six* months' instruction in the school of the British and Foreign Society. With this short training, they were thought perfectly fitted for their duties. When I entered the National School, I found a great, half-empty room, with two desks at the end, and two maps on the walls; and all the poor children standing before the teacher, as if to increase the difficulty of learning by the fatigue of the position. He told me, that they stood nearly the whole of every day in that manner; I remonstrated, and asked why he did not get desks and forms, and allow the poor children to sit; and I ventured to suggest that the standing must fatigue them, and render them listless, inattentive, and discontented; but I was immediately answered with the stupid reply,

"Oh no! it prevents them going to sleep." I felt inclined to ask, "Whose fault would it be, if they fell asleep over their lesson; would it not show, that you did not know how to interest them in their studies?" But what else could one expect from a half-educated peasant? He treated his children very much as a labourer would his cattle; kindly, but irrationally.

On my entering the other school, I found all the poor children standing, ranged round the walls, although there were plenty of desks in this school, and delivered to the charge of poor ignorant little boys of nine or ten years of age, who knew little more than the children themselves did. These so-called monitors were pretending to teach geography, while their poor scholars were leaning against the walls, playing tricks with one another, talking, and doing anything but learning; whilst the noise of all the different classes shouting at the same time, and in the same room, was so great, as to render almost inaudible the instruction, which the teacher himself was conveying. This school had, as I before mentioned, been just built at great expense, as a rival to the National School. After glancing my eye over the mere pretence of instruction, which was being given, I turned to the teacher, and asked him how he liked his situation: his answer was, "Oh, sir, I can hardly make my livelihood of it; I am married, and the committee allows me only 30*l.* per annum, my house, and the pence of the children, which amounts to very little, as the school is so poorly attended, and as the children only pay 1*d.* per week each."

Yet these are by no means unfavourable specimens

of even those of our parochial schools, which are not mere "*dame schools.*"

When I contrasted these schools, both modern, both under inspection, and both built under the auspices of a clergyman and parishioners, who professed themselves very zealous in the cause of the people's education, with the eight-roomed schools of Germany, with their eight classes and their eight educated teachers, I could not help feeling that if this be what we mean by EDUCATION, then indeed it is a dream to expect to raise the character of the people by its means. Such schools as these are penance chambers. They are only calculated to create unhappy associations with the name of the school, the teacher, the studies, and the Scriptures, which are first taught in such a place. How many have learned to hate the most beautiful works of the ancients, from the way in which these books were forced upon them in their childhood! The thought of unhappy school-days has often enveloped the pages of the school-books with miserable associations, and unhappy feelings. There can be no doubt, that many of our badly conducted schools are thus doing more to retard the progress of religion and morality, than any gin-palace in the land; for the gin-palace is at least free from the charge of surrounding virtuous maxims and ennobling pursuits with disgusting associations. It would be far, far better for many a parish in England to have no school at all, than to keep up those they have at present.

I have already shown, how well ventilated, how clean, and how well furnished the Saxon school-committees are required to keep their school-rooms; and how they are all furnished with desks and forms, at which each scholar has his appointed seat.

With respect to the education given in the primary schools, I may mention, that the laws of Saxony require every teacher to give instruction in the following subjects:—

1. Religion;
2. Reading and Speaking;
3. Writing;
4. Mental and Slate Arithmetic;
5. Singing and Chanting;
6. Elementary Instruction in
   Natural History;
   Physical and Local Geography; and
   History; especially the Geography and History of Germany.

As soon as a teacher has been appointed, he and the local inspector are required, to prepare a plan of daily instruction, to apportion the different school hours to the different studies, and to arrange the order and the time for holding the different classes. When this so-called lesson-plan has been once determined, the teacher is bound by it, and cannot vary the order of his class-instruction, without again consulting with the inspector.

The school duties are commenced every morning and closed every afternoon with prayer and singing.

A public examination of all the children is held once every half year in the school-room, and under the direction of the local inspector. Notice of the appointed day is given by the religious ministers from their pulpits;

and all the inhabitants of the parish are invited to attend. The school-committee is required by law to be present at these public examinations. These examinations serve to stimulate the efforts of both teachers and children, to interest the parents in the schools, and to encourage a spirit of healthy emulation among the scholars. At the end of the examination, the inspector pronounces his opinion on the progress of the children in the presence of the assembled parish; but all remarks upon the teacher himself are given to him in private, so as not to diminish the respect of the children for him, by showing them, that he does not fully understand how to instruct them in the most effective manner.

I have before mentioned that in this little and poor kingdom of Saxony EIGHT teachers' colleges have been established, for the education of the teachers of the people.

As an example of these admirable institutions, I shall describe one, that I had the pleasure of visiting several times. It is one of the two teachers' colleges, which have been founded in Dresden, and is under the direction and superintendence of that excellent man Dr. Otto, to whom the progress of the people's education in Saxony is so deeply indebted. During my stay in Dresden, Dr. Otto volunteered, in the most generous manner, to spend a portion of every evening with me, in order to explain to me the working of the admirable educational system now in force in Saxony.

The teachers' college, which I am about to describe, is situated in that part of Dresden called Friedrichstadt.

This college was first founded in 1787. On the 31st October 1835, it celebrated its 50th commemoration day: and at the end of 1842, it had educated and sent out above 655 teachers. The great significance of this last fact will be comprehended, when I have shown what a liberal course of education is given in this institution.

The number of the students, who attend the lectures and classes of the college, is limited to seventy; of these, sixty are lodged gratuitously in the institution; the remaining ten dwell with their parents or relations in the town. Twenty of the places in the college have been endowed by the government, and are therefore in its gift. The ablest of the candidates for admission are elected to them.

The examination of candidates for admission to the college is held every Easter. As the life in the normal college costs little or nothing, the lodging and education, if not the whole expenses, being, as I have said, given gratuitously; and, as a young man who distinguishes himself in the college is certain to be chosen by some school-committee afterwards as teacher, there are always plenty of candidates for admission from the middle and lower classes of society. All these are subjected to a rigorous examination; their acquirements, their character, and their past life, are most carefully scrutinised; and, from among them all the most promising are chosen for preparation for the teacher's profession. No candidate can be elected who is not healthy and strong, who has not a powerful and clear voice, or who is lame, short-sighted, or deaf. Every one must be at least sixteen years old, and must present to the examiners a certificate of a medical man of freedom from all organic complaints, and of sound health.

The course of education in this college, as in all the other colleges in Saxony, is of FOUR years' duration: no student can leave before the end of this time, and even then, he cannot obtain admission into the ranks of the teachers, unless he can pass the examination for diplomas, which I have before described. In England, it will be remembered, that a six months', and in some cases even a three months' training, is thought quite sufficient for the preparation of a teacher for his duties; while the candidate for admission into a Saxon teachers' college knows much more, generally, than a young man, at the completion of his course of education does in several of our colleges.

The students in the Dresden college are divided into three classes; each young man remains, during the first two years of his residence, in the third and second classes; but, during his third and fourth years' residence, he pursues his studies in the first class. The staff of professors and teachers in the college consist of, —

1st. The Director, Dr. Otto;
2nd. A Vice-Principal;
3rd. A Professor of Mathematics;
4th. A Professor of Music;
5th. Daily Teachers for Writing, Drawing, and Violin playing.

The director gives, every week, fourteen, the vice-principal sixteen, the third professor seventeen, and the fourth professor twenty-three hours' instruction to the students.

The following table will show, what the subjects of instruction are in the college, and how the time of residence is divided between them.

TIME TABLE IN DR. OTTO'S TEACHERS' COLLEGE IN DRESDEN.

Summer Half-Year. Number of Hours each Week in Class			Winter Half-Year. Number of Hours each Week in Class			Classes.
I.	II.	III.	I.	II.	III.	
2	2	2	2	2	2	1. Religion.
0	1	1	2	1	1	2. Explanation of the Scriptures.
0	1	1	0	1	1	3. Scripture history.
3	1	1	3	0	0	4. Catechism.
1	0	0	1	0	0	5. Religious exhortation.
2	0	0	2	0	0	6. Pedagogy.
0	3	3	0	3	3	7. Special methods of teaching.
2	1	1	2	0	0	8. I. Rhetoric and reading exercises; II. and III. Mental calculations.
1	1	1	1	1	1	9. Recitation.
2	0	0	2	0	0	10. Natural philosophy.
0	2	2	0	2	2	11. Natural history.
0	1	1	0	1	1	12. Geography.
1	0	0	0	0	0	13. Mathematical geography.
1	1	1	1	1	1	14. History.
1	2	2	1	2	2	15. German language.
2	0	0	2	0	0	16. Latin language.
2	2	2	2	2	2	17. Writing.
?	2	1	2	2	2	18. Arithmetic.
0	1	2	0	0	0	19. Geometrical drawing.
1	0	0	1	1	1	20. Geometry.
2	2	2	2	2	2	21. Drawing.
0	0	1	1	1	2	22. Singing.
1	1	1	1	1	1	23. Choral singing.
1	1	0	0	0	0	24. Quartet singing.
2	2	2	2	2	2	25. Concert singing.
6	3	2	3	1	6	26. Organ playing; II. and III. Violin playing.
13	19	19	7	12	6	27. Preparation and exercise hours.
2	2	2	2	2	2	28. Gymnastic exercises.
52	51	50	42	40	40	Total number of hours per week.

It is worth while calmly to consider this time table, and to remember, that this scheme of education is pursued unceasingly for four years, and that, too, after the students have already received quite as good an education in the primary schools of Saxony, as our teachers obtain in some of our teachers' colleges.

The students rise in summer at 5 o'clock, and in winter at 6 o'clock, in the morning: as soon as they are dressed, they meet in one of the class-rooms, where the director reads the morning prayers; their hours of study are from 7 to 12 A. M., and from 2 to 5 P. M.

Connected with the college is a primary school for children of that district of the city, in which the college is situated: this school is under the direction of a regularly appointed and experienced teacher, and is attended by 105 children, who are divided into three classes, to each of which is assigned a separate class-room, in one part of the college buildings. In these classes, a certain number of students from the college first practise teaching under the eye, and aided by the advice of the teacher. I attended two of these classes, and was much pleased to observe, how scientifically this branch of the students' education was conducted. It is much more difficult to teach in an effective manner, than to theorise about it, and hence the reason why the practice of teaching forms so considerable a part of the instruction, given in the German teachers' colleges.

The statistics of Saxon education form a strange contrast when compared with those of our own country.

ALL the children of Saxony between six and fourteen years of age are at this moment receiving daily instruction of the best kind in their parochial schools.

In the towns the children, instead of being left dirty and uncared for to demoralise one another in the streets, are *all* attending their respective schools beautifully clean, well dressed, and so civilised and gentle in their manners, as to be thought fit companions at the same desks and in the same school-rooms of the children of the richer classes.

There is in the whole of Saxony no class of children, which is worse educated or lower in the scale of civilisation than the children of our small shopkeepers. There is not in the whole of this country any class of children to be found at all similar, in their condition, to those poor outcasts of society, who attend our "ragged schools." In a Saxon town, during the regular school hours, no children are to be seen in the streets—they are all with their teachers, acquiring the knowledge requisite to fit them for the duties of citizens.

Besides the children, most of the young men of the poorer classes of Saxony attend the weekly schools, in order to improve themselves in the higher branches of instruction, which they commenced at the primary schools.

In the year 1843, there were in the kingdom of Saxony

1,719,800 inhabitants;

and for this population, not so great, be it observed, as that of London, there were in that year,

1908 Elementary Schools;
2925 Educated teachers;
or 1 Elementary School for every 901 inhabitants;
and 1 Teacher for every 588 "

There were also in this little country eight teachers'

colleges, *i. e.*, two-thirds as many colleges, as in the whole of England and Wales put together. And the young men, who are going to undertake the management of the village schools of Saxony, receive during their four years' residence in these great institutions a much more liberal and a much better education than nine-tenths of the under-graduates of either Oxford or Cambridge ever enjoy.

Dr. Otto furnished me with the results of some inquiries, which he had made, in order to find out the rate, at which the teachers in Saxony are paid. From them it appears, that, if we take into account the comparative value of money in England and Saxony, 2119 of the primary teachers of Saxony receive the following salaries, *independently of the lodgings, firing, &c., which is also, as I have shown, provided for them.*

Teachers	per annum, exclusive of all the perquisites of their office	£	s.	d.
607	receive not more than	30	0	0
531	" "	50	0	0
543	" "	70	10	0
306	" "	90	0	0
78	" "	95	0	0
25	" "	105	0	0
12	" "	120	0	0
9	" "	130	0	0
7	" "	138	0	0
1	" "	150	0	0
2119				

Of the salaries which the other teachers of Saxony receive, I have no return. But the above return will show that the teachers are paid much better in Saxony than in England, if we bear in mind, that the teachers of Saxony, besides the above-mentioned salaries, are provided by the parishes with comfortable houses, with all their firing, and generally with land enough for the cultivation of the vegetables required for their households, and for the keep of at least one cow.

The government has, lately, I believe, raised the salaries of all the teachers; as they think, that the money is not squandered which is expended in making a good teacher comfortable in his circumstances, and respectable in the eyes of the poor among whom he lives.

CHAP. XI.

THE EDUCATION OF THE POOR IN BAVARIA, WIRTEMBERG, AND THE GRAND DUCHY OF BADEN. — THE WORST SCHOOL IN MUNICH. — STATISTICS OF BAVARIAN EDUCATION. — A TOWN STREET IN THE MORNING IN WIRTEMBERG. — THE TEACHERS' COLLEGES IN WIRTEMBERG. — THE INDUSTRIAL CLASSES IN THE DUCHY OF BADEN. — THE SCHOOL BUILDINGS IN THE DUCHY OF BADEN. — THE STATISTICS OF EDUCATION IN THE DUCHY OF BADEN. — THE TEACHERS' CONFERENCES.

I HAVE given a minute account of what is being done to raise the intelligence of the people in Prussia and Saxony. I shall not describe the efforts of the governments of southern Germany nearly so fully, as, in all their leading features, the educational systems of southern Germany are precisely similar to those of Prussia and Saxony. Still I cannot pass over that part of the legislation of Bavaria, Wirtemberg, Baden, Nassau, and Austria, which relates to the civilisation of their poor, in silence, as their efforts have been so great, liberal, and successful.

In Bavaria, Wirtemberg, the Duchy of Baden, and Nassau, as much, and in Wirtemberg and Baden perhaps even more, has been done to promote the intelligence, morality, and civilisation of the lower orders of society, than in Prussia. In each of these countries, every village has a good school-house, and *at least* one learned and practically efficient teacher, who has been educated for several years at a college; every town has several well-organised schools, sufficiently large to receive all the children of the town, who are between the ages of six and fourteen; each of these schools contains from four to ten class-rooms, and each class-room is under the direction of a highly educated teacher.

In each of these countries, every parent is *obliged* to educate his children, either at home or at some school, the choice of the means being left to himself. In none of these countries are children left to grow up in vicious ignorance or with debasing habits.

In none of these countries, is there any class of children analogous to that, which swarms in the back streets, alleys, and gutters of our great cities and towns, and from which our paupers, our disaffected, and our criminals grow up, and from which our "ragged schools" are filled. All the children are intelligent, polite, clean, and neatly dressed, and grow up from their sixth to their fourteenth year under the teaching and influence of educated men.

In each of these countries a sufficient number of normal colleges has been founded, to enable it to educate a sufficient supply of teachers for the parishes and towns.

In each of these countries, all the schools of every sect and party, private as well as public, are open to public inspection, and are visited several times every year by learned men, whose business it is to examine both teachers and scholars, and to give the government, the chambers, and the country, a full and detailed account of the state, condition, character, and progress of every school, so that parents may know, where to send their children with safety; that good teachers may be encouraged, rewarded, and promoted; and that unworthy teachers may not be suffered to continue long in their situations.

In each of these countries, the laws prohibit any person being a teacher of any school, until he has proved his efficiency to the committee of professors, appointed by the state to examine candidates, and until he has laid before such committee, testimonials of character from his religious minister, his neighbours, and the professors of the college, at which he was educated.

It would take up too much of my space to narrate all I saw in these countries, and all I heard from the people themselves about the schools. A few anecdotes may not, however, be wholly out of place.

When I was in Nuremburg, in the kingdom of Bavaria, I asked a poor man, whether they obliged him to send his children to school: he said, "Yes; I must either send them to school or educate them at home, or I should be fined very heavily:" I said, "I suppose you don't like these rules?" he answered, "Why not, sir? I am a very poor man; I could not afford the time to teach my children myself, nor the expense of paying for their education myself; the municipal authorities pay all the school fees for my children, and give them good clothes to wear at school; both my children and myself are the gainers by such an arrangement; why should I object to it?"

In Ratisbon, I spent the whole of one day in company with a poor peasant, who acted as my guide. I said to him, "Have you any good schools here for your children?" He answered, with an air of astonishment, "Oh dear yes, sir: all our children go to school; the law obliges us to send them to school, and provides very good schools for them." I said, "But don't you dislike being *obliged* to send your children to school?" He answered, "Why should I, sir; the teachers are good and learned men, and our children learn from them many things, which enable them afterwards to get on in the world much better, than they would be able to do, if they were ignorant and incapable of studying." I asked again, "But what sort of men are the teachers?" He answered, "Oh, they are very learned men; they are all educated at the colleges." I said again, "But are the teachers generally liked by the poor?" He answered, "Oh, yes, they are learned men, and teach our children many useful things."

When I reached Munich, I engaged, according to my usual custom, a poor man as my guide. I asked him to take me to see some of the schools, where the children of *poor* people were educated, and told him, that I did not wish to visit the best, but the worst school in the city. He answered me, "Sir, we have no bad schools here; the government has done a great deal for our schools, and they are all very good." I said, "Well, take me to the worst of those you know:" he answered again, "I don't know any poor one, but I will take you to the one where my own children go. I am a poor man, and cannot afford to pay anything for the education of my children, and many of the children you will see there, are like my own, sent to the school at the expense of the city."

Accordingly, after passing several very large and handsome schools for primary instruction, we proceeded to the one, which the children of my poor guide attended. It was a lofty and handsome building, four stories high, and about 60 feet broad. In the two upper stories, all the teachers, of whom there were ten educated men attached to the institution, resided. On the lower floors, there were ten class-rooms, each about 20 feet long, 15 broad, and 14 feet high, and fitted up with parallel rows of desks, maps, drawing boards, and school-books. Five of these spacious class-rooms were for the boys, and five for the girls. The children were all classified, according to the time of entering the school. All those who had been less than a year in the school were put in the first class. These children, after remaining a year or a year and a half in the first class, moved on into the second class, and thence into the higher classes, the same teacher accompanying them through their five changes, and continuing to instruct them, until their leaving the school. Each school-room was filled with parallel rows of desks and forms; the desk of the teacher stood in front of them all, and the walls were covered with maps, pictures, and black boards.

The desks, forms, maps, pictures, and apparatus of each school-room were suited to the age, size, or attainments of the children for whom the class-room was destined.

The children sat during their first year or year and a half's education, in the first class-room, during their second year and a half's education in the second class-room, and so on.

I went first into the second class-room. The children were so clean and respectably dressed, that I could not believe they were the children of poor persons. I expressed my doubt to my guide. His answer was, "My children are here, Sir;" and then turning to the teacher, he requested him to tell me, who were the parents of the children present. The teacher made the children stand up one after another, and tell me, who their parents were. From them I learned, that two were the sons of counts, one the son of a physician, one of an officer of the royal household, one of a porter, and others of mechanics, artizans, and of labourers, who were too poor to pay for their children's education, and whose children were clothed and educated at the expense of the town. They all sat at the same desks together. They were all clothed with equal respectability. In their manners, dress, cleanliness, and appearance, I could discern no striking difference. My inference from this interesting scene was, that the children of the German poor must be in a very different state to that of the children of our English poor, to allow of such an intercourse, and to enable the richer classes to educate their sons at the same desks with the children of the peasants.

After spending some time in the different class-rooms, the quiet and order of which were admirable, I went to the town-hall to see the chief educational authority for the city itself. Outside his door, I found a poor woman waiting to see him. I asked her what she wanted. She said, she had a little girl of five years of age, and that she wanted to persuade the minister to allow her to send her little daughter to school a year before the legal age for admission, which in Bavaria, is the completion of the sixth year. I said to her, "Why are you so anxious to send your child to school so early?" She answered, smiling at my question; "The children learn at school so much, which is useful to them in after life, that I want her to begin as soon as possible." I thought to myself, this does not look, as if the people dislike being obliged to educate their children.

I had an interview with the head inspector of Bavaria, and asked him, whether he was certain, that all the young men below thirty years of age could read and write and understood arithmetic. He said, "I am certain of more than that; I know, that they all know their Scripture History, and that they all know something of geography, and of the elements of Natural History."

At the time I visited Munich, the Jesuit party was in power. The ministers, however, showed the greatest willingness to furnish me with all the information I required, and supplied me with all the statistics and documents I wished to procure.

I visited a priest, who directed one of the large educational establishments in the city. He told me, that they had established eight normal colleges in Bavaria for the education of teachers, and that two of these had been specially set apart for the education of Protestant teachers. He seemed to make very light of all difficulties arising from religious differences, and spoke of education as of a national work, which it was *necessary* to accomplish, by the joint efforts of all religious parties.

It is said, greatly to the honour of the late king, that, careless as his government was to many of the internal wants of the kingdom, and profuse and lavish as his expenditure was upon art, he never neglected the education of the people, but that he effected a great advance in this part of the national administration.

The Minister of the Interior for Bavaria supplied me with all the laws and statistics relating to the educational institutions of the country. The laws have been most carefully compiled and codified; and perhaps there is no country in Europe, which possesses such an admirable and minutely considered series of enactments on the subject of national education.

The statistics, with which the Minister furnished me show, that, in 1846, there were in the kingdom of Bavaria, for a population little more than double that of our own metropolis, a much more effective system of national education, and much more perfect means for the education of the people, than we have in England and Wales.

In 1846, the population of Bavaria was 4,440,000, and for this there were —

8 normal colleges for the education of teachers for the elementary schools;

696 students in the normal colleges, who were being educated as teachers;

7353 schools (many of them containing as many as *ten* class-rooms and ten teachers);

8978 classes open on Fridays and Sundays, for young people attending the manufactories, and for men and women desirous of improving themselves in any particular branch of instruction;

556,239 scholars of both sexes attending the schools;

565,876 persons of both sexes attending the Sunday and Friday classes;

8797 teachers, who have the management and direction of the schools and classes;

615 industrial schools, where some particular art is taught;

2517 teachers of the industrial schools;

85,681 persons attending the industrial schools.

These statistics give the following results; that, in 1846, exclusive of the number of persons attending the Sunday and Friday classes, and the industrial schools, about 1 person out of every 7 of the population was attending a daily school; that there was 1 normal college for every 555,000; 1 school for every 603, and 1 teacher for every 508 persons in the kingdom.

In the neigbouring kingdom of Wirtemberg, in 1846, the population was 1,600,000; and of this population, 1 in every 6 was attending a school conducted by a learned teacher.

Three normal colleges had been founded; two for the education of Protestant teachers, and one for the education of Romanist teachers. There were in this small kingdom, not containing so many inhabitants as London, 3201 teachers, or 1 teacher for every 500 inhabitants. All the parents in the kingdom are *obliged* to educate their children either at home, or at some school from their sixth to their fourteenth year, and afterwards to send them to the Sunday schools, until the completion of their eighteenth year.

I travelled through the kingdom of Wirtemberg from Ulm to a town in the interior, by night. My companions in the eilwagen, or diligence, were an Oxford Fellow, a German, and a Frenchman. The subject of our conversation, during one part of the night, was, the efforts of the Germany governments and people to educate the children of their poor. The Oxford Fellow would not credit the account I gave him of these efforts, and affected, moreover, to laugh at them as useless and chimerical. I saw it would be impossible to make a convert of him by argument, and so, to save words, I ended the conversation by saying, "Well, if you are ever in the streets of a German town between eight and nine o'clock, or between twelve and one o'clock, in the morning, observe what is then going on, and remember what I told you."

The next morning it so happened, that we stopped, about eight o'clock, to change horses, in a small town, about half way between Ulm and Stuttgard. It was just before the primary schools commenced their morning's work. All the children were on their way to their respective classes. I made the "Fellow" get out of the diligence, and regard what was going on in the streets at that early hour.

The street, in which we had drawn up, was full of clean, neatly-dressed children, each carrying a small bag of books in his hand, or a little goatskin knapsack full of books on his back. There were no rags, and no unseemly patched and darned clothes. The little girls were neat, their hair was dressed with a great deal of taste, their frocks were clean and tastefully made. Their appearance would have led a stranger to imagine, that they were the children of parents belonging to the middle classes of society. I said to my companion, — "These orderly, clean, and respectable-looking children are, many of them, the sons and daughters of the poorest artizans and labourers." In England they would have been the "ragged-school children," or the squalid players in the gutters and back alleys. There there was no perceptible difference between the children of the poorest labourer and the children of the shopkeeper or rich parent. They all looked equally clean, respectable, polite, and intelligent. I said to the Fellow, "Are you convinced now?" He turned to me and answered, "Yes, yes; this is, indeed, a very interesting and very curious sight. I do not any longer doubt the accuracy of all you told me last night. It is certainly very remarkable." That ten minutes taught my companion more, than he would have learned by days of argument.

The reflection, to which it leads every beholder, is, "are all the children of Germany like these? Is there no class of children in Germany like those, which grow up in the gutters and alleys of our English towns? No wonder then, if this be so, that there is so much less pauperism in Germany than in England, and that the poor are so much more prosperous, virtuous, and happy than our own."

To give an idea of the liberal scale, on which the

teachers' training colleges in Wirtemberg are regulated, I shall give the list of the professors and teachers attached to the colleges at Esslingen and Nurtingen; and the subjects of education taught in them.

I. The number of professors and teachers at the teachers' college at Esslingen in Wirtemberg, are—

1 Director, who officiates also as first Professor;
3 Professors of the Sciences;
1 Professor of Music;
2 Teachers;
1 Assistant for the Musical Professor;
1 Teacher of the Jewish religion (he conducts the dogmatical education of the Jewish students);
1 Teacher of Music for the model practising school attached to the College;
1 Treasurer and Accountant for the College;
1 Physician for the College;

The number of students at this college was eighty.

II. Number of professors and teachers at the normal college at Nurtingen, in Wirtemberg:—

1 Director, who acts as first Professor;
1 Professor of the Sciences;
2 Head Teachers;
2 Assistant Teachers;
1 Teacher of Music;
1 Teacher of Music, for the model school attached to the College;
1 Treasurer and Accountant;
1 Physician for the College.

The number of students in this college was eighty.

THE SUBJECTS OF INSTRUCTION in the teachers' colleges of Wirtemberg, are as follows: —

Religion;
Moral Philosophy;
German Language;
History — (General, German, and Scriptural),
Arithmetic;
Algebra;
Plane Geometry;
Logic;
The Principles of Natural History;
Physical Geography;
The Philosophy of the Human Mind;
Pedagogy;
Practice in Teaching;
Theory of Music;
The Piano-forte and Organ;
Chanting and Singing.

I beg my readers to look at these lists, and compare the efforts made by a small province of Germany not containing so many inhabitants as London, with those made by us; when the numbers of our working population are, like our commerce, increasing with such an astonishing rapidity.

The educational laws of Wirtemberg require the parishes to support, for every 90 children, one teacher; for more than 90 children, two teachers; for more than 180 children, three teachers; for more than 270 children, four teachers; and so on in like proportion.

If a country parish is very poor it is allowed, on proof of its inability to find funds for the support of the required number of teachers, to diminish the number, on two conditions; viz.: —

1st, That very able men are selected; and

2ndly, That one teacher is provided for every 120 children.

From the kingdom of Wirtemberg, I traveiled into the Grand Duchy of Baden, and as soon as I arrived in Carlsruhe, I put myself in communication with the director and professors of the Protestant teachers' college, which had been founded in the town, and through their kindness, I heard and saw a great deal of the educational institutions of the kingdom.

A law has been passed and is universally and stringently enforced in this, as in each of the other German states, regulating all the minutiæ of a great and perfect system of national education.

In every primary school of the country the following subjects at least *must* be taught: —

Religion;

German Language;

Writing;

Arithmetic;

Singing;

Drawing wherever practicable;

The Elements of Natural History;

Physical Geography, History, Geometry, and Gardening, and the art of taking care of the Health.

But besides these primary schools, three admirable kind of classes are held in the school-houses of this Duchy. A law was passed some years since, which enacted, that evening classes should be held twice a week during the winter, in every village and town; where young persons, who have completed their fourteenth year, and have left the primary school, may continue their studies in different subjects of instruction.

Sunday classes are also held every Sunday morning, in the class-rooms of the primary schools, which all young people who have completed the primary school course, are *obliged* to attend, in the towns for two years, and in the villages for three years, after leaving the primary schools.

The other kind of class is opened in all the school-buildings of the Duchy of Baden, both in the towns and in the country parishes, every afternoon, after the ordinary afternoon school.

These latter are the so-called "Industrial Classes," where the girls are taught to sew and knit. Similar classes are opened every afternoon in the primary schools throughout Germany; but as they have been more fully considered and regulated in the Duchy of Baden than elsewhere, I shall here give a short account of them.

Throughout Germany, as a general rule, to which there are however many exceptions, the girls are taught by men and not by women; and are often educated in the same class-rooms with the boys. In the towns, however, where the command of greater funds enables the school-committees to support larger school-houses, with a greater number of separate class-rooms and teachers; four or five class-rooms are often devoted to the exclusive use of the girls, and four or five others to that of the boys; and each of these is put under the care of a master. I have mentioned above, in my accounts of Prussian education, why masters are generally preferred to mistresses, even for the girls.

These two customs, however, render it impossible to teach the girls the useful, and to most of them the absolutely necessary, arts of sewing, knitting, &c. during the ordinary school-hours. The so-called industrial classes have, therefore, been instituted to supply this deficiency.

In all cases, where the teachers of the girls are men and not women, the school-committees are obliged by law, to engage respectable women to attend the schools for an hour or an hour and a half every afternoon, after the boys have left; in order to instruct the girls in all the mysteries of stitching, hemming, darning, gown and shirt making, knitting, &c. The inspectors are required to give a public account of the state and progress of these, as well as of all the other classes.

Sometimes the girls bring sewing from home with them —something which their mothers require for household use, or some clothes to make up for themselves or their relations; but when their mothers have nothing to send with them, the school-committees are required by law to provide them with materials, &c.

In the Duchy of Baden this industrial teaching is gratuitous. No school-fees are paid for it by the children. The whole expenses are defrayed by the school-committees. All the girls are obliged to attend these classes daily, from the completion of their eleventh year. All the girls of Germany are growing up reasonable and intelligent creatures, fit companions for the men, and instructed in the useful arts, which are needed to make them economical, tidy, and respectable housewives. How different this to the condition of the poor little girls, who are growing in all the immorality and neglect of our crowded streets!

In the words of the law of Baden: "The object of the schools for the people is, out of the child to raise up an intelligent and religious mannered man, and to instruct him in all the knowledge, which is useful to, or necessary for a member of the society of citizens.

"The instruction given in the people's schools must be so ordered, that whilst it is always elementary in its character, it may be at the same time (geistbildend), such as will tend to develope the powers and moral perceptions of the minds of the children.

"The scholar must not be merely mechanically taught, but he must be awoke to attentive observation, and to a capability of self-knowledge, self-government, and continued self-improvement. The memory is not to be merely mechanically exercised, but to be kept subservient to the intellectual faculties and moral feelings.

"The knowledge, which is imparted to the scholar, must not be taught him merely by way of rote, but the explanation of compound facts must be given him, wherever it is possible.

"The character of the school instruction should be synthetical. It should begin by teaching the simplest results of experience, and should proceed afterwards to the facts and knowledge, based upon a union of these simple elements." *

* See Das höhere und niedere Studien Wesen in Grossherzogthume Baden, p. 20.

Once every half year, in the Duchy of Baden, each school is publicly examined. At an appointed day, just before the Midsummer and Christmas holidays, the inspector of the district, in which the village or town is situated, goes down and examines the children in the presence of the school-committee, and of the people of the neighbourhood. But in addition to these fixed visits, each inspector is required to pay at least one visit each year to every school in his district, without giving the teacher notice before-hand; and, on his arrival, to hold another public examination in presence of the school-committee. The knowledge, that the inspector may arrive any day, keeps the teachers on the alert, that the school may be found in order, that the children may be found clean, and respectably dressed, and that nothing may betray carelessness or inattention on their parts.

The German teacher never knows when his school may be visited by one of the numerous inspectors. The religious ministers visit it almost daily; the union inspectors two or three times a year; the county magistrates once or twice a year; and the special messenger of the Minister of Education once in every one or two years.

Of most of these visits, no previous notice is given; so that the teacher never knows from hour to hour, when he shall be visited, or when his proceedings will be examined into and criticised. He, consequently, keeps his class-room and his class always in just a condition, as he knows would meet with the approbation of his superiors. Even if he be a naturally indolent or careless man, he is effectually prevented by these means from giving way to either indolence or carelessness; while the hope of pleasing those, who have the power of advancing him in his profession, stimulates him constantly to extraordinary efforts.

By the law of the Duchy of Baden, if the number of children in a village school exceed 120, there must be *two* teachers; if it exceed 240, there must be *three* teachers; and if it exceed 390, there must be at least *four* teachers appointed.

Each teacher must be provided with a separate class-room, and no teacher may instruct more than seventy children in the same class.

Several very important regulations have been put in force by the Baden Chambers, relative to children whose parents wish to employ them in factories. They are as follows: —

No child may be employed in any manual occupation, until it has completed its ELEVENTH year; nor may any child, even at the completion of its eleventh year, be employed in a factory, or in an industrial occupation, unless it then attends the so-called "*Factory Schools.*"

These schools correspond with those of Prussia, which I have described above, as far as their general constitution is concerned; so that I shall not do more than mention here a few special regulations affecting the Baden "Factory Schools."

The laws of the Duchy of Baden prescribe, that in the "Factory Schools" —

"No greater number of children than seventy may ever be educated together at the same time.

"The secular education given in them, must correspond to that prescribed by law, for the primary schools in general.

"No person may be selected, as a teacher of one of these schools, who has not obtained a diploma from the committee of public examiners for the Duchy.

"Each child attending a factory must receive, at least, two hours' instruction in the factory school.

"The hours of instruction should precede the morning and afternoon's working hours; but where this is impossible, an hour's relaxation must intervene between the hours of labour and the commencement of the hours of study.

"In the middle of the above-mentioned morning and afternoon working hours, the children must be allowed to take a quarter of an hour's exercise outside the mill, and in the middle of the day, there must be an interval of a full hour, between the morning and the afternoon working hours.

"Young people under the age of fifteen, are not to be employed more than twelve hours a day in the factory, and factory school together.

"Such young people are not to be employed in labour, before five o'clock in the morning, nor after five in the evening, nor on Sundays or holidays.

"All masters of factories, who employ young people under the age of fifteen, must render periodical lists of the children employed by them; giving the names, ages, places of residence, and names of the parents of such children.

"Any infringement of any of the above regulations will render the manufacturer offending liable to fines, the amount of which is fixed by law.

"The county magistrates are charged with the strenuous enforcement of these regulations.

"All the expenses of the education of the children attending a factory before the completion of their fourteenth year, must be borne by the owner of the factory which they attend."

Since 1830, the school-buildings and apparatus of the Duchy of Baden have been very much improved. At present, there is, perhaps, no country in Germany where the material of education is so perfect.

Herr Lohrer, one of the professors in the normal college at Carlsruhe, assured me, that the finest buildings, in the villages and small towns of the Duchy of Baden, were almost universally the school-houses.

No school-room may now be built less than ten feet in height, or allowing less than six square feet to each scholar.

I requested Herr Lohrer to show me the worst school-building in Carlsruhe. He took me to see one, which was built before the new regulations were put into force, and which he assured me was the poorest in the city.

It contained four large class-rooms, each ten feet high, by about twenty feet square, and well fitted up with rows of parallel desks and forms, black boards, maps, &c.

I afterwards visited one of the best. It also contained four class-rooms. They were loftier, more spacious and better lighted, than those in the former school. In this latter building, the class-rooms occupied the ground and first floors, while above them, were the apartments of the teachers. The class-rooms were very light, clean, and well-furnished with parallel desks and forms, maps, books, diagrams, black boards, &c.

I asked Herr Lohrer, whether any difficulty was experienced, in making the parents send their children to school regularly every day. His answer, which I took down directly afterwards, was in these words: —

"If a peasantry, totally unenlightened, and, therefore, destitute of all real appreciation of the benefits to be derived from education, are compelled by law to send their children to school every day, it is reasonable to suppose that they will kick against such regulations; but if the parents themselves, as with us, have been educated, and have experienced the benefits of instruction, you may rest assured, that they will be only too glad to second the efforts of the government to enforce such regulations. With us, the parents themselves have been educated and are only too glad to send their children to school. It is only now and then in the summer months, when there is a good deal of field labour, that the parents show any disposition to keep their children at home."

There are THREE large normal colleges for the education of teachers, in the Duchy of Baden. One of them is for the education of the teachers of the Protestant schools, and contains seventy-six students, six of whom are Jews; and the other two are for the education of Romanist teachers, and contain respectively eighty-five and eighty students.

These institutions are, like those of the rest of Germany, liberal alike in their endowment and in the education given in them. The teachers, who leave their walls after three years' residence there, to take the management of the peasant schools, are fit, from their character and acquirements, to educate the richer classes of any country.

I visited one of these colleges at Carlsruhe, and spent several days most profitably in the lecture-rooms and in the company of its professors; but as it corresponds in all its leading features with those I have described before, I shall not here say more of it.

The population of the Grand Duchy of Baden amounted in 1843 to 1,335,200, of whom about 900,000 were Roman Catholics and 23,000 Jews.

In 1843, there were in the Duchy, —

	582	Primary schools taught by Protestant teachers.
	1349	Primary schools taught by Romanist teachers.
	40	Primary schools taught by Jewish teachers.
Total	1971	Primary schools.

In 1843, there was, in the Duchy of Baden, about one primary school to every 677 inhabitants, of which schools, it is to be remembered, that those situated in the town contain, from four to six classes, each presided over by a learned professor.

In 1841, the population of the Duchy was 1,300,000, that is, about one-third less than the population of

London; and in that year, the duchy contained the following educational institutions: —

Primary schools	Protestant	586
	Romanist	1330
	Jewish	40
	Total	1956

Schools designed for girls exclusively	8
Normal Colleges for the education of teachers	8
Latin schools, or schools expressly designed for giving a classical education	12
Superior primary schools, where the children of shopkeepers and of the poorer part of the middle classes and the most promising of the children of the peasantry continue their education, after leaving the primary schools, and where they study the elements of the sciences and the rudiments of the classics	12
Schools, where poor boys who wish to become teachers and to enter the Normal Colleges, are educated	7
Gymnasia, or schools for the richer classes, where the children of the gentry are educated in Hebrew, the classics, the modern languages, science, mathematics, history, geography, rhetoric, drawing, singing, and religion	10
School for the blind	1
School for the deaf	1
School of practical science	1
Universities	2
Military school	1
Veterinary school	1
Seminary for the education of Roman Catholic priests	1
Several industrial schools.	

There is one part of the educational regulations of the Duchy of Baden, which deserves particular notice. It is that, which relates to the periodical meetings of all the teachers of a union.

In describing the educational regulations of Prussia, I showed the object and usefulness of periodical assemblies of great bodies of teachers in one place. I shall now show, how the teachers' conferences are regulated in the Duchy of Baden.

In each union (using the word "union" here, as I have hitherto employed it, viz., to designate the German Kreis), the union inspector is obliged, every September, *i. e.*, during the holidays, to send notices to every teacher in his district, to assemble at a place and time specified in the notice.

Every teacher, who receives the notice, is required by law to assemble at the place and time therein mentioned.

Notices are sent also to each of the religious ministers of the union, that those, who are able, may meet the teachers. The educational magistrate of the county, or some one representing him, is also always at the meeting.

The notices are sent round as early as the month of May, preceding the meeting. The inspector, when he issues them, sends at the same time to each teacher in his district, one or two questions on some point, connected either with the practice, or the methods of teaching, or with some of the various subjects of instruction, and upon which there has been some difference of opinion or practice.

Each teacher is required to send to the inspector an answer to these questions by the month of August.

When the inspector has received these answers, he reads them carefully through, and writes a short and concise criticism of each answer, and reads it to the teachers when assembled at the conference.

After the inspector has read the answers and criticisms to the meeting, the teachers proceed to debate the subject among themselves, rising one after another and addressing the meeting upon it, by turn.

When this debate is concluded, three teachers, who had been chosen by the previous meeting, are then called upon to instruct a class of children before the rest of the assembly, in different branches of instruction. Their performances are then criticised and discussed by the others, who had been looking on as spectators.

This plan serves two important ends: —

1st. It stimulates each of the teachers to aim at continual self-improvement; in order that he may excel his competitors at the yearly meetings, and prove himself worthy of recommendation by the inspector to the more lucrative situations, as they fall vacant, and also that he may win the respect and approval of his professional brethren.

2ndly. It obliges the teachers to *think* over the various methods of instruction; to consider how they may teach in the most effective manner; to avoid bad and slothful habits with their scholars, and to observe how best to catch and retain the attention of their scholars, and how most effectually to interest them in the subjects of instruction.

At these meetings, also, the teachers arrange the affairs of their book-clubs. Every teacher in each union is a member of the teachers' union book-club. They each pay a small sum monthly, and with the sum thus collected, a few books are purchased and sent round from one to another. At the September meetings, they choose the treasurer of their book-club, and determine what books are to be purchased.

Before the meeting is dissolved, a short account of all the proceedings is drawn up; and is then signed by the inspector, the magistrate present at the meeting, and all the teachers, and forwarded to the chief magistrate of the county, in which the union is situated.

The expenses of each teacher, incurred by attending these yearly conferences, are defrayed by the state.

CHAP. XII.

EDUCATION OF THE POOR IN THE AUSTRIAN EMPIRE.

It is very remarkable to observe, what gigantic efforts the late despotic government of Austria made to educate the poorest classes of its citizens. True it is, that neither the educational system nor the character of the education given in the schools was nearly so liberal, as those of Germany; but still, as compared with our own efforts, those of Austria deserve great commendation.

In that great empire, where, until only a few months since, there was literally no such thing as political liberty known; where the press could not publish any political article whatever; and where its voice, in almost every other matter, was literally stopped; where people could not move from one town to another without obtaining a special passport; where the people had no representation, no share in the government of the empire, and no interest in the soil; where some of the worst features of the feudal system still survived; where there was no jury, no open courts of justice, and no greater security for property, personal freedom, or life, than the will of the minister or his subordinates; where offenders against the tyranny often disappeared, and were cut off from all their friends, without a trace of their place of imprisonment being left behind; where all thoughts of gaining liberty had long been suppressed by the presence of an army of 400,000 soldiers; and where the secrets of every family were violated by a hideous system of espionage, rivalling in its villany that of Fouché under Napoleon; in this empire, a system of education has been for many years in operation, which, in its vastness and in its effects, far exceeds the efforts made in our country.

It is a fact, of which the old government of Austria may well be proud, that throughout the vast territorial extent of that part of this immense empire, which is composed of the regal province of Bohemia, a part of Poland, the great province of Moravia, the ancient territories of Styria and Illyria, the provinces of Dalmatia, Carynthia, and Carniola, the Duchies of Upper and Lower Austria, and the Tyrol; varying as the people of these provinces do, in character, habits, and religion, composed as they are of Romanists and Lutherans, Moravians, Greeks, Jews, and Unitarians; every child between the ages of six and ten, and almost every child between the ages of six and thirteen, is receiving daily instruction in the truths of Revelation and science, and in the duties of a citizen and a man. I shall show very briefly, how this great result has been obtained.

Every parent then, in the Austrian Empire, is obliged by law, to satisfactorily prove to the inspector of the district, in which he resides, that he is either educating his children, who are between the ages of six and twelve, at home, in an efficient manner, or that he sends them to some school.

The law requires, that every child throughout the empire, except in the manufacturing districts, shall be educated, either in a school or at home, from the completion of its fifth to the completion of its twelfth years. The parent may educate it as much longer as he pleases, but he is obliged to educate it to the completion of its twelfth year, whether he pleases or not.

In the manufacturing districts, the law prevents any child being taken from school and sent into a manufactory, before the completion of its ninth year. At this age, it may enter a manufactory, but from that time, until the completion of its twelfth year, it is obliged, by law, to attend the classes opened in all schools in the manufacturing districts, on Friday evenings and on Sunday mornings.

Accurate registers of all the children, between the ages of six and twelve, are kept in each parish, and a copy is furnished to each teacher, giving him the name, address, and age of every child, who ought to be regularly attending his classes. The teachers note down daily, in these lists, the attendance or non-attendance of each child who ought to be present. These lists, thus entered up, are forwarded once every year to the magistrate of the parish, with a table annexed, showing the number of times each child has been absent during the year. If the attendance of any child has been very irregular, and the parent cannot satisfactorily explain such irregularity, the latter is fined by the magistrate.

Even after the completion of the twelfth year, young people are not exempted in the Austrian Empire from school attendance. From that time, until the completion of their fifteenth year, they are still obliged to attend the classes, which are opened in every school, on the Friday evenings and on the Sunday mornings. So that it may be said, that nearly all the young people of Austria between the ages of six and fifteen, are receiving education in the parochial or town schools of the Empire. The only children exempted from the operation of the above law, are children, who regularly attend the higher schools, or are educated at home until the end of their fifteenth year.

Heavy fines are by law imposed on parents, who omit, either to send their children to one of the higher schools, or to the evening classes, or to educate them at home, until the completion of their fifteenth year.

The children are not instructed as many hours a day in Austria, as in Germany. In the town schools, in each of which there are several distinct class-rooms and teachers, the children are instructed four hours a day; but in those villages, where there is only one teacher and one class-room, the whole of the children are divided into two sections, — one of which attends the school three hours every morning, whilst the other, which generally contains the younger part of the village children, attends the school two hours every afternoon.

They understand education too well in Austria to attempt to educate two classes in the same room and at the same time, as we do in England, and the consequence is, that the children often learn much more in Austria in three hours, than they do here in the whole day. I often used to think, how a German teacher would laugh, if he could look into one of our crowded school-rooms, where four or five classes, and sometimes between 200 and 300 children are pretending to learn, and are shouting together, confusing and confused.

The great task of supplying all the parishes and towns of Austria with school-buildings, books, and apparatus, has been accomplished, despite all the difficulties arising from the great number of their religious parties and from the ascendency and multitude of the Romanist priesthood.

I shall show how it has been effected.

The political division of the country is exactly similar to that of Prussia; save, that there is an additional division called the school district, of which I shall speak immediately, and that, until the late revolution, the county magistrates were much less independent than those of Prussia, and were much more the creatures of the central power.

In each parish of the Austrian Empire, whose population is WHOLLY Romanist, the superintendence and direction of the parochial schools are committed to one of the priests, who is chosen and appointed by the parochial magistrates, in conjunction with the district overseer, of whom I shall speak presently. This religious minister is, in these cases, empowered and required by law to superintend and direct the religious and the secular instruction given in the schools; to take care that no person is appointed teacher, who is not a man of religious principles and of correct habits; to enforce the regular attendance of all the children of his parish; to stimulate their industry, and to report on the progress of the schools, teachers, and scholars to the overseers of the school district, in which the parish is situated.

Austria is divided into what are called SCHOOL-DISTRICTS. These divisions are less than the unions or kreis; but greater than the parishes. Each union contains several school-districts, and each school-district several parishes.

In each district, in which there are any Romanists, one of the priests is selected by the county magistrates as "school overseer," and to him is entrusted, the inspection, direction, and superintendence of the education of all the children of the Romanist parents residing in his district.

I shall show hereafter, to whom the direction of the education of children of Protestants is entrusted.

The law requires every "school overseer," after his appointment, to take care: —

1st. That his district is supplied with a sufficient number of school-buildings; and for this end, he is empowered, in conjunction with the village or town magistrates, to levy a school-rate upon the householders of his district.

2dly. That all the new school-buildings, which are erected from time to time in his district, are built in healthy situations, not near any noisy workshops, or any swamp or bad smells; that the class-rooms are built according to the plans, which have been prescribed by Government; that the class-rooms are well provided with desks, forms, writing-boards, maps, and all necessary school apparatus.

3dly. That the school-buildings are kept in good

repair, well and frequently whitewashed, and well warmed and lighted.

4thly. That a good and suitable house is provided for the teachers and their families, and that it is kept in a good condition and fit for their use.

5thly. That the *curé* of each parish regularly inspects his school; that he watches the conduct and character of the teacher; that he examines the scholars frequently; and that he aids the teacher by his counsel, advice, and assistance.

6thly. That the parishioners send all their children, who are between the ages of six and twelve, to school regularly, and that they pay the weekly school-fees in a regular manner.

7thly. That each parochial magistrate is zealous, in enforcing a regular school attendance, in supporting the teachers, and in protecting them from the least disrespectful treatment.

8thly. That regular periodical reports of the state and progress of the schools in his district are forwarded to the county educational magistrates; who, in their turn, are required to forward a general report of the progress of education in the whole county to the Minister of Education in Vienna.

By these means the government in Vienna is informed every year of the actual state and progress of education, throughout every parish of their great empire; of the wants and difficulties of those districts which require assistance; of the results of particular experiments in particular schools, in the remotest provinces; and of the actual number of children in each county, who have not attended the classes with sufficient regularity.

From this brief abstract, it will be seen, that the clergy have a much greater share in the direction of primary education in Austria than in the rest of Germany. Yet, although the clergy do really direct the educational affairs of the different school districts throughout the empire, they are by no means left at liberty to direct that education exactly as they please. The clergy are not empowered to prescribe how much, or how little, secular instruction shall be imparted in the schools; or how the schools shall be built and furnished; or what books shall be used in them. All these matters are regulated by minutely considered laws.

The clerical overseers are not the managers of the schools; they are only the superintendents commissioned and obliged to execute the mandates of the central government, and to foster and watch over the religious character of the school instruction.

Still the Austrian system, although so much better than doing nothing, is very unsatisfactory. It deprives the people of any real share in the management of the schools, and therefore of much of that interest, which they would otherwise feel in their prosperity. It confides the superintendence of the secular education of Romanists to a set of men, who are by no means necessarily interested in promoting it, and it renders it but too likely, that the schools are often employed as instruments of superstition and tyranny.

The most interesting and satisfactory feature of the Austrian system is, the great liberality, with which the government, although so stanch an adherent and supporter of the Romanist priesthood, has treated the religious parties, who differ from itself in their religious dogmas. It has been entirely owing to this liberality, that neither the great number of the sects in Austria, nor the great difference of their religious tenets, have hindered the work of the education of the poor throughout the empire. Here, as elsewhere, it has been demonstrated, that such difficulties may easily be overcome, when a government understands, how to raise the nation in civilisation, and wishes earnestly to do so.

In those parishes of the Austrian empire, where there are any dissenters from the Romanist Church, the education of their children is not directed by the priests, but is committed to the care of the dissenting ministers. These latter are empowered and required by government, to provide for, to watch over, and to promote the education of the children of their own sects, in the same manner, as the priests are required to do for the education of their children.

In each county, a dissenting minister is chosen by the magistrates, as the general superintendent and inspector of the education of all the dissenters of his county. This minister, accompanied by one of the county magistrates, is required to visit and inspect all the dissenting schools in his county, at least once in every year, and to report thereon to the county magistrates. He is also required and empowered to enforce the building of schools in districts inhabited by dissenters alone, but unsupplied with schools; to oblige all the dissenters of his county, either to send their children to some school, or to educate them efficiently at home; to punish them, when they neglect to conform to the educational regulations; to take care that the children of dissenters, who attend Romanist schools, receive regular religious instruction from some minister of their own sect; and to oblige the dissenting ministers to give religious education to the children of their own sect.

In those parishes, where dissenters reside, but where there is only a Romanist school, the dissenters are obliged, either to educate their children at home, or to send them to the school; and the committee and managers of the school are obliged to receive them into the classes of the school, to give them education in all the subjects of secular instruction, and to allow them to leave the school during the hours, when religious instruction is given to the Romanist children.

To facilitate the carrying out of these liberal and excellent regulations, a law has been made, that, in schools containing members of different religious sects, the religious instruction must be always given either in the first or last of the daily school hours; in order, that the children of parents, who profess religious dogmas different to those of the teacher, may easily, and without disturbing any class of secular instruction, or running any risk of missing any part of such instruction, absent themselves from the school.

In those districts, where there is no Romanist school, but only a Protestant one, arrangements such as those I have mentioned, as framed for the benefit of dissenters, are put into force for the benefit of the Romanists. But in each case, the law is very strict, in requiring the inspectors of the minority to see, that the children who thus absent themselves from the religious lessons given in the schools, receive a sound religious education from their own religious ministers.

Whenever the minority of any parish, whether Romanists, Protestants, or Jews, desire to establish a separate school for their children, and to support a teacher of their own denomination, they are at liberty to separate from the majority, and to provide alone for the education of their children; but, by one means or another, each parish is obliged to provide for the education of *all* its children, and each householder to contribute his share of the funds necessary for this purpose; and, whether separate or mixed schools are established, all are made subject to public inspection, so that the public may know the real character of each establishment; that no demoralising school, or inefficient or immoral teacher, may be allowed to exercise a baneful influence upon the youth of the empire; and that the instruction in useful and civilising knowledge may not be sacrificed in any degree to the dogmatical teaching of the different sects.

In each of the town primary schools of Austria, there are generally several class-rooms, and an equal number of teachers; in the villages, it is not often, that the school-committees can afford to bear the expense of more than one teacher.

The law requires the head teacher of each school, in conjunction with the religious minister of the majority of the scholars, who frequent the school, to hold, at stated periods, a public examination of the school, to which the school-committee and the parents of the scholars are invited. The scholars are then examined in all the subjects of instruction, and the parents are enabled to judge for themselves, what progress the scholars have made since the last examination, and whether the teacher has instructed them efficiently; the teacher is stimulated to exert himself, in order that the school authorities may not be dissatisfied with the progress of the children; and the scholars themselves to work industriously, in order to avoid being disgraced in the eyes of their acquaintances and neighbours. When the examinations are over, prizes are publicly distributed to those who have the most distinguished themselves.

Several very interesting and instructive laws have been made concerning the school-buildings, among which are the following: —

"Wherever, on account of the numbers of the children, several teachers are required, a separate class-room must be provided in the school-building for each teacher.

"As it is important, that the scholars should not be disturbed in their studies, by the domestic employments of the wife, children, or servants of the teacher, and that the class-rooms should never be used for any other purpose than teaching, the house of the teacher must always be separated from the school-house.

" The class-rooms must be kept well warmed and lighted, and must be provided with double windows, so as to render them sufficiently warm in winter.

" The class-rooms must be furnished with desks and forms. These latter must not be too narrow or too high, to allow of the scholars sitting comfortably upon them; and the former must be furnished with places, in which the scholars can put their slates, books, &c.

" The desks and forms must allow, in length, 5 feet 2 inches for three scholars, 7 feet for four scholars, 8 feet 9 inches for five scholars, and 10 feet 6 inches for six scholars; and in breadth, 2 feet 2 inches for each scholar. The space between two rows of desks must be 2 feet 6 inches.

" A great black-painted board for copies and dictation exercises, and for arithmetical exercise and remarks, must be put up in a light part of the class-room opposite the scholars' desks. At one side of this board the teacher's desk and seat must be placed, raised a little above the floor of the class-room, so that he may be able to see all his scholars easily.

" The plan of the daily studies and a copy of the school regulations must, where possible, be framed and hung up in a convenient place, on the walls of the class-room.

" A chest must be provided to contain the books, &c. of the poor children, to whom these things are given gratuitously, and two chairs must be kept in each class-room for the use of the inspector, clergyman, and civil magistrates, on their visits to the school.

" The class-room must not be used for any other purpose than instruction.

" The committee must provide for the teacher and his family a separate, warm, and convenient parlour, a room for his children, a kitchen with an oven for cooking, a bed-room, and a place for his fuel.

" An additional chamber must be provided for each of the assistant teachers.

" If any of these regulations are not observed, the overseer of the district must communicate with the county magistrates, and take all necessary measures for supplying the deficiency, in as cheap a manner as possible.

" Where new school-buildings are required, the local authorities must take care, that a good site is selected, on a dry ground and in a dry place, not near water, nor in a dark place, nor in the neighbourhood of any noisy business; but in a healthy, pleasant, and quiet situation, and as near as possible to the centre of the district, for which the school is intended.

" The plans of every school-house must be laid before the county magistrates, and their sanction must be obtained, before the building may be commenced.

" Each class-room, for between 40 and 50 scholars, must be 21 feet long, and 18 feet broad; and for between 50 and 60 scholars, 23 feet long, 18 feet broad, and at least 10 feet high. The ground-floor rooms must be raised a little height above the ground, that the floors may be dry; the windows must be raised so high above the floor, that the scholars may not be able to see through them and be disturbed by what passes outside. The teacher's desk must face the children, and be placed, so that the light may fall on his left side.

"In every new school-house, which is built after the issuing of these laws, and which is to contain only one class-room, a second small room must be built, in which instruction in sewing and in spinning may be given, and in which accidental business, which would distract the attention of the scholars, if transacted in the class-room, may be attended to."

Several very important regulations have also been made, relating to the part, which the great landed proprietors are required to take in the erection and furnishing of the school-buildings, and in the payment of the teachers for the poor on their estates. It would occupy too much space to enumerate them all; but some of them are too important and too instructive to be altogether omitted.

In Austria, as in England, great tracts of land belong to individuals, and many villages and small towns belong exclusively to one or two proprietors. *In these cases, the whole expense of educating the children of the peasants residing as labourers on these estates is imposed by law upon the landlords themselves.*

This is the very least that a country ought to do for the peasants, where the laws are so framed, as to encourage the accumulation of all the land in a few hands, and to prevent the peasants from becoming independent proprietors themselves. Throughout nearly the whole of western Europe, as I have already shown in the first chapter of this work, the majority of the peasants are themselves proprietors, and are generally very much better off, than the peasants of Austria and England, who are nothing but labourers on the soil of others. In the former countries, therefore, they have always, until the last year, paid for the education of their own children. But as the Austrian government has perceived, that a system like that of England and Austria, necessarily renders many of the peasants much poorer and much more unable to help themselves, than those of countries, where the opposite system prevails, they have, as a certain kind of recompense to the peasants living on the great territories of the feudal lords, made these latter provide almost all, and in certain cases, all the funds necessary for the education of the children of the peasants living on their lands.

The landlords are obliged, in these cases, to furnish all the materials necessary for the erection of the school-buildings; to give the land on which the buildings are to be erected; to provide, in most cases, all the interior furniture of the buildings and class-rooms; to pay a great proportion of the funds required to build the school, &c., and to regularly provide the fuel for warming the class-rooms and teachers' dwellings.

The regulations respecting the education of the teachers are not nearly so satisfactory, as those of Prussia and the other German states; but, as they are far in advance of what we have done, it will be instructive to mention them.

No person can officiate, even as an *assistant* teacher in Austria, until he has obtained a *certificate* of competency, and no one can officiate as a *head* teacher, until he has obtained a *diploma.*

To obtain a *certificate,* it is necessary for the candidate to pass an examination, conducted by the teachers of one of the superior schools. One of these examinations is held once a year, in one of the superior schools of each union, for the purpose of testing the capabilities of all candidates for the teachers' profession. If a young man is sufficiently well educated to pass the examination creditably, he receives a certificate, sealed with the seal of the school, where the examination is held, stamped with a legal stamp, and engrossed with the words—

"Fit to be an assistant teacher."

A young man who has gained such a certificate may then take a situation in a school as *assistant* teacher; but he cannot take a situation as *principal* teacher, until he has gained a diploma, of which I shall speak presently. Until a candidate has passed one of the above-mentioned examinations in a creditable manner, he is shut out altogether from the teachers' profession.

When a young man has obtained the above-mentioned certificate, and when he has officiated as assistant teacher for *at least* a year, and has completed the twentieth year of his age, he may then, *but not before,* apply for a teacher's diploma.

In order to obtain this *diploma,* the young man is obliged to obtain from the overseer, and from the civil authorities of the parish, and from the principal teacher of the school, in which he has officiated as assistant teacher, certificates of his efficiency in the management of a class of children, and in the art of instructing children; of his character; of his temper, and of his fitness to be a teacher. These certificates he is obliged to lay before the principal educational authorities of the province, in which he has been officiating as assistant teacher. After this is done, the educational authorities appoint a day for an examination of candidates, to which he is invited. This examination is a very searching one, and comprises all the subjects of elementary instruction. Unless the young man passes it, he cannot obtain a teacher's diploma. If he passes this second severe examination, he receives a formal stamped diploma, bearing the words —

"Worthy to be appointed teacher."

This diploma, thus obtained and endorsed, is a proof to all the world, that the owner is an able and an educated man, fit to be entrusted with the management of a school.

The examiners are obliged by law to be very strict in granting diplomas to none, but the ablest of the candidates.

The law also prescribes certain penalties for any individual, who ventures to officiate as teacher in Austria, without having obtained a diploma.

Many teachers in Austria belong to the clerical body. These are also, however, obliged to undergo similar examinations, and to obtain certificates of competence, before they may officiate as teachers in any school.

The following miscellaneous regulations of the Austrian government, with respect to the teachers and to the instruction to be given in the schools, are very admirable, and serve to show, how much attention they have paid to the subject of national education, and to even the minutiæ of the system.

The law prescribes, that

"The teacher of a primary school must be a person of good sense, having a good, clear pronunciation, good health, and a sound constitution.

"The teacher must not merely understand the science of pedagogy, but he must be able to practise it. In order that he may do this, he must not be satisfied with merely having obtained his diploma; he must afterwards seek to perfect his knowledge by the study of able and scientific works upon this science; he must make and note down observations on the results of different methods; he must not feel ashamed to learn from other teachers, or even from his own assistants; and he must attend to the remarks and advice of the inspectors.

"He must be careful to speak clearly and loud enough to be heard by all his class, when giving instruction.

"He must be careful not to neglect any of his scholars, by attending too exclusively to the more clever children.

"He must be particularly careful to make his scholars obedient, orderly, and quiet in their classes, industrious, modest, clean, and polite.

"He must never endure a lie, and must prevent tale-telling, teazing, and vexing of one scholar by another, buying, selling, and exchanging in school, eating during the hours of instruction, frequent going out of the class-room, careless sitting postures, and *concealment of the hands.*

"He must be most careful to prevent any unnecessary loitering in coming to school, or in returning home, all rough handling of the school-books, loud and unseemly shouting and screaming, and mingling of the boys and girls, &c.

"He must take care, that the children are clean; that they come to school with clean hands and faces, with cut nails, with combed hair, and with tidy clothes.

"He must warn the children not to drink, or to lie down upon the cold ground, when they are hot.

"He must warn the children against eating roots or berries, whose properties they do not know, and against playing near deep water, or in public streets.

"In winter he must take care, that the children shake the snow from their clothes and shoes outside the school door.

"He must send unhealthy children home again, and prevent them mingling with the others.

"He must take care, that the school-room is kept sufficiently warm; that it is well aired when the children are out, and that it is well cleaned every second day.

"In order to make the scholars industrious and obedient, the teacher must win the respect of his scholars: he cannot do this by a sullen, angry countenance, or by using the ruler, or by making a noise; but by evincing knowledge of his business, by command over himself, and by a manly, sensible, and *unchangeable* behaviour.

"If the teacher leaves his class-room often in the day, or is inattentive or careless in his manner of imparting instruction, or is lazy, impatient, or irritable, the consequence will be, that his scholars will be disorderly, and will gain little or no good from their school attendance.

"The teacher must guard against the extremes of both kindness and harshness; he must act like an affectionate, but sensible father; he must make a great distinction between his manner of reproving acts of mere childish carelessness, and actual sins; he must never employ severe punishments, as long as he can hope to succeed by milder means; and he must avoid anything like unfairness in his praises and punishments.

"The teacher must carefully avoid hastily resorting to the rod; he must never box a child's ears; or pull or pinch them; or pull its hair; or hit him on the head, or any tender part; or use any other instrument of punishment, than a rod or stick; and that only in cases of great faults. Even in these cases, this kind of punishment may only be administered after having obtained the consent of the overseer, and of the parents of the child, and in their presence.

"The teacher must take care to be polite and friendly to the parents of his scholars; if he is obliged to complain to any of them of their children, he must do it, without showing anything like personal irritation; he must never send his complaints to them by any of his scholars, or by third persons; for, by such means mistakes are easily made, and unkind feelings are often excited.

"If the teacher is obliged to speak severely to any one, he must be careful not to do so in the presence of his children.

"The teacher must not engage in any trade or

or business; he must not keep a shop, he must not play music at public festivities, and he must avoid all companies and places, which would be likely to throw any suspicion on his character, or to injure his reputation."

In order to protect and defend the teachers from ill-judged interference, and from the effects of personal prejudices, to encourage worthy and to check careless teachers, to stimulate the efforts of both teachers and scholars, and to foster and promote the improvement of all the materials of national education, a great system of public inspection has been established in Austria.

I mentioned, in the commencement of this chapter, how the school overseers are appointed, and what some of their duties are.

Each of these school overseers, throughout the whole empire, is obliged by law to visit all the primary schools in his district once every year. Each of them is required to divide all the schools in his district into two parts, and to visit one of these in the latter part of one year, and in the early part of the succeeding year, so as to see each school in spring and winter alternately.

The overseer is required to give public notice some time previously of his intention to visit any school, and of the day upon which he will publicly examine it.

The law *requires* the parochial magistrates, the religious minister, to whose sect the school belongs, and a committee of the householders of the parish, to be present at the examination, and imposes a penalty on any of these persons, who absents himself without satisfactory excuse. The overseer is required to write down the names of the absentees, in order that the magistrates may be informed, and may impose the legal fine to which their absence renders them liable.

The teacher is required by law to give all his children notice of the day, on which the examination will take place, and to order them all to attend at a certain hour. He is also required to bring the book, in which the daily absentees are marked down, the copy-books and exercises of the scholars, the monthly register of the way, in which each child has attended to his work, an account of the progress the classes have made in the several subjects of instruction, and any notes or observations he may have made in his note-book for the inspector. These several documents are laid before the overseer at the public examination, and are examined by him. The knowledge that this will be done stimulates both scholars and teachers, as each is as unwilling to be reproved for carelessness or incompetence, as he is anxious to be praised for industry and skill.

The law next directs each overseer—

1. To examine what character the teacher has borne in his neighbourhood; how he acts towards his scholars, and towards those who live about him; whether he teaches skilfully or not; what methods of teaching he pursues; whether he is industrious and zealous in his work, and whether he continues to aim at self-improvement.

2. To examine the registers of the school, and to observe, how often each child has been absent from the

classes; to observe the manners of the children in the classes and in the playground, the manner in which they answer the questions put to them, their demeanour to one another and to their teachers, their appearance, cleanliness, and the state of their health.

3. To observe what interest the parishioners and parents take in the state of the school, and in the education of their children; how far they assist the teacher to secure a regular attendance; what excuses they generally make for the occasional absences of their children; with what degree of respect they treat the teachers; and whether they pay the weekly school-pence regularly.

4. To observe the state of the school-buildings, whether they are built in a healthy locality, and after a good and reasonable plan; whether the class-rooms are dry and light; whether they are furnished with sufficient school-apparatus; and whether they are supplied with sufficient quantities of fuel for the daily consumption during winter.

5. Whether the religious ministers of the sect, to which the majority of the scholars belongs, visits and inspects the school-classes often; whether he treats the teachers in a wise and judicious manner; whether he uses his influence among the parents to secure a regular attendance at school; and whether he attempts to diminish any little misunderstandings between the teachers and parishioners, when any such arise.

6. Whether the civil magistrates are strict in punishing any infraction of the school regulations.

The law then proceeds to require, that as soon as the

overseer has examined the lists, &c. laid before him, he shall commence the examination. It is formally opened by a short prayer and a speech. After this the overseer examines the children, class after class, beginning with the first.

He first requires the children to read aloud something selected from their school-books, and then questions them about the subject matter of the exercise.

He selects some particular child to answer each question he asks, and does not allow the whole class to shout an answer to it simultaneously, so as to conceal the idleness and ignorance of some by the knowledge and ability of others.

The overseer then dictates something to the school, and requires them to write from his dictation. The scholars are then made to write a copy, and are afterwards examined in arithmetic and mental calculation.

The overseer is particularly required to observe, during the course of the examination, whether there are any scholars, who appear to have been neglected by the teachers, or whether the instruction has been bestowed equally upon all.

The law requires the overseer at the end of the examination, to read aloud to the whole meeting, the names of the twelve scholars, who in his opinion have made the greatest progress in their studies, or who have evidently been the most industrious; to praise them publicly for their industry and ability, and to encourage them and all the rest of the scholars to renewed exertion.

The overseer is next required to publicly reprove

any scholar, who has been very idle or negligent in his studies, or in his attendance, and then to urge the children to make fresh exertion to prepare for the next public examination.

After the examination is concluded, the overseer orders whatever repairs the school-buildings stand in need of, and whatever books and apparatus are required for the class-rooms. He then asks the parochial magistrates and clergy privately, if they have any fault to find with the teachers, and if they have, he examines into the cause of complaint, and acts between the parties as impartial judge. On the other hand, if the teachers have any cause of complaint against the parochial authorities, they state it to the overseer, and he, after examining into the matter, decides upon it as an arbitrator, and as a protector of the teachers.

I have no need to point out how these visits of the representative of the central governments stimulate all the teachers, children, and parishioners. Each is afraid to be found behindhand in the performance of his duties; and each is desirous to merit public praise for his efforts and success. The teacher is protected from neglect, insult, or injudicious interference, while he is at the same time kept under a wholesome check. His close connection with the emissary of the government of the empire, gives him a standing among his neighbours, and covers himself and his office with the respect of the people.

The Austrian government has indeed so strongly felt the importance of making the teachers respected, that one of the laws expressly requires the overseer to address the teacher at the public examinations, with the title of Mr. and Sir, and forbids the overseer to allow himself to treat the teacher with any undue familiarity or carelessness before his pupils.

Besides these wise enactments, a series of laws has been framed, by which a pension and livelihood is secured to every superannuated teacher, and to the orphans and widow of every deserving teacher, who dies in the public service. These enactments are for the most part similar to those, which I have already described as in force in Prussia.

By these means, the teachers are released from all anxiety about providing for the support of themselves in old age, or of their families in case of their own decease, and are, consequently, freed from any temptation to divert any of their thoughts from their school duties to mercantile, or money-making pursuits, and are enabled to devote the whole of their faculties, thoughts, and energies to the duties of their profession.

Besides these advantages, the people are by these different regulations impressed with a high consideration and respect for the profession, as they see it an object of the anxious solicitude of the government. They know, that the teachers must be learned men, or they could not have gained their situations, and that they must be men of high character, or they would not be allowed to hold their offices. They see the teachers in continual correspondence with the agents of the imperial government. They see how respectfully the teachers are treated by the overseers and civil magistrates. They perceive how careful the government is of the teachers when aged or infirm, and of their orphans and widows after their decease; and, influenced by these observations, the people have acquired a deep respect for these instructors and guardians of their children.

This respect reacts upon the children in the most beneficial manner. They see the teachers welcomed at home, honoured by the agents of the imperial government, cared for by the government in sickness and old age, comfortably lodged, and treated by every one with respect. This begets in the minds of the scholars a respect for their instructors, makes them pay attention to their advice and instruction, makes them anxious to win their good opinion, and thus gives a double weight to all the counsels, advice, and admonitions of these excellent monitors.

It is impossible to exaggerate the value of the labours and of the influence of such a body of men working among the poor.

The statistics of the Austrian empire prove, that the liberality of the laws, which I have been describing, have enabled the Austrian government to triumph over all the difficulties arising from the ignorant hostility of religious dogmatism and sectarianism. The great work of national education was commenced in several provinces of the Austrian empire as early as the year 1806, under the laws and regulation of the Emperor, Francis I., but in a great part of the empire, little was done until the year 1820. In that year, however, the government began to devote its energies and its funds to the great enterprise, and the results have been most magnificent.

In 1842, the population of the Austrian empire, including Lombardy, but excluding Hungary, was, 25,304,152. For this population, 20,293 primary day-schools had been founded, that is, 1 primary day-school for every 1247 inhabitants, besides 11,140 repetition or evening class schools!

For these 20,293 primary schools, 41,809 teachers had been appointed and salaried, each of these teachers having obtained a certificate of competence, before being allowed to officiate as an instructor of youth. There were, therefore, in 1842, about one teacher for every 600 inhabitants in the whole empire of Austria, excluding Hungary, and rather more than two teachers on the average to every primary school!

The subjoined table will show how many children are actually attending school, how many are of a proper age to attend schools, how many persons are attending the repetition schools open on the Fridays and Sundays, and how many persons are actually attending the primary schools in each province of the Austrian empire. It is well worthy consideration, as it will show how very universal the diffusion of knowledge and intelligence must be among the youth of the empire, and how very few persons are now left to grow up in ignorance and brutality. It will also give a still clearer idea of the vast character of the efforts made to educate the labouring classes of this great empire.

Provinces.	Number of Children who ought to be attending Primary Schools.	Number of Children actually attending the Primary Schools every Day.	Number of Persons attending the Repetition Schools.	Total Number of Persons attending the Primary School Classes.
Austria -	249,326	244,032	108,398	342,430
Styria -	107,556	81,491	36,308	117,799
Carinthia and Carniola -	85,245	28,256	16,489	44,745
Kustenland -	62,462	12,707	3,934	16,641
The Tyrol -	102,731	104,763	50,181	154,944
Bohemia -	542,143	511,444	226,539	737,983
Moravia -	290,033	277,481	174,852	452,333
Galicia -	536,125	81,584	36,061	117,645
Dalmatia -	13,254	3,708	148	3,856
Lombardy -	346,476	193,654	7,623	201,277
Venice -	260,212	82,949	851	83,800
Siebenburgen	99,918	60,897	- -	60,897
Militärgränze	127,083	71,317	22,190	93,507
Total -	2,822,564	1,754,283	673,574	2,427,857

From the latter table, it will be seen that in 1842, if we take into consideration, the number of children always detained from school by sickness and accidents, as well as the number, who are educated either at home or in the higher schools, and those who, in the manufacturing districts, leave the morning and afternoon primary schools, at a somewhat earlier age, all the children in a condition to attend the day schools throughout Austria Proper, Styria, the Tyrol, Bohemia, and Moravia, were attending the daily classes of the primary schools, and receiving a careful education from men of high character, and respectable attainments. But in addition to the great number of young people receiving instruction in the primary schools, there were also great numbers attending the special and higher schools.

In 1842, there were in the Austria empire, not including Hungary: —

8 Universities;

29 Academies;

12 Lyceums;

49 Theological Colleges;

53 Philosophical Colleges;

188 Gymnasia or Public Schools;

126 Special Schools;

1252 Private and non-described schools.

These institutions were attended regularly by 155,746 young people. Adding these to the number of persons attending the primary school classes, viz. 2,427,857, we obtain this result, that in 1842, there were in the Austrian empire, not including Hungary, 2,583,603 persons; *i. e.* more than ONE TENTH of the whole population, receiving regular instruction from teachers carefully selected for their character and ability.

CHAP. XIII.

EDUCATION OF THE PEOPLE IN SWITZERLAND.—WHEN THE CANTONS BEGAN TO EDUCATE ALL THE CHILDREN.—THE LAWS OBLIGING PARENTS TO EDUCATE THEIR CHILDREN. —THE NORMAL COLLEGES.—EDUCATION IN THEM GRATUITOUS.—THE MANUAL LABOUR IN THE SWISS COLLEGES. —ITS OBJECTS AND EFFECTS.—VEHRLI'S OPINION.—THE RESULTS OF VEHRLI'S TEACHING.—THE BERNESE NORMAL COLLEGE.—VEHRLI'S COLLEGE.—VEHRLI.—HIS OPINIONS ON THE EDUCATION OF TEACHERS.—HIS FARM.—HIS MODEL SCHOOL.—THE AGRICULTURAL SCHOOLS OF SWITZERLAND.—THEIR EFFECTS ON AGRICULTURE.—VEHRLI'S OPINIONS ON THE EFFECTS OF EDUCATION IN SWITZERLAND.—SIR JAMES P. KAY SHUTTLEWORTH'S ACCOUNT OF VEHRLI'S COLLEGE.—THE EDUCATION IN THE PARISH SCHOOLS.—THE SYSTEM OF INSPECTION IN SWITZERLAND. —THE PROGRESS OF EDUCATION IN THE DIFFERENT CANTONS.—THE EDUCATION OF THE GIRLS IN THE ROMAN CATHOLIC CANTONS.

I VISITED Switzerland in 1844, and examined the progress of primary education, and the state of the people in the cantons of Neuchatel, Geneva, Vaud, the Vallais, Tessin, Berne, Fribourg, Lucerne, Uri, Schweitz, Unterwalden, Zug, St. Gall, Thurgovie, Zurick, Schaffhouse, and Argovie. I visited all these cantons, and put myself in communication, with the governments, professors, teachers, and people; and I think I may safely express a confident opinion upon the progress and character of the people's education.

Perhaps, of all countries, Switzerland offers the most instructive lesson to any one desirous of investigating the comparative merits and effects of different systems of national education. Switzerland is divided into twenty-two cantons; each of which has an executive and representative assembly, for the special direction of its own internal affairs. Owing to the existence and power of these local executives, which were then much more independent of the central Diet of Switzerland than they are now, the educational systems of the different cantons differ from each other very materially in many respects. For this reason, and because the members of each canton are accustomed to observe and examine the peculiar merits of the different systems, the traveller is enabled to compare the various results, and to avail himself of the experience of educational authorities, whose opinions have been matured by great opportunities of observation.

The advantages accruing from these causes are still further increased by the great difference of the religious beliefs of the cantons. Thus, the population of the canton of Vaud, for example, is decidedly Presbyterian; that of Lucerne is almost exclusively Romanist; whilst those of Argovie and Berne, are partly Romanist and partly Protestant. The traveller may therefore observe the manner, in which the people of the several cantons have overcome the difficulties arising from the existence of several religious sects under one government.

The great development of public education in Switzerland dates from 1832, after the overthrow of the old oligarchical forms of cantonal government, and the establishment of the present democratic forms. As soon as the people got the reins of government into their own hands completely, they issued a series of the most stringent regulations respecting national education, and put them at once in force. From that time to the present, each year has witnessed continued improvements in the schools, apparatus, methods, education of the teachers, and the condition of the youth in Switzerland, and, at this time, the educational operations of the cantonal governments form their most weighty and important duty.

Throughout all the cantons, with the exception of Geneva, Vallais, and the three small mountainous cantons situated on the Lake of Lucerne, viz., — Uri, Schweitz, and Unterwalden, where the population is too scanty, too much scattered, and too poor to allow of the erection of many schools, education is compulsory,—that is, all parents are obliged to educate their children, either at home or at a school, from the completion of their fifth to the completion of their fourteenth, and, in some cantons, to the completion of their sixteenth year. In some of the manufacturing districts, the children are permitted to leave school and enter the mills at the age of eleven years, on condition that they first obtain from the inspectors, a certificate of being able to read and write, and that they afterwards attend school a certain number of hours periodically, until they attain the age of fourteen or fifteen. In the canton of Argovie, however, which is one of the manufacturing districts of Switzerland, the children are not allowed to enter the mills, until they attain the age of thirteen.

In the cantons of Berne, Vaud, Argovie, Zurick, Thurgovie, Lucerne, and Schaffhouse, where the education of the poor has made the greatest progress, all the children between the ages of six and fifteen are receiving daily instruction in the Scriptures, and in reading, writing, arithmetic, history, geography, singing, and drawing.

The children in Switzerland are as regularly engaged in their school duties and exercises, as their parents in their daily occupations, so that none of the young are neglected and left to grow up in a state of filth and degradation; but all are tended, watched over, trained and instructed, with as much care as the children of our gentry. The health, the bodily strength and activity, the habits, manners, personal cleanliness and neatness of the scholars are all taken care of in the schools of Switzerland. It is thought, that the duty of the teachers is not merely to cram the children's heads with a few facts, but rather to rear up prudent, strong, active, polite, moral, and intelligent citizens, capable of understanding, that the interests of one class in the community are inseparably connected with the interests of all the others, and capable of assisting to advance the general prosperity of the whole nation. These are the real objects of national schools.

In the towns of the Protestant cantons, there is no class of children similar to the class of our "ragged children." No children are to be seen during the greater part of the day in the streets, or in such a degraded condition as the poor, half-clothed, dirty, and ill-mannered little wretches, which crowd the back alleys of all our towns. All the poor children of the towns are in as good and happy a condition as those of our better shopkeepers. Instead, therefore, of the Swiss towns being, like all our English ones, nurseries of juvenile degradation, and, consequently, of adult vice, they afford only still better opportunities than the rural districts, of rearing up a fine race of children and citizens.

This one fact alone is sufficient of itself to explain the great difference between the condition of the Swiss and of the English peasantry.

Each town and village in Switzerland is obliged by law, to provide sufficient school-room for all its children, and to engage and find salaries for a sufficient number of teachers. This is managed nearly in the same way as in Prussia. In the town, the handsomest building is generally the primary school, intended for the education of the children of all people both rich and poor. It often contains five or six class-rooms, each of which is managed by a teacher educated in one of the colleges. The rooms are large, well lighted, ventilated, and coloured, and full of rows of desks and forms, and of all the apparatus necessary for instruction.

This small country beautified, but impoverished by its Alpine ranges, and containing a population less than that of Middlesex, and not one half of its capital, supports and carries on an educational system, greater and much more complete, than that which is maintained here for the whole of England!

Knowing that it is hopeless to attempt to improve

the education or the condition of the poor, without first improving the character and position of the teachers, Switzerland has established, and, at present, supports thirteen normal colleges for the education of the teachers, whilst in England and Wales, we have not more than ten worthy of notice.

Eleven of these colleges are permanent, and are open during the whole of the year; the remaining two are only open for about three months in the year, for the purpose of examining monitors recommended by the teachers of the primary schools, and desirous of obtaining diplomas, to enable them to officiate as teachers. Four of these colleges contain each from eighty-five to one hundred, and each of the others from forty to eighty students, preparing to be teachers of the poor.

In the majority of these colleges, members of the different religious sects are educated together, and receive their religious instruction in separate rooms, from the religious ministers of their respective creeds. This liberal regulation does not proceed from any carelessness about the religious education of the teachers; for one of the fundamental laws of almost every canton of Switzerland is, that no person shall officiate as teacher, until he has obtained a diploma of fitness from the government of his own canton, and that no such diploma shall be granted, until the applicant has presented a certificate from his religious minister, stating the excellence of his character, and his fitness to be entrusted with the religious education of the young, and also certificates from the professors of his normal college, stating his fitness to be entrusted with the secular instruction of youth, his industry, and the excellence of his attianments.

M. Gauthey, a Presbyterian clergyman and the Director of the Normal College at Lausanne; M. Vehrli, Director of the Normal College near Constance; the Professors of the Normal College in Argau; M. Schneider von Langnau, the Minister of Public Instruction in the canton of Berne; M. Fellenberg, of Hofwyl; the Père Girard, the celebrated monk of Fribourg, and many others, all assured me, that no inconvenience was found to result from the instruction of children of different sects in the same school. Those children, who differ in faith from the teacher, are always, throughout Switzerland, allowed to absent themselves from the classes, whilst the religious lessons are being given, and are, in such cases, required by law to attend one of their own clergy, in order to receive doctrinal instruction from him.

Even in Fribourg, a canton which was at the time of my visit governed by priests, who were under the influence of the Jesuits, the children of Protestants were instructed in the same schools and in the same classes with the children of the Romanists, and were allowed to absent themselves during the religious lessons; and, in Argovie, a canton which distinguished itself by its opposition to the Jesuits of Lucerne, I found that several of the scientific professors in the normal college intended for the Protestant teachers were Romanists, and that the utmost tolerance was manifested to all the Romanists who attended the cantonal schools.

The Swiss soon discovered, what every other European nation but England has long found out, that without the direct interference of the state, it is impossible to find sufficient funds to educate a people, and that the state cannot interfere at all, unless it aids one religious party just as much as another,— unless it leaves religious education entirely and exclusively in the hands of the people, — and unless it confines its own efforts solely and exclusively to the secular education of the children, only taking care that the religious ministers do *bonâ fide* and earnestly foster the religious education of the young of the respective sects.

In the canton of Neuchatel, at the time of my visit, there was no normal college. The teachers were selected from among the most efficient monitors in the primary schools. Notwithstanding their greatest exertions, however, to improve the class of the monitors, and to choose the most promising of them, I was assured by a very intelligent teacher in Neuchatel, that this system was found wholly insufficient; that they could not obtain good teachers, unless they founded a college for them and educated them for two or three years expressly for their work; and that they felt, that they should be obliged to found a normal college.

In the cantons of Fribourg and Schaffhouse, the normal colleges were only open for three months in the year, in order to give a course of lectures to those, who were preparing to be examined for diplomas, and to examine the candidates at the end of the course. But so totally inadequate had they found this system to provide them with good teachers, that the priests at Fribourg informed me, that their government was going to found a permanent college; while in Schaffhouse, one of the directors of the public education assured me that, it had only been the want of funds which had prevented the government of Schaffhouse founding one also.

The priests of the one canton and the Protestant clergy of the other, both said, that it was impossible to obtain efficient and good teachers, unless young men were trained expressly for the work.

Switzerland would not require quite so many normal colleges, if the teachers were paid better than at present. The cantons are not rich, and do not pay the teachers large salaries, and the consequence is, that many, after spending four or five years in the profession, desert it and seek some more lucrative occupation. Wherever I went, the educational authorities said to me,—"If you educate your teachers well, you must pay them well. You cannot expect highly educated men to remain long satisfied with a very poor salary, when they are qualified to seek situations where they would receive much larger salaries. We pay our teachers but poorly, and educate them very well, and the consequence is, that many of them, when the time of their engagement to government, in return for their gratuitous education, is over, leave the profession for more lucrative situations, and oblige us to send to the college for others to supply their places. The number of new teachers required from the colleges is, therefore, much greater than it would be, if none but vacancies occasioned by deaths had to be supplied; and we are, therefore, obliged to found larger colleges, and more of them, than we should otherwise require, in order to accommodate the number of students who are required to fill the vacancies occasioned by those who leave the profession."

I visited and examined very carefully the normal colleges of Lausanne, Argau, Constance, St. Gall, Zurich, Solleure, and Berne. Most of them are institutions deserving the highest praise. The education given in them to the young students who are preparing therein for the teacher's profession, is at once practical, scientific, and religious.

The students are educated, in most of the Swiss colleges, at the expense of the cantonal governments. They are chosen from among the most able of the monitors in the village schools, and receive a very excellent education both in pedagogy and in reading, writing, arithmetic, geography, history, and the Scriptures, before they are even received into the colleges. They remain in these colleges from two to three years, and are educated there very highly, while at the same time they are accustomed to the most humble duties, and are made to labour harder than the poorest peasant. The students, whilst studying history, geography, mathematics, music and drawing, are obliged to take care of their own beds, to serve one another at meals, to peel the potatoes for their dinners, to cultivate all the vegetables necessary for the supply of the college dining-table, to wait upon the directors and professors, and to take care of a farm attached to the institution.

All the educational authorities of Switzerland were unanimous on three points: viz.—

1st. That, in order to raise the people by education to a higher state of civilisation and morality, it is necessary to educate a class of teachers specially for the work of instruction in the village and town schools, as the effect of the instruction and example given by a narrow-minded, ill-tempered, or uninstructed man is much more to be dreaded than utter ignorance.

2ndly. That a teacher cannot be properly trained for his duties in less than three years, even if he were well educated, when he entered the college; as the habits and manners form so important a part of a teacher's character, and cannot be formed or developed in less than three years of unremitted attention.

3rdly. That manual labour ought to form a prominent feature of the education given in every teachers' college.

In the Bernese normal college, situated near Hofwyl; in the normal college of Kreuitzlingen, on the Lake of Constance, which is conducted by Vehrli, the philanthropic successor of Pestalozzi and de Fellenberg; and in the normal colleges of the cantons of Lucerne and Solleure, the young students are obliged to labour in the farms attached to these institutions, a certain number of hours every day.

Each of these colleges is surrounded by a large piece of land, which is cultivated and managed by the students, in the hours set apart for the out-of-door exercise. The farms attached to five of the Swiss colleges, are sufficiently large to employ the students two hours per diem in their cultivation. I have seen the young men who had only just left classes, where thev had been studying mathematics, pedagogy, history, and music, cultivating these farms, clothed in coarse frocks, such as those worn by the peasants, with thick wooden shoes on their feet; toiling in the company of the directors and professors, in cultivating the vegetables necessary for the use of the household during the winter months, as well as some for the neighbouring markets; and looking just like a set of young peasants at their daily labour, working for their bread. Besides this out-door labour, the young student in a Swiss college is also obliged, as I have before mentioned, to attend to all his household duties; so that his life, whilst he remains in the college, is one of real humility and hardship: he is never allowed to lose sight of the class from which he sprung, and with which he will afterwards have to labour and associate. He is never allowed to forget his sympathies with the peasants, or with their habits, hardships, or necessities. He is accustomed to these laborious duties, in order to make his after life appear easy, and pleasant to him, when compared to his college career, and to prevent him imbibing any disgust for the patience-trying duties of his profession, by accustoming him to duties still more arduous, and still more harassing during the period of his education.

By these means the cantonal governments avoid the danger, which always attends the education of a peasant, when that education is confined to a mere intellectual training, viz. of rendering him dissatisfied with a peasant's life, and with a peasant's hardships, and disgusted with the humble companions and laborious duties of his after life. The peasant who enters a Swiss normal college to be trained for admission into the teacher's profession, retains all his peasant's habits, is kept accustomed to hard and humble toil, and finds his sympathies with his class increased, rather than weakened, by his residence and education there. When he enters upon his duties in some distant and secluded village, he finds himself, consequently, in his proper sphere; that in which he was born, and in which he has always lived. Instead of feeling dissatisfied, and sighing for a town life, and for literary society, he finds his situation much easier, and much less laborious than anything to which he had formerly been accustomed. He settles down, therefore, contented, and perfectly satisfied with his condition, duties, and associates; and, by his very satisfaction and contentment, he makes the peasants respect and love him more, and renders his advice and his example much more influential than they otherwise would have been.

Owing to this system, the Swiss teachers live in their respective villages as the coadjutors of the clergy, associating with the labourers in their homes, and at their firesides, aiding them with advice, sympathising with them in their troubles, and at the same time exhibiting the highly beneficial example of Christian-minded and learned men, professors in science and peasants in habits, living proofs of the benefits to be derived from education, and examples to the peasants of the nobility of their own class, whenever that nobility is sought by proper means.

In speaking of the Swiss system of educating teachers,

Vehrli said to me, — "Your object in educating a schoolmaster ought to be to prepare a teacher of the people, who, whilst he is considerably elevated in mental acquirements above those, amongst whom he will be obliged to live, shall thoroughly sympathise with them, by having been himself accustomed to hard manual labour. If you take pupil-teachers into your normal colleges, and content yourselves, with merely cultivating their mental powers, you will find that, however carefully you tend their religious instruction, you have educated men who will soon, despite themselves, feel a disgust for the population with whom they will be called upon to associate, and for the laborious duties which they will have to perform; but if, during the whole of their residence at the normal college, you accustom them to hard and humble labour, when they leave, they will find themselves in higher, easier, and more comfortable situations than those of their school and college days: they will, from early habits and education, sympathise with their poor associates; they will feel contented and satisfied with their situation; and, feeling satisfied and happy, they will work with more energy and success, and exercise a better and a happier influence over the poor around them."

The truth of Vehrli's teaching is felt throughout Switzerland; the college directors and the cantonal governments are gradually adopting his views and plans, and regulating their colleges on the model of the admirable one, over which Vehrli himself presides. In Argovie they have resolved to adopt Vehrli's suggestions, and to add a farm to their college, which, until lately, has been a school of learning, rather than of habits. In the canton of Vaud, where, up to the time of my visit, the students of the normal college had not been obliged to submit to any manual labour during their residence, I was assured, that the teachers constantly became dissatisfied with their humble duties and associates, after leaving the literary society of the college, and settling down to their humble duties in some country village.

The best and most practically efficient colleges, that I saw in Switzerland, were, the one conducted by Vehrli at Kreuitzlingen on the borders of the lake of Constance, and about a mile from the gate of the city of Constance, and the college of the canton of Berne, situated close to Hofwyl.

To this latter one I paid a visit in company with M. de Fellenberg, the son of the celebrated educationalist. It is a large roomy building, with a good farm attached to it, and is situated in a beautiful, undulating part of the country, which is here covered with vast pine forests, and bounded by the magnificent and lofty chain of the Bernese Alps, conspicuous among which rises the snowy mass of the majestic Jungfrau. In the midst of this splendid scenery, the young candidates for the teachers' profession, selected from among the monitors of the schools of the Bernese towns and villages, are educated for three years, in a manner, which in England would fit them to be tutors to the children of our nobility, but which, in Switzerland, combined with the healthy discipline under which they live while in the college, prepares them to act, as the teachers of the children of the poorest, as well as of the richest citizens. When I visited the college with M. de Fellenberg, the young men, 100 in number, were in their class-rooms, listening to the lectures of the professors. As I entered the college, the first thing which met my eye, was the collection of spades, hoes, &c. belonging to the students. Each student had his own field tools, and his own peg on which to hang them; while near them were placed the thick wooden clogs used in the fields, but left with the tools, when the young men entered the lecture rooms. Every thing in the college was plain, simple, and perfectly unostentatious, but clean and substantial.

The education given in the class-rooms was of the most liberal and efficient character. There is no attempt in Switzerland to disguise the feeling, which is impressed on the minds of all, that they are a Republic, — that the people are the electors of the rulers, — that the electors must be enlightened, in order that they may be able to exercise their liberties aright, and to make the best use of their resources, — and that the teachers to whom the great duty of educating the citizens is entrusted, must be thoroughly efficient, strong-minded and learned men; capable of unfolding the principles of others, and of teaching sound and true maxims of self-government and of political economy. An Englishman, accustomed to his country's ideas of the teachers' profession, would indeed be astonished, could he observe what an education the teachers receive in Switzerland, Germany, and Holland. The student comes to the normal college much better educated than the vast majority of our teachers are, when they commence the management of schools. During the three years the Swiss teachers remain in the college, they receive daily instruction from learned men in history, physical and local geography, mathematics, practical science, music, drawing, pedagogy, and agriculture. How much superior such men are, when they leave the college, to the majority of our teachers, I leave my readers to imagine.

There are 100 students in this normal college; about 33 leave it every year to take the charge of primary schools in the canton. But this number does not suffice to supply the number of annual vacancies in teachers' situations in the canton. The government has, therefore, established two other normal colleges, one for the education of school-masters, and the other for the education of school-mistresses. In all three of these colleges, Romanist and Protestant students are educated together, although the directors are Presbyterian ministers. The Romanist students are allowed to absent themselves during the religious lectures, and receive religious instruction from one of their own priests.

The population of the canton of Berne in 1843 was 407,913, and there were more normal colleges provided for this small population than for that of London, which is nearly five times as numerous!

I went through the lecture-rooms of the Berne college in company with the director and M. de Fellenberg. I found the different classes of the students sitting in their separate lecture-rooms at their desks, receiving a much more liberal and efficient education from the professors of the college, than the majority of the sons of our gentry ever enjoy.

The students were very plainly but neatly dressed. They had exchanged the clogs which they used in the fields for light shoes. They had left their field dresses with their tools in the places set apart for them. They had washed and cleaned themselves after their out-door labour, and set at their work,—as fine, healthy, and intelligent looking a set of young men as any one could have wished to see; attentive and respectful to their tutors, but inspired with that feeling of self-confidence, which the union of intelligence, health, and political freedom invariably bestows. In looking at them, one felt that the teaching of such men must lay a sound foundation whereon to build the prosperity, manly virtue, and happiness of a nation. Men trained in such a manner as this feel a real pleasure in labour, understand the habits and feelings of peasants, sympathise with them, associate with them without restraint and embarrassment, and, without lowering themselves, make the peasants feel that their own class is capable of being as refined as the richest classes in the community, and of joining to that refinement a masculine simplicity and energy of character, which their own particular sphere of life is better qualified than any other to foster and develope.

But the most interesting of all the Swiss teachers' colleges is that directed by Vehrli. About a mile from the gates of the old city of Constance, close to the shore of the vast and beautiful lake of the same name, and upon a rising ground which slants gradually upwards from the water, stands an old-fashioned looking building, in the style which the nobles of Germany were so fond of about three hundred years ago. This ancient, turreted house was formerly the palace of the abbot of the vast convent situated about half-a-mile distant, and still occupied by monks. On all sides it commands magnificent views. Close below it, and spread out seventy miles in length, and twenty miles in breadth, lies the beautiful lake of Constance. To the left, at about a mile distant, rise the ancient, time-honoured towers of the council and martyr famed city, stretching out the white stone pier of its harbour into the blue waters of this inland sea. Far to the right, are seen above the sea the lofty, snow-clad peaks of the mountains of Appenzell. In front, appear just above the horizon, the forest-covered hills of the kingdom of Wirtemberg. Behind, rises the great mass of the convent, and round the palace, lies its well-cultivated and fertile farm. This commodious and beautifully situated building has been set apart by the republican government of the canton of Thurgovie for the teachers' college, and to become its director, Vehrli was tempted to leave De Fellenberg, whose comrade and assistant he had to that time been.

I visited Vehrli several times. The first time I walked to the college, Vehrli was on his fields superintending some field labour. One of the students, however, was in the hall, and promised to go and tell the director I wished to see him, begging me to enter and look at anything I wished to see while he was absent. I accepted the invitation and walked through the bed-rooms and class-rooms. Every part of the furniture of the college was of the plainest and most unostentatious kind. The bed-linen was coarse, the chairs and tables simple deal; but the books in the class-rooms, the diagrams of the last mathematical lessons chalked upon the blackboards, the drawings of the students, and the music books, served to show the visitor, that he was in a college, where the instruction given to the students, formed a strange contrast to the simplicity of their domestic life.

In a short time, Vehrli made his appearance. He was dressed in a coarse tweed coat, an old weather-worn hat, and thick farming shoes; his hands and face were brown like those of a peasant; but his bright eye and strong marked features told me, that he was a man of practical ability and of action, and no mere theoriser on the improvement of mankind.

When I next visited him he was busily engaged with the students in repairing the wooden furniture of the college, and the handles, &c. of his farming tools.

Almost his first words to me were*, "You must not expect to find any grandeur in my house; my boys are all to be engaged among peasants, to live among them, to associate with them, to advise them, and to be their friends and the instructors of their children. It is a

* I took down this conversation immediately after leaving Vehrli, and I think that some of my readers will not think the experience of this good and able man, who has devoted his whole life to the education of the poor, devoid of interest or undeserving consideration.

difficult thing for an educated man to do this, unless his habits are properly disciplined during the period of his education; and the object of my labours is, so to discipline my students, that they may be able to do all this, when they are learned men.

"It is necessary, that teachers of the poor should learn and should be accustomed to labour; for labour gives humility, and teaches how to respect the labourer.

"After a long experience in teaching both the children of rich and poor, it is my firm opinion, that all children should be accustomed, while they are young, to labour with their own hands for a certain time every day. No school ought ever to be situated in a town. All ought to be situated in the country; and every boy, no matter who his parents are, ought to be obliged to labour upon the soil. Labour makes the children healthy, capable of bearing fatigue and robust, and it teaches the children of the rich to get rid of all those notions which riches are too apt to stimulate; to understand the feelings of the poor better; to treat them better, and to associate with them better; it thus diminishes the artificial distance between classes, and, with the distinction of this artificial distance, it diminishes also the jealous feelings, which false mannerism on the part of the rich too often engenders.

"But important as labour is in my own opinion, as a part of the training of *all* youth, it is absolutely necessary in the education of teachers of the poor.

"The object of a normal college is to train men, who will be capable of educating the poor, *i. e.* of teaching them the doctrines of religion, the laws of morality, a knowledge of letters, the principles of the sciences, how to make the most of their opportunities, what is expedient in their different careers of life, the great importance of prudence and foresight, if they would improve their positions in the world and attain independence, and the intimate dependence of all classes of society upon each other. To enable us to give such an education as this to the poor, we must rear a class of teachers, who will be at once the instructors, the friends, and the associates of the poor. How can we attain this end?

"Will it be sufficient to give a good education to the young men, to educate them in a gentlemanly and luxurious manner, and surrounded by many of the elegancies and comforts by which the middle classes are surrounded? Should we train them for years together in large and comfortable colleges, with great rooms, and in good clothes, as the children of the rich are educated? Is there anything in the life of a teacher in a poor, remote village, separated from all literary society, which is at all similar to the life of such a student, or which would enable the teacher of the village to gratify the tastes acquired in such a college? If there is not, ought we to be astonished, if a young man, who has left such a college and entered into the village school and upon his arduous school duties, should be dissatisfied with the change, and should begin first to wish and then to strive to get another situation, more suitable to the habits he had acquired in the college? This is the reasonable, the almost inevitable result of such an education. The money which any government spends in educating the teachers of the poor in such a manner, will be generally found in the end to have been expended in educating a good clerk of some merchant's house, while the schools will be deserted and will want teachers.

"You must, if you wish to avoid these consequences, make the student's college life as simple, and even more humble and laborious, than the teacher's village life. You must accustom the teacher to a peasant's life and to a peasant's hardships. You must make his college life a life of greater drudgery than his village life, and then, however highly you instruct him, however learned you make him, he will, when he settles down in his village, find his life one of less toil, of greater ease, and of more enjoyment, than that to which he had been for three years accustomed in his college.

"I think that every normal college ought to be situated in the country, and that it ought to have a piece of land attached to it, of sufficient size to employ the young men four hours every day in cultivating it. The farm attached to my college is large enough to do this, and I find, that by cultivating the vegetables necessary for our household, and by selling all, that we do not require for our own use, I can diminish what would otherwise be the annual expense of our household, by one-fifth ; so that the out-door labour, besides rendering the education of the college more efficient in a moral point of view, saves the government of our canton a considerable annual expenditure in the sustenance of the college itself; and by making the teachers satisfied with their situations in the villages, lessens the number of annual vacancies in the teachers' situations, occasioned in other cantons by the teachers' dissatisfaction with their duties, and, consequently, lessens materially, the number of new teachers, and, therefore, the number of students, who would otherwise be annually educated in the colleges to supply those vacancies.

"The chambers, the repasts, all the comforts and the manners of life in the college ought to be inferior, and not superior, to those which the teacher will enjoy afterwards in his village life.

"In our college, our students do every thing for themselves. They clean their own chambers, brush their own boots, clean the knives and forks, cultivate all the vegetables, prepare them to be cooked, and set out the meals. But notwithstanding all this, they work in their class-rooms eight hours every day, and study the Scriptures, history, geography, arithmetic, mathematics, the elements of the sciences, music, and drawing."

The students, before they enter this admirable college, have received an excellent education in the primary and secondary schools of the canton. They remain two years, however, in the college, before they are entrusted with the management of any school.

Vehrli said, "The students ought to remain four, or at least three years in the college; it is impossible to form good habits in a shorter period. But our government has not thought it necessary to allow me to keep my students more than two years."

"I have heard that in England you do not give the greater part of your teachers any special education whatever; but that you advertise for a teacher, and choose the best of all the candidates who apply. Your countrymen will act very differently in a few years. It is strange, that so great a people as the English, should have done so little for the education of their poor, especially considering how much poverty there is in England; but I suppose it is the jealousy of your religious parties, which has hindered you thus far. Here, in Switzerland and Germany, we are firmly persuaded, after much experience, that no one can officiate well as teacher, unless he has been educated specially and for a long time in the particular knowledge, habits, and manners, which a teacher must possess, in order to fit him for the proper performance of his duties. The education of the young is a very delicate and difficult work. It is a fatal error to imagine, that *any* one is fit for it, without preparation."

I walked over the farm with Vehrli, saw his young men at work in the fields, and spent a considerable time with the students, while Vehrli himself was engaged with other people. I was very much pleased with the manners of the young men. They were gentlemanly, but quite unaffected in their way of addressing any one. They spoke with pleasure of their work, with affection of the director, and with a tone of healthy feeling about every thing, which showed me, that the wholesome discipline of the college was producing its proper effect upon them. They were fine, healthy, active-looking fellows, capable of bearing fatigue, and accustomed to simple and self-denying habits.

Vehrli said to me, " Go amongst my boys alone, and

talk to them, and ask them whatever you please. See every thing for yourself." I did so, and the more I saw, the more I was convinced that the college was no mere show-place, but that it had been established for an end, which it was carrying out.

The second time I visited the college, the students were preparing to give Vehrli a fête on his birthday. They had decked their dining-room with flowers, and ornamented the director's part of the room and his great arm-chair with wreaths and devices formed of flowers. On the walls, flowers were arranged so as to form the words—"Vehrli, our father, God bless him."

I dined one day with Vehrli and his wife. The dinner was one of the simplest description. The table was spread in their bed-room, which, as is often the case in Germany and Switzerland, served the purposes of library, sitting-room, and bed-room. Vehrli said to me, "I hope you will excuse my humble fare. Remember you are visiting people, who in their manner of life are simple peasants. We have made no difference for you, for you did not give us any notice of your visit."

I went to see his model school. It was a large village school, situated close to the college. The children of the neighbourhood attended every morning and afternoon, and were educated by an able teacher. A party of the students, who take this duty by turns, was sent to this school from the college every morning and afternoon, to practise teaching under the direction and advice of the head teacher. In this school the students of the college first begin to learn the art of teaching.

We afterwards walked into the country to see two *agricultural schools,* one of which was then in the course of erection. These agricultural schools are institutions intended for the completion of the education of the sons of farmers, after they have left the primary schools. The scholars receive an excellent education in the science of agriculture, as well as in chemistry, mathematics, history, geography, and the languages. A large farm is attached to each of these institutions, well stocked with cattle, farming implements, &c., where the boys learn farming for five or six hours every day, under the direction of an experienced farmer. The produce of these farms enables the institutions, I believe, to support themselves without assistance, and to afford the board and education at so low a rate, as to bring it within the reach of the poorest farmers. A great many of these institutions have been established throughout Switzerland. They are improving the system of farming more than any thing else that could have been devised; and for a country of small farms like Switzerland, they are of inestimable importance. I found that nearly all the cantons, either had established, or were thinking of establishing such schools. In these institutions, the farmers get a very cheap and scientific education for their children, while by their means the country gets better farmers, and much more scientific and economical farming. If we except Saxony, there is no country in Europe, where the farming is so good; and where all the means of cultivation are so carefully made use of, as in the Protestant cantons of Switzerland. This is entirely owing to two causes, — the subdivision of the land among the peasants themselves, and the excellent education which the farmers receive.

Vehrli spoke very highly of these agricultural schools, and of their results. He seemed very anxious to increase their numbers, and told me, that they were about to found a very large one, as a model for all the others, and as a monument in honour of the first great teacher of Switzerland — Pestalozzi.

M. de Fellenberg also took me to see an agricultural school, he had founded near his great institution, and assured me, that the importance and usefulness of these schools for farmers could not be over-estimated. The young students learn, chemistry and agricultural chemistry — how to treat different kinds of soils — how to make good manures — how to collect and employ all the waste of the farms in the making of manure — how to drain the farm-yards — how to manage sickly cattle — how to drain the fields, and how to avoid waste in every part of the farming operations.

The consequence is, as I have before said, that the farming operations in Switzerland give a greater return in proportion to the outlay, than those of almost any other country in Europe. On a Swiss farm nothing is wasted. Every thing that can be converted into manure, such as the drainings of the yards, stables, cow-houses, kitchens, offices, &c. is collected and spread over the fields, after having been prepared in such a manner, as to suit the particular character of the soil of each farm. No room is lost in the arrangements of the fields and plots of land. No stones or rubbish is left upon the land to injure the crops. The soil is cleaned as well as if it were garden land. It is always well drained, and is never injured by a too frequent repetition of the same kind of crops.

The cattle too are well tended. Their ailments are understood, and the kind of treatment proper for their cure. A richer milk and butter is thus obtained, as well as more of it; and, as I have before said, a given amount of capital expended in farming produces much more in Switzerland than in England, because there is less waste in the farming operations of Switzerland than there is in those of England; because the farmers of Switzerland are much better educated, and understand farming much better, than the farmers of England; and last, but not least, because the farmers of Switzerland are proprietors of their own farms, and much more interested in the good cultivation of their own estates, than the farmers of England, who cultivate the land of another and do not know how long they will remain in possession of the farms, which are let to them.

I was very much interested in all I saw and heard whilst with Vehrli. He is a man, who has perhaps had more experience in educating the children of peasants than any other person in Europe. He has, for forty years, watched the progress and effects of education in Switzerland. He has been a general referee and adviser. People have visited him from all parts of Europe to consult him on systems and methods; to see his college; to ask his opinions, and to tell him of the progress and effects of national education in their own districts. He is therefore of all men in Europe, perhaps the best qualified to express an opinion, both on the effects to be expected from education, and upon the way in which that education ought to be given.

He expressed himself positively and decidedly on the effects, which education was producing in Switzerland. He said that pauperism was diminishing; that the prudential habits of the people were rapidly improving; that their tastes were rising; that they were beginning to dress better and better; to build better houses; to furnish them better; to lay by more against bad times; and, in a word, to become more intelligent, civilised, independent, and happy. He said his decided opinion, based upon wide experience, was, that the more intelligent a people were, the more prosperous and virtuous they would inevitably be.

But he also said to me over and over again: "You cannot educate your peasants, unless you educate your teachers first. To make a good teacher requires a very careful, long, and special education. A bad teacher or a stupid teacher does much more harm than good. It is very incomprehensible to us here, that you English, with your enormous pauperism, should have done so little for the education of your poor, while Germany, Switzerland, France, and Holland have been making such great efforts, and with such very satisfactory results. Teach the people to think and they will take care of themselves, and will not require to be supported by your charity."

I cannot take leave of this most interesting institution, without inserting the Report upon it, published some few years ago by Dr. Kay (now Sir James P. Kay Shuttleworth) and Mr. Tufnell). They say:—

" The normal school at Kreuitzlingen is in the summer palace of the former abbot of the convent of that name, on the shore of the lake of Constance, about one mile from the gate of the city. The pupils are sent thither from the several communes of the canton, to be trained three years by Vehrli, before they take charge of the communal schools. Their expenses are borne partly by the commune, and partly by the council of the canton. We found ninety young men, apparently from 18 to 24 or 26 years of age, in the school. Vehrli welcomed us with a frankness and simplicity which at once won our confidence. We joined him at his frugal meal. He pointed to the viands, which were coarse, and said, ' I am a peasant's son. I wish to be no other than I am,—the teacher of the sons of the peasantry. You are welcome to my meal; it is coarse and homely, but it is offered cordially.'

" We sat down with him. ' These potatoes,' he said, ' are our own. We won them from the earth, and therefore we need no dainties; for our appetite is gained by labour, and the fruit of our toil is always savoury.' This introduced the subject of industry. He told us that all the pupils of the normal school laboured daily some hours in a garden of several acres, attached to the house, and that they performed all the domestic duty of the household. When we walked out with Vehrli, we found some in the garden digging, and carrying on other garden operations, with great assiduity. Others were sawing wood into logs and chopping it into billets in the court-yard. Some brought in sacks of potatoes on their backs, or baskets of recently-gathered vegetables. Others laboured in the domestic duties of the household.

"After a while the bell rang, and immediately their out-door labours terminated, and they returned in an orderly manner, with all their implements, to the court-yard, where having deposited them, thrown off their frocks, and washed, they re-assembled in their respective class-rooms.

"We soon followed them. Here we listened to lessons in mathematics, proving that they were well grounded in the elementary parts of that science. We saw them drawing from models, with considerable skill and precision, and heard them instructed in the laws of perspective. We listened to a lecture on the code of the canton, and to instruction in the geography of Europe. We were informed, that their instruction extended to the language of the canton, its construction and grammar; history, and especially the history of Switzerland; arithmetic; mensuration; such a knowledge of natural philosophy and mechanics, as might enable them to explain the chief phenomena of nature and the mechanical forces; and some acquaintance with astronomy. They had continual lessons in pedagogy, or the theory of the art of teaching, which they practised in the neighbouring village school. We were assured, that their instruction in the Holy Scriptures, and other religious knowledge, was a constant subject of solicitude.

"The following extract from Vehrli's address at the first examination of the pupils, in 1837, will best explain the spirit, that governs the seminary, and the attention paid there to what we believe has been too often neglected in this country — the education of the heart and feelings, as distinct from the cultivation of the intellect. It may appear strange to English habits to assign so prominent a place in an educational institution to the following points; but the indication here given *of the superior care bestowed in the formation of the character, to what is given to the acquisition of knowledge,* forms in our view the chief charm and merit in this and several other Swiss seminaries, and is what we have laboured to impress on the institution we have founded.

" To those who can enter into its spirit, the following extract will not appear tinctured with too sanguine views: —

" ' The course of life in this seminary is threefold:

" ' 1st. Life in the home circle, or family life;

" ' 2nd. Life in the school-room;

" ' 3rd. Life beyond the walls in the cultivation of the soil.

" ' I place the family life first, for here the truest education is imparted; here the future teacher can best receive that cultivation of the character and feelings, which will fit him to direct those, who are entrusted to his care, in the ways of piety and truth.

" ' A well-arranged family circle is the place, where each member, by participating in the other's joys and sorrows, pleasures and misfortunes, by teaching, advice, consolation, and example, is inspired with sentiments of single-mindedness, of charity, of mutual confidence, of noble thoughts, of high feelings, and of virtue.

" ' In such a circle can a true religious sense take the firmest and the deepest root. Here it is that the principles of Christian feeling can best be laid, where opportunity is continually given for the exercise of affection and charity, which are the first virtues that should distinguish a teacher's mind. Here it is that kindness and earnestness can most surely form the young members to be good and intelligent men, and that each is most willing to learn and receive an impress from his fellow. He who is brought up in such a circle, who thus recognises all his fellow-men as brothers, serves them with willingness whenever he can, treats all his race as one family, and loves them, and God their Father above all, how richly does such an one scatter blessings around! What earnestness does he show in all his doings and conduct! What devotion especially does he display in the business of a teacher! How differently from him does that master enter and leave his school, whose feelings are dead to a sense of piety, and whose heart never beats in unison with the joys of family life!

" 'Where is such a teacher as I have described most pleasantly occupied? In his school amongst his children, with them in the house of God, or in the family circle, and wherever he can be giving and receiving instruction. A great man has expressed, perhaps too strongly, "I never wish to see a teacher who cannot sing." With more reason I would maintain, that a teacher to whom a sense of the pleasures of a well-arranged family is wanting, and who fails to recognise in it a well-grounded religious influence, should never enter a school-room.'

" As we returned from the garden with the pupils, on the evening of the first day, we stood for a few minutes with Vehrli in the court-yard by the shore of the lake. The pupils had ascended into the class-rooms, and the evening being tranquil and warm, the windows were thrown up, and we shortly afterwards heard them sing in excellent harmony. As soon as this song had ceased, we sent a message to request another, with which we had become familiar in our visits to the Swiss schools; and thus in succession we called for song after song of Nageli, imagining that we were only directing them in their usual hour of instruction in vocal music. There was a great charm in this simple but excellent harmony. When we had listened nearly an hour, Vehrli invited us to ascend into the room, where the pupils were assembled. We followed him, and on entering the apartment, great was our surprise to discover the whole school, during the period we had listened, *had been cheering with songs their evening employment of peeling potatoes, and cutting the stalks from the green vegetables and beans, which they had gathered in the garden.* As we stood there, they renewed their chorusses till prayers were announced. Supper had been previously taken. After prayers, Vehrli, walking about the apartment, conversed with them familiarly on the occurrences of the day, mingling with his conversation such friendly admonition as sprung from the incidents, and lifting his hands he recommended them to the protection of Heaven, and dismissed them to rest.

"We spent two days with great interest in this establishment. Vehrli had ever on his lips, — 'We are peasants' sons. We would not be ignorant of our duties but God forbid that knowledge should make us despise the simplicity of our lives. The earth is our mother, and we gather our food from her breast; but while we peasants labour for our daily food, we may learn many lessons from our mother earth. There is no knowledge in books like an immediate converse with Nature, and those that dig the soil have nearest communion with her. Believe me, or believe me not, this is the thought that can make a peasant's life sweet, and his toil a luxury. I know it; for see my hands are horny with toil. The lot of man is very equal, and wisdom consists in the discovery of the truth, that what is *without* is not the source of sorrow, but that which is within. A peasant may be happier than a prince, if his conscience be pure before God, and he learn not only contentment, but joy, in the life of labour, which is to prepare him for the life of heaven.'

"This was the theme always on Vehrli's lips. Expressed with more or less perspicuity, his main thought seemed to be that poverty, rightly understood, was no misfortune. He regarded it as a sphere of human exertion and human trial, preparatory to the change of existence, but offering its own sources of enjoyment as abundantly as any other. 'We are all equal,' he said, 'before God; why should the son of a peasant envy a prince, or the lily an oak: are they not both God's creatures?'

"We were greatly charmed in this school by the union of comparatively high intellectual attainments among the scholars, with the utmost simplicity of life, and cheerfulness in the most menial labour. Their food was of the coarsest character, consisting chiefly of vegetables, soups, and very brown bread. They rose between four and five, took three meals in the day, the last about six, and retired to rest at nine. They seemed happy in their lot.

"Some of the other normal schools in Switzerland are remarkable for the same simplicity in their domestic arrangements, though the students exceed, in their intellectual attainments, all notions prevalent in England of what should be taught in such schools. Thus, in the normal school of the canton of Berne the pupils worked in the fields during eight hours of the day, and spent the rest in intellectual labour. They were clad in the coarsest dresses of the peasantry, wore wooden shoes, and were without stockings. Their intellectual attainments, however, would have enabled them to put to shame the masters of most of our best elementary schools.

"Such men, we feel assured, would go forth *cheerfully* to their humble village homes to spread the doctrine, which Vehrli taught of peace and contentment in virtuous exertion; and men similarly trained appeared to us best fitted for the labour of reclaiming the pauper youth of England to the virtues, and restoring them to the happiness, of her best instructed peasantry."*

The result of this simple life is, that while in other parts of Switzerland, teachers, who have been admirably instructed at normal colleges, but who have never had the advantage of the excellent discipline of the habits, which Vehrli's pupils receive, often become discontented with the drudgery of a teacher's life; the young men, who have left Vehrli's college, are found to persevere,

* Reports on the Training of Pauper Children, p. 208.

with cheerfulness and christian enthusiasm, in the work of social reform and social reformation.

Throughout Switzerland, Vehrli's college is regarded as a model, and in all the other normal colleges, they are gradually adopting his views on the education of the teachers.

I have thus particularly noticed the necessity of a great simplicity in the daily life of a pupil teacher, as I fear this important part of a schoolmaster's training is almost entirely neglected in several of the few normal colleges we at present possess. We seem to imagine, that it is a perfectly easy thing for a man, who has acquired habits of life fitting him for the higher circles of society, to associate with the poor, without any previous training. No mistake can be more fatal to the progress of the religious education of the poor. An instructed man, accustomed for several years to the society of intellectual professors as companions, without having anything to remind him of, still less to habituate him to, communication with, the humble class among whom he is afterwards to live, must feel considerable reluctance, if not decided disgust, when he finds himself called on to associate with the simple, rude, and uneducated poor. To enable him to do this, requires as careful a training as to enable him to teach; and although men are found, whose sense of duty and whose Christian philanthropy triumph over the defects of their education, yet, in the majority of cases, the dissimilarity of tastes between the teacher and his associates, must at least curtail his power of doing good, even if it does not actually cause him to neglect altogether the principal of his duties, from that natural repugnance which he cannot surmount. If we would teach the poor effectively, we must choose the teachers from among themselves; and during their education, we must continually accustom them to the humble character of their former lives, as well as to that of their future associates.

The Roman Church has always clearly understood this truth. She perceived from the first, with that sagacity, which has marked all her worldly policy, that to obtain men, who would really understand and sympathise with the poor, and who would feel no disgust for the greatest duty of a priest's life, — the visitation of the meanest hovels, — she must take her teachers from the poor themselves, and keep their minds continually habituated to a toilsome and humble life, whilst being educated and fitted to be the religious teachers of the people. The greater part, therefore, of her priests are chosen from the poorer classes. The poor know, that these priests can understand their necessities, sympathise with their sufferings, and visit their simple firesides without disgust. Whilst, therefore, the Romanist peasant respects his priest for the sacred character of the office he fills, and for the education he has received, there is none of that painful sense of separation between them, which exists where the peasant feels that his religious minister belongs to another class, and can never perfectly comprehend the situation, the wants, and the troubles of the poor. Still less does such a religious minister feel any difficulty in his communications with the poor. He visits the meanest hovel without disgust, he associates with the labourer without any danger of exhibiting an insolent air of worldly superiority, and knowing what a labourer's feelings are, he communicates with him without embarrassment, without reserve, and above all, without superciliousness.

In the Romanist cantons of Switzerland the priest is not only the spiritual adviser, but he is also the friend and companion of the labourer, and that too, naturally, without any difficulty to himself, and with infinite advantage to the poor. An Englishman would scarcely believe me, were I to describe how the priests, in the Romanist cantons, may be seen associating with the peasants in their cottages, markets, and amusements.

In this country, where the clergyman is so far separated from the poor man by his station in society, his associations, habits, and education, it becomes doubly important, that the teachers should be a connecting link between the religious minister and his flock. He ought to be fitted by his education to be the assistant of his religious minister, and strictly united by his habits to the poor, among whom he ought with cheerfulness to labour.

It is, then, a great pity that in some of the few normal colleges we have established, we have not only abandoned the idea of labour being a necessary part of the discipline of such an institution, but that we are accustoming the pupil-teachers to manners of dress and living *far*, *far* above those of the poor, amongst whom they must afterwards live, and with whom they ought continually to associate. The life of a pupil-teacher in a normal college ought to be such, that when he leaves it for his village school, he shall find his new position one of greater ease and comfort than the one he has left, and consequently feel pleased and not disgusted with the laborious drudgery that must fall to his lot in such a situation.

It must naturally follow, that a young man educated in the society of intellectual professors and companions, and accustomed to the comforts of a large, roomy, comfortable, and handsome establishment, such as the Stanley Grov eor the Battersea colleges, without being daily enured to the actual hardships of a peasant's life, will feel acutely the great difference of his situation, when he leaves to become the teacher of a village school in some agricultural or manufacturing district, where the people, with whom he ought to mingle, are gross and uneducated farm labourers, or equally uncivilised operatives.

But whilst the Swiss cantons are thus careful to prepare the pupil-teachers for the practical duties of their lives, they do not neglect their intellectual instruction; as they are fully convinced, that the instruction given in a village school, by an ignorant man, must not only be very meagre in kind, but very unattractive in character. In order to attain a certain standard of instruction in a village school, the education of the teacher should be very much elevated above it; and in order to make the poor prize the village school, it is necessary that they should have a very high opinion of the character and learning of the teacher.

The accompanying tables will show the character of the instruction given in two normal colleges of Switzerland, which may be fairly taken as specimens of the greater part of the others, as far as the instruction given in them is concerned. The two, however, to which the tables refer, are in a less satisfactory condition, as far as their moral discipline is concerned, than the normal colleges of Berne, Thurgovie, Lucerne, and Solleure, where a very much greater attention is paid to the domestic training of the teachers and to the true formation of the habits of their minds. (See Tables, pp. 387, 388, 389.)

The education given in the parochial schools includes —

1. Religious instruction.
2. Reading.
3. Writing.
4. Linear drawing.
5. Orthography and grammar.
6. Arithmetic and book-keeping.
7. Singing.
8. The elements of geography, and particularly of the geography of Switzerland.
9. The History of Switzerland.
10. The Elements of Natural Philosophy, with its practical appplications.
11. Exercises in composition.
12. Instruction in the rights and duties of a citizen, and a general acquaintance with the laws of the canton.

Let my readers compare this with the meagre instruction given in most of even the best of our parochial schools.

No teacher is allowed to undertake the charge of any

TABLE I.

Showing the Distribution of the Lessons in the Normal College of the Canton of Zurich.

SUBJECTS OF STUDY, &c.	HOURS PER WEEK.		
	Third, or Highest Class.	Second Class.	First, or Lowest Class.
Religious instruction	2	3	3
Mode of communicating religious instruction	—	2	
German language	4	3	10
Elocution	—	2	
French language	11	5	5
Geography	2	3	3
History	2	3	3
Arithmetic	3	3	3
Geometry	3	3	3
Natural history	2	2	3
Natural philosophy	3	2	
Pedagogy	3	3	
Writing or drawing	—	5	5
Geometrical drawing	4		
Vocal music	2	3	3
Gymnastics	3	3	3
Art of building	1½	1½	1½
Instrumental music	2½	2½	2½
Total number of hours' instruction per week	48	48	48

The students remain three years in this college, studying the various subjects of instruction mentioned above; and at the end of each year they are examined publicly, to ascertain the progress they have made.

There is a large garden attached to this College, where the pupil-teachers labour a certain number of hours per week, but the industrial training occupies, in this otherwise admirable institution, too subordinate a place.

TABLE II.

Showing the Lectures given in the Normal College at Lausanne during the Summer.

Hour of the Day.	MONDAY.	TUESDAY.	WEDNESDAY.	THURSDAY.	FRIDAY.	SATURDAY.
5	- - -	Book-keeping. — Senior Pupils. Writing. — Junior Pupils.	Geography.— Senior Pupils.	Geography. — Senior Pupils. Writing. — Junior Pupils.	- - -	Writing. — Senior Pupils.
6	Prayer, Reading, and Religious Instruction. — All.	Same as Monday.	Same as Monday.	Same as Monday.	Same as Monday.	Same as Monday.
7	Composition.—Senior Pupils. Arithmetic. — Junior Pupils.	Arithmetic. — Senior Pupils. Theme. — Junior Pupils.	Composition.—Senior Pupils. Geometry. — Junior Pupils.	Arithmetic. — Senior Pupils. Theme. — Junior Pupils.	Composition. — Senior Pupils. Geometry. — Junior Pupils.	Arithmetic. — Senior Pupils. Composition.—Junior Pupils.
9	Pedagogy. — All.	Use of the Globes. — All.	Pedagogy. — All.	Instruction in the laws of the canton.	Pedagogy. — All.	Instruction in the laws of the canton. — All.
10	Geography. — Senior Pupils. Mental Arithmetic. — Junior Pupils.	Grammar. — Senior Pupils. Geography. — Junior Pupils.	Geometry.— Senior Pupils. Grammar.— Junior Pupils.	Analytical Reading. — All.	Grammar. — Senior Pupils. Geography.— Junior Pupils.	Geometry. — Senior Pupils. Grammar. — Junior Pupils.
11	Natural History.—All.	Physics. — Junior Pupils.	Natural History.—All.	Natural History.—All.	Pedagogic exercises in the physical sciences. — Jun. Pupils.	Reading. — Senior Pupils. Arithmetic. — Junior Pupils.
2	Theme. — Senior Pupils.	Drawing. — Senior Pupils. Composition. — Junior Pupils.	Theme. — Senior Pupils.	Drawing. — Junior Pupils.		
3	Gymnastics. — Junior Pupils.	Drawing. — Senior Pupils. Composition. — Junior Pupils.	Geography of Switzerland. — Senior Pupils.	Drawing. — Junior Pupils.	Gymnastics. — Junior Pupils.	
4	Reading. — Junior Pupils.	Reading. — All.	Chanting. — Senior Pupils. Arithmetic.—Junior Pupils.	Reading. — All.	Chanting. — Senior Pupils. Arithmetic.— Junior Pupils.	Practical Geometry. — Junior Pupils.
5	Mental Arithmetic. Senior Pupils.	Chanting. — All.	Chanting. — Junior Pupils.	Chanting. — All.	Chanting. — Junior Pupils.	

TABLE III.

Showing the Lectures given in the Normal College at Lausanne during the Winter.

Hour of the Day.	MONDAY.	TUESDAY.	WEDNESDAY.	THURSDAY.	FRIDAY.	SATURDAY.
8	Prayer, Reading, and Religious Instruction. — All.	Same as Monday.	Same as Monday.	Same as Monday.	Same as Monday.	Same as Monday.
9	Pedagogy. — All.	General History. — All.	Pedagogy. — All.	Use of the Globes. — All.	History of Switzerland. — All.	Laws of the canton. — 1, 2. Composition. — 3.
10	Geometry. — 1, 2. Anthropology. — 3.	Arithmetic. — 1, 2. Theme. — 3.	Theme. — 1, 2. Arithmetic. — 3.	Composition. — 1, 2. Mental Arithmetic. — 3.	Arithmetic. — 1, 2. Theme. — 3.	Theme. — 1, 2. Arithmetic. — 3.
11	Botany. — 1, 2.	Writing. — 1, 2, 3.	Chemistry or Zoology. — 1, 2, 3.	Same as Wednesday.	Writing. — 1, 2, 3.	Same as Wednesday.
1	- -	- -	- -	- -	Physical sciences. — 1, 2.	Writing. — 3.
2	Grammar. — 1, 2, 3.	Drawing. — 1, 2. Reading — 3.	Grammar. — 1, 2, 3.	Drawing. — 3. Mental Arithmetic. — 1, 2.	Geometry. 3. Composition. — 1, 3.	Geometry. — 1, 2.
3	Gymnastics. — 1, 2.	Drawing. — 1, 2.	Gymnastics. — 3. Book-keeping. — 1.	Drawing. — 3. Reading. — 1, 2.	Pedagogic exercises in Mathematics. — 1, 2.	
4	Geography. — 3.	Geography. — 1, 2.	Reading. — 1, 2. Geography. — 3.	Reading. — 3.	Swiss Geography. — 1, 2, 3.	
5	- -	Geography. — 3.	- -	Geography. — 1, 2.		
7	- -	Chanting. — 3.	Chanting — 1, 2, 3.	Chanting. — 1, 2.	Chanting. — 1, 2, 3.	

N.B. The figures refer to the different divisions of the College: 1. to those of the first year; 2. to those of the second year; and 3. to those of the third year. The extraordinary attention which, this table shows, is paid in Switzerland to the education of the teachers, is well worthy the very serious attention of every Englishman, who is really interested in the best interests of the poor.

school, until he has obtained from the council of his canton, whose duty it is to examine candidates, a diploma stating his capability of directing the education of a school. This diploma is only granted, after a very severe examination, which the candidate must pass, before he can become a teacher. Besides this, he must have obtained a certificate of character from the director of the normal college, in which he was educated; and, in many cantons, another from a clergyman of his own sect, stating his capability of conducting the religious education of a school. This latter point is always strictly inquired into, either by the council of inspection, which examines the candidates, or by a clergyman of the sect, of which the candidate is a member. The character and abilities of the teachers are not considered, in Switzerland, as matters of small concern; but, on the contrary, every precaution is taken to guard against the possibility of a man of low character or poor education obtaining such a post. It is happily understood in the Swiss cantons, that such a teacher is much worse than none at all. The influence of such an one on the young is demoralising in the extreme, and does infinite mischief, by creating in the minds of the children associations connecting the school and the school studies with unhappy thoughts, and thus often actually engendering a spirit of hostility, not only to education, but also to the religious precepts, which were professedly taught at school.

Each canton in Switzerland is divided into a certain number of communes or parishes, and *each of these parishes is obliged by law to furnish sufficient school-*

room for the education of its children, and to provide a certain salary, the minimum of which is fixed by the cantonal government, and a house, for each teacher it receives from the normal college of the canton. These parochial schools are, in the majority of cases, conducted by teachers professing the religion of the most numerous sect in the parish, unless there are sufficient numbers of the different religious bodies to require more than one school, when one school is conducted by a teacher belonging to one sect, and the other by a teacher belonging to another. The children of those parents, who differ in religion from the teacher, are permitted to absent themselves from the doctrinal lessons, and are required to obtain instruction, in the religious doctrines of their own creed, from clergy of their own persuasion.

The inspection of the cantonal schools is conducted in the most satisfactory manner. Each canton has a board of inspectors, or council-general of instruction, which is presided over by the Minister of Public Instruction for the canton, and whose duty it is to visit all the schools of the canton at least once in the year, and to report to the government and to the PEOPLE of the canton, the state of each of the schools, the progress of each of the pupils, the character of the instruction given by each of the teachers, and the character of the attendance of each child of the commune.

But besides the *cantonal* board of inspectors, there is also in each *parish* a board of inspectors, who are elected annually from among the clergy and educated men of the parish, and who visit the parochial schools at least once each year, and report to the Minister of Public Instruction for the canton, on the progress of EACH of the children in the parochial schools. *The head inspector of the canton of Solleure showed me samples of the handwriting, composition, accounts, &c. of all the children in the canton.* By these means, each teacher is encouraged in his exertions, as he feels that the eyes of his canton are upon him, and that he is regarded as a most important public functionary, to whom is committed a great and momentous trust, for the proper discharge of which it is but right his canton should receive constant assurance.

By these means, also, the different communes or parishes are immediately interested in the progress of their schools, whilst the government is insured against the possibility of a school being wholly neglected; as every school is sure of being examined several times a year by the government inspectors, even if the parochial authorities should fail to visit them, or should not pay them sufficient attention.

This is the true theory of a system of inspection. There ought always to be a system of *local* inspection, because local authorities are able, when active, to discover better than any stranger can possibly do, the peculiar wants and requirements of their localities, as well as the *real character* of their teachers, and because a system of local inspection provides a continual check upon the schoolmaster; but, as persons, who have other and pressing duties upon their hands, and who are deeply engaged in business, or in agricultural pursuits, are very likely to neglect at times, and often altogether, the important duty of attending to the schools of their neighbourhood; and as schools which receive no *surveillance* from persons qualified to judge of their particular merits or demerits, are always *sure* to degenerate, and are liable to become seriously demoralised; and as, moreover, it is deeply important that every government, for the sake of social order, and of the happiness and morality of its subjects, should have every security that the people are really educated, and not demoralised by a sham of education; so in every well-governed state, where the government takes any interest in the promotion of the education of the poor, it is necessary, that it should have the power of examining the interior of every school, together with the character of its discipline, studies, and teachers, and that it should be obliged to publish an annual report of the merits and character of every educational institution in the country. By these means, if the local inspection is neglected, the public supplies its place: vicious teachers are checked, and kept from demoralising their children; good teachers are encouraged, and stimulated by public notice to make renewed exertions, and parents are informed what schools are really good, and where they may safely send their children.

Both parents and teachers, but especially parents, gain great advantages from such an arrangement. At present a parent has no means in England of testing the real character of the school, to which he sends his children. He is induced to trust his children to the care of the teacher, either by some advertisement which the teacher himself has published, or by the statements of other parents, founded for the most part on what their children have told them. Hence the general distrust of schools that is on all hands expressed. No one knows how to find out the real character of any particular institution. All people feel, that in sending their children to school, they are running a great, and, under present circumstances, an inevitable risk.

But in Germany, Holland, Switzerland, Denmark, France, and Austria, *every* school, for the children of either rich or poor, is open to inspection, and is examined several times every year by some learned man skilled in the science of pedagogy. If a parent wishes to learn the character of any particular institution, he can apply to the inspector of his district. A bad school is thus immediately found out and deserted, whilst the really efficient ones are crowded with scholars. The inspection, therefore, ruins the bad schools; and improves the good ones, by filling them with scholars, by stimulating the teacher to exert himself, and by making him feel that his efforts will be speedily appreciated and recompensed by the public. By these means the character of all the schools is considerably raised, immoral schools are unable to exist long, and the parents are enabled to find out, which are the best schools for the education of their children.

I shall now give a few interesting details relative to the progress of education in the different cantons.

In the canton of Neuchatel all children are obliged by law to attend some school or other from the age of six to the age of fifteen. The education given in the schools is perfectly gratuitous. The educational expenses are paid out of the district rates. The religious education of the children of each sect is directed by the religious ministers of that sect.

In the canton of Lausanne there are two normal colleges, one for the education of schoolmistresses, the other for that of schoolmasters. The normal college for young men contains about fifty students. Twenty of these, however, are teachers, who have been sent up from the country districts by the inspectors, to receive a few months' training in some branch or branches of knowledge in which they have appeared deficient.

The normal colleges have a staff of THIRTEEN professors and teachers attached to them. The instruction given in these colleges is perfectly gratuitous, and is provided by government. The time, which is fixed for continuance in the college, is THREE years, but if a young student is able to gain his diploma before the expiration of this period, he is allowed to do so, and to take a school immediately afterwards. All parents are obliged by law to send their children to school from the age of six to the age of sixteen. The inspectors forward to the government of the canton, once every year, a report on the state and progress of each school in the canton.

The Minister of Education for this county assured me, that nineteen twentieths of all the children in the canton were attending the schools.

In the canton of Fribourg every parent is required by law to send his children to school from the age of six to the age of fifteen. When, however, a scholar in any of the schools can write, read and cipher, he is allowed to discontinue his attendance at school. Many of the children continue to attend school until the age of *sixteen.*

The education given in the schools is perfectly gratuitous, so that in this, as in nearly all the cantons of Switzerland, the children of the rich and of the poor attend the same schools, and are brought up together at the same desks.

In the canton of Lucerne, every parent is obliged to send his children to school, from the age of seven to the age of *sixteen.* There is a normal college in this canton, where all the teachers are educated. The students remain in the college *three* years. The education given in the college, and in the primary schools, is perfectly gratuitous. All the schools and universities in the different cantons are open to all children. The education given in them is gratuitous. Every child is obliged to go through the regular course of education in the primary schools first; afterwards, if his parents are willing, he can enter the higher schools or the universities. I have seen sons of the poorest peasants and labourers working in the colleges and high schools, at the highest branches of knowledge, with the children of the rich. These young men return afterwards to their little farms or humble occupations, and make the best peasants in the world. The maxim in Switzerland is, that education unfits no one for any situation, however humble. *Lucerne is a Romanist canton.*

Many of the sons of the Swiss peasants receive as good an education, as the young men at our English universities, and often a much more liberal one. I have seen at Lausanne, Fribourg, Geneva, Neuchatel, Berne, and Lucerne, young men of all ranks in the social scale receiving instruction in the colleges together, in the sciences, philosophy, the classics, history, music, and religion. This, let it be remembered, is done in a country, which can boast the most industrious, independent, and least pauperised peasantry in Europe.

In the canton of Zurich, all the children attend school from the age of six to the age of *fifteen*. There is an admirable normal college in this canton, for the education of teachers. The students are admitted at the age of seventeen, and remain three years in it.

I visited also the normal colleges of the cantons of Argovie, Solleure, and St. Gall, and the schools or educational directors of the cantons of Schaffhouse, Zug, Uri, Geneva, and Tessin.

In the canton of Berne, the population amounted in 1843 to 407,913, and in 1844, I found, that the number of children in the elementary schools in that year was 1 in every 4·3 inhabitants! The government of the canton supports *three* large normal colleges for the education of teachers, two for schoolmasters, and one for schoolmistresses. The pupil-teachers, after having completed their education in the primary schools, are educated for *three* years in these institutions, before being allowed to take the charge of a school. All the parents of the canton are obliged to send their children to school from the age of seven to the age of fifteen.

In the canton of Thurgovie, education is nearly as far advanced, the proportion of scholars to the population being at least 1 in 4·8! The population in 1837 was 84,124, and for the education of a sufficient number of teachers, they have an admirable normal college, containing eighty pupil-teachers, who remain there under Vehrli's instruction for two years. In 1837, 1 in every 4·8 of the population was attending a school!

In this, as indeed in all the cantons, with the exception of Vallais, Schweitz, and Uri, in the two latter of which, the population is too thinly scattered over the mountains, all parents are *obliged* by law to send their children to school, from the age of seven to the age of fifteen; but in the manufacturing cantons, the children are permitted to begin work before the age of thirteen, on condition that they attend evening classes all the year, or that they attend daily schools, during certain stated periods of the year, until they attain the age of fifteen.

The proportion of scholars to population in ten of the cantons is as follows: —

			Scholar.		Population.
Vaud	1844	at least	1	in	6
St. Gall	1843	about	1	in	5·5
Argovie	1843	at least	1	in	5·5
Zurich	1844	"	1	in	5
Neuchatel	1838	"	1	in	6
Fribourg	1839	"	1	in	6·5
Solothurn	1844	"	1	in	7
Lucerne	1844	about	1	in	6
Schaffhouse	1844	"	1	in	6
Geneva	1844	"	1	in	6
Berne	1844	"	1	in	4·3
Thurgovie	1844	"	1	in	4·8

Education is also very satisfactorily advanced in the cantons of Zug*, Basle, and Appenzell. But I am not so well acquainted with the exact progress it has made

* I was assured by the Minister of Education in this canton, that *all* the children of the canton were receiving education in the primary schools.

in them, as in the above-mentioned cantons. Comparing, however, the actual results of the measures pursued by the other cantons, of which I possess certain and credible statistics, with the probable results of the efforts, now made by these cantons, I should say, that about one in every seven of their population is at school.

The cantons, where the education of the poor is least advanced, are Vallais, Tessin, Grisons, Glarus, and the three small mountainous cantons on the lake of Lucerne; but still it is far from being wholly neglected even in these; for in several* of them, there are regulations, which *oblige* all the children to learn at least to read and write, although, beyond that, little instruction is given. The proportion of children, who receive this amount of instruction, as compared to their whole population, is about one in ten; but this is only a rough guess, based on nothing but the information received from individuals. Generally speaking, the instruction given in the Romanist cantons of Switzerland, is very much below the standard of that given in the Protestant cantons, being confined almost always to reading, writing, arithmetic, and religious instruction. This education, however, meagre as it is, is very widely diffused among the people, so that at the present time it may be truly said, that in nearly the whole of Switzerland *every* boy and girl below the age of seventeen years can read and write. The education of the girls is, perhaps, in a more satisfactory condition in the Romanist cantons than in the Protestant. It is confided to the

* Tessin, Grisons, Schweitz, and, I believe, Unterwalden.

special care of the nuns; and I can bear testimony to the gentle, patient, and religious spirit, in which these excellent women affectionately tend the progress of the young girls. The self-denying life, which the Romanist nuns lead, and the excellent education they receive in the nunneries, admirably suit them for the important duties confided to their charge in these cantons. After having examined the schools conducted by some of the nuns in Fribourg, the abbess of one of the convents allowed me to visit her house, in company with a very intelligent priest, with whom I had been spending some days. We went over it in company with one of the sisters. We were ushered first into the entrance hall, where we found about twenty of the nuns, under the direction of a venerable old abbess of about eighty years of age, seated at a long table, engaged in making clothes and household linen for the poor.

After we had conversed for some time with the abbess, two of the nuns took us over the convent, and showed all the interior arrangements.

The apartments of the sisters were of the plainest possible description. They were in beautiful order, and exquisitely clean; but furnished very meagrely, and literally destitute of everything that was not absolutely necessary. The sisters had no servants and no assistants. In turn they prepared their own food, cleaned their own chambers, took charge of the dining-room, hall, and chamber of the abbess, and performed all the humblest duties of domestic servants. They also gave a very excellent education to the young persons destined to take the veil, comprising reading, writing, arithmetic, history, geography, grammar, and singing. The noviciates are therefore, in every way, admirably prepared for teaching in the primary schools. This they undertake in the female schools, after having taken the veil. The humble life, to which they are accustomed during the years of their noviciate, and during the rest of their lives, makes them admirably well qualified for intercourse with the poor, and renders them patient, gentle, and persevering in their efforts in the schools. They certainly are living examples of the class of teachers a good training is capable of producing.

To give an idea of the way in which education is diffused among the people of Switzerland, I beg to call the reader's attention to the following remarkable statistics of the canton of Vaud:—

State of Education in the Canton of Vaud in the Month of April, 1841.

Number of children between the ages of 6 and 16, during which time they are obliged by law to attend the schools		32,484
Number of children actually attending schools		30,525
Scriptures.	Number of children who understand what is read to them out of the Bible	7,370
Catechism.	Know it well	9,234
Reading.	Can read fluently	10,826
Writing.	Can write well	7,456
———	Can write accurately	4,577
Grammar.	Know the principal rules	6,575
Exercises.	Can write a letter, a tale, or an exercise	3,645
Arithmetic.	Understand the rule of three and its applications	5,357
———	Understand only the four simple rules, with whole and fractional numbers	3,570
———	Understand only the four simple rules	4,413
Mental arithmetic.	In the four simple rules	6,132
Book-keeping.	Understand this art	5,196

Singing.	Can sing the Psalms - - - -	14,055
———	Can sing difficult pieces of music - - -	9,845
Physical geography.	Know the principles of - - -	5,436
———	Know the principles of that of Switzerland	5,951
Mathematical geography.	Know its principles - -	3,300
History of Switzerland.	Know it - - - -	4,503
The principles of the laws of the canton - -	Know them - - -	3,504
Natural history.	Know something of it - - -	4,009
Linear drawing.	Know its principles - - - -	6,072
Geometry.	Know its principles - - - -	2,633
Mensuration.	Know something of it - - - -	2,544
Housewifery.	Girls who are educated therein - - -	2,269

CHAP. XIV.

EDUCATION OF THE POOR IN FRANCE, HOLLAND, HANOVER, DENMARK, SWEDEN, AND NORWAY.

VAST as the efforts are which the German and Swiss states are making to educate their people, the great and minutely considered system of public education, which is now in operation throughout every commune in France, rivals them in its comprehensiveness, efficiency, and liberality, and in the completeness and well considered nature of its details.

The master mind of Napoleon perceived the importance and necessity of educating the people, and in the short intervals of peace, which varied his stormy career, he made and put in force many laws calculated to promote the enlightenment of the lower orders.

The continued wars, however, in which he was engaged, prevented the full realisation of his great plans for the attainment of this object, and after his overthrow the government ceased to take any interest in the question, until the Revolution of July obliged and enabled French statesmen once again to devote their minds to the development of the means requisite for raising the condition and the character of the people.

In 1833, M. Guizot, then Minister of Public Instruction, laid before the Chambers a great and comprehensive scheme of national education, which received their assent, and was immediately put into operation throughout the whole of France.

It was long a question of great doubt among French legislators, in what manner the difficulties arising from religious differences, could be overcome. The different religious parties in France were as earnest in their demands, as the church and dissenting parties in England at the present day.

The Chambers were called upon to decide;

Whether they would establish separate schools for all the different sects; or,

Whether they would establish mixed schools, where no religious education should be given, and where the children of all sects should be instructed together; or, Whether they would allow the parishes to found their own schools, and elect teachers educated in the religious belief of the majority of the parishioners; merely requiring, as an indispensable preliminary, that the children of the minority should be allowed to avail themselves of the secular instruction given in the schools, and to leave the class-rooms when the religious instruction was given there; on condition, however, that their parents provided in some other manner for the efficient education of their children in their own religious belief.

The Chambers felt, that to adopt the first course, would be to leave the education of many children totally unprovided for, in the cases of those communes, where there was not a sufficient number of some one sect in a commune to enable the government to establish a separate school for them; that, to adopt the second alternative, would be to leave the most deeply important part of education either wholly neglected, or at least most indifferently provided for; and that to deny the master the liberty of giving practical religious education in the school, was to deprive him of the most powerful means of improving the character of his children. They, therefore, adopted the third alternative, and resolved to place each of the normal colleges of the different departments, and each of the primary schools of the different communes, under the management of a professor or teacher, selected from the most numerous Christian sect of the department or commune, in which the college or school was situated. They further determined, that the parents, who differed in their religious belief from the director of the college, or from the teacher of the school, should have the power of requiring their children to absent themselves during the periods of religious instruction; on condition, however, that such parents provided elsewhere for the religious education of their children.

This liberal and excellent scheme has been undeservedly taunted with irreligion. The cries of the French Jesuits, raised from purely interested motives, have found an echo in the mouths of English Protestants, and this belief, strengthened by our laudable fear of excessive centralisation, and by our national prejudices against the French, have prevented us doing justice to the magnificent efforts, which they are making to educate their people, and by that means to raise their virtue and their happiness.

The importance of the religious element in the education of the children, is put forward in great prominence by the French statutes and regulations upon the subject. In the words of the Statute of April 25th, 1834, upon the elementary schools: —

"In all the divisions (of each school), the moral and religious instructions shall rank *first*. Prayers shall commence and close all the classes. Some verses of the Holy Scriptures shall be learned every day. Every Saturday, the Gospel of the following Sunday shall be recited. On the Sundays and Fast-days the scholars shall be conducted to Divine Service. The reading-books, the writing copies, the discourses and exhortations of the teacher shall tend continually to penetrate the soul of the scholars, with the feelings and principles, which are the safeguards of morality, and which are proper to inspire the fear and love of God."

And M. Guizot in the letters, which he addressed, while Minister of Public Instruction to each of the teachers of France, says —

"Among the objects of instruction, there is one which demands of me particular notice; or, rather, it is the law itself, which, by placing it at the head of all the others, has committed it more especially to our zeal; I refer to moral and religious instruction. Your labours, in this respect, ought to be both direct and sometimes indirect.

"If by your character and by your example, you have succeeded in obtaining in your school all the authority, with which I desire to see you clothed; the moral lessons, which you will give, will be received with deference; they will be something more than an instruction for the mind of the pupils; they will supply the insufficiency of the primary education so incomplete, and often so vicious in the present state of our morals and of our intelligence.

"Do not neglect any means of exercising this salutary influence; increase it by means of conversation with individual scholars, as well as by means of general lessons; let it be your constant thought and your constant duty.

"It is absolutely necessary, that popular instruction should not be confined to the development of the intelligence; it should embrace the whole soul; it should awaken the conscience, which ought to be elevated and strengthened according as the intelligence is developed. It suffices to tell you, sir, what importance the religious instruction ought to have in your eyes. The teachers, who will be called upon to give this instruction in the elementary schools, ought to have been well prepared for this duty, by having themselves received a sound and religious education in the normal colleges. Do not, however, satisfy yourself with the regularity of forms and appearances; it is not sufficient, that certain observances should be maintained, that certain hours should be consecrated to religious instruction; it is necessary to be able to assure ourselves of its reality and efficiency. I invite you to make known to me the exact state of religious education in your own school. In concert with the bishops and religious ministers, I will neglect nothing in order to attain this end. You will yourself contribute very materially to it, by taking a constant care that none of the difficulties, unfortunately still too common, should be raised between you and those, who are more especially charged with the administration of the sacred functions; that neither your conduct, nor your language should, in this respect, furnish any pretext either for prejudice or jealousy. You will thus secure to our establishments, that good feeling of the families, which is so important for us; and you will inspire a great number of worthy persons, with that feeling of security in our future morality, which events have sometimes shaken, even in the case of the most enlightened men."

Hitherto, the parents of France have not, as in the German counties, and in Italy and Sweden, been obliged by law to educate their children.

In France, as in England, a parent is left by the laws, at perfect liberty to train up his children in vice, or in virtue, just as it pleases him. The state does not interfere to prevent crime, but only to punish it. A selfish or immoral, or merely careless parent, rears immoral children, who become immoral citizens, and contribute their share to the pollution of the social system. The selfish man, for the sake of his own gains, deprives his children of all mental and of all moral culture. The immoral man laughs at the idea of his children deriving any benefit from that, which he has either never enjoyed, or the influence of which he has since stifled; while the careless man never thinks about the subject, or does not understand it. In each of such cases, the state ought to be ready to interpose its intelligence and its authority to rescue the children of such parents from vice, and to preserve the country from any addition being made to the numbers of its vicious citizens. If it is the duty of the state to promote virtue and to repress vice, it surely is its duty to take care, that no child is educated from its earliest years in *immorality.* But every child whose mind is never cultivated, who is left every hour of every day among demoralised companions, who is never brought into connection with good and intelligent beings, and whose younger years are embittered by toil and constant association with vice, is, it would seem, enjoying a perfect system of education in *immorality.* And yet, how many such instances must there always be, in every country, where the state only punishes vice when committed, and does not interfere at an earlier period for its prevention.

There is no law in France similar to those of Germany, by which a parent is obliged either to send his children to school, or to educate them at home. In the agricultural departments of France, where the children can be profitably employed in the field at an early age, a child does not enjoy instruction for so many years; and therefore does not receive, in general, so complete an education as the German children.

In the manufacturing districts of France this evil is, in some degree, obviated, by a law, which prevents any child being employed in manufacturing operations, until he has attained the age of nine years. But even this is much too early a period, at which to remove a child from training, and to introduce him to the all-engrossing and severe labour of his future life. It must be but too evident, that his character cannot be nearly formed at so early an age, and that hs is but too likely to forget all that he has learned at school, and to lose all the influence of his education, by a constant connection with low-minded and degraded associates.

But although France has not yet imitated the German and Swiss States in this most important feature of their educational systems, she has followed their examples in several others of almost equal significance, as will be seen from the following sketch of the French system: —

Each department of France is subdivided into arrondissements, and each arrondissement into communes or parishes. Each commune IS OBLIGED by law, either alone, or in conjunction with one or more neighbouring communes, to support *at least one* elementary primary school. Where the population is large enough to require more than one school, it is *invited* to establish another. If it neglects this duty, the government is empowered to interfere. The means of instruction are thus placed within the reach of every parent throughout the kingdom of France. If the government had left it to each commune to please itself, whether it would establish schools or not, the result would have been similar to the one, which is still disgracing us. Many of the communes would never have put themselves to the expense of erecting schools, and supporting teachers.

I shall explain how the communal organisation is arranged, and how the difficulties arising from religious differences have been overcome: —

1st. In communes, in which all the inhabitants belong to the *same* religious sect.

In each of these cases, a committee is formed, composed of the mayor, president, *curé* or religious minister, and one or two of the inhabitants of the commune, who are nominated by the committee of the arrondissement, of which I shall speak presently. The latter members of the committee are elected for three years, and are then re-eligible.

2ndly. In communes in which there are *several* of the religious sects, which are recognised by the state (*i. e.* Romanists, Protestants, and Jews).

In each of these cases, the inhabitants may please themselves, whether they will establish separate or mixed schools, and whether they will have a separate committee for each school or one central committee for them all; but they are *obliged* by law to adopt one of these courses.

If one central committee is constituted for all the schools of the commune, it is formed of the mayor, the president, a religious minister of each of the different sects of the commune, and two or three inhabitants selected by the committee of the arrondissement.

The French law in this respect agrees with the different German systems. It obliges each parish or commune to provide the means of education, but it leaves it to the inhabitants of each parish to determine, whether they will do this in concert or not.

If a mixed school is established, and a teacher professing the same religion as the majority of the inhabitants of the commune is appointed to instruct, and direct its classes, the parents who differ with the teacher in religious belief are at liberty, if they feel so disposed, to remove their children from the classes during the time in which religious instruction is given.

The chief towns of each department and every commune not being a chief town of a department, but whose population exceeds 6000, are also required to support a *superior* primary school for the education of poor children, who have finished their course of instruction in the *elementary* schools, and whose parents wish to keep them at school, and give them a better education than that afforded by the primary schools.

The law requires that in every elementary school in France, instruction shall be given in —

1. Religion;
2. Morality;
3. Reading;
4. Writing;
5. Arithmetic;
6. The French Language;
7. The legal System of Weights and Measures;
8. Geography (particularly of France);
9. History (particularly of France);
10. Linear Drawing; and
11. Singing.

The teachers are required to pay especial attention to the *religious* education of the children. The law requires, that each of the classes shall be commenced and terminated by a short prayer that the scholars shall learn by heart a few verses of the Bible every day, and that every Saturday, the children shall learn by heart the Gospel for the next Sunday.

Every elementary school is divided into *three* divisions, in which the pupils are placed, according to the progress they make in their studies.

The first generally comprehends children of from six to eight years of age, and their education consists of religious lessons, reading, writing, and the elements of arithmetic.

The second generally comprehends children of from eight to ten years of age, and their education consists of the study of the Holy Scriptures, a continuation of their former exercises in reading, writing, and arithmetic, and instruction in the French grammar.

The third generally comprehends children of ten years of age and upwards, and their education comprises, the study of the Christian doctrines, a continuation of their former exercises in reading, writing, arithmetic, and French grammar, and instruction in the elements of geography and history, particularly of the geography and history of France, and in music and linear drawing.

No books are allowed to be used in these schools, but such as are sanctioned by Government; but the teachers are permitted to follow the method of instruction, which they themselves think preferable. Every teacher of a primary school is required at the end of each month, to furnish the local committee with an account of the state and progress of instruction in his school, during the past month. Each school is subjected to an examination twice a year, in the presence of the members of the local committee, and of one member of the committee of the arrondissement; and at the end of these examinations, a list is made out of the names of all the pupils in order of merit, and is fixed upon the walls of the school, where it remains until the next examination. This stimulates the efforts of both teacher and pupils, as they feel that the eyes of their district are upon them, watching their progress.

There are, as I have said, two local committees: — one of the arrondissement, and one of the commune.

The former is specially charged with the general *surveillance* and encouragement of primary education throughout the arrondissement. It consists of the mayor of the chief town in the arrondissement, the *juge de paix*, the *curé*, a minister from each of the recognised sects in the arrondissement, a professor, *a primary schoolmaster*, three members of the council, of the arrondissement, and those members of the council general of the department, who live within the arrondissement.

The committee of the commune consists, of the mayor, the president, the *curé* or pastor, and one or two of the most influential inhabitants of the commune.

These committees meet at least once a month. The communal or parochial committee inspects the condition and progress of the schools in its district, and reports to the committee of the arrondissement. This latter committee has the right of examining all the schools of the arrondissement. Some one of its members is generally present at each local examination, and it reports to the Minister of Public Instruction on the state and progress of the education of its district.

But besides this local inspection, which serves so well to stimulate and encourage the efforts of both the teachers and the resident gentry of the different parishes, and to inform the Minister of Public Instruction of the true wants of different localities; there is another great system of general inspection directed by the Minister of Public Instruction, which deserves particular attention. By an ordinance of February 1835, it was decreed, that an inspector should be appointed for every department in France, and that these principal inspectors should be each of them assisted by one or two sub-inspectors, according as the urgency of the case might require. All the travelling expenses of all these inspectors are defrayed out of an annual sum granted for that purpose; the residue of which, when it is not entirely expended, is distributed among those who have laboured most assiduously in the service of the state.

The inspectors are required, several times a year, to visit and inspect each of the primary schools of their several districts, without giving the teachers notice beforehand, and to send in a report to the Minister of Public Instruction.

1st. Upon the state of each school-house and its classes;

2nd. Upon the moral character of the school;

3rd. Upon the instruction given, and the methods followed, by the teacher.

They are also required to pay particular attention to the state of the normal colleges in their several districts, and to visit them frequently; to correspond with the local authorities, and to inform them of any defect in the management, &c. of the schools, which they consider to require immediate remedy; and once in every year to present a report to the prefects of their several departments on the condition and progress of education in each of the schools.

Each department is obliged, either alone or in conjunction with other neighbouring departments, to support ONE NORMAL COLLEGE *for the education of its teachers.* The expenses of this establishment are borne by the department; whilst the direction of the education given in it is vested in the Minister of Public Instruction, who is responsible to the Assembly, of which he is an ex-officio member, for the right exercise of his power. The directors of these normal colleges, and of the primary classes, which are annexed to them, are nominated by the Minister of Public Instruction, on the presentation of the prefect of the department, and of the rector of the academy. Their salaries are paid from the public funds set apart for the public instruction.

The instruction given in the normal colleges of France comprehends —

1. Moral and religious instruction;
2. Reading;
3. Arithmetic;
4. French grammar;
5. Linear drawing, surveying, and the other applications of practical geometry;
6. The elements of the physical sciences;
7. Music;
8. The elements of geography and history, and more particularly of the history of France;
9. The grafting and the cutting of trees.

I have no need to remark how grievously inferior the education of the majority of our parochial teachers is, to the above standard of French primary education. In the majority of the schools we at present possess, the education comprises nothing more than religious instruction, — often of the most meagre kind, — reading, writing, and a little arithmetic. The generality of our schoolmasters are not capable of giving a more liberal education than this, and are often incapable of giving even this; and even where there is an efficient teacher, he hardly ever possesses the apparatus necessary for carrying out the education of his scholars.

The university, the departments, the communes, and private individuals, are enabled to settle upon the normal colleges pensions for the maintenance and education of poor but worthy young men, desirous of being educated as teachers.

No candidate can be *admitted* into a normal college, unless he comply with the following conditions: —

1. He must be at least sixteen years old.

2. He must produce certificates of good character, and a certificate of a physician, that he has been vaccinated, and that he is not subject to any infirmity, incompatible with the proper exercise of the duties of teacher.

3. He must pass an examination before a departmental committee, charged with the examination of candidates, desirous of obtaining *brevets de capacité*; of his being able to read and write correctly; of his having a knowledge of the rudiments of French gram-

mar and of arithmetic; and of his having a satisfactory acquaintance with the principles of the religion he professes.

The examiners are not *bound* to receive a candidate, who complies with these conditions, unless they are satisfied with his disposition, his character, and his intelligence.

No one can be admitted into a college unless he binds himself to serve as teacher, in a communal school, *at least ten years;* and if the candidate is under age, he cannot be admitted, unless his father, his mother, or his guardian, contracts for him.

If a young man, who has thus bound himself, quits the profession of a teacher, before the time of his engagement is ended, he is obliged by law to repay to the department the whole expense of his education in the normal college. The teachers of the department are allowed to attend the courses of instruction given in the normal college, in order to perfect their knowledge in branches of knowledge, in which they feel themselves deficient, or to learn the new methods of teaching, which have been adopted as more effectual, since they left the college.

The department committee, of which I have formerly spoken, has the power of granting assistance to those teachers who attend the normal colleges for the purpose of improving themselves.

The normal colleges admit members of all religions. All dogmatical instruction is avoided in the *general* lessons. The students receive this instruction at hours set apart for it, from clergy of their own church.

No student can officiate as teacher, in any school whatever, until he has obtained a certificate of his proficiency in the doctrines of his own religion, from a minister of his own church, until he is eighteen years old, and until he has presented to the mayor of the commune in which he wishes to conduct a school —

1. A certificate of his capability (*un brevet de capacité*) of conducting a school, which certificate must be obtained from the departmental committee, appointed to examine candidates desirous of conducting schools.

2. A certificate of moral character, which must be obtained from the mayor of the communes, or of each of the communes, in which he has lived during the last three years.

Whoever ventures to conduct a primary school without having complied with these regulations, and without having obtained from the departmental commission à *brevet de capacité*, is liable to a fine of 200 francs. His school will be closed.

I have spoken several times of the departmental commission charged with the examination of all aspirants to *brevets de capacité*. The law requires that there must be, in each department, at least one commission of primary education; charged with the examination of all candidates for a *brevet de capacité*, with the power of granting these brevets, and with the examination of all young men desiring to enter the normal colleges.

The members of these commissions are named by the Minister of Public Instruction.

The examinations are public, and the periods when

they take place are fixed and publicly announced by the minister. They are always conducted in the chief town of each department.

The commission is formed of at least seven members, three of whom are nominated from the members of the body of public instruction; a fourth must be a minister of religion. In the words of M. Kilean, who has collected all the enactments relative to primary education in France,—

"La loi a mis l'instruction morale et religieuse en tête de l'instruction primaire: il faut donc que l'instituteur ait prouvé qu'il saura transmettre aux enfans confiés à ses soins ces importantes notions, première règle de la vie. Nul doute que tout fonctionnaire de l'instruction publique, tout père de famille qui, sur la proposition des recteurs, aura été nommé membre d'une commission d'examen, ne soit en état d'apprécier l'instruction morale et religieuse des candidats; mais il convient que les futurs instituteurs fassent leurs preuves de capacité en ce genre, sous les yeux des hommes que leur caractère propre et leur mission spéciale appellent plus particulièrement à en être juges."

The number of the commission is not limited to seven.

On the contrary, besides six laymen, who ought to form part of it, there ought to be joined to it a minister of each of the three religious sects, recognised by the state; (viz. the Romanist, the Protestant, and the Jewish), which is to be found in the department.

In the scientific examinations, the commission may avail itself, if necessary, of the aid of scientific men.

If the candidate passes an examination in a satisfactory manner, he receives a *brevet de capacité* enabling him to conduct a primary school. I ought to add, that the examination varies, according as the candidate is destined to conduct an *elementary* or *superior* primary school.

The following are the forms of the certificate of examination, and of the *brevet de capacité* granted by the commission of inspection:—

" PROCÈS-VERBAL D'EXAMEN POUR L'INSTRUCTION PRIMAIRE, ÉLÉMENTAIRE, OU SUPÉRIEURE.

" Instruction primaire, élémentaire, ou supérieure.

" Procès-verbal de l'examen subi par le Sieur . . . ., né le . . . . département de . . . ., à l'effet d'obtenir le Brevet de capacité pour l'instruction primaire, élémentaire, ou supérieure.

" Matières de l'Examen.	Résultat de l'Examen.	Observations.
. . . .	. . . .	. . . .
. . . .	. . . .	. . . .

" Nous membres de la Commission d'Instruction primaire réunis en la salle de . . . . au nombre de . . . . membres, après avoir fait subir publiquement au Sieur . . . . l'examen qui précéde,

" Avons jugé que le Sieur . . . . était digne d'obtenir le Brevet de capacité pour l'instruction primaire, élémentaire, ou supérieure.

" En foi de quoi nous avons signé le présent procès-verbal dont un duplicate sera aussitôt transmis à M. le Recteur de l'Académie.

"A' . . . . ce . . . ., 184 .

"Signature du récipiendaire . . . .

"BREVET DE CAPACITÉ.

"Instruction primaire, élémentaire, ou supérieure.

"Président et membres de la Commission d'Instruction primaire séant à . . . ., chef lieu de l'arrondissement ou du département de . . . ., académie de . . . ., nommé par M. le Ministre, secrétaire d'état du département de l'Instruction publique, et chargés à ce titre: 1. d'examiner les aspirants au Brevet de capacité pour l'instruction primaire, élémentaire, ou supérieure: 2. de délivrer le dit brevet aux aspirants qui en auront été jugés dignes, ... Vu le procès-verbal par nous dressé ce jourd'hui, et constatant que le Sieur . . . ., né le . . . . à . . . ., canton de . . . ., arrondissement de . . . ., département de . . . ., a été examiné par nous, sur [énumérer les divers objets de l'examen, conformément aux articles 8 ou 9 du réglement], ainsi que sur les procédés méthodes d'enseignement de ces diverses connaissances; vu les articles 4 et 25 de la loi du 28 Juin 1833; et les articles 1, 5, 8, 10, 11, et 12, du réglement du conseil royal, en date du 15 Juillet 1833,

"Estimons, que le candidat a fait preuve de la capacité requise pour donner l'instruction primaire, élémentaire, ou supérieure, et, en conséquence, avons accordé au dit Sieur . . . . le présent brevet, pour lui servir et valoir ce que de raison.

"Délivré à . . . . , le . . . . 183 .

"Signature de l'impétrant . . . .

"Au nom et sous l'autorité de M. le Ministre de l'Instruction Publique.

"Les Membres de la Commission d'Instruction Primaire."

It remains for me now to explain, how the funds for the maintenance and working of this great and liberal system of national education are defrayed.

The expenses of the normal colleges are paid out of the departmental treasures; or, as we should say in England, out of the county rates.

If a department is not rich enough to support a normal college, the prefect of the department is empowered to concert with the prefects of the neighbouring departments, for the establishment and maintenance of one joint normal college for several departments, the expenses of which are borne by them proportionally to their population. It is not left to the departments to define, what number of professors is necessary in such a college, or what salaries should be given to them: these are matters regulated by the state; for it is felt, that unless good and sufficient salaries are provided for the professors and teachers *by law,* the standard of attainment amongst them would soon be lessened; as the departments are too immediately interested in the reduction of the heavy, but necessary expenses of supporting the colleges, and often too little interested in a matter of such vital importance to the nation as the education of its citizens.

They have, therefore, wisely concluded that the state alone can be entrusted with these important regulations.

There are NINETY-TWO great colleges in France, established for the education of teachers, while in England and Wales we have not more than ten deserving of notice!

The number of young men in the normal colleges of France, in 1843, was 3012. These students were divided thus: —

Number of students, supported by exhibitions, founded by the state - - - - - -	249
Number of students, supported by exhibitions, founded by the departments - - - - -	2,244
Number of students, supported by exhibitions, founded by the communes - - - - - -	86
Number of students who pay for their own education - -	389
Number, who are admitted for instruction only, free of expense -	44
Total - - -	3,012

So that, out of the whole number of students, who receive instruction in the normal colleges, only 389 pay for it.

This appears to me to be a very wise arrangement. If we only admit into the normal colleges, those, who will pay a certain part of the expense of their education, it is true, that we can generally ensure a more respectable class of young men; but this class is not generally so well suited to the humble though honourable drudgery of a village schoolmaster's life, as the sons of the peasants themselves, who cannot afford to pay anything towards their education.

It would seem to be advisable for government to

encourage the founding of exhibitions at the normal colleges, for defraying the expense of the education of peasants' sons as teachers.

Besides SEVENTY-SIX normal colleges, which are now established for the education of schoolmasters, sixteen others have been opened in France for the education of schoolmistresses. The departments contribute annually towards the expense of these latter colleges the sum of 60,459 francs, the state 11,430 francs, and the pupil-teachers themselves 13,558 francs.

The number of young women in these colleges, in 1843, was 283, divided as follows: —

Number supported by exhibitions founded by the state	33
Number supported by exhibitions founded by the departments	174
Number paying for their own education	28
Number admitted to the classes free of expense	48
Total	283

Eight of these colleges are directed by members of religious associations, and the schoolmistresses belonging to these religious societies are found to be much more serviceable than the lay schoolmistresses. In this respect the Roman Church has a great advantage over us. Had we institutions, where females desirous of devoting themselves to a religious life, and to the education of the poor, could be educated; we should soon have them filled, and should thus secure to the country a body of religious, zealous, and enlightened teachers of poor girls. Without institutions of this kind, we shall always find it very difficult, to obtain a sufficient supply of good female teachers. For not only are the duties of a schoolmistress such as most young women fear to encounter alone, without the protection and support of a husband; but even, if we could find a sufficient number of young women to supply the village schools of England and Wales, the desertions from their ranks would always be very numerous and frequent, as marriages would be more frequent amongst them, than amongst any other set of women; from the value set upon sensible and well-educated wives by the poor, and even by the middle classes. From this cause, the annual vacancies in schoolmistresses' situations in France are very much more numerous in proportion to the number of situations, than the annual vacancies in schoolmasters' situations.

In the institutions directed by members of religious associations, the French government most wisely claims the right of inspecting the schools and classes, and forbids any young woman engaging in the duties of schoolmistress, until she has obtained from the local committee a *brevet de capacité*.

The number of schoolmasters' situations annually vacant in France is 1888, and that of schoolmistresses 787. There are two causes for the number of the former vacancies being so numerous.

One is, that the payment of the masters of France is not good, the other, that industrial training is not yet sufficiently developed in of the normal colleges. As long as a country will educate a set of intellectual *gentlemen* for the management of *pauper* schools, so long, despite of all its efforts, it will find, that the number of desertions from the teachers' ranks will be great. The first of these defects is now being remedied by the present French government. The second will not long escape observation in a country paying such attention to the question of primary education.

In addition to the great number of colleges for the instruction of teachers, of which I have spoken, there is another establishment for the same purpose, to which I cannot advert without feelings of the deepest gratification. I mean the normal college and religious foundation of the Frères Chrétiens at Paris. No one interested in the progress of true Christianity, and in the advancement of the best interests of the people, should fail to visit these excellent men, and to witness a spectacle, which truly exhibits, in these active days, a realisation of the apostolic times.

The Frères are a society of men, *devoted entirely and exclusively to the education of the poor.* They take the vow of celibacy, renounce all the pleasures of society and relationship, enter into the brotherhood, and retain only two objects in life — their own spiritual advancement, and the education of children of the poor. Before a young man can be received into the society, he is required to pass an intermediate period of education and trial, during which he is denied all the ordinary pleasures of life, is accustomed to the humblest and most servile occupations, and receives an excellent and most liberal education. During this period, which lasts three years, he is carefully instructed in the principles of the Romanist religion, in the sciences, in the French and Latin languages, in history, geography, arithmetic, writing, &c., while he is, during the same time, required to perform the most humble household duties. The frères and the young men, who are passing through their first novitiate, manage in turn all the household duties — as the cooking, the preparation of the meals, and all the ordinary duties of domestic servants. These duties, together with their simple and perfectly plain costume, and their separation from the world and from their friends, who are only permitted to visit them at long intervals, accustom them to the arduous and self-denying life, they are called upon afterwards to lead in the primary schools.

By these means, is formed a character admirably fitted for the important office of a teacher.

The frères never leave the walls of one of their houses, except in company. One frère is not permitted to travel without being accompanied by another; and when a department or commune requires their services in a primary school, *three* are sent out, one of whom manages their domestic concerns, whilst the other two conduct the school classes. When, however, there is in any town, more than one school conducted by frères, they all live together under the superintendence of an elder frère, who is styled director.

If, at the end of the first novitiate, the young man is still willing and desirous of entering the brotherhood, he is admitted by gradual advancement and preparation into the bosom of the society. He is then at the disposition of the principal of the order, who sends him, in company with two brothers, to some district, which has requested a teacher from them.

What remains of their salaries, after defraying the expenses of their frugal table, *is returned to the trea-*

sury of the society, by which it is expended in the printing of school-books, in the various expenses of their central establishment, and in works of charity.

Before a frère is allowed to conduct a primary school, he is obliged to obtain, in like manner as all the other teachers of French, a *brevet de capacité;* government demanding in all cases assurance, that every teacher has a certain amount of knowledge, and that a certain amount of secular instruction is given in their schools.

All the schools of this order are open as well to the inspectors of government, who regularly visit, examine, and report upon them, as to the periodical examination of several of the elder of the brotherhood, who travel at the expense of the society, and examine with great strictness the conduct and progress of the frères in all their different schools, and report to the principal of the order in Paris.

This society exists in various countries, and the following table, extracted from some statistics recommended to my notice by the principal of the order in France, will show the number of schools conducted by Frères in 1844, and the number of children educated in them, throughout Europe.

	Number of Schools conducted by Frères.	Number of Children in these Schools.
France - -	658	169,501
Belgium - -	41	9,535
Savoy - -	28	5,110
Piedmont - -	30	6,490
Pontifical States -	20	4,199
Canada - -	6	1,840
Turkey - -	2	580
Switzerland - -	2	444
Total - -	787	197,699

The education given in their schools is very liberal, and the books used very good. The frères consider that if they neglect to develope the intellect of their pupils, they cannot advance their religious education satisfactorily; they consequently spare no pains to attain the former development, in order that the latter, which is the great end of their teaching and of all instruction whatsoever, may not be retarded.

I annex a few of the regulations of the society, referring all, who wish to know more of this interesting association, to a work recently published at Paris, entitled "De l'Association en général et spécialement de l'Association Charitable des Frères des Ecoles Chrétiennes, par M. Rendu": —

"1. The Institution des Frères des Ecoles Chrétiennes is a society, which professes to conduct schools gratuitously.

"The design of this institution is to give a christian education to children. With this object in view, the frères conduct schools, where children may be placed under the management of teachers from morning until evening, so that the teachers may be able to teach them to live honestly and uprightly, by instructing them in the principles of our holy religion, by teaching them christian precepts, and by giving them suitable and sufficient instruction.

"2. The spirit of the institution is a spirit of faith, which ought to encourage its members to attribute all to God, to act as continually in the sight of God, and in perfect conformity to his orders and his will. The members of this association should be filled with an ardent zeal for the instruction of children, for their preservation in innocence and the fear of God, and for their entire separation from sin.

"3. The institution is directed by a superior, who is nominated for life. He has two assistants, who compose his council, and aid him in governing the society. These assistants live in the same house with him, assist at his councils, and render him aid, whenever necessary.

"4. The superior is elected by ballot, by the directors assembled at the principal houses; the two assistants are chosen in the same manner; and these latter hold office ten years, and can then be re-elected.

"5. The superior may be deposed; but only by a general chapter, and for grave causes.

"6. This chapter is composed of thirty of the oldest frères, or directors of the principal houses, who assemble by right once every ten years, and whenever it is deemed necessary to convoke an extraordinary meeting.

"7. The private houses are governed by frères-directors, who are appointed for three years, unless it appears advisable to the superior and his assistants to name a shorter period, or to recall them before the end of it.

"8. The superior names the visitors. They are appointed for three years, and make a round of visits once every year. They require of the directors an account of the receipts and expenses, and as soon as their visits are completed, they present a report to their superior of the necessary changes and corrections to be made by him.

"9. No frère can take priests' orders, or pretend to

any ecclesiastical office, neither can he wear a surplice, or serve in the churches, except at daily mass; but all confine themselves to their vocations and live in silence, in retreat, and in entire devotion to their duties.

"10. They are bound to the institution by three simple religious vows, which are taken at first for only three years, as well as by a vow of perseverance, and a renouncement of any recompense for the instruction they give. These vows can only be annulled after dispensation granted by the Pope.

"11. They are not admitted to take the vows, until they have been at least two years in the institution, and until they have passed one year in the noviciate, and one year in the school.

"12. They are only admitted after a severe examination, and then only by the votes of a majority of the frères of the house, in which they have passed their novitiate.

"13. They have two noviciates—one to which young men between thirteen and sixteen years of age, and the other to which older men, are admitted. But all young men, below the age of twenty-five, who enter the society, must renew their vows every year, till they attain that age.

"14. They banish from the society every frère, who conducts himself unbecomingly. But this is only done for grave offences, and by a majority of votes, at a general chapter.

"15. The same regulation is observed, when a frère desires to leave the society, and to obtain a dispensation from his vows.

"16. The frères will not establish themselves in the dioceses without the consent of the bishops, and will acknowledge their authority as their spiritual government, and that of the magistrates as their civil government.

"19. The frères shall instruct their pupils after the method prescribed to them by the institution.

"20. They shall teach their scholars to read French and Latin, and to write.

"21. They shall also teach them orthography, arithmetic, the matins, the vespers, le Pater, l'Ave-Maria, le Credo et le Confiteor, the French translations of these prayers, the commandments of God and of the Church, the responses of the holy mass, the catechism, the duties of a Christian, and the maxims and precepts, which our Lord has left us in the Holy Testament.

"22. They shall teach the catechism half-an-hour daily."

They also teach geography, French, and universal history, drawing and singing. Their school books are very excellent, and the education given in their schools very liberal and sound. There is no attempt to diminish the quantity or quality of secular instruction; but, on the contrary, every effort is made by the frères, by giving a good instruction to their children, to prepare their minds for the reception of religious truths; that they may become practical and consistent Christians, instead of superstitious and inconsistent men. I visited one of their private schools at Paris, and was very much delighted with the quiet of the class-rooms and with the manners, and great intelligence of the children.

"27. The frères may not receive from the scholars or their parents, either money or any other presents at any time.

"30. They must exhibit an equal affection for all their poor scholars, and more for the poor, than for the rich, because the object of the institution is the instruction of the poor.

"31. They must endeavour to give their pupils, by their conduct and manners, a continual example of modesty and of all the other virtues, which the children ought to be taught, and which they ought to practise.

"37. They must take the greatest care to punish their children as rarely as possible, as they ought to be persuaded, that by refraining as much as possible from punishment, they will best succeed in properly conducting a school, and establishing order in it.

"38. When punishment has become absolutely necessary, they must take the greatest care to punish with the greatest moderation and presence of mind, and never to do it under the influence of a hasty movement, or when they feel irritated.

"39. They must watch over themselves, that they never exhibit the least anger or impatience, either in their corrections, or in any of their words or actions; as they ought to be convinced, that if they do not take these precautions, the scholars will not profit from their correction, (and the frères never ought to correct, except with the object of benefiting their children), and God will not give the correction his blessing.

"40. They must not at any time give to their scholars any injurious epithet or insulting name.

"41. They must also take the greatest care not to strike their scholars with hand, foot, or stick, nor to push them rudely.

"42. They must take great care not to pull the ears, hair, or noses of their scholars, nor to fling anything at them: these kinds of corrections ought not to be practised by the frères, as they are very indecent, and opposed to charity and Christian kindness.

"43. They must not correct their scholars during prayers, or at the time of catechising, except when they cannot defer the correction.

"44. They must not use corporal punishment, except when every other means of correction has failed to produce the right effect.

"58. The Frère-director shall be an inspector over all the schools in his town, and when more than one inspector is necessary for one house of Frères, the other inspector shall report to the Frère-director twice a week on the conduct of each frère, on the condition of his class, and on the progress of his scholars.

* * * * * *

* * * * * *

"Signé Jean Baptiste Herbet dit Frumence, Vicaire-Général des Frères des écoles chrétiennes;
Barthélemy Garnier, dit F. Barthélemy;
Jean Baptiste Dié, dit F. Emery;
Aflabel, dit F. P. Célestin."

Each commune, as I have before said, is required, either alone or in association with one or more neighbouring communes, to establish at least one primary school, to pay at least one teacher, and to furnish him with a comfortable house. If a commune cannot, either alone or by association with others, afford to provide sufficient school-room for its population, it applies for assistance first to the council of the department, and if the council is not able to render the required aid, it forwards an application to government, which is always ready to assist local efforts in the development of national education.

The following table will give an idea of the condition of primary education in the different communes in 1843 : —

Number of arrondissements - - - -	363
Number of communes - - - -	37,038
Population - - - - -	34,230,178
Number of communes provided with primary schools -	34,578
Population of communes provided with primary schools -	33,080,002
Number of communes not yet provided with a primary school	2,460
Population of the communes not yet provided with primary schools - - - - -	1,150,176
Number of communes which require several primary schools and which possess only one - - -	23
Number of communes which are required by law to support one superior primary school - - -	290
Number of communes which ought to support superior primary schools, and which do support them - -	222
Population of these communes - - -	4,177,047
Number of communes which ought to support several superior primary schools, and which support only one - -	23
Number of communes which are not required by law to support a superior primary school, and which do support one -	103
Total number of primary schools elementary and superior, for boys and girls, established in France in 1843 -	59,838
Total number of primary schools in the 86 departments of France visited in 1843 by the 87 inspectors and 113 sub-inspectors - - - - -	50,936

In addition to these schools for children, there ought to be added 6434 classes for the labourers, which are conducted by the primary school teachers in the evenings after the day's work, or on the Sundays, and in which 95,064 adult labourers received instruction in 1843 ; and also a great number of infant schools, which have been recently opened in the departments, and which are receiving great encouragement and attention from the government.

Before I close this imperfect account of the great and admirable system of primary education in France, I ought to mention two other wise and beneficial regulations. One is the formation of funds in each department, for the relief of the old and superanuated teachers, and of the widows and children of teachers who die in the exercise of their important functions. In each department every teacher is required to subscribe yearly one-twentieth part of the salary he receives from his commune, and the sum which he thus pays, together with the interest upon it, is returned to him when he retires, or to his widow and children, if he dies before retiring.

The other regulation to which I referred, is the awarding of silver and bronze medals by government, to those teachers who distinguish themselves in the management of their schools. This encourages and stimulates them to continued efforts, by offering honourable marks of the approbation of their country to those who distinguish themselves, and by reminding them that the whole nation is interested in their success.

Since the French Revolution of 1848, the salaries of

the communal teachers which were formerly too small, have been considerably augmented, and the social position of the national instructors has, in consequence, been considerably improved. This is an act worthy of the Republic, and will be productive of great good, as it makes the teachers' profession more worthy the aspirations and labours of able men of the lower classes of society.

A law is at present under the consideration of the Assembleé Nationale, which, if passed, will give the préfects, or chief magistrates of the departments, much greater powers, than they at present possess, both in the appointment of the teachers and in their suspension, when necessary. But its fate is so uncertain, that I purposely abstain from mentioning it further.

At the present moment, France has 76 normal colleges for the education of schoolmasters, and 16 for the education of schoolmistresses, making in all 92 normal colleges. To 52 of these colleges land is adjoined, for the purpose of teaching the students agriculture or horticulture. The course of instruction lasts 2 years in 49 of these schools, and 3 years in the rest.

The force of inspectors consists of 87 chief inspectors, and 114 subinspectors; and I find that in the year 1843 these gentlemen visited 30,001 communes, and inspected 50,986 schools.

The French government grants 2,000,000*l*. per annum for the furtherance of national education. This is in addition to the enormous local funds, which are expended annually on the same object by the departments and communes.

In England the government grants 120,000*l.* a year for the same purpose.

TABLE showing the Number of Primary Schools belonging to the different Sects recognised by the State.

Schools	Type	Sex	Number	Subtotal	Total
Primary Schools specially set apart for the Roman Catholics - -	Public Schools.	Boys	33,207	40,867	56,812
		Girls	7,660		
	Private Schools.	Boys	17,098	15,945	
		Girls	8,847		
Primary Schools set apart for the Protestants -	Public Schools.	Boys	702	761	1,080
		Girls	59		
	Private Schools.	Boys	163	39	
		Girls	156		
Primary Schools specially set apart for the Jews	Public Schools.	Boys	33	37	115
		Girls	4		
	Private Schools.	Boys	74	78	
		Girls	4		
Mixed Schools open for all three Sects - -	Public Schools.	Boys	948	4055	1,831
		Girls	107		
	Private Schools.	Boys	326	776	
		Girls	450		
Total Number of Primary Schools in France in 1843 -					59,838

I shall now give a very brief sketch of the admirable educational system of HOLLAND.

In England not one in every 12 of the population is receiving primary instruction; in the Dutch provinces of Drenthe and Over Yesel, in 1835, the proportion was about one in six, and throughout Holland generally it was one in eight. There is scarcely a child of ten years of age, and of sound intellect in Holland, who cannot both read and write; almost every every one receives instruction at some period, the expense of which is for the most part, and in some instances entirely, defrayed by the state, without the inculcation of any particular creed; the interference of government being exerted only to exclude improper and incompetent teachers, and to regulate the mode of instruction by a system of inspection.

Mr. Nicholls, in his interesting Report on the Condition of the Labouring Poor in Belgium and Holland, published in 1838, from which I quote by his permission, says —

"Nothing can exceed the cleanliness, the personal propriety, and the apparent comfort of the people of Holland. I did not see a house or fence out of repair, or a garden that was not carefully cultivated. We met no ragged or dirty persons, nor any drunken men; neither did I see any indication that drunkenness is the vice of any portion of the people. I was assured, that bastardy was almost unknown; and, although we were, during all hours of the day, much in the public thoroughfares, we saw only two beggars, and they in manners and appearance scarcely came within the designation.

"The Dutch people appear to be strongly attached to their government, and few countries possess a population, in which the domestic and social duties are discharged with such constancy. A scrupulous economy and cautious foresight seem to be the characteristic virtues of every class. To spend their full annual income is accounted a species of crime. The same systematic prudence pervades every part of the community, agricultural and commercial, and thus the Dutch people are enabled to bear up against the most formidable physical difficulties, and to secure a larger amount of individual comfort than probably exists in any other country."

But what has led to this happy social state? How

has Holland improved the social condition of her people? I answer, by providing for their education, and by teaching them to think and to care for themselves. Holland has the honour of having been one of the first among the European nations which recognised the truth, that an uncivilised and degraded peasantry are always more immoral and wretched, than one whose minds have been disenthralled, and whose tastes have been raised by a religious, moral, and intellectual education; and she has the still greater honour of having been one of the first to throw off the shackles of uncharitable and unchristian sectarianism, and to assert and to act on the assertion, that the doctrines in which all Christian sects agree, are immeasurably more important, than the doctrines in which they differ.

I shall give a very brief sketch of the organisation and present condition of primary education in Holland.

The department of Public Instruction is directed by the Minister of the Interior, aided by the "Inspector General of Public Instruction." This latter person is, in reality, the Minister of Education. There is no further centralisation than this. There is neither a council nor any other central inspectors than the Inspector General.

It is only since 1800, that primary education has re ceived the serious attention of the Dutch government. M. Van der Palm, in that year, introduced into the Chamber of the Representatives of the Batavian Republic, a great scheme of national education, which was modified and altered by M. Van den Ende, and finally adopted in February 1806.

This code of instruction is so well suited to the

spirit and genius of the country, that it has survived three great revolutions without receiving any great alteration.

In each province, there is a commission of primary instruction. This commission is composed of all the inspectors of the different school districts into which the province is divided. In each of these school districts, there resides an inspector of the schools, who is required to visit and inspect each school in his district, at least twice a year. Each inspector is the director of the primary education of his district. Before he has examined and approved a candidate, no one can exercise the office of either public or private instructor, nor can any teacher obtain advancement, without his permission. The parochial school societies have no power to do anything without his assent, and he is either president or influential member of all in his district.

Three times a year, all the inspectors of each province assemble at its chief town, where the governor of the province presides over their meetings. Each of these conferences lasts two or three weeks, during which time each inspector reads aloud his report of the progress and state of education in his district, and refers to the meeting any questions on which he may desire to have their decision.

Each province has its own special regulations on primary education, founded on the general law of the country. The meeting of the inspectors examines whether the acts of the inspectors have conformed with these regulations, and prepares a general report on the state and progress of education in the province, which is forwarded to the Inspector-General, together with such proposals for changes or modifications in the provincial regulations as may seem advisable to the meeting.

Thus each inspector is responsible to the provincial board for the progress of education within his district, whilst the provincial boards are themselves responsible to the government.

Before a candidate can become a teacher, he must obtain, besides a certificate of moral character, brevets of—

1. General Admission;
2. Special Admission.

He must obtain a brevet of general admission to the profession of teacher, by passing an examination before the provincial commission composed of the inspectors of the districts of the province. When he has obtained this general admission, he becomes an authorised candidate; but he is not yet at liberty to exercise the functions of either public or private teacher. If the candidate wishes to be a private teacher, it is necessary for him to obtain the authorisation of the municipal authorities, which cannot be granted without the consent of the inspector. If the candidate wishes to be a teacher in a public school, he is obliged to pass another examination before a local committee, where the inspector sits as one of the judges; and should the inspector think the decision of the commission unwise, and that the candidate is not worthy to be entrusted with the care of a school, the inspector has a right to appeal against the decision of this commission to the minister. Even when elected by the commission, the candidate is obliged to visit the inspector, and obtain his sanction. Such are the great precautions, which Holland takes in the election of her teachers; whilst with us, in the great majority of cases, any one is considered sufficiently qualified to fill this important office. I myself have seen men entrusted with the care of schools, whose immorality and lowness was so marked with indelible lines upon their countenances, that I would on no account have entrusted them with the duties of the humblest menial.

The suspension or dismissal of the teachers is pronounced, when it is necessary, by the municipal or provincial authorities, but only on the proposition of the inspectors.

The inspectors themselves are appointed and paid by the state.

The inspectors are charged to take care that no books are employed in the primary schools, but such as are authorised by government.

The law of 1801 proclaims, as the great end of all instruction, the exercise of the social and Christian virtues. In this respect it agrees with the law of Prussia and France; but it differs from the law of these countries in the way by which it attempts to attain this end. In France, and all the German countries, the schools are the auxiliaries, so to speak, of the churches; for, whilst the schools are open to all sects, yet the teacher is a man trained up in the particular doctrines of the majority of his pupils, and required to teach those doctrines during certain hours, the children who differ from him in religious belief, being permitted to absent themselves from the religious lessons, on condition that their parents provided elsewhere for their religious instruction. But, in Holland, the teachers are required to give religious instruction to all the children, and to avoid most carefully touching on any of the grounds of controversy between the different sects.

Mr. Nicholls says: "As respects religion, the population of Holland is divided, in about equal proportions, into Catholic, Lutheran, and Protestants of the reformed Calvinistic church; and the ministers of each are supported by the state. The schools contain, without distinction, the children of every sect of Christians. The religious and moral instruction afforded to the children is taken from the pages of Holy Writ, and the whole course of education is mingled with a frequent reference to the great general evidences of revelation. Biblical history is taught, not as a dry narration of facts, but as a store-house of truths, calculated to influence the affections, to correct and elevate the manners, and to inspire sentiments of devotion and virtue. The great principles and truths of Christianity, in which all are agreed, are likewise carefully inculcated; but those points, which are the subjects of difference and religious controversy, form no part of the instructions of the schools. This department of religious teaching is confided to the ministers of each persuasion, who discharge this portion of their duties out of school; but within the schools the common ground of instruction is faithfully preserved, and they are, consequently, altogether free from the spirit of jealousy or proselytism. We witnessed the exercise of a class of the children of notables of Haarlem (according to the simultaneous method), respecting the death and resurrection of our Saviour, by a minister of the Lutheran church. The class contained children of Catholics, Calvinists, and other denominations of Christians, as well as Lutherans, and all disputable doctrinal points were carefully avoided. The Lutherans are the smallest in number, the Calvinists the largest, and the Catholics about midway between the two; but all appear to live together in perfect amity, without the slightest distinction in the common intercourse of life; and this circumstance, so extremely interesting in itself, no doubt facilitated the establishment of the general system of education here described, the *effects of which are so apparent in the highly moral and intellectual condition of the Dutch people.*"

Education is not compulsory in Holland, as it is in Switzerland and in all the German countries; but the inspectors throughout the country, whose number is about eighty, have so excited the zeal of the departmental and communal committees, and have been so well seconded in their efforts by the ministers of religion in their parochial visitations, in their sermons, and in their lectures, and by the excellent administration of public relief, *which is invariably refused, unless the children of the parents applying for relief are sent to school;* that the necessity of compulsory regulations has not been felt; and we find, that in several parts of the kingdom, the proportion of children attending school, to the whole population, is as great as *one in every six;* whilst the proportion generally of the children receiving instruction to the whole population, *is one in every eight.*

These admirable results have been obtained slowly. The causes which have most contributed to them, are the excellence of the schools, the talent of the teachers, and, above all, the respect and honour the teachers have gradually attained by the honourable and independent situation, in which they have been placed by the government.

Nothing can be a more fatal delusion, than to suppose that the poor are indifferent to the character and acquirements of the teacher. I have seen the most remarkable instances to the contrary, and I could mention more than fifty instances, which have come under my own knowledge, where the schools conducted by able and high-minded teachers have been filled to overflowing, where, previously, the schools being conducted by inefficient and low-minded men, hardly contained sufficient numbers for one small class. It is shameful to suppose, that the poor, even where they themselves have never enjoyed any education, are indifferent to these matters. Natural love and affection are not the results of education, but, on the contrary, are found generally much stronger in the cottage than in the palace; and they teach the parents, no matter how ignorant, to keep their children under their own eye at home, rather than to expose them to the misery and moral degradation of the instruction of a narrow-minded and ignorant man. As long as we are content to fill any of the teachers' situations with wholly unfit persons, and as long as we are content to leave the teachers to work in the schools without any constant inspection by the central authority, so long shall we continue in many instances to do positive injury to the poor, instead of conferring benefit upon them. We are creating miserable and demoralising associations in connection with all the humanising influences of a good education. The Bible, and the books used in the classes, remind of the hated classes, where the child was miserable under the caprice of an ignorant and low-minded teacher, and they are laid aside as producing disagreeable sensations, reminiscences of the school-days.

The Dutch government has not defined the minimum of the teachers' salaries, as the French, Swiss, and German governments have done, but it has enjoined (réglement A, art. 30.) upon the parochial committees to take care, that they pay their teachers well, and it has promised its assistance to any parish, which is too poor to raise the necessary funds. The inspectors have, as I have shown, sufficient power to enforce the actual observance of this injunction; and it appears that the teachers throughout the country are satisfied with their situations.

Mr. Nicholls says, "The schoolmasters of the primary schools in Holland are supported in respectability and comfort. Their functions are held in high estimation, and we were assured, that they were generally content with their lot; but there is no positive provision fixing their salaries. The law only enacts, generally, that the municipal and departmental authorities shall secure a sufficient income to the teachers, and *that they shall not be left dependent upon payments from the parents of their scholars.*"

This last regulation is very wise, as it is highly important that the teachers' incomes should be certain as well as sufficient to secure them a respectable maintenance. The Dutch think it advisable to oblige all the parents, who send their children to school, and *who can afford it,* to pay some small weekly sum for the education of their children. They think that by doing this, the parents become more interested in the progress of their children, and that, on the other hand, the teacher is interested in pleasing the parents, and in the improvement of the children, as the greater the progress they make, the greater will generally be the numbers of his school, and the greater will be his weekly gains.

In the great part of Germany, however, primary education has been made entirely gratuitous since the revolutions of 1848.

I again quote Mr. Nicholls, who says: "To the schools thus provided, the people, without any exception or distinction, are entitled to send their children on payment of certain fixed sums monthly, or at shorter periods. These payments are regulated with reference to the nature of the education to be afforded; but the whole charge, even for the highest class, is of small amount. *In the case of parents so poor, or so burdened with large families as to be actually unable to pay, the local authorities are empowered to remit the charge;* and thus the means of education are secured to the lowest, as well as to the highest. We were assured that no abuse of the power of exemption had ever occurred, and that no charge of partiality had ever been made. The people acquiesced cheerfully and contentedly in every arrangement, and were as desirous of sending their children to be educated, as the government and local authorities were to impart the benefits of education. In Haarlem, with a population of 21,000, we were informed *there was not a child of ten years of age, and of sound intellect, who could not both read and write,* and throughout Holland it is the same."

There are two normal colleges in Holland for the instruction of teachers; one at Groningen, for the province of Friesland, Drenthe, and Overyssel, and the other at Haarlem, for the rest of Holland.

It was in 1816 that the Dutch government first established normal colleges, after having in vain tried all other methods for obtaining a sufficient supply of efficient teachers.

I visited the college at Haarlem in 1848: it was under the direction of the celebrated educationist Herr Princen; it was one of the first normal colleges ever established in Europe.

There were forty students in the college; the students remain in the college FOUR years, before they leave to undertake the management of the elementary schools.

The subjects of instruction in the college are —

The Scriptures;

Arithmetic;

Writing;

History of Holland;
General History;
Geography;
Mathematics;
Natural History;
Botany;
Singing;
The Art of Teaching.

The education given in the college IS PERFECTLY GRATUITOUS: all the expenses of the college are borne by the States. Before a candidate can be admitted into the college definitely, he is obliged to pass through a trial of three months; if nothing is discovered during this trial, which proves him to be unfitted to be a teacher, a report is made to the minister on his character, conduct, and general fitness for a teacher's duties; and, if this report is satisfactory, the candidate is admitted into the college.

I have mentioned, before, the two kinds of examinations which each candidate is required to pass before he can obtain permission to conduct a primary school. By far the most important of these is the examination of general admission; this examination is perfectly organised in Holland.

The brevets granted to those who pass an examination are of four kinds; varying according to the merits of the teachers: they consequently constitute four ranks among the teachers. The towns never admit any teachers but of the first and second rank; a brevet of the first rank cannot be obtained, until the candidate has attained the age of twenty-five years. The brevet of the third rank only confers the right of conducting a village school, and the brevet of the fourth rank only confers the right of acting as assistant teacher in some town or village school, or of conducting a village school where the pay is very poor, if such a school can be found.

The examinations embrace the scientific attainments of the candidates, their methods of instruction, their power of disciplining and governing a school, and a strict inquiry into their character and religious education. After the examinations are concluded, the brevets are delivered with the ranks of their respective candidates inscribed upon them, as well as a short *résumé* of their characters and attainments. The names and ranks of the different candidates are then published in the official Journal of Public Instruction.

It is not necessary for me to point out what emulation this plan begets among the pupil teachers in the normal colleges, and among the teachers in the lower classes of the primary schools: they know that by improving themselves, they may raise themselves to the highest ranks of their profession.

But as M. Cousin justly remarks, however well organized the examinations themselves may be, their real efficiency must entirely depend on the persons who are selected to form the commissions of examinations. If men, who have never given their thoughts to education, were chosen, the examinations would degenerate into a mere empty farce, as ridiculous as they would be injurious to the community. But here again, the Dutch have made some very wise and important regulations. The commissioners, who conduct these examinations, are the inspectors themselves, assembled in the provincial meetings; men who have spent years in studying the best way of promoting the education of the poor; men who thoroughly understand what ought to be required of a man, wishing to enter into the honourable profession of the teachers; and men, also, who are personally interested in obtaining good and able men for their several districts.

Every district inspector is required by law to convene, either at his own house in the district, or at some other place, as shall appear most convenient to himself, at certain fixed periods, an educational conference, to which he is required to invite all the teachers of his district. At these conferences the general progress of education in the district, and the best means of promoting and furthering its further developments are discussed, and the teachers are reminded that they are not struggling singly and unaided, but that each one is a member of a well-disciplined army, all engaged in the same great enterprise, the moral reformation of their country.

As regards the proportional number of teachers and scholars, it is ordained; that if the number of scholars attending a primary school is under seventy, one teacher only need be provided; but that if it exceeds seventy, the commune must either alone, or with the assistance of government, support two teachers.

When a scholar leaves the primary school in which he has been educated, he receives, if he has conducted himself well and made a satisfactory progress in his studies, an honorary certificate, which of course is of great assistance to him afterwards when seeking a situation.

As I mentioned before, the same plan is adopted in Prussia, and with the most admirable results, as it stimulates the scholars to distinguish themselves by their attention to their studies, and to gain the approbation of their teachers by their orderly deportment in the school. But it is highly important that the power of granting these certificates should not be left to the teachers alone, as it enables a tyrannical and capricious man to blast the future prospects of a poor child, merely perhaps to gratify some unreasonable prejudice or dislike, arising from an unintentional or slight personal affront offered him by the scholar.

M. Cousin thinks, that Holland ought to have five instead of two normal colleges; and certainly, when we consider the numbers which are found necessary in France, Prussia, Saxony, Austria, Switzerland, Hanover, and Bavaria, it would seem that two are not a sufficient number for 2,600,000 inhabitants. The reason why Holland does not require so many as other countries is, that she seems to have provided a more comfortable livelihood for the primary teachers than the other European nations have done. I have mentioned several times before, that it is found to be very bad economy to stint the pay of the teachers. The worse they are paid, the shorter time they will stay at their posts; for it cannot be expected, that the majority of the teachers will be so philanthropic as to forego the good pay, which their education will enable them to obtain in other situations, for poor pay and hard work as a village teacher.

The school-buildings in Holland are very good. I inspected several of them in different parts of the country. Each school-house contains from one to six class-rooms. The children are divided into classes, according to their proficiency in their studies, and are separated in the different class-rooms. One or two teachers direct the studies of the children in each room. There are, however, generally two or three times as many children in one class-room in Holland, as in Prussia.

The class rooms in Holland, as in the rest of Europe, are each fitted up with parallel rows of desks and forms where the children sit. They are kept beautifully clean, are constantly whitewashed, and are very well ventilated. All necessary apparatus is also provided. The excellent condition and character of the school-buildings prove how warmly interested the people themselves feel in the education of the young.

The appearance of the children is as beautiful as in Prussia.

I, and a friend with whom I was travelling in Holland, used to go out into the streets in the middle of the day to see the children come out from the schools, and walk home. It was a beautiful sight. The little girls, with their clean and well-made frocks, with their well-arranged hair, and with their clean hands and faces; and the boys, with their neat clothes, free from unseemly patches, with their well-brushed hair, and with their well-washed hands and faces, form a strange and almost incredible contrast with the children to be seen in the streets of our towns.

The children in Holland do not, as in Germany, carry their books home with them. In Germany, each child carries a bag or a knapsack, and whenever they go home they carry their school-books with them. The Dutch children leave their books, &c. at school. I think the German plan is the better of the two. It interests the children more in the books themselves, and in their preservation, and it impresses them with the feeling, that the books are their own property. It enables them to show their parents what they have been learning or reading. It gives them an opportunity of working at home, and of preparing for their class duties. It makes the children feel that they are trusted, and it connects the school in some degree with the home.

Such is the system of national education in Holland.

In Hanover, as, indeed, throughout all the German kingdoms, the education of the people has made very satisfactory progress, despite all the difficulties arising from religious differences. In fact, it is always easy enough to overcome these difficulties, wherever the higher classes are really interested in the people's progress.

The population of Hanover is divided into different religious sects in the following proportions:—

Lutherans - - -	1,356,000
Calvinists - - -	102,850
Roman Catholics - -	212,300
Jews - - -	11,000
Memnonites - - -	1,850

Six normal colleges have been established in the principalities of Hanover, Hildesheim, Stade, and Osnabruck; in which the teachers are educated and trained for their duties. The proportion of the children attending school, as compared with the whole population, is about 1 in every 7.

Education in Denmark is very widely diffused, there being very few persons, even among the lowest classes, who are unable to read and write. In Denmark, a general code of regulations for schools has existed since 1817. The condition of primary education has, since that period, made a continuous and very satisfactory progress. Primary schools are established in all the parishes; and here, as in Prussia, attendance at school is not optional; for, by a late law, all children between the ages of seven and fourteen years are *obliged* to attend some public school. The children, whose parents are unable to pay the usual school-fees, are educated at the public expense. The instruction given in the primary schools, besides reading, writing, arithmetic, and history, includes geography, and natural history.

The elementary schools of Denmark, amounted, in 1838, to 4600, and contained 278,500 scholars. The population in 1835 was 2,033,865, and the number of children of an age to go to school was 300,000; so that the whole of the juvenile population of Denmark may be said to have been receiving instruction.

In Sweden and Norway the education of the people is quite as satisfactorily advanced, and in the former country it is said, that there is not more than one person in every thousand who cannot read and write!

"It was from the German states that the influence of advancing civilisation spread into Switzerland, Sweden, Denmark, and Holland. The wars which succeeded the French revolution, kept back for a time the educational institutions of these states; yet even under a foreign yoke, and in the confusion consequent on rapid political changes, a gradual progress was made: every interval of quiet was in Germany and Prussia applied to the reparation of the consequences of foreign invasion; and the peace was no sooner proclaimed, than the government of every Protestant state on the continent sought to rescue the people from the demoralisation consequent on a disorganising war, and to prepare the means of future defence in the developement of the moral force of her people. England alone appears in this respect to have misunderstood the genius of Protestantism. With the wealthiest and the most enlightened aristocracy, the richest and most influential church, and the most enterprising middle class, her lower orders are, as a mass, more ignorant and less civilised than those of any other large Protestant country in Europe." *

* Recent Measures for the Promotion of Education in England.

CHAP. XIV.

THE PRESENT STATE OF PRIMARY EDUCATION IN ENGLAND AND WALES. — THE COMMITTEE OF COUNCIL ON EDUCATION. — HOW WE MIGHT PROVIDE SUFFICIENT MEANS FOR THE EDUCATION OF THE PEOPLE.

SINCE the year 1801, the population of England and Wales has nearly DOUBLED. In 1801, the population, inclusive of the army and navy, amounted to only 8,872,980, while at the present time it amounts to nearly 17,000,000, exclusive of the same forces. In 1831, the population, exclusive of the army and navy, amounted to only 13,897,187; so that, in the short space of EIGHTEEN years, it has increased by more than 3,000,000 souls!

We have, within the last four years, freed our trade and commerce from nearly every impediment to their fullest developement.

We have repealed the duties on corn, which tended formerly to prevent corn-growing countries from bringing their corn to our markets, in order to exchange it for our manufactured products; we have opened our ports to the ships of all nations, and have invited them all to come and take away our goods; we are rapidly destroying the system of piracy, which has hitherto infested the seas of China and the Eastern Archipelago, and greatly hindered the progress of our commerce in those regions; we are about to open the vast and almost unexplored markets of India by railways, and by the flat-bottomed steam-boats on the great rivers; our people are spreading themselves over all the colonies faster and faster, carrying with them a taste for, and thus forming vast markets for the sale of, English manufactures; the American people are increasing prodigiously in numbers, and the more they increase, so much the more of our products are they demanding; the American corn and cotton growers are beginning to cry out for free trade, in order that they may be able to sell us more of their corn and cotton in exchange for more of our productions; and, lastly, our own people are increasing rapidly in numbers; and as they do so, they also require more and still more from our manufacturing districts. All this must of necessity rapidly and prodigiously develope our commercial and our manufacturing system. It will augment the numbers of our operative population faster and faster, and will enormously swell the size of our manufacturing towns, and the crowd of labourers in the sea-port towns and in the manufacturing and mining districts.

To those who know, from personal experience, what the present state of those districts is, their further growth in their present condition is a terrible alternative. Upon the way in which we legislate for them during the next twenty years, depends the fate of the British Empire.

Times of terrible distress must necessarily recur at regular intervals, owing, partly, to the gluts of foreign and of home markets, produced by the ever-increasing rapidity of production by machines, and partly, also, to the disturbance of the markets by bad harvests, by wars, and by periodical speculations.

But if the population should increase in those districts during the next twenty years, as it inevitably will do, and if no *vast* plan is carried into operation, whereby to raise the moral and religious tone of those districts, it is frightful to contemplate what may be the result in some season of distress of concentrating such a mass of such a people as the present operatives upon so small an area.

I have already shown the condition of the labourers of this country, and the neglected state of the juvenile population of the towns.

What are we doing to remedy this state of things, and to prepare for the future?

I will give a short summary of the present state of primary education in England and Wales, as collected from the reports, of Her Majesty's Inspectors, of the Commissioners of Inquiry in Wales, of the National Society, of the Statistical Society, and of the city mission; from Mr. Redgrave's reports from some very able articles in the North British Review and from numerous personal inquiries in various parts of England and Wales.

1. It has been calculated that there are at the present day, in England and Wales, nearly 8,000,000 persons who cannot read and write.

2. Of all the children in England and Wales, between the ages of five and fourteen, more than the half* are not attending any school.

* The following table was put into my hands in the autumn of 1849, by the Rev. Charles Richson, clerk in orders of the Cathedral of Man-

3. Even of the class of the farmers, there are great numbers who cannot read and write.

4. Even of those children of the poor, who have received some instruction, very few know anything of geography, history, science, music, or drawing. Their instruction in the village schools has hitherto generally consisted of nothing more than a little practice in reading, writing, and Scripture history.

5. Of the teachers, who are officiating in many of the village schools, there are many who cannot read and write correctly, and who know very little of the Bible, which they profess to explain to their scholars.

6. A very great part of our present village and town-schools are managed by poor and miserably instructed dames, who thus seek to make a livelihood, and who literally do no good to the children, except it be keeping

chester, as representing the state of the education of the poor in Manchester in that year. If such is the state of the education of the poor in this town, where so much has been done of late years, it may be comprehended what its state is, in the poorer and less intelligent districts of this country.

MANCHESTER CATHEDRAL AND PARISH CHURCH DISTRICT.

Return of the Children of the Poor, between the Ages of Three and Fifteen, in the District between Long Millgate and Shudehill, attending Day School or otherwise.

No. of Families visited.	No. of Children		No. of Children attending some Day School.	No. of Children at work.	No. of Children at Home		No. of Children who have *never* been at Day School, out of Tables A and B.
	between 3 & 10	between 10 & 15			from various excuses except poverty. A	from alleged poverty. B	
917	1693	518	754	392	625	440	* 407
			1146		1065		
Total.	§ 2211		2211				* Between 3 & 15

§ Many of these go to Sunday School.

them for a certain number of hours in the day out of the dirt and out of worse society.

7. Many of these dame schools are so wretchedly managed, as to do the children a very great deal more harm than good, — by uniting miserable associations with the sacred writings, and with the subjects of the wretched instruction given in these schools.

8. Very many of our town-schools are held in small and unventilated cellars or garrets, where the health of the children is seriously impaired.

9. If we except only the *worst* part of the dame-schools, we have not even then *one-half* as many school-buildings as we require, for the *present* numbers of our population.

10. By far the greatest part of our school-buildings have only *one* room, in which all the classes are instructed together, in the midst of noise and foul air.

11. Many of our present school-rooms have no forms and no parallel desks, — both of which are to be found in every school-room throughout Western Europe, — and in all such schools the children are kept standing the whole day.

12. Very few of our school-rooms are properly supplied with maps, books, or school apparatus.

13. The majority of our town-schools have no play-grounds; and in all these cases the children are turned out into the streets during the hours of recreation.

14. Scarcely any schools throughout the country have more than *two* class-rooms; the classification of the children is therefore very deficient, and the instruction is thereby much impaired.

15. Very few schools have more than one teacher.

16. Great numbers of parishes and districts throughout England and Wales have no school-room at all, and no place, in which their children can be instructed.

17. Of these latter districts, many are too poor or too careless to raise anything towards the erection of school-buildings, and in none of these cases does the Committee of Council give any assistance.

18. In many other districts, the inhabitants are so divided in religious opinions, that they find it impossible to act in concert, in providing for the education of their children, and in these cases the Committee of Council renders no assistance.

19. In most of our schools, it is necessary in order to provide salaries for the teacher, and funds for the support of the school, to charge from 2*d.* to 4*d.* a week per head for the instruction of scholars. This absolutely excludes the children of all paupers, and of all poor persons, who cannot afford to pay so much out of their small earnings, whilst throughout the greatest part of Western Europe, the education afforded in the primary schools is quite gratuitous.

20. There is no public provision for the proper payment and maintenance of our teachers, and these latter are therefore generally placed in so very humiliating and dependent a position, as in many cases virtually to prevent any man of ability and education from accepting such an office.

21. A great part of our village teachers are only poor uneducated women, or poor men who are not fit

for any other office or employment, and who are themselves miserably educated.*

* To give an idea of the character of the teachers' profession in our country, I append here a remarkable and curious statement taken from Mr. Lingen's very able report on the state of education in South Wales.

"The present average age of teachers is upwards of 40 years; that at which they commenced their vocation upwards of 30; the number trained is 12·5 per cent. of the whole ascertained number; the average period of training is 7·30 months; the average income is 22*l.* 10*s.* 9*d.* per annum; besides which, 16·1 per cent. have a house rent-free. Before adopting their present profession, 6 had been assistants in school, 3 attorneys' clerks, 1 attorney's clerk and sheriff's officer, 1 apprentice to an ironmonger, 1 assistant to a draper, 1 agent, 1 artilleryman, 1 articled clerk, 2 accountants, 1 auctioneer's clerk, 1 actuary in a savings-bank, 3 bookbinders, 1 butler, 1 barber, 1 blacksmith, 4 bonnet-makers, 2 booksellers, 1 bookkeeper, 15 commercial clerks, 3 colliers, 1 cordwainer, 7 carpenters, 1 compositor, 1 copyist, 3 cabinetmakers, 3 cooks, 1 corndealer, 3 druggists, 42 milliners, 20 domestic servants, 10 drapers, 4 excisemen, 61 farmers, 25 farm-servants, 1 farm-bailiff, 1 fisherman, 2 governesses, 7 grocers, 1 glover, 1 gardener, 177 at home or in school, 1 herald-chaser, 4 housekeepers, 2 hatters, 1 helper in a stable, 8 hucksters or shopkeepers, 1 ironroller, 6 joiners, 1 knitter, 13 labourers, 4 laundresses, 1 limeburner, 1 lay-vicar, 5 ladies' maids, 1 lieutenant R. N., 2 land-surveyors, 22 mariners, 1 millwright, 108 married women, 7 ministers, 1 mechanic, 1 miner, 2 mineral agents, 5 masons, 1 mate, 1 malster, 1 militia-man, 1 musician, 1 musical-wiredrawer, 2 nursery-maids, 1 night-schoolmaster, 1 publican's wife (separated from her husband), 2 preparing for the church, 1 policeman, 1 pedlar, 1 publican, 1 potter, 1 purser's steward, 1 planter, 2 private tutors, 1 quarryman, 1 reed-thatcher, 28 sempstresses, 1 second master R.N., 4 soldiers, 14 shoemakers, 2 machine-weighers, 1 stonecutter, 1 sergeant of marines, 1 sawyer, 1 surgeon, 1 ship's cook, 7 tailors, 1 tailor and marine, 1 tiler, 17 widows, 4 weavers, and 60 unascertained, or having had no previous occupation.

"In connection with the vocation of teacher, 2 follow that of assistant-overseer of roads, 6 are assistant-overseers of the poor, 1 accountant, 1 assistant parish-clerk, 1 bookbinder, 1 broom and clog-maker, 4 bonnet makers, 1 sells Berlin wool, 2 are cow-keepers, 3 collectors of taxes, 1 drover (in summer), 12 dress-makers, 1 druggist, 1 farmer, 4 grocers, 3 hucksters or shopkeepers, 1 inspector of weights and measures, 1

22. In proportion to our population, we have scarcely one-fourth part as many colleges for the instruction of teachers, as any of the countries of Western Europe; and not one-fourth part as many are necessary for the education of a sufficient number of teachers for our poor.

23. In nearly all the few colleges we have established for the instruction of teachers, the education is very limited and meagre in its character; as these colleges depend upon voluntary aid, and cannot afford to give the students more than a year's or eighteen months' training; while throughout Western Europe the teachers receive *three years'* training in the teachers' colleges at the expense of the government.

24. The colleges we have established are so poor, that they cannot afford to support nearly so large and complete a staff of teachers and professors as are to be found in almost all the teachers' colleges throughout Western Europe.

25. A great part of our schools and teachers are never visited by any public inspector, or by any private person, or committee of persons from the year's beginning to the year's end. In many of these cases,

knitter, 2 land-surveyors (one of them is also a stone-cutter), 2 lodging-house keepers, 1 librarian to a mechanics' institute, 16 ministers, 1 master of a workhouse, 1 matron of a lying-in hospital, 3 mat-makers, 13 preachers, 18 parish or vestry-clerks (uniting in some instances the office of sexton), 1 printer and engraver, 1 porter, barber, and layer-out of the dead in a workhouse, 4 publicans, 1 registrar of marriages, 11 sempstresses, 1 shopman (on Saturdays), 8 secretaries to benefit-societies, 1 sexton, 2 shoemakers, 1 tailor, 1 teacher of modern languages, 1 turnpike-man, 1 tobacconist, 1 writing-master in a grammar-school, and 9 are in receipt of parochial relief."

bad teachers are left to do great injury to their scholars unchecked and unheard of, and in many other cases, good and able teachers are left without encouragement or advice, to labour on unknown, disheartened and alone.

26. In most of our schools, owing to the teacher either not having been trained at all, or not having been educated for a long enough time in a college, the methods of teaching are miserable and ridiculous. The noise in the school-rooms is often so great, that it is with difficulty that any individual can make himself heard. The children are often kept standing the greater part of the day, and are wearied beyond endurance, so that the lessons, and all the associations connected with the subjects of instruction are rendered hateful ever afterwards. The highest religious subjects are thus often made odious to the children, who during their after life avoid as much as possible recurring to what awakens so many disagreeable recollections. In most of our schools, there is little or no attempt to interest the children in their studies, or to teach them to think or reason. The instruction is mere parrot work. They are taught by rote, and forget again almost as soon as they have left the school.

27. Great numbers of the school-buildings in the more remote country districts are of the most wretched and miserable character.

An idea of some of these may be formed from the following descriptions, selected from the able report of Mr. Lingen on the state of education in South Wales, published in 1848. These are fair specimens of schools, which may be found throughout England and Wales.

Mr. Lingen says: "There was no room for making furniture and apparatus separate considerations in most of the schools throughout the remoter districts, exhibiting, as they did, every form of squalid destitution. I subjoin a few instances out of many others perhaps more striking.

Of one school, he says: —

"The furniture consisted of one desk for the master, two longer ones for the pupils, and a few benches, all in a wretched state of repair. The room was not ceiled. In one corner was a heap of spars, the property of the master, for the purpose of thatching his house. In another place was a heap of culm, emptied out on the floor. The floor was boarded, but all the middle of it was in holes."

Of another, he says: —

"The school was held in a miserable room over the stable; it was lighted by two small glazed windows, and was very low; in one corner were a broken bench, some sacks, and a worn-out basket; another corner was boarded off for storing tiles and mortar belonging to the chapel. The furniture consisted of three small square tables, one for the master, two larger ones for the children, and a few benches, all in a wretched state of repair. There were several panes of glass broken in the windows; in one place paper served the place of glass, and in another a slate, to keep out wind and rain; the door was also in a very dilapidated condition. On the beams which crossed the room were a ladder and two large poles.

Of another, he says: —

"The school was held in a room built in a corner of the churchyard; it was an open-roofed room; the floor was of the bare earth, and very uneven; the room was lighted by two small glazed windows, one third of each of which was patched up with boards. The furniture consisted of a small square table for the master, one square table for the pupils, and seven or eight benches, some of which were in good repair, and others very bad. The biers belonging to the church were placed on the beams which ran across the room. At one end of the room was a heap of coal and some rubbish and a worn-out basket, and on one side was a new door leaning against the wall, and intended for the stable belonging to the church. The door of the school-room was in a very bad condition, there being large holes in it, through which cold currents of air were continually flowing."

Of another, he says: —

"This school is held in a dark miserable den under the town-hall; the furniture comprised only a few old benches and tables; in the corner was a litter of broken cups and a bottle; there was a starling of the master's loose in the room, which, by flying about, greatly disturbed the children during my visit."

Of another, he says: —

"In one corner was a heap of culm, in another a bench or two, piled against the wall, and various litter; at the bottom of the room lay a gravestone, on which the master had been chalking the letters which the village mason was to cut as an inscription: on the table lay a jug and pipe."

I might quote endless instances to prove the miserable character and ill effects of the present school-buildings in Carmarthenshire and Pembrokeshire. Indeed, Report after Report is too often only a wearisome repetition of such particulars. It will suffice for me to subjoin a few instances, by way of illustration, taking them almost at hazard.

Of another school, he says: —

"The school was held in a room, part of a dwelling-house; the room was so small that a great many of the scholars were obliged to go into the room above, which they reached by means of a ladder, through a hole in the loft; the room was lighted by one small glazed window, half of which was patched up with boards; it was altogether a wretched place; the furniture consisted of one table, in a miserable condition, and a few broken benches; the floor was in a very bad state, there being several large holes in it, some of them nearly half a foot deep; the room was so dark that the few children whom I heard read were obliged to go to the door, and open it, to have sufficient light."

Of another, he says: —

"This school is held in the mistress's house. I never shall forget the hot, sickening smell, which struck me on opening the door of that low dark room, in which thirty girls and twenty boys were huddled together. It more nearly resembled the smell of the engine on board a steamer, such as it is felt by a sea-sick voyager on passing near the funnel. Exaggerated as this may appear, I am writing on the evening of the same day on which I visited the school, and I will vouch for the accuracy of what I state. Every thing in the room (*i. e.* a few benches of various heights and sizes, and a couple of tables) was hidden under and overlaid with children."

Of another, he says: —

"This school is held in a ruinous hovel of the most squalid and miserable character; the floor is of bare earth, full of deep holes; the windows are all broken; a tattered partition of lath and plaster divides it into two unequal portions; in the larger were a few wretched benches, and a small desk for the master in one corner; in the lesser was an old door, with the hasp still upon it, laid crossways upon two benches, about half a yard high, to serve for a writing-desk! Such of the scholars as write retire in pairs to this part of the room, and kneel on the ground while they write. On the floor was a heap of loose coal, and a litter of straw, paper, and all kinds of rubbish. The vicar's son informed me that he had seen eighty children in this hut. In summer the heat of it is said to be suffocating; and no wonder."

Of another, he says: —

"In the school-room, which, at six square feet per child, is calculated to hold 28 scholars, I found 59 present, and 74 on the books: some of the children are drafted off into the master's dwelling-house."

Of another, he says: —

"The school is held in a room over the stable, which is a very small one. The children were much crowded.

There was a very comfortable fire in the room on the day of my visit. Some 10 or 12 of the senior boys were obliged to sit in the adjoining chapel, on account of the smallness of the room. The chapel had no fire in it, and was very cold and uncomfortable."

Of another, he says: —

"The school-room is part of a dwelling-house, on the ground-floor, and the smell arising from so many children being crammed in such a small room was quite overpowering. There was a large fire in the grate at the time. The window was a small one, and was kept closed. The floor, walls, and the room altogether were in bad repair. I observed, after the scholars went out at noon (for there was no seeing anything but children while they were in the room), 1 square table for the master, 2 long tables for the writers and cipherers, 5 benches, and 1 chair."

Of another, he says: —

"This school is kept upstairs in two rooms of the master's house. There is a door to each room from the landing at the top of the stairs, but the master cannot see all the scholars from one room while they are in the other. He generally sits with the elementary classes."

Of another, he says: —

"The floor was of the bare earth, very uneven and rather damp. There was a fire in an iron stove placed in the middle of the room. The steam which arose from it was quite insufferable, so much so that I was obliged to keep both door and window open to enable me to breathe. The master remarked that it was 'bad to a stranger, but nothing to those who were used to it.'"

Of another, he says: —

"This school is held in the church. I found the master and four little children ensconced in the chancel, amidst a lumber of old tables, benches, and desks, round a three-legged grate full of burning sticks, with no sort of funnel or chimney for the smoke to escape. It made my eyes smart till I was nearly blinded, and kept covering with ashes the paper on which I was writing. How the master and children bore it with so little apparent inconvenience I cannot tell."

Of another, he says: —

"The day-school (which used to be held in private houses) is now held in an old Independent chapel, no longer used for religious purposes, and rented by the master. There was a raised hearth of brick in the room, with a grate on the top, but no chimney. There was a fire of culm burning on it; the heat and vapour made the room almost insufferable to one coming from the fresh air."

Of another, he says: —

"The floor of the chapel was of earth and lime, very uneven and broken: it contained a few pews, a pulpit, a table, and a couple of desks, with a few benches in use, others being heaped together at one end of the chapel; there was a grate full of culm* in the middle of the chapel, but no chimney."

Of another, he says: —

"The room in which this school is held is a most

* This is the name of the common fuel in Wales, which is anthracite coal made up into balls with clay. It burns without smoke, but with a glowing vapour like charcoal.

miserable hut, not fit to shelter cattle in, as the thatched roof would be anything but proof against bad weather. The master said that he often suffered from the rain; and there were large quantities of straw inside the roof to shelter in some degree himself and pupils."

Of another, he says: —

"The boys' free school was held in a most miserable hovel, lighted by four small windows. The floor was of the bare earth and excessively damp. The door was in a very dilapidated state, and the rain was coming through the thatch when I was in the school-room."

Of others, he says: —

"I am about to enter on one of the most painful subjects of my inquiry. It is a disgusting fact that, out of 692 schools, I found 364, or 52·6 per cent., utterly unprovided with privies."

These are not isolated instances. I could quote hundreds of such descriptions of schools situated in all parts of England and Wales. I have myself seen many which are held in cellars, garrets, chapels, and kitchens, badly warmed, wretchedly ventilated, dirty, unfurnished, dark, damp, and unhealthy. Are the miserable hours spent in these miserable places likely to leave good impressions afterwards? Are they likely to create happy, moral, and healthy ideas and associations in the minds of the children? Are they likely to make the children love what they learned in such scenes and places, and remember it with reverence and with a desire to act upon it afterwards? Are they not much rather likely to make the children hate and shun everything which would remind them of the school and the miserable school-day?

28. By far the greatest majority of the criminals who are convicted every year in England and Wales, are persons *who have never been educated at all.* Very few persons, who have received even a tolerable education, are found among the great numbers annually committed.

29. Whilst throughout the agricultural districts of Western Europe, the children remain in school until they have completed their fourteenth year, and very often until they have completed their sixteenth year, very few even of those children who go to school at all in our agricultural districts continue to attend school beyond their ninth year; whilst very many do not continue to attend them beyond their eighth year. So that of the children of the poor, who do go to school in England and Wales, the greatest number discontinue their attendance long before they have received anything worthy the name of education.

30. The present system is bearing very unfairly, and very oppressively upon many conscientious and benevolent clergymen in the remote rural districts.

The nation is entirely ignorant of the almost marvellous efforts which some of the clergy are making in the remote rural districts, to provide schools for the poor.

Many poor clergymen, with not 150*l.* of annual income, are out of that small stipend supporting their schools and teachers themselves, wholly unaided either by the public or by their neighbours. How they can do it God only knows, but that many of them, in all parts of the country, do effect this prodigy of self-denial, all the inspectors unanimously attest. These good men receive and expect no public praise as their reward. They are labouring unheard of, and unknown by their fellows, and are looking for their reward to Heaven alone.

But what a disgrace it is to us, as a nation, to impose such a burden upon any of our clergy! What a shame it is, that the small stipend of a religious and benevolent man should be made still smaller, by forcing him to pay, what ought to be borne by the nation at large! And what a precarious means of support for these schools! It is not reasonable to expect, that each succeeding incumbent can or will be equally self-denying; and when one fails to give the accustomed support, such a school must necessarily be closed.

Such is a short summary of the state of education of the poor in England and Wales, as attested by the inspectors of schools, by the government and by the clergy. Whilst foreign countries, by the aid of the central authority, have established such perfect systems, and have accomplished such magnificent results, the system of leaving the education of a nation dependent upon the efforts of charitable individuals finds us, in 1849, in the situation which I have described.

I have shown in Chap. IX. of this work, that, notwithstanding the very large size of the primary schools in the towns of Germany and Switzerland (many of them containing as many as *ten* class-rooms and *ten* teachers, and scarcely any containing fewer than *four* class-rooms), there were: —

In Prussia

1 primary school for every	653	inhabitants.
1 teacher for every	522	„
1 normal college for every	377,360	„

In Saxony

1 primary school for every	900	inhabitants.
1 teacher for every	588	„
1 normal college for every	214,975	„

In Bavaria

1 primary school for	508	inhabitants.
1 teacher for every	603	„
1 normal college for every	550,000	„

In the Duchy of Baden

1 primary school for every	700	inhabitants.
1 normal college for every	500,000	„

In Switzerland

1 teacher for every	480	inhabitants.
1 normal college for every	176,923	„

In France

1 primary school for every	568	inhabitants.
1 teacher for every	446	„
1 normal college for every	356,564	„

and that supposing we required fewer schools, fewer teachers, and fewer normal colleges than any other country, and that we should be sufficiently provided if we had

1 primary school for every	700	inhabitants.
1 teacher for every	600	„
1 normal college for every	400,000	„

we should then require, for our population,

23,581 *large* schools,
26,500 teachers, and
41 normal colleges.

There are four principal defects in our present educational system, which I would here more particularly notice.

I. THE WANT OF NORMAL COLLEGES.

When all the normal colleges in course of erection are completed, there will then be only sixteen in the whole of England and Wales. There are only twelve colleges finished, while at the very lowest computation we require forty-one,—each capable of accommodating one hundred students and six professors,—if we are to have a sufficient supply of educated teachers. We should not even then have so many colleges in proportion to the numbers of our population, as the greater part of Western Europe.

Most of the counties and several of the most populous dioceses of this country have no normal college at all, and are obliged to content themselves with teachers, who have never received anything worthy the name of education, and who are as fit to manage a school and teach children, as they are to drill and command a regiment. Nearly all these men do their scholars much more harm than good.

The smallness of the numbers of our normal colleges is felt all the more, in consequence of the small number of efficient teachers at present in the primary schools, and of the constant change going on in their ranks, owing to the smallness of their pay, and the abject dependence of their situations.

The great demand for teachers, and the imperfect ideas at present afloat of the character of the education required to make an efficient schoolmaster, are rendering several of the few colleges, which have been founded in this country, quite worthless; for the directors of some of these establishments, imagining that it is better to supply a great number of inefficient teachers than a smaller number of efficient and well-educated instructors, or perhaps ignorant of what ought to be expected from a teacher, permit the young students to leave and undertake the charge of primary schools after a year's, and in some cases after six months' residence! Mr. Coleridge, on the contrary, justly considers that the most important duty of the principal of a normal college is, to form the *habits* and *disposition* of his students, and he is well convinced of the soundness of the conclusion, to which all foreign countries have come, viz. that it is ridiculous to hope to remodel the *habits* of a young man, to inspire him with high and religious aims, and to instruct him sufficiently for the important post of a teacher in the short space of twelve months. The greater part of the first year's residence at the normal college is always required, for the *preparation* of the student's mind, for what is *afterwards* to be instilled. It is the *second*, and still more the *third* year, which is the most valuable period for the development of his character, and for the education of his mind. If we could have more than this, it would be really advisable, but certainly we ought not to have less.

A long training in the normal college not only makes the future teacher much more efficient, but it ensures his remaining longer at his post; for the more thoroughly the habits of his mind are moulded to his future occupations, and the more thoroughly we habituate him to the peculiar life that is marked out for him, the less capable will he be afterwards of changing his career. To imagine, that we can in *twelve months* not only sufficiently instruct, but also religiously and morally educate a young man,—that in *twelve months,* we can change or remodel the habits of his mind, or instil into him so strong an enthusiasm for his profession, as to make him proof against the temptations to forsake it that will present themselves,—is perfectly absurd. Vehrli of Kreuitzlingen, the Frères Chrétiens of Paris, and those master trainers, the Jesuits, all tell us a very different tale.

It would be much better to turn out fewer and more efficient teachers,—men who would be unwilling afterwards to forsake their posts,—than to send out a set of pedantic young men, who have gained a little knowledge and no new habits in the normal schools, and who will be ready to forsake their profession whenever they can do so with advantage to themselves.

Mr. Coleridge, in an interesting report on the normal school at Stanley Grove, speaking of the plan of training teachers, says, that it "proposes *to form* the character, both generally and with especial reference to the scholastic office. Thus principally, yet at the same time to give them every *appropriate* acquirement,—in fact, a very much larger amount of acquirements (though this be a subordinate end) than could be otherwise commanded. Agreeably to this idea, *youths* only are admitted and are kept in training for a period of time measured by years, not months. The force of habit and association—early and long-continued impressions—favourable influences of many kinds—the daily sight and sound of good—the means and opportunity of discipline, moral, physical, and intellectual—such are the advantages, which in this way it is intended to secure; and to these are added every facility for special instruction. Yet must this statement be received with limitation. The object is indeed to *form* the character; yet, as the institution cannot be open to children or very young boys, a groundwork of good must have been laid beforehand. There must be evident signs of towardness in the youth at his admission; for though much may be done for him afterwards, *much* cannot be undone. It is not a school of correction. The principle of selection, therefore, cannot be dispensed with—it rather stands out with increased force."

It will not be necessary for me to speak of the pretended system of training for six months. The utter fallacy of the idea is self-apparent, and still more when instruction only, without any good domestic training, is given, as in some of our so-called training establishments.

But can we do without normal colleges?—I might just as well ask, can we do without teachers? I see no difference whatsoever between the questions. We can do without them certainly, if we are resolved not to educate the people. We may as well hope to educate the people by means of teachers, who have never been trained, as to educate them without schools. Or, if education consists in merely teaching to read and write, and forcing instruction into the child by means of the ruler and the cane, then we may do without normal colleges. Or, if the profession of a teacher is one, for which *any one* is fitted, and to which *any one* may turn as his last shift in the world for obtaining a decent maintenance, then we may do without normal colleges: or, if it is impossible for a badly organised school to do harm, and most grievous harm, and to demoralise, instead of improving youth, then we may do without normal colleges. In short, if the education of the people is a visionary scheme, on which none but enthusiasts speculate, or, if it is doubtful, whether it will advance the cause of religion, morality, prudence, foresight, and order; or, if it is merely a plaything, wherewith to soothe and gratify the people, then assuredly we have no need of normal colleges. But I think very differently of education combined with good government. I look to Europe, and regard the mighty change, which has, since 1800, been wrought in the character of the Swiss, German, and Dutch people, and the great difference between them and the Italians, and I feel confident, it is no dream to hope and believe, that we might effect the same in our own land, if we adopted similar means. But, so long as we commit the education of the poor to a set of men, as ignorant and low-minded as the majority of our present primary teachers are, so long, instead of advancing, we shall positively retard the moral progress of the people. Mere instruction, unaccompanied with the true development of the mind,—the moral and religious education of the man,—is a positive harm. It awakens his intellect sufficiently to render it a powerful and dangerous auxiliary to his unbridled and to his unruly passions; whilst the religious and humanising influences of his soul remaining dormant, leave him like a vessel with its canvas spread, but without a rudder, on a dark and stormy sea. He is then no longer dull, stupid, and totally without capabilities of reasoning, as the labourers in our agricultural districts, but sufficiently enlightened to indulge, not only the mere sensual appetites and demands of his ill-governed body, but the restless, wild, and rebellious promptings of his scarce-awakened and unreflecting mind.

The establishment of normal colleges is of such great importance, that the efficiency of the education of our poor may be considered wholly ruined, so long as we are unsupplied with them; and the efficiency of the normal colleges themselves is destroyed, so long as we continue to send out teachers from them after a twelvemonths' training.

II. THE WANT OF A CERTAIN AND SUFFICIENT MAINTENANCE AND OF AN HONOURABLE POSITION IN SOCIETY FOR THE TEACHERS.

Let me ask, is there any thing, if we consider the *majority* of the existing English schools, without choosing out certain honourable exceptions, — is there any thing in the present situation of a village schoolmaster in this country, to tempt a well educated man to engage in such a despised and laborious profession, as long as any hope remains of his earning an independent livelihood by any honest, however humble trade?

Is the pay in the majority of the schools good enough? — Is the support and encouragement the teacher receives from the rich and powerful sufficient to compensate for the want of good pay?—Is the honour paid to the profession of a teacher in England great enough to make up for all or any of the other disadvantages? —Is the want of education so fully undertood by the poor themselves, as to insure the teacher their gratitude at least, for his exertions? Is not the contrary of all these suppositions too true?

The salaries in most cases are miserable, and in very many cases so poor, as to oblige the teacher to follow other occupations in connection with his office, in order to gain a livelihood. The teachers in the schools have therefore in most cases hitherto been men or women of such very miserable education, and so utterly ignorant of the nature of their duties, that the name of "schoolmaster" has almost become a byword and reproach; whilst the importance of their work has been so little understood by either the gentry or the poor, that in many cases, they have received no encouragement from the former, while by the latter they have been almost wholly neglected. I know that of late years a great change has been effected, but still it is to be remembered, as I have before said, that hardly one *half* of the country is properly supplied with schools, and that of this half, there are many schools directed by dames or half-educated men, or which are the private enterprises of vulgar and low-minded men, who having failed in every other attempt to gain an honest livelihood, have turned to school-keeping as to their last resource.

In very many cases, I might perhaps say with truth, in nearly one-half of the schools now in existence, the incomes are too poor to induce any *man* to accept the place of teacher, so that the wives of peasants or common mechanics manage them, — women, who have not had the least previous training, and who have all their domestic concerns to attend to while they conduct the imperfect *instruction* of their classes. What is the character of the education given in these schools? Reading, the poorest and most meagre description of writing, a little arithmetic and the most injudicious and injurious description of religious instruction. Whether I am right or not in setting down this class of schools, as answering the description *of half* our present supply of primary schools, I will not say; but it is notable, that the majority of those established in the agricultural districts are only "dame" schools.

Then how are the salaries of the teachers obtained? Generally, either entirely from the precarious and uncertain pay of the scholars, or partly from this source, and partly from a small yearly sum proceeding, either from the school endowments, or from the voluntary subscriptions of inhabitants of the locality, or from the liberality and exertions of the clergyman.

What is the consequence? Even supposing that the teacher is a well-educated man, which is very rarely the case, he is entirely and wholly dependent on the caprices, either of the clergyman of the parish, or of the local subscriber or subscribers to the school, or of the parents of his scholars. Now, although it is most important that the religious ministers should be *ex officio* inspectors of their schools and of the religious instruction given there, still it does seem to me, that it is putting the teacher into a most invidious position, to subject him to the uncontrolled caprice of any individuals of his locality. What is and what must often be the consequence of such a position? It very often happens, that the teacher of a school, from his previous training, supposing him to have had any, knows very much more about the minor details of school management, than either the clergyman or the inhabitants of the locality. In such cases he very naturally wishes to follow out the directions, which have been given him, by the learned professors of the normal college where he was educated. If the clergyman who has not been educated in pedagogy, should think differently, a dispute often ensues on some point of school management, and either the parish dismisses an able teacher, or the teacher is rendered discontented, and is hindered in the improvement and instruction of his children. As long as his position is one of such dependence on the whims of those about him, his usefulness and contentment must both be lessened. There ought always to be an impartial arbitrator between the teacher and those who object to his method of instruction, &c.; and that arbitrator ought to be well educated in pedagogy, and removed above the influence of personal enmities and personal vexation. Whether this arbitration be vested in the government, or in the school societies in London, it matters little; but it certainly ought to be vested in some person or persons at a distance, who might defend the teachers against unreasonable caprices, and at the same time take care that they performed their duty, and that all sound objections to them were immediately attended to. To leave them in their present position is to cripple their powers of doing good, and to make the profession contemptible in the eyes of every honest, independent, and intelligent man.

In all foreign countries this evil is most carefully guarded against. The teachers cannot be discharged from their situations, unless the central power concurs with the local authorities; but every complaint of the local committees, or of the local clergy, is *immediately* attended to; their causes are investigated by the inspectors, and full redress is afforded for every real grievance. In Germany, as I have shown, the parochial clergy are *ex officio* inspectors of their several schools; and if the teacher neglects his duty, or is guilty of any unbecoming conduct, they have first the right of reprimanding him; and if that reprimand fails in convincing him of the impropriety of his conduct, they can report him to the inspector of the district, who immediately examines into the complaints, and then, if he finds those complaints well founded, he reports to the provincial consistory, which at once dismisses the teacher. In this way, the clergy are insured good teachers, and these latter are defended against the whims and caprices of peevish or ignorant clergy. In France, Holland, Denmark, and Switzerland, the teachers are also most carefully protected from subjection to local influence; whilst in all these countries local influence and local superintendence are considered most necessary adjuncts to the moderating influence of the central power.

If a teacher feels, that his continuance in office depends entirely on the pleasure of people, who are living near him, his independence and honesty are generally diminished; his power of doing good is curtailed; his satisfaction with his work and with his situation is lessened; his own education in a college is in a great measure thrown away, by making others, who have not been so educated, the directors of the instruction given in his schools. It degrades and enervates the teacher to subject him so entirely, as we now do, to the influence of any local authority, which is much oftener exercised in a manner biased by personal feelings, than that of some person living at a distance. Of course, if we are to employ teachers as uneducated and low-minded as the majority of those employed at the present day, it makes little matter by whom the control of them is exercised; but *if* we are desirous to make the office such, that men, like those educated by Sir James P. Kay Shuttleworth at Battersea, or by Mr. Coleridge at Stanley Grove, shall be willing to accept it; and if we are desirous of increasing the efficiency of such men, when they have accepted situations, we must alter this state of things.

Besides this, good salaries ought to be provided for the teachers, independent of the school-pence, or *schulgeld*, as the Germans call it; and the amount of these payments ought to be defined by other authorities than the school-masters, whilst these latter should be interested in the increase of the numbers of their scholars, by being permitted to receive, as additions to their fixed incomes, the school-pence of all their children. At the same time it ought to be provided here, as in France, and Germany, and Holland, that when the parents are really too poor to pay these small sums, their children should be allowed to attend the school free of expense.

But what will be the consequence of our pursuing our present course, of leaving the payment of the teachers entirely dependent on the precarious payments of individuals? Why, so long as we do this, the educated men, who leave our normal colleges, will find scarcely any situations worth their taking; and if they do accept some of the present miserable places, it will be with discontented, and justly discontented minds, and with a resolution to leave as soon as the term of their apprenticeship is ended. For we need not think, that good situations will be wanting to them. There are plenty of warehouses in Lancashire where, with their education, they would be received with joy, and where they would obtain 50*l.*, 80*l.*, or 100*l.* per annum, for work not one-half so laborious as the management of a village school. The difficulty of applying for and obtaining such places exists no longer. The letter of application for a place in Manchester, sent by a schoolmaster of the south, formerly cost 14*d.* or 15*d.*, or even 18*d.*; now that letter may be sent for 1*d.*; and the journey, which a few years back, from its expensiveness and tediousness, was a positive check on emigration to those great and ever-increasing fields of labour, may now be accomplished, even from the shores of Sussex in half a day and for a few shillings.

The Committee of Council has attempted to do something to remedy this state of things; but what can it effect with only 125,000*l.* per annum in its hands, out of which it has to support its system of inspection, to assist in building schools and colleges, and to aid the teachers of the whole of Great Britain?

We may, however, rest assured that, until we provide a better situation for our teachers, we shall never be able to improve the profession, or to renovate the schools.

An income of at least 50*l.* per annnm, the school-pence, a comfortable house, a garden, and a field for a cow, ought to be *secured* to every teacher; and until these are secured to them, we shall never be able to obtain educated men for the village schools. I know that several of the nobility are paying more than this. There are several instances, which have come under my own observation, where they are paying more than *double* this sum: but then, in these instances, gratifying as they are, there is no *security* for the continuance of this payment; and even if it were certain that each successive head of the house would take an equal interest in the school; yet still the position of the teacher is one of the most distressing dependence, where he is afraid, at each step, of the parents of his scholars misrepresenting him to his patron; where he is fearful at each word of giving offence; and where, consequently, his position is in the highest degree enervating and injurious to his moral character, which ought to be at least as fully developed in him as in any other citizen of the state.

But until the state will come forward and assist the Church and the dissenters, as is done in France, Holland, Germany, Switzerland, and Austria, in providing for the maintenance of the schoolmasters and schoolmistresses, things must go on as at present.

III. The want of local and public inspection.

Before I venture to offer any remarks on the necessity of inspection, let me remind my readers of the state of inspection in several of the European nations. In Holland, there are EIGHTY inspectors appointed and paid by government, who have, in reality, the management of the education of the country. In France, besides the local committees of inspection, there is one head inspector in each department; and where the number of schools is too great for one inspector to examine them sufficiently often in the year, one or two assistants are joined to him, according to the size of his department. At present, there are altogether in France 200 inspectors appointed and paid by government; and I find that the number of schools inspected and reported on by them in 1843 was 50,986. In Switzerland, there is in each canton at the seat of government a central board of inspectors, numbering generally about four or five, who have the inspection of all the primary and normal schools of the canton: and in each parish of the canton there is a school society, formed of the parish clergy or priests and several heads of families, who inspect the progress of *each individual* child in the commune and report to the central board, who in their turn report to the government. In Prussia, the clergy or priests are *ex-officio* inspectors of their respective parish schools, whilst there is also in each union a regular inspector, appointed by government, whose duty it is to visit all the primary schools of his canton several times in the year, and to report on them to a magistrate of the department within which his canton lies. This magistrate is also the general inspector of the department; he can, if he thinks it necessary, visit any of the schools or normal colleges in his department; he corresponds with the inspectors of the cantons in his department and with the parochial clergy, receives their reports, and reports himself to government on the state of education in his department. The same plan is also followed out in all the other German states; and in Bavaria, with only 4,000,000 of inhabitants, there are 286 inspectors.

Now, the very fact of this general adoption in foreign countries of the plan of a central and local inspection, is an *à priori* argument in its favour; and whoever reads the reports of the few inspectors we have yet appointed in England and Wales, will clearly understand, much better than from any thing I can say, the necessity of this encouragement and assistance to the clergy and teachers of this country. Where the religious minister is a good and zealous man, the school is certain to receive some part of his attention; but in very many cases it is not possible for him to visit it often; whilst from the trustees of the school, gentlemen engaged sometimes in the pursuit of pleasure, and sometimes in business or in the management of estates, there is often still less chance of the teacher receiving any notice, advice, or encouragement. If the teacher is a really honest man, and sincerely desirous of promoting the good of the school, he may perhaps go on tolerably well without any supervision; but how much more encouraged would even such an one feel, if he knew that there was some one to whom he could always apply for advice, and if he felt that his country was watching his exertions, and that his succsss was certain of meeting with reward and encouragement! France has fully comprehended this; and her government stimulates the exertions of all the teachers by the distribution, annually, of a number of silver and bronze medals to those who are the most praised by the inspectors for the management of their school classes, and for the progress of their children.

But if inspection is an encouragement and a stimulus to good and honest teachers, still more truly is it a check and restraint upon the undeserving. It may be said there is that restraint at present—that there are the religious ministers. This, in some cases, is no doubt true; but will any one deny that there are many cases where the religious ministers are forced,—by their having already far more to attend to than they have time or strength for,—wholly to neglect this additional demand upon their exertions? Will any one deny, also, that where there are lay trustees to a school, who ought to watch the progress of the schoolmaster, the duty of inspecting the school is still more frequently neglected, and that there exist at the present time numerous examples of schools possessing ample funds for the payment of the teacher and the support of the school, which, from the want of some person, whose business it is to visit and inspect them from time to time, and to inquire into the character and conduct of the teachers,—have degenerated in the most distressing manner; the teachers sometimes becoming careless, or immoral, sometimes neglecting the school altogether, or leaving it in the care of half-instructed monitors, whilst they themselves attend to other concerns; and sometimes venting their evil passions on the children,—thus diminishing the numbers of the school, and positively rendering it to the few, who remain, a miserable recollection, which they associate with the highest and most humanising principles of a Christian education. In this way many schools throughout the country have become hot-beds of immorality, rebellion, and infidelity, and, instead of promoting the progress of religion and civilisation, have been the most fruitful source of the corrupting principles now at work among the poor.

But what is the state of things in England in the *great majority* of the schools throughout the country, with the exception of the 3226 schools now open to the inspection of the Committee of Council? They receive no public inspection, and very often *no local inspection whatever.* To conduct the inspection of all the schools necessary for this country in a *tolerably* efficient manner—I mean in any manner that could be compared to the inspection the Swiss, French, German, Danish, and more particularly the Dutch schools receive—would require a force of at least 150 inspectors for England and Wales, and this force would even then be little more than one half as great, as the number of inspectors now employed by the Bavarian government. How wholly inefficient our present system of inspection is, will appear therefore, when I mention, that there are only 19 inspectors for the whole of England and Wales!

There is still another reason why an official force of inspectors ought to be supported, either by the school societies themselves, or by government, viz. the unfitness of many of the clergy to act as *sole* inspectors of the schools. I will explain myself. Is a gentleman, who has never given his attention to the practical details of school management, who has never studied the respective merits of different methods of teaching, who has never paid any attention to many of what ought to be the subjects of instruction in every school or to the minutiæ of class direction, school order, manners of master, manners of children, and all the numerous details so important to the sound progress of a school, and upon all of which the teacher has been carefully lectured in the normal colleges by able professors, who have themselves given a serious and deep attention to these matters—is, I repeat, a gentleman who has never in his life given any attention to these matters, and who may actually have a fancy for methods and plans of instruction, totally at variance with all that the teacher has been taught, and who at any rate cannot possibly have any good standard of perfection whereby to measure the progress of his school, or the excellence or faultiness of the methods pursued by the teacher—is such a gentleman the best qualified, is he at all qualified to be the *sole* inspector of a school? I say *sole*, because I willingly allow, that although other inspectors are necessary, the clergy and dissenting ministers ought undoubtedly to be *ex-officio* local inspectors of their schools; for they and they alone are the proper guardians, fosterers, and inspectors of the religious part of national education. On this ground, in Austria, Germany, France, and Switzerland, the parochial clergy and priests are always the *ex-officio* guardians and inspectors of their parochial schools.

What I wish to say is, that this inspection, *wholly indispensable as it is,* is not sufficient. We require, in addition, a body of men who, by constant attention to all the subjects of instruction and to all the minutiæ of school management, and by constant attendance at, and examination of the best normal, model, and parochial schools, should be well-versed in all that is necessary to the perfection of a school, and should thus be able —*in conjunction with* the clergy and ministers of their different districts,—to *advise* and *counsel* the teachers; encourage them to persevere when in a right course, and to check them when pursuing a wrong one; to prevent a school being ruined from want of superintendence and *surveillance;* to stimulate the teachers to renewed exertions by reporting all those who deserved honourable mention, and by thus drawing the attention of the public upon them; to acquaint government of those poor districts, wholly without schools and destitute of local funds, which require its assistance, and in these different ways to guard against the possibility of any district being left to languish without the means of obtaining a sound and Christian education.

The duty of such inspectors would be to advise the teachers and religious ministers; to receive the reports of the latter on the religious and moral conduct of the schools; to act as arbitrators between the teachers and the school committees; to examine the schools, and to report to the nation on the progress of national education.

This would encourage both teachers and clergy, some of whom in distant parts of the country, unnoticed and forgotten, are making efforts so laudable, so truly noble and so Christian, as to demand the nation's gratitude, of whom we now know little or nothing; but who ought to be held up as bright examples to stimulate others to do likewise. It is to be hoped, that if we ever do arrive at that happy time when the government, the clergy, and the dissenting ministers will aid one another in carrying out this great work, that we shall then adopt that plan, which is pursued with so much advantage in France at the present moment—I mean the awarding of medals signifying the approbation of the sovereign, and through the sovereign, of the people, to those teachers, who labour most successfully in the cause of the education of the people. Our Committee of Council might do it now in the few schools, which are open to them, and conjointly with that, they might publish a short monthly or quarterly official gazette of education, mentioning those, who have gained this recognition of a nation's gratitude, and giving the results of the examinations in the normal colleges for brevets of admission to the profession of schoolmasters, as well as all other interesting intelligence connected with the progress of education during the past month or quarter. Each inspector should be invited to send a short account of the school which he considered most deserving notice in his district, or of some one, in which some ingenious and excellent method of teaching was employed, or a short treatise on some subject connected with school management. By these means, and especially by encouraging teachers' conferences, of which I have spoken before, the feeling of a great and united body would be encouraged among the teachers; no one would fancy he was forgotten, but each would feel that the country was interested in his individual success.

Nor is this any ideal picture of what national education in England might be, would all but unite in furthering it; for all this, and much more than this, is actually effected abroad, and with the greatest success and happiest results.

I am not aware of any foreign country which has seriously undertaken the education of its people, that has not recognised the absolute necessity of maintaining a large body of efficiont and well-trained inspectors, who should act in concert with the local clergy and local authorities, and who should be at the same time a check upon, and an encouragment to the schoolmasters. Far from wishing these inspectors to be in the stead of local influence, I am only desirous of seeing them acting in unison with the clergy and dissenting ministers, aiding them to foster and promote the moral and religious progress of their several localities. The only reasons we have not long since had an effective body of these inspectors, are, that the state has not sufficiently explained what would be the special duties of those officers; that the clergy have consequently feared that the *surveillance* of their parochial education, which is one of their principal duties, would be taken out of their hands, instead of the inspectors for the Church being chosen from the clergy themselves, and being directed to act in unison with them; and that the whole country has had far too low an idea of what the education of the people ought to be, so that we have imagined any one fit to be a schoolmaster; that it did not matter what the teacher did, after he was put at the head of the school, and therefore, that he required neither checking nor encouraging in any way or by any person.

I have thus briefly sketched the present state of the means of educating the people of England.

What is the Committee of Council on Education doing to improve this state of things?

When we have scarcely one half as many schools, as we require, not one third as many teachers' colleges as are necessary, and not one third as many inspectors as we require; when many populous districts have no school, and cannot raise any thing towards building one; when most of our teachers are ignorant men or women, and are so poorly paid, that it is hopeless to persuade any well-educated man to take their places; when most of the normal colleges we do possess, are so poor, that they cannot afford to support a sufficient number of professors, or to keep the students long enough to give them an education nearly adequate to fit them for their work; when most of our schools and colleges are wretchedly provided with books, furniture, and apparatus; and when nearly half of our present school-buildings are disgracefully wretched and inefficient; all that our government is doing, is to dole out 125,000*l.* per annum to remedy the numerous and great deficiencies I have mentioned! When one considers the enormous sums, which are being expended annually, both by the governments and parishes of Western Europe, in promoting the education of the poor, and when one regards the present state of education in England, it is hardly possible to believe, that in the nineteenth century the efforts of the English government in this great work should be so miserably and absurdly inefficient. If the Committee of Council is really to remedy the consequences of our past neglect, and to supply us with even a moderately efficient system of public education, it will require funds to the amount of at least 3,000,000*l.* per annum. If it had even this amount of funds at its disposal, it could not even then, under the present system, unless local activity were very much increased, supply us with the means of public education so well, as the educational systems of the countries of Western Europe, combining as they do local and central activity, have supplied those countries.

I would not be understood to disparage in the least the very great and admirable labours of the Committee of Council. Nearly all the advancement which national education has made during the last ten years in this country, may be said to be owing to the labours of men connected with that Committee. Fifteen years ago, before the Committee of Council began to show what national education really meant, and how it was to be effected, there was not a single teachers' college in England or Wales; there were scarcely fifty teachers in either country, who were even *decently* acquainted with the subjects or methods of instruction; the schools were wretchedly arranged; most of them were *wholly* unfurnished, and without even a desk or form, unventilated, badly situated, and wretchedly built; inspection of schools was not thought of; no one knew its use or its necessity; there was not one inspector in England or Wales; any one was thought good enough to be a teacher; the idea of a previous training being necessary was ridiculed; the subjects of instruction were confined almost always to reading, writing, arithmetic, and the most meagre and injudicious Bible instruction, and the books used in the schools were ridiculously poor.

About ten years ago, my brother, Sir James P. Kay Shuttleworth, reformed the industrial school at Norwood, and accepted the situation of Secretary to the Privy Council on Education, and shortly afterwards he and Mr. Tufnell founded the first English normal college at Battersea. Since that time twelve normal colleges have been built—four others are in the course of completion—nineteen inspectors have been appointed —3226 schools have been opened to public inspection, —several thousand monitors have been trained—many schools have been furnished with parallel desks, rising one above another—many school-rooms have been well furnished with maps, books, and apparatus—many excellent school-books have been published—the subjects of instruction have been extended—many excellent school-buildings have been raised—people have begun to be ashamed of the "dame schools"—and as far as the amount of funds raised by voluntary efforts will allow, the country has, under the teaching and example of the Committee of Council, improved the means for the education of the people.

All this has been effected, be it remembered, notwithstanding the opposition of some, the lukewarmness of others, the taunts of those who sneer at education, the fears and outcries of the religious parties, and the slanders of those who wished to make the education of the people a means of increasing their own influence and power. Nothing but an enthusiastic earnestness of purpose, and inflexible impartiality, has enabled the committee to succeed thus far.

But to enable us to advance any further, we must have improved and very greatly enlarged means. We want, in short, much more money. The ridiculous insufficiency of the funds at the command of the Committee of Council is apparent, when we consider what we have to do. The normal colleges, the schools, and, in fact, all parts of the organisation, by which we are to effect the education of the people, are languishing, and losing the greater part of their efficiency from want of funds. The annual funds of the Committee of Council *would not suffice for the education of Cheshire*, but they have to be sprinkled over the whole of England, Wales, and Scotland.

Moreover, the Committee of Council does not assist those districts which most need assistance; viz.

1. Those, which have either no school or not sufficient school room, and which are too poor to raise any parts of the necessary funds themselves.

2. Those, which are too ignorant or too careless to make any effort themselves.

3. Those, which are so divided between different religious parties as to be unable to make combined effort, however, small.

Now there are vast numbers of each of these three classes of cases, and none of these are assisted at all by the Committee of Council, and yet these are the very cases which more than any others stand in need of assistance.

And even in those cases, in which the Committee might, in accordance with its constitution and regulations, render assistance, its capability of doing so is confined within very narrow limits, owing to the absurdly small funds put at its disposition, amounting as they do to only 125,000*l.* per annum.

We want a system, which would create us at least twice as many schools, as we have at present; which would enable the towns to establish large schools containing each of them ten to fourteen teachers and class-rooms, where the children might be well classified, and assist instead of hindering one another's improvement; we want a system, which would enable us to pay our teachers so well, that we might hope to see men of ability entering the profession; which would enable us to support our normal colleges efficiently, to supply each of them with a sufficient number of professors, and to keep the students in them at least THREE years; which would enable us to inspect each school in the country several times a year, and to publish a *public* report once every year, on the progress of each teacher and school in every part of the country; *which would enable us to distribute copies of the report on each county among all the religious ministers, teachers, and magistrates of the county, in order to interest them all in the progress of the schools around them;* which would enable us to furnish every school throughout the country with desks, forms, maps, books, all necessary apparatus, and with a good play-ground and garden; and though last, not least, *which would enable us to educate* GRATUITOUSLY *the children of all those poor, who cannot afford to pay any thing for the instruction of their offspring.*

The educational systems of the nations of Western Europe have enabled those countries to realise all these great objects. We, however, are still far removed from the attainment of this end. Surely it is not impossible for us to accomplish, what nations less rich and less active than ourselves have succeeded in effecting.

The *possibility* no one doubts. The only question to be solved is, by what means is this great end to be attained?

But difficult as the solution of the question, "How shall we effect the education of the people?" undoubtedly is, it would be the extreme of folly to imagine, that there is no solution of it, *but a revolution;* and that what Germany, Holland, Norway, Sweden, Denmark, and Austria have accomplished in times of social tranquillity, cannot be undertaken here, until, as in France and Switzerland, a social earthquake has levelled the obstructions to the settlement of this question. Still, though I believe that we want in England nothing but the will, and though I am convinced that it would be easy to carry out this great work of social reformation did that will exist, I freely confess that I see no prospect of its being done, until the people accomplish it for themselves; as I see it opposed by the bigoted sectarianism of one party, by the ignorant hostility of a second, by the selfish ambition of a third, by the blind indifference of a fourth, and by the luke-warmness of even its real friends.

Let it not be thought, that I am at all desirous of superseding local efforts, or of taking the direction of the parochial schools out of the hand of local authorities; far otherwise: I only wish to see the local efforts aided, where without aid they are confessedly impotent, and a security given to the country, that some one shall provide for the wants of those localities, which cannot do anything for themselves.

Nor do I wish to interfere with the educational societies further than we now do, that is, by assisting them in every possible manner; by assisting the diocesan boards to realise their present desire to establish and support normal colleges, and by assisting the Church and the Dissenters to educate efficient teachers for their schools, and to provide an efficient system of inspection for them all. Government ought to give every possible guarantee to the different religious bodies, that it will not attempt in any way to undermine the influence, which they legitimately claim to exercise over the religious education of the people, whilst at the same time it should require sufficient guarantees, that the secular education of the people shall be properly attended to.

But whilst the church and the dissenting bodies both continue so suspicious of all government interference whatever, what can we hope to do? Without the aid of Government, I have shown that the efforts to raise sufficient funds for the education of the people have always failed and must always fail, and that on the other hand, the government will always be crippled in its efforts to promote national education, if it does not act cordially with the religious bodies, and if it attempts to carry on the work alone. I sincerely hope, then, that it will not be thought by any, that I am desirous of undermining the influence of our clergy, or that I think the education of the country can be carried on without their most cordial co-operation. I fully agree with them, that the great end of all human education is to develop the religious character of mankind, and I cannot wonder, that they are suspicious of every public interference, which appears to overlook this great truth. But let them take great heed, that this suspicion is not carried too far, and that it is not expressed, when no cause for it exists; let them avoid exciting a belief, that their opposition does not proceed from this holy feeling, but that it is stimulated by the desire of raising their order, and increasing their political influence. If such a suspicion ever attaches itself to them, from that day the fall of the church will be sealed.

We stand on dangerous ground. We know not now how far the mine has been excavated. We know not how strong the enemy is; but certain it is that a spirit omnipotent for evil, a spirit of revolution, irreverence, irreligion, and recklessness, and, more dangerous than all, a spirit of unchecked, unguided, and licentious intelligence is abroad, which will be the most dangerous enemy, with which Christianity has hitherto had to cope. Remember, that it is utterly impossible in these days to stop the rapidly unfolding intellect of the people, even if it were desirable, and that *uneducated* intellect is the worst enemy to the best interests of mankind. Cheap literature, which may be had for the asking, cheap postage, cheap and rapid communication between different districts, the continually increasing interest, which the people take in political transactions; the lessons, *the practical lessons,* they are daily receiving on the effects of combination, and the wholly unfettered exercise of thought and speech in this country, have utterly precluded the possibility of their remaining stupefied, and have ensured their *intellectual* advancement beyond a doubt. Cannot we, then, see the consequence of all this? If religious teachers are not found, and that soon, for this people, where will the church be fifty years hence? Where the French church was in 1796 — overthrown by an infidel multitude. Can any one think our social condition to be compared to that of Holland? Can any one look on, for the next half century without dismay? Are not the cause of religion, the cause of morality, the cause of social order, and the future prosperity of this country, all compromised, deeply compromised, by our present inaction?

And yet what are we doing? Behold us, in 1850, with one of the most pauperised, demoralised, and worst educated people in Europe; with the greatest accumulated masses in the world; with one of the most rapidly-increasing populations in the world; behold us, in 1850, developing our productive powers, giving the most tremendous stimulus to our manufactures and our population — resolved to turn the North into one vast city — to collect there the labourers of the world, and to leave them without a religion! Not only are we fearfully careless of the best interest of our brethren, not only are we acting, as if we were ourselves convinced that our religion was a lie; but we are blind to the absolute necessities of the commonwealth. The very heathens would have laughed our policy to scorn. They all saw, that even if there were no God, it was necessary to invent one for the peace of mankind; they bound their people by religious formulas, wanting although these were of all true vitality; whilst we, in an age of the world when the intelligence of the multitude is advancing with giant strides, we stand still, saying to one another, it is impossible to do anything with our neighbours, for this party differs from one religious dogma we have started, and that party differs from another: each thus assuming for himself that perfection and that infallibility, which he scorns his neighbour for pretending to; whilst, alas! all are too ready to omit the inculcation of the weightier matters of the law — judgment, and justice, and mercy.

Moreover, the very genius of the Protestant religion requires, more than any other ever did, that its members should be educated, in order that they should be influenced by it. The different religions of the old world and the Roman Catholic religion have retained their hold upon the mind of the multitude by striking and affecting ceremonies, and by means of the senses have established their empire over the spirit of mankind.

But Protestantism has thrown aside almost all, and many forms of Protestantism have thrown aside all the ceremonies, which so strongly affected the mind of the unthinking people, and which so powerfully contributed, and in many countries at the present day still so very powerfully contribute, to excite a reverential and religious feeling among the ignorant; and we boast, that ours is not a religion merely of the feelings, but peculiarly one of the understanding. But do not Protestants perceive, that in order that an intellectual religion should affect the people, it is absolutely necessary, that their intellects should be fitted for the exercise, or that the religion will lose its hold upon them and be entirely neglected? What has contributed to the spread of many of the lowest kinds of dissent in this country? Simply because they have appealed to the *feelings* of the people. And so it will be, as long as we offer an intellectual and spiritual religion to a people incapable of reflection or of thought, and who cannot take any pleasure in a service, which to them appears cold, meaningless, and formal. In this way does the English Church contribute to the increase of the Ranters, the Mormonites, and all the wild and visionary enthusiasts, who have so great a hold upon the minds of the people in North Wales and in our manufacturing and mining districts, and who know right well, that a religion, which appeals to the feelings and passions is the only one which can have any influence over an ignorant multitude. It is impossible for the intellectual and unimaginative Protestantism of the English Church ever to affect the masses, until the masses are sufficiently educated to dispense with all need of mental excitement, which they never will be able to do, until they can think. If, then, the Protestants of England are not willing to prepare the people for the reception of our pure and spiritual religion, and as there can be no doubt that some form of religion, even although erroneous, is better for mankind than the absence of all religion whatsoever, it surely would be better for us, if we had the ceremonial religion of the Romanists, with all its faults, capable, as it would be, of affecting and influencing an unthinking multitude, than the spiritual religion of the Protestants, requiring an educated mind for its reception, when the English Protestants have seemingly resolved they will not educate the people. Much better to have a faith for the people, although it be erroneous, than to have no faith at all.

Why is it, that in Protestant countries like England and America, where nearly all the poor above thirty years of age are wholly uneducated, we find so many of the very lowest forms of the expression of religious belief, as the Mormonites, the Ranters, &c., whilst in countries like Holland, Wirtemberg, and Baden, where the people have been fitted for the reception of a higher species of Protestantism, there is hardly anything analogous to these religious extravangancies? Why is it, too, that in Romanist countries, where an objective religion is given to the people — where the uneducated are not required to accept a religion requiring an educated mind, — why is it, that in these countries there is nothing like the extravagant religious enthusiasm, or the still more lamentable atheism, which is found existing among our poor?

The reason is, that in each case the governments have wisely judged, that it was of primary importance to the people and to the state, that the people should have a faith, and where that faith has not been one, like Romanism, suited to captivate the ignorant, but one, like Protestantism, fitted only for the educated, they have wisely educated their people, so as to fit them for its reception, not in a low and degraded form, but in its highest and purest spiritual development.

I repeat that the great majority of the people in the great towns of this kingdom have no religion. They are not fitted for the reception of Protestantism, or if they are so in a few cases, it is only for the reception of a corrupted and *corrupting* phase of it; and we have taken from them the only religion capable of influencing them in their present state.

How deeply, then, does it behove us, as true Protestants, and especially as members of a church boasting, and boasting truly, to offer to the people the purest and most beautiful form of Protestantism! but a form, whose very purity and freedom from the captivating errors, which have rendered other religions more influential on the ignorant poor, more urgently requires, that the people should be educated to accept it; — how deeply does it behove us, to be tenfold more diligent than Romanist countries, to prepare the people, by means of education, for the reception of its tenets. And yet, alas! Romanist countries have far outstripped us in the eagerness with which they are promoting the education of their people. They understand the signs of the times, but we have yet to learn them. Then, and not till then, shall we understand the real necessities of the poor.

I cannot imagine anything more injurious to the clergy, more hostile to the influence they ought to possess over the people; I cannot imagine anything more certain to separate the people from them, than that it should be fancied for one moment, that they oppose government interference (after sufficient guarantees have been offered them that it is not intended to take the direction and surveillance of the moral and religious education of the people out of their hands,) merely from a vain desire to manage and direct the education of the people themselves, especially after they have given such proofs of their utter inability to raise a tithe of the funds necessary for such a purpose. They are doubtless the fit and proper guardians of the religion and the morality of the country, and they are only performing their high duty, when they oppose any measure, which may seem likely to undermine the religious and moral influence they ought to have; but let them be most careful they do not demand more. Let them take care that they do not reject the assistance of government, after having shown the country that they cannot raise one paltry half-million for the primary education of a nation of 16,000,000 souls. Far from thwarting government, it behoves them, *if* they can discern the signs of the times, to be the first to demand the co-operation of the state, and to confess their inability to carry on the education of the people without it, instead of appearing for one moment satisfied with, and still less venturing for one instant to vaunt, the miserably small progress that education has yet made.

First, then, let me again briefly state what we have to do, referring as proof of what I lay down here to the deeply interesting reports of her Majesty's inspectors.

I. We require twice as many schools as we at present possess; nor is this want confined to either towns or country, but is equally felt in each.

II. We require an annual provision for the payment not only of nearly all the teachers we at present have, but for all that we shall find it necessary to appoint for the education of our numerous and increasing population.

III. We require, as I have before shown, annual funds for the efficient support of at least forty-one normal colleges, for the education of teachers.

IV. We require, also, an annual outlay of 70,000*l.* on the support of an efficient body of inspectors; those for the church-schools being chosen from the ranks of the clergy, with the sanction of the ecclesiastical authorities, and those for the schools of the Dissenters being chosen from among them, sufficient guarantees being at the same time given them, that no one shall be chosen, to whom they can honestly object.

First, then, how can we provide sufficient school-rooms for the population?

The present plan both of the government and the educational societies is, to wait until some locality provides about two-thirds of the necessary funds and applies for aid, and then to furnish the other third, requiring guarantees for the proper outlay of the money, as well as the right of inspecting the progress of the school. What is the consequence? There are many districts, as the reports of the inspectors only too plainly show, where no one takes the least interest in the education of the young; so that no voluntary local efforts are ever likely to be made, and where, consequently, no assistance is ever likely to be given, and which remain at the present day wholly without schools or teachers; — there are many other districts where there is literally no one, who knows how to make an application, even if sufficient local funds could be raised, the population being wholly composed of small farmers and labourers, or of manufacturing operatives or miners; — and there are many other districts, where, although the clergy or ministers have succeeded in raising two-thirds of the funds necessary for one or two schools, they are *utterly* unable to raise more, and where several more schools are imperatively required; under this class will fall nearly all the larger towns of the kingdom, where, from the vast numbers of the poor, a great number of schools are required, and where it is utterly hopeless to raise sufficient funds from the few inhabitants of the district, who happen to understand the necessity of education. And though it may be answered, that the National Society has assisted several of these districts, even when local funds could not be raised, yet it requires no demonstration to show, how utterly incapable that society is to meet the disheartening deficiency in the manufacturing districts, with the ridiculously small funds at its disposal. Why, it would require at least a million of money to provide schools for the districts in the north, which are *now* unable or unwilling to do any thing for themselves, and are wholly without, or very deficiently provided with, school-room, for the population.

Whenever we do resolve to undertake the education of the country, it will be necessary for government so to increase its force of inspectors, as to obtain information of the exact condition of the means for education in every parish throughout the kingdom. The state of the different parishes should, then, be ranged under the following heads: —

1. Parishes, which are already supplied with sufficient school-room.
2. Parishes, which have some school-room, but require more, and are able to provide what is wanted.
3. Parishes, which have some school-room, but require more, and are unable to provide what is wanted.
4. Parishes which have no school-room, but which are able to provide sufficient.
5. Parishes which have no school-room, and are not able to provide any.

Now, as I have already shown, and as the reports of the inspectors still more clearly show, there is no hope of anything being done in very many parishes capable of great local efforts, unless government requires it of them. As several of the inspectors show, over great tracts of country, there does not at present exist a single school. It is evident, therefore, that the present voluntary system cannot, with all our efforts, provide the country with schools, and that if we are to have them, *government must interfere and oblige each parish, as far as it is able, and assist it when unable to provide itself with sufficient school-room for its population.*

In each parish, all tenants of houses, whose rent amounts, say to at least 10*l.* per annum, might be made liable to a certain rate, to be apportioned according to the wants of the parish and the number of the householders who are liable to the rate. Each of these householders might have a vote in the election of a committee of eight or ten members, for the administration of the educational expenditure of the parish. Of this committee, the clergy and the dissenting ministers ought to be, as in all European countries, the ex-officio members.

Before this committee, when elected, the inspector for the district should lay an account of the exact state of education in the parish, showing the quantity of school-room required for the population; where the required school or schools should be situated, so as best to suit the convenience of the poor of the parish, and also how many houses for teachers should be provided. The committee might then deliberate, whether it would supply the wants of the parish by mixed schools for the different religious sects, or by separate schools for each sect, and whether it would at once provide for all the schools required, or by the imposition of separate rates in separate years. At these deliberations the clergy, the dissenting ministers, and the inspectors should be entitled to assist, the latter, by affording all necessary information as to the exact wants of the district.

I am firmly of opinion, that were the government to OBLIGE each parish to provide itself with sufficient school-room, and to leave it to the option of the several parishes, whether they would support separate or mixed schools, that there would be little difficulty. Wherever any one party was decidedly too small to establish a school for itself, it would concur in the arrangement for a mixed school. It is when government endeavours itself to decide upon it, that all parties are alarmed, and begin to suspect ulterior designs, and to fear the effects of a scheme, over which they have had no control. All that government should do, *is to oblige each parish, as far as it is able, to supply itself with sufficient school-room,* and to leave to its own decision the *manner,* in which this should be done. I am confirmed in my opinion that mixed schools would not be objected to, if the establishing of them were left to the inhabitants of the different parishes, by the experience I have had in the North, where I have frequently found schools expressly intended for the church, filled partly with the children of dissenters, who did not object in the least to their children remaining, even during the religious lessons given in the school. But whenever a power from without endeavours to force mixed schools upon a locality, then the clergy and the dissenting ministers, and many of the parents, begin to be alarmed. Of course government ought to require, when a school was established for two sects, and the schoolmaster was chosen from the most numerous sect, that the children should either attend the religious lessons given in the school, or should receive daily religious instruction from one of the ministers of their own sect.

In those cases where the committee could not agree

to provide a mixed school, and where the minority was too small to support a school for themselves, the majority should be obliged and empowered to levy the rate and build the school, on condition that the minority should be allowed to send their children to the secular instruction, and remove them during the religious instruction given in the school. We should soon find, that the minority would not object to their children attending the secular instruction given at the school, and receiving their religious instruction from their own minister. Many parishes, moreover, would require *several* schools, and in these cases the committee could easily arrange, if desired, that the schools should be appropriated to the different sects, according to their respective numbers.

Where a parish was not capable of doing more than it had already done, or of making any but very inefficient efforts, government ought to be prepared to give the necessary assistance, instead of confining its grants, as at present, to those parishes alone, which are able to raise a considerable part of the necessary funds. But in the poorest parishes, where several schools were required, the householders ought to be consulted, whether they wish to have *separate* or *mixed* schools.

These parish committees might be called on to meet at certain periods, to examine the state of the school-buildings, and to provide, by the levying of a small rate on the householders, for all the repairs required for all the schools and schoolmasters' houses in the parish; and when the population was increased so much, as to require another school, for the building of another school in the parish. The inspectors of the district would inform them of the exact wants of the parish. *It would be also wise to give these parish committees the power of requiring the attendance of all the children at school between certain ages, and of enforcing that attendance, whenever they saw fit to do so.* In many districts, the parochial authorities would not object to put this regulation into force, while government will be wholly unable for some time to enforce a general regulation of this kind. The people would not object to it, if it issued from themselves, although they would call it unwarrantable interference on the part of government. And although, doubtless, very many districts would not consent to enforce such a regulation for some years to come, yet it would be a great gain to the country, if the inspectors could induce *any* of the towns or parishes to make such a regulation. But, whether they would do so or not, yet a general encouragement would be given to parents to send their children, if the inspectors reported yearly to the committees the names of those parents who neglected this duty, and urged the members of the committees to use their influence with them in inducing them to allow their children to be educated.

The mere fact of the attention of their parish being directed to their negligence would induce many parents, who are now wholly careless about it, to promote the education of their children, by sending them to the parochial schools.

Another thing which might, with great advantage, be left to the decision of these parochial committees, would be the fixing of the amount of the weekly school fees. They would be better acquainted, than any other persons, with the exact condition of the inhabitants of the parish, and with the sums they would be able to pay. A power ought, however, in all cases to be given to the clergy or dissenting ministers, in conjunction with the schoolmasters, to allow those children to attend the schools, whose parents were notably too poor to pay any part of the settled weekly fees, and in these cases, the parish committees should be required to pay the fees to the teacher out of the parochial school funds.

In all those cases where there was in a parish a national school, or a school belonging to some sect of the dissenters, and the numbers of the other sects in the parish were very small, the committee would inquire of the minister of the sect, to which the school belonged, whether he would allow the children of other religious denominations to attend the secular instruction given in the school. In very many cases, this would be done willingly, but where it was refused, the committee should, unless the numbers of the other sects were too small, be required to establish another school in the parish.

Where such permission was granted, then the parochial committee should be required to support such schools, and provide all the funds necessary for its repair, for the salaries of the teachers and for the necessary apparatus, &c.

But how should the teachers for these schools, and for all the schools in the country, henceforward be chosen? In the case of all schools at present established, directed by trustees, school societies, religious congregations, or private individuals, I would, of course, leave the selection of the teachers in the hands of the persons in whom it is now vested, reserving for government, however, the right of examining by means of its inspectors the persons chosen, and the power of annulling the election, if the candidate was found upon examination to be unfitted for the exercise of his important duties. In the case of schools erected by the parochial authorities, the teachers should be always chosen, if the school was intended for only one sect, from that sect, by its school committee, and if for several sects, by the minister and members of the school committee, who belonged to the most numerous sect in the parish, subject, however, in every case to the approval of government. When we have a sufficient number of normal colleges, of course no person should be permitted to be a candidate for the situation of teacher, but one, who had been educated in such a college, and who had obtained a certificate from its director and professors of high moral character, and of satisfactory intellectual attainments.

It is very important that government should have the right of examining every candidate for the situation of a schoolmaster, and the power of rejecting him, if found upon examination unworthy of the situation. Until government is entrusted with this privilege, we shall always be liable, in the event of the trustees or managers of a school being careless, (which does and will constantly happen) to have men chosen, who not only are wholly unfitted by their want of any previous education, but who are capable of doing the greatest possible mischief to the children committed to their care, by their exceeding low moral character. I have seen men occupying the post of schoolmasters, who had been elected by the managers or trustees of the schools, and who were positively doing a great moral injury to the children in their schools, and who were unfitted in every respect for their situations.

It is monstrous, that this should be even *possible*, much more that it should be of constant occurrence. But it is the necessary consequence of leaving the selection of the teachers to men burdened with other affairs, who have not sufficient time for a truly laborious and difficult duty, and who, in the generality of cases, are wholly unfit to be judges of the capability of any one for such a post. Imagine one of our country farmers choosing a schoolmaster! The very idea is absurd. And yet, I have seen farmers performing this responsible duty in their capacity of managers of country schools, attended by nearly one hundred children, and choosing men who were unworthy to be even the monitors in the lowest classes. Government need not interfere with the rights of trustees and managers, further than to require to be satisfied of the capability of the candidates, but so far it undoubtedly ought to interfere, making it the law of the land here, as it is in Holland, Prussia, Saxony, France, Hanover, Baden, Wirtemburg, Bavaria, Switzerland, and Austria, that no one should be allowed to be henceforward chosen, as teacher of a school for the poor, until the country had been satisfied of his capability of conducting the religious and secular instruction of a school. Every teacher should be required to obtain a certificate of high moral character from the director of the normal college at which he was educated; a certificate of capability to conduct religious instruction of children from the clergyman or dissenting minister who directed the religious superintendence of the college, and a certificate of capability to conduct the secular instruction of children from the inspector of the district, in which he desired to be a teacher. By this means, followed universally abroad, we should raise the profession of teachers in the public estimation, we should secure a set of men of high character and qualifications for these important posts, and we should raise the standard of religious, moral, and secular education throughout the country.

II. We require an annual provision for the payment, not only of all the teachers we at present possess, but of all those we shall be obliged hereafter to appoint.

Each teacher ought to have a certain salary of at least 50*l*. per annum provided him, as well as a house and garden and the school-fees, which, however, as I have before mentioned, should be so limited by the parish authorities as not to prevent, any, but the very poorest parents, who were unable to pay anything, sending their children to school; and in the case of these parents, the clergy or dissenting ministers should have the power of admitting their children into the schools free of all expense, on ascertaining that their plea of poverty was a true one.

We must provide good situations for the teachers, or we shall never obtain well-educated teachers for the schools.

We should therefore be prepared to provide a salary of at least 50*l*. per annum for every teacher at present appointed to a school, on his presenting one certificate from the clergyman or dissenting minister, who directs his school, of his religious and moral character, and of his capability of directing the religious education of his school; and another from the inspector of his district of his capability to conduct the secular instruction of his school. But no salary should be paid, unless these certificates were first obtained; and in the case of any teacher appointed in future, a third certificate of character should be required to be obtained from the director of the normal college, in which the candidate was educated. Where any school is endowed, the annual income settled on the teacher should be raised, where deficient, to 50*l.* per annum, on condition that he presented the above-mentioned certificates. But even where any school is so endowed, that the income secured to the teacher amounts to at least 50*l.* per annum, the government should demand the right of inspecting the school, and of having a veto on the appointment of any teacher in future.

The reports of the inspectors prove only too plainly, that the country can have no security against the negligence or ignorance of local authorities, until government has the *surveillance*—I do not say the direction, but the mere *surveillance*—of all the primary schools in the country, and a veto on the appointment *and dismissal* of all the teachers in the country. It is what all foreign countries, where education has made any progress, have granted their government, and it is what our government must have sooner or later. Until government has this direct influence on the choice and dismissal of the teachers, the education of the country, left in the hands of careless local authorities, all engaged in other affairs, and having little time to look after the schools, will remain what it is at present—defective, unproductive of any satisfactory results, and in many cases positively hurtful and demoralising.

Of course out of our present schools there would be but few teachers, who would be able to obtain the necessary certificates of character and competence; and of the few respectable teachers we have, most of them are at least temporarily provided with sufficient salaries; so that the *immediate* provision required for this purpose would be comparatively very trifling. Now there are several ways in which this annual outlay might be provided, did we but take any real interest in the education of the people. But I confess that, as far as I am able to judge, one method appears to me to offer many advantages that no other does. I have in the course of the observations I have ventured to make on the state of the English poor pointed to the way in which the out-door expenditure of the Poor-Law Unions of England and Wales has been steadily and rapidly increasing. It is needless for me to remark how very much better it would be for the poor themselves, if this relief could be *gradually* withdrawn. The evil effects of a public charity of this kind, in the stimulus it gives to improvidence and carelessness among the poor, is now too generally admitted to need any notice from me. It is however impossible, as I have before observed, to withdraw this relief suddenly. We have, by our own neglect of the poor, fostered the growth of our present pauperism; cruel therefore, in the extreme, would it be to *suddenly* withdraw the stimulant, which we have made necessary to the people. We have pauperised the people by our own ignorant sectarianism, so that we could not, in common justice, or in common humanity, deny them that relief, which we ourselves have rendered necessary.

But we can provide for the education of their children in habits of temperance and prudence, and having done this, we might then withdraw that relief, of which they would no longer stand in need. As I have before shown, the payment of the teachers at first would amount to a comparatively small sum. This sum I think the unions should be required to provide from the poor-rates. Each union should be required to *check the increase* of its expenditure in out-door relief, and to provide for the payment of such of its teachers as obtained the certificates mentioned above. The sums required for this purpose at first would be very small, and as they increased, the out-door relief might be slowly and gradually withdrawn in the same proportion; so that in fifteen years from this time, we might hope to have substituted the expenses required for the support of the teachers in places of honourable independence for a part of the present enormous expenditure on out-door relief. An auditor might be attached to each board of guardians for the purpose of managing the educational expenses of the union; and to this officer the inspector of the district might send information of the teachers whom he, in conjunction with the clergy and dissenting ministers, had deemed worthy of receiving their salaries from the union. Moreover, the unions might be required to supply the school apparatus necessary for those schools, whose teachers had obtained the necessary certificates. Of the apparatus necessary for the use of the school, the clergyman or dissenting minister, who had the direction of the school, in conjunction with the schoolmaster and inspector, might decide; and on an application forwarded by them jointly, the union might be required to furnish the necessary outlay.

This plan would not interfere with private munificence or local benevolence, but it would always provide for the failure of those supplies, and it would secure to a good schoolmaster a sufficient and independent livelihood, so that he would be satisfied with his situation and would be able to devote his undivided attention to his duties.

Of course, as I have said before, government should, through its inspectors, require to have a veto on the dismissal as well as on the appointment of every teacher, so as to secure a worthy teacher from all risk of losing his situation through any mere caprice on the part of the local authorities who elected him. The annual expenditure in out-door relief is now about 3,000,000*l.* per annum, and the annual expenditure of the unions in the national education, supposing they supported the normal colleges, provided the incomes of the teachers and the apparatus for the schools, would not for many years amount to more than 2,000,000*l.* per annum, and would not amount to even that sum, until many of the present race of uneducated and low-minded teachers had become superannuated or had died at their posts.

If then, government were to limit the annual expenditure of the unions on out-door relief and on education to 3,500,000*l.*, never allowing them to exceed that expenditure, it is manifest, that the retrenchment of the out-door relief would be so very gradual, as scarcely to be felt, whilst it would not be superseded by the educational expenditure for many years, as population must have considerably increased ere, we should require 3,500,000*l.* per annum for the school apparatus and for the education and support of the teachers of this country, in addition to the present endowments and to the efforts of private benevolence.

There are two reasons, which point to the adoption of a plan such as the one I have very briefly and imperfectly sketched; one is, that we have the organisation necessary to obtain the local funds already provided — an organisation, moreover, admirably suited for the purpose, since it would interest the local authorities in the progress of the education of their localities, as they would not like to feel, that they were bearing such expenses and reaping no returns; another is, that it would not only tend to check the rapidly spreading pauperism of the country — by applying a remedy to the root of the evil; but it would also enforce the *very gradual* withdrawal of that out-door relief, which very greatly contributes to the spread of that disease which is threatening the very vitals of our commonwealth. I look on the withdrawal of this demoralizing expenditure as only second in importance to the education of the people. I believe this expenditure is demoralizing the poor. I am certain, from its effects on districts, which have fallen under my own observation, that it is contributing very greatly to the pauperism, immorality, and degradation of our poor. I have seen it bestowed in the most careless and indiscriminate manner, as if it were intended to encourage to the utmost the spirit of improvidence, now, alas, so generally existing among the poor. I have known poor families (who, if they had not had this injurious benevolence to depend upon, would have provided in their prosperous days against the return of slack times,) living in a careless and profuse manner, whilst their prosperity lasted, without the least idea of providing against a return of adverse seasons, spending all their earnings in drink and good living, with no idea of providence or foresight, knowing that, however careless they were, it mattered little, as they could easily persuade the Union to assist them, if they should be overtaken by adversity. What can be worse than such a system? Can it be too strongly reprobated? Is it not offering a premium to improvidence, and a stimulant to pauperism? I can imagine no better plan of demoralising the country, than by continuing to dispense this false, injurious, and absurd charity in our present injudicious manner, and by confining our efforts to our present contemptible sham of national education.

III. We require, as I have before shown, annual funds for the efficient support of *at least* forty-one Normal Colleges for the education of teachers.

As I have mentioned in the last chapter, in several of the dioceses, attempts have been made to establish normal colleges, which have in great measure failed from the want of sufficient funds. Until government comes forward, and assists the bishops and the Dissenters to carry out these laudable efforts, we shall continue without any sufficient supply of teachers fitted to carry out the education of the country. However great the deficiency of these training establishments for the Church, the Dissenters are still worse provided for in this respect. As I have shown, a public provision is set apart for the support of the normal establishments in each of the European countries, of which I have so often spoken, and the benevolence of private individuals is exercised in creating endowments for the education of poor but worthy aspirants to the teacher's ranks. This is a way in which private benevolence may be very beneficially encouraged; but certainly it is not right, that institutions of such great public importance as training establishments for teachers should be left dependent on such benevolence. Government should therefore be prepared to enable each diocese to support at least one good and efficient normal college for teachers for the schools of the Church, where the pupil-teachers should receive at least a *three* years' training, before they were permitted to undertake the management of a village or town school. But in addition to these, government should be prepared to provide for the support of a second normal college in the diocese of Bangor for the teachers of the schools of the Methodists in North Wales; of two others in the populous diocese of Manchester, one for the teachers of the Methodists and the other for the teachers of the Baptists and Independents; of another also in the dioceses of Lichfield and Coventry,

St. David and Durham, for the education of the teachers of the schools of the Dissenters in these populous districts; of two others in the populous diocese of York, one for the Methodists, and another for the Baptists and Independents; of four in the diocese of London, two for the Church and two for the Dissenters; of two in the diocese of Exeter, one for the Church and one for the Dissenters of Devonshire and Cornwall; and of two others in the diocese of Norwich, one for the Baptists and Independents, and another for the Methodists.

All the government normal colleges should be open to members of any religious sect, who would consent to observe the rules and regulations of the institution; and if any such entered a college set apart for a religious sect different to their own, they should be permitted to be absent from the religious lessons and exercises, on condition that they received regular religious instruction from some religious minister of their own sect.

The whole number of normal colleges required for the different dioceses would then be as follows: — (See next page.)

I will suppose that forty-one colleges for teachers would suffice for 17,000,000 inhabitants. The question then arises, how shall we provide for their support? Now the expenses of the normal colleges and of the annual payment of the teachers, together with the provision of the necessary school apparatus, would not amount, probably, to more than 2,000,000*l.* per annum for our present population. I should be prepared to throw the whole of this expenditure, together with that

Number of Normal Colleges for the Education of Teachers, which ought to be provided for England and Wales.

Diocese.	No. of Normal Colleges.	For what Sect intended.
St. Asaph -	1	Church.
Bangor - -	2	1 Church. 1 Methodists.
Bath and Wells -	1	Church.
Bristol - - -	1	—
Canterbury - -	1	—
Carlisle - -	1	—
Chester - -	1	Church.
Chichester - -	1	Church.
St. David - -	2	1 Church. 1 Congregationalists.
Durham - - -	2	1 Church. 1 Congregationalists.
Ely - - -	1	Church.
Exeter - - -	2	1 Church. 1 Dissenters.
Gloucester - -	1	Church.
Hereford - -	1	—
Landaff - -	1	—
Litchfield and Coven- Coventry	2	1 Church. 1 Dissenters.
Lincoln - - -	1	Church.
London - - -	4	2 Church. 1 Methodists. 1 Congregationalists.
Manchester - -	3	1 Church. 1 Methodists. 1 Congregationalists.
Norwich - - -	3	1 Church. 1 Methodists. 1 Congregationalists.
Oxford - - -	1	Church.
Peterborough -	1	—
Rochester - -	1	—
Salisbury - -	1	—
Winchester - -	1	—
Worcester - -	1	—
York - - -	3	1 Church. 1 Methodists. 1 Congregationalists.
Total -	41	28 for the Church. 13 for the Dissenters.

required for the support of the teachers, upon the unions, substituting it *gradually* for the greater part of the present expenditure of out-door relief, now given in the *encouragement of pauperism.* I would require all the Poor Law Unions, within the different dioceses, to provide the necessary sums for the building and support of the diocesan normal colleges. I would leave the normal colleges of the Church in the hands of the bishops, giving to them the appointment of the principals and professors, and only requiring for government the inspection of the colleges, and a veto on the appointment of the principals. So in like manner with the normal colleges for the Dissenters. Government should select the principals, in the case of the colleges for the Methodists, from the Methodists, and, in the case of the schools for the Congregationalists, from the most numerous of their sects in the diocese; and a requisition signed by a certain number of the ministers of the Methodists or of the Congregationalists should be able to annul the selection, which had been made by the government. In these cases also, government should, of course, require the right of inspection. I have not mentioned the normal colleges for female teachers, because I am willing to own that I see great difficulties in the way of the education of the schoolmistresses. But I think, supposing it is possible to educate efficient schoolmistresses in the same manner as we have commenced to educate the schoolmasters; I mean by selecting young girls of a religious character, and by placing them for three years in a training establishment, that a normal school for mistresses might be established in every two or three dioceses, and the support of it be thrown upon all the unions in those dioceses.

I offer these suggestions with diffidence, knowing the extreme difficulty of the subject, of which I have ventured to treat, but feeling the deep importance of doing something, instead of leaving every thing to work its own way unchecked and unguided. It is impossible to educate the people without good teachers; it is impossible to obtain these, unless we have a sufficiency of training establishments; and it is impossible for us to retain them at their posts, when we have obtained them, unless we provide certain and sufficient salaries for them. Why then do we leave all these things undone? Is it that the country is not so able to bear the expenses of an educational system as Holland or Switzerland? Is it that an educational system is not so necessary for a country like ours, where the masses of poor are so great and so rapidly increasing, as for one, where their numbers are much smaller, and the rate of their increase much slower? or is it, that we do not care for the happiness or improvement of the people, and that we cannot see the evident tendency of events, with our present demoralised masses?

IV. We require a much greater number of inspectors. I have already said so much on this head, that little more remains to be noticed. I have already shown, that we require at least 150 inspectors; and I have also shown, that it is impossible to do anything, until we have ascertained, by their agency, the actual state of education throughout the country. On this point we are at present in the profoundest ignorance. We only know *that we have not more than one-half the schools we require* for our population; but as to the exact wants of the different parishes throughout the kingdom, we know nothing. It behoves government, therefore, to examine this matter, and to increase its staff of inspectors in such a manner, as to enable it to obtain exact statistics of the state of education throughout the kingdom. The State has given the Church a veto on the appointment of the inspectors for the Church schools; it has also given the same security to the Dissenters, that no inspector shall be chosen to visit their schools, to whom they can object.

Let government only come forward and assist the ministers of religion, and let it continue to avoid any attempt to undermine their influence, or to take the entire direction of education into its own hands, and it will meet with no opposition; but, on the contrary, it will find among them the fullest appreciation of the necessity of education, and of the importance of the State's assisting the religious teachers in giving it to the nation. But as long as the State and the religious ministers exhibit so much distrust, the one of the other, nothing can be done; but that day will be advanced, when, after the turmoil of a fierce political strife, the people will create an educational system for themselves, and will reject the interference of the clergy altogether, having learned to associate their names with the idea of an unwillingness to advance their improvement; and the consequence will be, that an educational system will be established void of all religion, thoroughly atheistical and revolutionary in its tendency, and which will completely overthrow all that influence, which it is most important, for the best interests of the people, that the clergy should have on the education of the nation.

Before I conclude, there is one other point, which I would shortly advert to, and that is the need of assistants for the masters. Every schoolmaster, having the care of more than fifty scholars, ought to have the assistance of *well-trained* monitors, capable of conducting the instruction of the younger children. The reports of Her Majesty's Inspectors will show this much better than anything I can say. Now we can never obtain the services of efficient monitors unless we pay them; for if they are not paid, they will always leave the school before they are old enough to be entrusted with the care of the junior classes. Very few children remain at school after attaining the age of twelve, and it is manifest that a child of twelve years old is not capable of being of much assistance to a schoolmaster. But if we paid the monitors of the village schools about as much as they could earn, if they went to work, we should be enabled to keep them much longer, and should provide useful assistants for the schoolmasters. Here would be an ample field for the exercise of private benevolence. Private individuals should be encouraged to provide small salaries for monitors in all schools, where the number of the children exceeded thirty. Moreover, another good result would ensue from this plan. We should in this way educate a number of candidates for the normal colleges, who would be admirably fitted to be trained as teachers, as their education would have all along prepared them for this life, would have accustomed them to its arduous duties, and would thus have ensured their perseverance afterwards in the exercise of the toilsome duties of a profession, to which they had been accustomed from their earliest years. So let it not be said, that in throwing the maintenance of the schoolmasters upon the country, we should take away the means for the exercise of private charity, (I have heard this absurd argument used,) for we should then leave a field open for the exercise of that charity, so vast that all the efforts of the educational societies, and of all the benevolent individuals in the country, would not suffice to supply it.

The committee of council has attempted to enable the parochial schools to educate monitors; but its efforts in this respect, as in every other, are thwarted by the small amount of funds at its disposal.

With these few and imperfect suggestions I take my leave, for the present, of a subject on which I may not, perhaps, have offered valuable counsel, but in which I have long taken the profoundest interest. I hope, however valueless the observations I have made may be, that they will at least lead some to reflect on the rapidly unfolding of the democratic tendency of the times, and of the imperative necessity of providing beforehand for it. I would ask them to regard Europe, where nothing at all similar to our social condition exists, and to ask themselves, why it is that Prussia, Germany, France, Holland, Denmark, Sweden, Norway, Switzerland, and even Austria, have judged it absolutely necessary to consider this great question so seriously; and then I would beg them to turn their gaze on our own land, and to ask themselves, whether it can be really true, that with our social symptoms we are really so miserably provided with educational means as the reports of government would have us believe? Alas! it is only too true. Here, with our vast accumulated masses; with a population increasing by 1000 per diem; with an expenditure on abject pauperism, which in these days of our prosperity amounts to 5,000,000*l.* per annum; with a terrible deficiency in the numbers of our churches and of our clergy; with the most demoralising publications spread through the cottages of our operatives; with democratic ideas of the wildest kinds, and a knowledge of the power of union daily gaining ground among them; — here, too, where the poor have no stake whatever in the country; where there are no small properties; where the most frightful discrepancy exists between the richer and the poorer classes; where the poor fancy they have nothing to lose and every thing to gain from a revolution; here, too, where we are stimulating the rapid increase of our population by extending and steadying the base of our commercial greatness; where the majority of the operatives have no religion; where the national religion is one utterly unfitted to attract an uneducated people; where our very freedom is a danger, unless the people are taught to use and not to abuse it; — and here, too, where the aristocracy is richer and more powerful than that of any other country in the world, the *poor are more depressed, more pauperised, more numerous in comparison to the other classes, more irreligious, and very much worse educated than the poor of any other European nation, solely excepting Russia, Turkey, South Italy, Portugal, and Spain.*

Such a state of things cannot long continue.

TABLE I.

Showing the Proportion of Scholars in Elementary Schools, to the whole Population in different European Countries.

		Scholars.		Inhabitants.
Berne, Canton of Switzerland -	1843	1	in every	4·3
Thurgovie „ „ -	1837	1	„	4·8
Vaud „ „ -	1844	1	„	5
St. Gall „ „ -	1843	1	„	5·5
Argovie „ „ -	1843	1	„	5·5
Neuchatel „ „ -	1838	1	„	6
Lucerne „ „ -	1844	1	„	6
Schaffhouse „ „ -	1844	1	„	6
Geneva „ „ -	1844	1	„	6
Zurich „ „ -	1838	1	„	6·3
Fribourg „ „ -	1839	1	„	6·5
Solothurn „ „ -	1844	1	„	7
Saxony - - - -	1841	1	„	5
Six departments of France (each)	1843	1	„	6
Wirtemberg - -	1838	1	„	6
Prussia - - - -	1838	1	„	6
Baden (Duchy) - - -	1838	1	„	6
Overyssel (Province of Holland) -	1838	1	„	6
Drenthe „ „ -	1838	1	„	6
Friesland „ „ -	1838	1	„	6·8
Tyrol - - - -	1843	1	„	7·5
Norway - - - -	1837	1	„	7
Denmark - - -	1834	1	„	7
Holland (generally) - -	1838	1	„	8
Bavaria - - - -	1831	1	„	8
Scotland - - - -	1842	1	„	8
Bohemia - - - -	1843	1	„	8·5
Austria Proper - - -	1843	1	„	9
France (generally) - -	1843	1	„	10·5
Belgium - - - -	1836	1	„	10·7
ENGLAND ! - - -	1850	1	„	14

TABLE II.

Showing the comparative state of the Education of the Poor in several of the European Countries.

Name of Country.	Population.	Number of Normal Colleges for the Education of Teachers.	Number of Schools for the poor open to the inspection of Government.	Children of different religious sects educated together.	The Teachers supported in honourable and independent situations by Government.	No one but a person of high character and attainments ever allowed to be a Teacher.	The Government has a veto on the appointment of Teachers whose characters and attainments it does not think sufficiently high.	All children are *obliged* by law to attend School between the ages of seven and thirteen.	Government takes care that school-houses shall be provided for all the people.	The different religious sects unite in assisting Government to promote the education of the people.	All the parishes well supplied with school-room.
Wirtemberg	1,600,000	3	all the schools.	Yes.	Yes.	Yes.	Yes.	Yes.	Yes.	Yes.	Yes.
Bavaria -	4,000,000	8	7,353	Yes.	Yes.	Yes.	Yes.	Yes.	Yes.	Yes.	Yes.
Grand Duchy of Baden	1,335,200	3	1,971	Yes.	Yes.	Yes.	Yes.	Yes.	Yes.	Yes.	Yes.
France -	34,000,000	92	59,838	Yes.	Yes.	Yes.	Yes.	No.	Yes.	Yes.	Yes.
Denmark -	2,100,000	5	4,600	Yes.	Yes.	Yes.	Yes.	Yes.	Yes.	Yes.	Yes.
Hanover -	1,700,000	6	3,428	Yes.	Yes.	Yes.	Yes.	Yes.	Yes.	Yes.	Yes.
Holland -	2,600,000	2	2,832	Yes.	Yes.	Yes.	Yes.	No.	Yes.	Yes.	Yes.
Prussia -	14,100,000	42	23,646	Yes.	Yes.	Yes.	Yes.	Yes.	Yes.	Yes.	Yes.
Switzerland	2,200,000	13	all the schools.	Yes.	Yes.	Yes.	Yes.	Yes.	Yes.	Yes.	Yes.
Saxony -	1,719,000	8	- -	Yes.	Yes.	Yes.	Yes.	Yes.	Yes.	Yes.	Yes.
England & Wales	17,000,000 population *rapidly* increasing.	only 12 worth mention !!	Not 4,000 !!	No !	No ! quite the contrary.	No ! quite the contrary.	No !	No !	No !	No ! quite the contrary.	No ! Great numbers of districts without any schools at all, or insufficiently supplied.

LONDON: SPOTTISWOODES and SHAW, New-street Square.